WOODLAND HILLS BRANCH LIBRARY
22200 VENTURA BLVD
WOODLAND HILLS CA 91364

IDIOT'S
GUIDES.
AS EASY AS IT GETS!

P9-DCV-619

MAY 0 3

due
7-18-22
8-29-22
9-19-22
11-25-2022

The GED® Crash Course

Second Edition

by Courtney Mayer, Sandra McCune, Shannon Reed, and Jane Burstein

373.0973
M468
2018

ALPHA

A member of Penguin Random House LLC

MAY 0 2 2018

DK Penguin
Random
House

Publisher: Mike Sanders
Executive Managing Editor: Billy Fields
Cover Designer: Lindsay Dobbs
Book Designer: William Thomas
Compositor: Ayanna Lacey
Proofreader: Lisa M. Starnes
Indexer: Celia McCoy

Second American Edition, 2018
Published in the United States by DK Publishing
6081 E. 82nd Street, Indianapolis, Indiana 46250

Copyright © 2018 Dorling Kindersley Limited
A Penguin Random House Company
18 19 20   10 9 8 7 6 5 4 3 2 1
001-308596-April2018

All rights reserved.
Without limiting the rights under the copyright reserved above, no part of this
publication may be reproduced, stored in or introduced into a retrieval system, or
transmitted, in any form, or by any means (electronic, mechanical, photocopying,
recording, or otherwise), without the prior written permission of the copyright owner.

Published in the United States by Dorling Kindersley Limited.

IDIOT'S GUIDES and Design are trademarks of Penguin Random House LLC

ISBN: 9781465470232
Library of Congress Catalog Card Number: 2017952180

Note: This publication contains the opinions and ideas of its author(s). It is intended to
provide helpful and informative material on the subject matter covered. It is sold with
the understanding that the author(s) and publisher are not engaged in rendering professional services in the book. If the reader requires personal assistance or advice, a
competent professional should be consulted. The author(s) and publisher specifically
disclaim any responsibility for any liability, loss, or risk, personal or otherwise, which
is incurred as a consequence, directly or indirectly, of the use and application of any
of the contents of this book.

Trademarks: All terms mentioned in this book that are known to be or are suspected
of being trademarks or service marks have been appropriately capitalized. Alpha
Books, DK, and Penguin Random House LLC cannot attest to the accuracy of this
information. Use of a term in this book should not be regarded as affecting the valid-
ity of any trademark or service mark.

DK books are available at special discounts when purchased in bulk for sales promo-
tions, premiums, fund-raising, or educational use. For details, contact: DK Publishing
Special Markets, 345 Hudson Street, New York, New York 10014 or SpecialSales@
dk.com.

Printed and bound in the United States of America

Contents

Introduction

Are you thinking about taking the GED? Perhaps you've already made that decision and are beginning to review and prepare for the tests. Or maybe you've taken one or all of the GED tests but need a little help getting a passing score when you retake them. At whatever stage you are now, *Idiot's Guides: The GED Crash Course, Second Edition,* can help you move to the next level so you can accomplish your educational goals.

Passing the GED provides proof you've achieved the level of education equivalent to a high school diploma. So if you missed out on getting a high school diploma for whatever reason, now's your chance to get one. This achievement can be an important step in getting a better job, moving ahead in your career, or even getting further education beyond high school if you want. Getting a GED credential also can build your confidence and help you gain more respect from others.

In other words, if you're on a path that leads toward passing the GED, you've made a smart decision.

How This Book Can Help

If you've decided you need to review the information and practice the skills you'll need to pass the GED, you've made another smart decision. The tests aren't easy. In fact, only about two thirds of those with high school diplomas can pass them. This book provides a crash course for each of the four subject areas covered on the GED—language arts, social studies, science, and mathematics. It reviews the skills you need to master and provides practice questions similar to those on the actual GED. Reviewing these chapters and practicing with the sample questions will improve your chances of passing each of the tests.

Idiot's Guides: The GED Crash Course, Second Edition, starts at square one and progresses in a simple, straightforward manner so you don't get lost or confused along the way. The book is broken down into 29 chapters, making it easy to find what you're looking for, work through each chapter, plot your progress, and complete your preparation before test day.

Although this book is easy to use, don't be fooled—it's focused on serious learning. It won't show you tricks that help you "beat" the tests, but it will help you develop the knowledge and practice the skills you need to pass the GED. Choosing this book is yet another smart decision you've made.

How This Book Is Organized

Idiot's Guides: The GED Crash Course, Second Edition, is designed to be flexible and adaptable to different needs. You can work through it from beginning to end, or you can prioritize and focus first on the areas where you feel less confident. Develop your own plan, and use it in the way that makes sense to you.

For ease of use, this book is divided into four parts:

Part 1, Reasoning Through Language Arts Test, is divided into 10 chapters designed to help you develop the reading and writing skills on which you'll be tested. We review good writing and grammatical skills and also evaluate reading comprehension and interpretation skills, focusing on different types of reading: nonfiction and fiction, including poetry, drama, and prose. Two chapters cover the Extended Response (better known as the essay) and offer guidance on planning, writing, and editing it.

Part 2, Social Studies Test, reviews five key subject areas: U.S. government and civics, U.S. history, economics, world history, and geography.

Part 3, Science Test, reviews what you need to know in life science, physical science (chemistry and physics), and earth and space science, providing a basic understanding of science and scientific inquiry.

Part 4, Mathematical Reasoning Test, covers four major areas: number operations and number sense; geometric measurement; data analysis, statistics, and probability; and algebraic expressions and functions. It also includes a chapter on taking the Mathematical Reasoning Test.

At the end of each part, you'll find a final chapter that provides a half- or full-length practice test containing questions that reflect those on the actual GED. Don't skip these chapters. They give you a sneak peek at the types of questions you'll encounter and enable you to practice your test-taking strategies and pacing. They also give you a sense of how well you're doing and whether or not you need further review and practice.

Extras

Throughout this book you'll find four types of sidebars, each providing something extra you can use. Here's what to look for:

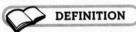 **DEFINITION**

These sidebars define and clarify words, giving you a better understanding of important terms you may encounter on the GED.

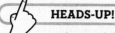

HEADS-UP!

These sidebars provide cautions to help you steer clear of trouble when studying for and taking the GED.

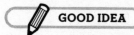

GOOD IDEA

These sidebars are tip-offs to proven strategies or actions you can take to increase your chances of success.

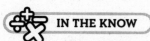

IN THE KNOW

These sidebars provide key information that will help you understand the subject content and do better on the tests.

Acknowledgments

Sandra Luna McCune wishes to thank her family for their love and support. Shannon Reed thanks her co-authors; her family; and Grace Freedson, Billy Fields, and Lori Cates Hand. Jane Burstein offers many thanks to her family and colleagues for their support. Special thanks goes the Villa 10 for their humor and patience.

Reasoning Through Language Arts Test

The Reasoning Through Language Arts Test is the longest of the GED® tests and divided into three parts: 95 minutes of questions on Language (formerly known as "writing") and Reading, a 10-minute break, and an Extended Response (essay) section that's allotted 45 minutes.

The Language assessment consists of two passages, which likely contain documents similar to emails, ads, or job-related forms. Four times in each passage, drop-down fill-in-the-blank questions are provided from which you must choose the best answer. The Reading assessment asks you to read and interpret six to eight passages of 900 words or fewer by answering a few questions about each. About 75 percent of those passages are informational; the remaining 25 percent (anywhere from one to three passages) are literary—fiction, poetry, or drama. These questions could be multiple choice, drop-down fill in the blank, or drag and drop (asking you to reorder the events in a passage correctly, for example).

Part 1 covers what you need to know for the Language portion of the test by reviewing essential English grammar rules, including sentence structure, some parts of speech with a focus on verb tense, and grammar and punctuation. We help you prepare for the Reading portion of the test by studying nonfiction, prose fiction, poetry, and drama examples, focusing on determining meaning; comprehending what you're reading; reading for main ideas, details, and inferences; and using context clues to determine the meaning of unknown words. Part 1 also helps you prepare for the Extended Response by reviewing ways to prepare for, outline, and write your essay in the time provided. This is often the most stressful portion of the test, but our tips and samples will help ease your way. Throughout all the review chapters, we offer plenty of practice questions, along with answers so you can check your work.

At the end of Part 1, we give you a sample Reasoning Through Language Arts Practice Test presented in the same format as the current GED, again with answers so you can see how you did.

Writing Correct Sentences

You probably have daily reasons to write, whether for work, a course you're taking, or personal communication. Whatever your motive, you want to present your thoughts clearly and correctly. In fact, because your writing is another way to express yourself to friends, family, colleagues, and others, you need to use correct English to present yourself in the best possible manner.

In this chapter, we review sentence structure. Your English sentences will function well if you remember a few basic rules about creating complete thoughts.

Foundations of the English Sentence: Subjects and Verbs

All sentences must contain a subject (the person, place, or thing doing or being something) and a verb (the word that shows the action or state of being). If a group of words lacks either a subject or a verb, it's not a complete sentence.

On the GED, you need to be able to match your subject and verb correctly. You do not need to worry about diagramming or identifying the parts of a sentence. You also don't have to explain what errors you've spotted or suggest what grammatical rule has been broken. You only need to choose the correct form of the words provided.

In This Chapter

- Grammar rules for English sentences
- Pointers on establishing subject-verb agreement
- Tips on avoiding fragments, run-ons, and comma faults
- Sample GED®-style questions to practice the skills on which you'll be tested
- Answers and explanations for all questions

What Makes the English Sentence a Complete Thought?

You may see a group of words that contains the name of a person or thing and an action word. That doesn't always mean it's a complete sentence. For example:

> Because the car stalled.

Car is the name of a thing and, therefore, the subject. *Stalled* is an action word, or verb. So how is this an incomplete thought if it has a subject and a verb? If you read the sentence aloud, you can hear that the thought is incomplete. You want to ask what happened when the car stalled. Why did it stall? The complete thought might be this:

> We rolled to the side of the road because the car stalled.

Which word in the original sentence makes the sentence incomplete? *Because.*

It's important that you can see the difference between the two groups of words. The first is a common error called a *fragment*.

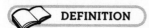 **DEFINITION**

A **fragment** is a group of words that looks like a sentence but is incomplete. The sentence cannot stand by itself.

Later in this chapter, in the "Words that Make a Sentence Incomplete" section, you learn more about words such as *because*. For now, read the following sentences and complete the incomplete thoughts. Ask yourself what's missing in the sentence, the subject or the verb?

Practice

1. A lost child.

2. Rainy to dry.

Answers

You can complete each sentence in several ways. Here are some possibilities:

1. A lost child cried. (subject, *child*; verb, *cried*)

2. The day changed from rainy to dry. (subject, *day*; verb, *changed*)

Run-On Sentences

Remember that too much of a good thing can be wrong as well. Sentences that go on and on without punctuation can be a problem. Read this sentence:

> I left home very early I got to the beach early enough to get a good parking place it was less than a quarter mile from the ocean.

How many thoughts can you find in this sentence? (1) I left home very early; (2) I got to the beach early enough to get a good parking place; and (3) it was less than a quarter mile from the ocean.

The three separate thoughts in this sentence are strung together, one after the other. This is called a *run-on sentence*. Later in this section, you'll learn to build more interesting sentences with connecting words. For now, just add correct punctuation and capitalization to correct the run-on error:

> Because I left home very early, I got to the beach early enough to get a good parking place. The space was less than a quarter mile from the ocean.

Or:

> Because I left home very early, I got to the beach early enough to get a good parking place less than a quarter mile from the ocean.

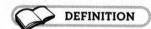 **DEFINITION**

A **run-on sentence** is one in which two or more complete thoughts or sentences (called independent clauses) are strung together incorrectly, without proper punctuation.

Practice

Some of the following sentences are run-ons. Correct them with simple punctuation changes. You can insert a period between two complete thoughts, or you can use a comma and a connecting word such as *and* or *but*. Leave the correct sentences as they are. The first sentence is corrected for you.

1. My boss gave us our new schedules mine is worse than before.
   Correction: My boss gave us our new schedules, but mine is worse than before.

2. I thought I was signing up for half days, but I found out I was wrong.

3. There are four dogs kept in that enclosure the black Lab is my favorite.

Answers

2. Correct as is.

3. There are four dogs kept in that enclosure, and the black Lab is my favorite.

Wordiness

Sometimes the GED presents a sentence that is not quite grammatically wrong but is guilty of wordiness, or using many words to say the same thing over and over. Take a look at this example:

> I wanted to apologize for missing class yesterday. I was not feeling well, and that is why I decided to miss class. I would not have made the decision not to come to class if I had not been feeling well.

This example could be simplified to:

> I apologize for missing class yesterday. I was ill.

Comma Faults

The following sentence contains a *comma fault*. Can you explain why?

> Some computer-related injuries occur on the job, many are associated with overuse at home.

The sentence contains two complete thoughts, yet a comma alone cannot connect two complete thoughts. To correct the sentence, insert a comma and a connecting word, or separate the thoughts with a period:

> Some computer-related injuries occur on the job, although many are associated with overuse at home.

> Some computer-related injuries occur on the job. Many are associated with overuse at home.

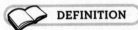 **DEFINITION**

A **comma fault** occurs when you link two or more complete thoughts with commas. A complete thought needs to end in a period or be connected to another thought with a semicolon or a comma plus a connecting word.

Chapter 1: Writing Correct Sentences **7**

Practice

Look for fragments, run-ons, wordiness, and comma faults in paragraph 1. Insert punctuation or correct marks where needed.

Paragraph 1:

(A) Having many questions about health-care coverage and retirement funds as well. (B) Ask about continued benefits while you look for a job, any company that interviews you should be able to answer your questions about continued benefits, finding a job you'll be ready to pick your health-care coverage and retirement funds

In paragraph 2, rewrite the fragments to make complete sentences. Look for comma faults and run-on sentences, and separate them into complete thoughts.

Paragraph 2:

(A) There are many safety issues linked to children's clothing, flammability is a primary concern, that's why federal regulations were written. (B) The law says that sleepwear for children 9 months or older must be flame resistant or snug fitting that's because 300 child-burn injuries are treated in emergency rooms yearly and the law is supposed to help prevent those accidents

For each question, decide which is the best way to write the underlined portion of paragraph 3. Note that this question is in the style you'll be asked on the GED.

Paragraph 3:

(A) At work, I learned that I had <u>a one-week vacation the only</u> condition was that I had to take it before August 1. (B) <u>When we bought airplane tickets</u> for Disneyland on a flight that leaves at 7:30 A.M. (C) <u>Having to set our alarm</u> for 4 A.M. in order to get to the airport in time. (D) <u>Rushing and making it through security just in time.</u> We collapsed into our seats once we were on the plane.

1. What correction should be made to the underlined portion of sentence A?

    (1) a one-week vacation that the only

    (2) a one-week vacation so the only

    (3) a one-week vacation. The only

    (4) a one-week vacation of which the only

    (5) a one-week vacation after which the only

2. What correction should be made to the underlined portion of sentence B?

   (1) Buying airplane tickets

   (2) Having bought airplane tickets

   (3) Since buying airplane tickets

   (4) We bought airplane tickets

   (5) Because of buying airplane tickets

3. What correction should be made to the underlined portion of sentence C?

   (1) We had to set our alarm

   (2) We were having to set our alarm

   (3) When we have to set our alarm

   (4) Since setting our alarm

   (5) While setting our alarm

4. What correction should be made to sentence D to make it complete?

   (1) While rushing and making it through security just in time.

   (2) Since rushing through security just in time.

   (3) After rushing and making it through security just in time.

   (4) Because we rushed, we were able to make it through security just in time.

   (5) Although rushing and making it through security just in time.

Answers

Paragraph 1:

Sentence A is a fragment. When a sentence begins with an *-ing* verb (*Having*), you need to be especially careful to complete the thought. Here is what the writer meant:

> If you lose your job, you'll have many questions about health-care coverage and retirement funds as well.

Sentence B is a comma fault with three thoughts all combined with commas. Instead, create three separate and complete thoughts:

> Ask about continued benefits while you look for a job. Any company that interviews you should be able to answer your questions. When you finally find a job, you'll be ready to pick your benefits.

Sentences B and C both contain wordiness. It's unnecessary to rewrite "about continued benefits" and "in the form of health-care coverage and retirement funds." Those facts are already clear.

Here's the rewritten paragraph:

> If you lose your job, you'll have many questions about health-care coverage and retirement funds as well. Ask about continued benefits while you look for a job. Any company that interviews you should be able to answer your questions. When you finally find a job, you'll be ready to pick your benefits.

Paragraph 2:

Sentence A contains a comma fault. Correct it by changing the comma to a period:

> There are many safety issues linked to children's clothing.

Correct the run-on sentence with a comma and a connecting word *and:*

> Flammability is a primary concern, and that's why federal regulations were written.

Sentence B is a run-on sentence. Correct with a period and capital letter:

> The law says that sleepwear for children 9 months or older must be flame resistant or snug fitting. That's because 300 child-burn injuries are treated in emergency rooms yearly.

Sentence B also contains wordiness by closing with the phrase "and the law is supposed to help prevent those accidents." That is clear from the sentence already, so that phrase can be cut.

An even better sentence would be:

> Because 300 child-burn injuries are treated in emergency rooms yearly, the law says that sleepwear for children 9 months or older must be flame resistant or snug fitting.

Paragraph 3:

1. (3) As it stands in the paragraph, this is a run-on sentence. Two complete ideas are run together with no punctuation to show where one ends and the other one begins. The correct answer inserts a period between the two complete thoughts.

2. **(4)** The word *When* makes the sentence incomplete. Delete it, and the sentence has a clear subject (*We*) and verb (*bought*).

3. **(1)** *Having* makes the sentence incomplete. Correct it by substituting *We had to*.

4. **(4)** The original sentence has no subject. The addition of a subject, *we*, makes it correct. None of the other answers solves that problem.

Words That Make a Sentence Incomplete

The words *when, before, because, since, as soon as, while, although,* and *as,* among others, are examples of *conjunctions,* or connecting words. If you start a sentence with one of these words or phrases, be sure you complete the thought. For example:

Incomplete thought: When I last saw Jason.

Complete thought: When I last saw Jason, we had a big disagreement.

 **IN THE KNOW**

There are many other conjunctions such as *and, but, or, yet, for, nor,* and *so.*

Practice

Read the following examples of incomplete thoughts. How would you finish them? The first one is done for you.

1. Because I like that teacher so much.
   Correction: Because I like that teacher so much, I'm taking the other course she teaches.

2. Since our train left at noon

3. While you slept

Answers

You can finish these sentences in many ways. Here are some possibilities. The important thing is to recognize that an introductory group of words, or clause (for example, *when you go to work*), needs a completing thought.

2. Since our train left at noon, we brought lunch with us.

3. While you slept, I finished cleaning the basement.

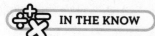 **IN THE KNOW**

How is a clause different from a sentence? After all, *While you slept* has a subject (*you*) and a verb (*slept*), so it should be a sentence, right? No. Even with both a subject and a verb, a clause does not provide a complete thought. An example of a complete sentence would be *While you slept, I read my assignment.*

Agreement Between Subject and Verb in Number

Among the most frequent errors in English is lack of agreement between the subject and verb in number. Agreement between the subject and verb in number simply means that if the subject you use is singular (one), the verb form must be singular as well. Here's an example:

> A cat chases its tail.

You know the subject (*cat*) is singular because it does not end in *s*. This is not always true—some singular nouns end in *s*, such as *bus*—but it is true often enough to be helpful. However, verbs often are the opposite because verbs that end in *s* are often required with singular subjects, such as *chases* with *cat*. See what happens when the plural subject requires a plural verb:

> Two cats chase their tails.

Cats indicates more than one cat. *Chase* is the plural form of the verb and agrees in number with *cats*.

Always be aware that subjects and verbs form their plurals differently. Is the following sentence correct? Before you answer, find the verb and then the subject.

> The chips in the cupcake makes it so crunchy.

To decide if the subject and verb are in agreement, find the two of them first: verb (*makes*) and subject (*chips,* plural).

If you still don't know if the verb is singular or plural, use the pronoun test. Substitute *they* for the plural subject *chips:*

> They makes it so crunchy.

That's clearly wrong. You were correct not to add an *s* to the verb. It may not seem logical, but although a plural subject is spelled with an *s*, a plural verb is not spelled with an *s*.

What's the other problem you face when you choose the correct verb form in this sentence? The answer is that the subject and verb are separated by a phrase. You need to simplify the sentence to decide whether the verb should end in *s*. The verb form *makes* is incorrect in the following sentence:

> The chips in the cupcake makes it so crunchy.

Which phrase would you delete to make this a more straightforward sentence? In other words, which words stand between the subject and verb? If you said *in the cupcake*, you are right! To choose the correct verb form, remove the interrupting phrase.

Practice

For the following questions, find the subject and verb in each sentence. Draw one line under the subject and two lines under the verb. Then, decide if the subject and verb agree in number.

1. Maia and Hector cook some delicious recipes.

2. At the senior center, volunteers helps with the activities.

Now we'll add interrupting phrases to some of these sentences. For the following questions, find the verb, find the subject, and decide if the subject and verb agree.

3. Ben and Eden, and sometimes their mom, collects shells at the beach.

4. A desk and a chair, although big and heavy, fits nicely in that room.

Look for fragments, run-on sentences, wordiness, and comma faults in the following sentences, and correct the errors.

5. When a classroom is filled with students who have the freedom to express themselves for who they are and along with a great teacher tied in with a strong curriculum it allows us a chance to explore education deeper than ever before. A classroom with a very good teacher and very strong curriculum, that is.

6. Diversity is a commitment to recognizing and appreciating the variety of characteristics that makes individuals unique, they represent the many ways we are different.

7. If I were to write a list of my philosophies as a teacher I would be sensitive to differences and I will understand that everybody is different and not everybody is as gifted with athleticism, but I would expect everyone to do their best.

8. Read the following paragraph to find errors in subject-verb agreement. One sentence is a fragment. Can you find it?

   (A) When it comes to the classroom, there is two different aspects of diversity. (B) The first one deal with people who may have special needs, whether they are learning or physical disabilities. (C) Teachers who have a good understanding of these people's issues is sensitive to challenging problems. (D) These teachers helps make all students feel comfortable. (E) The second aspect of diversity in the classroom are all the different cultures, ethnicities, and sexual orientations we have. (F) It is important for children to admire and respect different cultures. (G) While also realizing that minority groups has been exposed to a large amount of unnecessary hostility.

Answers

1. Subject: *Maia and Hector.* Verb: *cook.* Do the subject and verb agree? Yes.

2. Subject: *volunteers.* Verb: *helps.* Do the subject and verb agree? No. The plural noun *volunteers* needs a plural verb: *help.*

3. Incorrect. The subject (*Ben and Eden*) is plural, so *collects* needs to take the plural form (no *s*), *collect. Correction:* Ben and Eden, and sometimes their mom, collect shells at the beach.

4. Incorrect. The subject (*A desk and a chair*) is plural, but the verb (*fits*) ends in *s,* which makes it singular. *Correction:* A desk and a chair, although big and heavy, fit nicely in that room.

5. The first paragraph is one long run-on sentence. The last sentence, although grammatically correct, is not necessary because it repeats information that's already been given and can be cut. To correct the run-on sentences:

    There are ways we can explore education more deeply than ever before. We need classrooms in which students have the freedom to express themselves in their own distinctive voices. Along with that freedom, we need great teachers and a strong curriculum.

6. The second paragraph consists of one sentence with a comma fault. Two complete sentences were connected with a comma and no connecting word. Here is a possible correction:

    Diversity is a commitment to recognizing and appreciating the variety of characteristics that makes individuals unique. The various characteristics represent the many ways we are different.

7. In the third paragraph, there is no division of ideas. With all ideas connected by *and,* it is one long run-on sentence. There are several ways to correct the paragraph. Here is one:

    If I were to write a list of my philosophies as a teacher I would first list sensitivity to differences. A teacher needs an understanding that not everybody is gifted in the same way. For example, not everybody is gifted athletically, but everyone can do his or her best.

8. (A) *Correction:* there *are* two different aspects

Be careful of sentences that start with *there is/are,* and avoid them if possible. The subject is hidden, so it's difficult to know whether the subject is singular or plural. In this sentence, the subject is *aspects*—a plural subject—so your verb needs to be plural, *are.*

(B) *Correction:* The first one *deals*

What is the verb? *Deal* is the verb, and it's plural. What is the subject? The subject is *one,* and it's singular. What needs to be changed? Add an *s* to *deal* to make it singular also.

(C) *Correction:* Teachers who have a good understanding of these people's issues *are* sensitive

You may run into a problem when the subject and verb are far apart in the sentence. The verb is the singular word *is.* The subject is the plural word *teachers.* Change *is* to the plural form, *are.*

(D) *Correction:* These teachers *help*

The plural noun *teachers* needs a plural verb, *help.* Remember that plural verbs don't end in *s.*

(E) *Correction:* The second aspect *is*

The subject is singular, *aspect.* Change the plural verb, *are,* to the singular, *is.*

(F) is correct.

(G) This sentence has two errors. Error 1: The sentence begins with *While,* a word that makes the sentence an incomplete thought. It is a fragment. *Correction:* Add the fragment to the previous sentence:

> It is important for children to admire and respect different cultures while also realizing that minority groups has been exposed to a large amount of unnecessary hostility.

Error 2: that minority groups has been

The subject *(groups)* and the verb *(has been)* don't agree. *Correction:* groups *have been* exposed

Verbs

As you probably already realized, verbs are key. If you understand how they work in a sentence—and better yet, which form of a persnickety verb you should use—you're on your way to a grammatically accurate sentence that clearly conveys your meaning. Conversely, messing up the verb is one of the most common mistakes people make. Therefore, you'll need to find and correct lots of verb errors in the Language questions on the Reasoning Through Language Arts Test.

In this chapter, we focus in on verbs to ensure you understand all their possibilities and quirks. Remember, a verb provides the action or being in a sentence. Verbs don't describe, and they're not people, places, things, or ideas. They're the motors of sentences.

In This Chapter

- Verbs and how they work in sentences
- Sample GED®-style questions to practice the skills on which you'll be tested
- Answers and explanations for all questions

Verb Tenses

Verbs change their form in sentences so readers can understand what time the sentence tells about. Those changes in form are called *tenses*. The Reasoning Through Language Arts: Language Test includes many questions that require you to find and fix errors in *verb tense*. You don't have to identify which verb tense is in use, but simply choose the answer that corrects the errors in the sentences.

Past, Present, and Future

There are three basic tenses: past, present, and future.

Past tense tells readers about something that happened in the past:

> Danielle *wrote* the letter last week.
>
> Yu *emailed* the complaint over a year ago.
>
> Sam *walked* home after the party.

Those things all happened before this present minute, so we use the past tense.

For things that are happening in the present—right now—it's correct to use *present tense:*

> Danielle *writes* the letter.
>
> Yu *emails* the complaint right now.
>
> Sam *walks* while I read.

For things we expect to happen in the future, we use *future tense:*

> Danielle *will write* the letter.
>
> Yu *will email* her complaint.
>
> Sam *will walk* after the party.

Notice that the future tense often includes a *helping verb*—that is, a linking verb that helps the main verb.

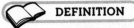 **DEFINITION**

> **Helping verbs** help the main verb by making the tense more clear. Common helping verbs include *will, may, could, must, should, would, might,* and *can.*

Practice

Choose the correct verb from those provided. Use cues from the other words in the sentence to help you figure them out.

1. Alice *bikes/biked* before winter came, but now it's too cold.

2. At the party tonight, she *wears/will be wearing* the necklace we gave her.

Answers

1. Biked (The sentence makes it clear that winter has arrived—no more biking!)

2. Will be wearing (The sentence is referring to an event that will happen.)

Present Perfect, Past Perfect, and Future Perfect

Now verb tense gets a little more complicated. You should be able to spot three other tenses on the Reasoning Through Language Arts: Language Test. Remember, you need to be able to fix the errors you see in the sentences, although you do not need to explain which verb tenses are in use.

Present perfect tense is for when you're writing or speaking about a specific action or state of being that happened at an unspecified time before now. Present perfect can *never* be used with a specific time (or words that designate a specific time, such as *yesterday, last week, on October 9 …*). Here are a few examples of sentences in the present perfect tense:

> I've heard that song so many times.
>
> She has walked away from him before.
>
> We have chosen to move.

Notice that present perfect tense always involves a helping verb, such as *have* or *has*.

Past perfect tense indicates something that happened *before* something else that happened in the past. Here, the examples might be less confusing than the explanation:

> He had moved to Miami before we went to college.
>
> Nigel had purchased that farm before Grandmother died.
>
> They had let the sled go before they realized there was a crash.

In the first example, he moved *before* we went to college—two events that happened in the past, put into their proper order. That's past perfect tense.

Future perfect tense expresses the idea that something will be completed before something else in the future. For example:

> By 2019, I will have completed my GED.
>
> When it's Christmastime again, I'll have mastered my fruitcake recipe.
>
> By next Tuesday, Nora will have broken up with him.

It might be difficult to believe, but there are actually more complicated verb tenses than these, and specific names for all of them—past perfect conditional, anyone?—but for the GED, and general usage, knowing these six will be more than sufficient.

Practice

Name the verb tense for each of the following sentences:

1. The dog had stopped barking by the time the police arrived.

2. My farm lies to the west of the highway.

3. Next year, we'll have completed our conversion to gas heat.

4. The taxi waited for you.

5. Nedra will go to the concert.

6. Gladys has asked that question 30 times already.

Answers

1. Past perfect

2. Present

3. Future perfect

4. Past

5. Future

6. Present perfect

Irregular Verbs

Many verbs follow the conventions of spelling and usage, but some do not. For example, *to call* is a standard verb, and its past tense is *called*. That's logical. But when we try the same construction with *to bring*, we see that something went wrong in the past tense. There's no *bringed* in the English language. Occasionally, a question on the test will include one of these confusing irregular verbs. To help you prepare for the GED, the following table offers a handy review.

Irregular Verbs

Verb	Past	Present	Future
To bring	Brought	Bringing	Will bring
To choose	Chose	Choosing	Will choose
To do	Did	Doing	Will do
To come	Came	Comes	Is coming

In addition, some words are irregular *and* have two different forms of the past tense, depending on whether a helping verb is involved, as shown in the following table.

Verb	Past	Present	Future
To grow	Grew, have grown	Growing	Will grow
To know	Knew, have known	Knowing	Will know
To give	Gave, have given	Gives	Will give
To break	Broke, have broken	Breaking	Will break
To drink	Drank, have drunk	Drinking	Will drink
To eat	Ate, have eaten	Eating	Will eat
To run	Ran, have run	Running	Will run
To ring	Rang, have rung	Ringing	Will ring
To ride	Rode, have ridden	Riding	Will ride
To sing	Sang, have sung	Singing	Will sing
To see	Saw, have seen	Seeing	Will see
To speak	Spoke, have spoken	Speaking	Will speak
To swim	Swam, have swum	Swimming	Will swim
To throw	Threw, have thrown	Throwing	Will throw
To wear	Wore, have worn	Wearing	Will wear
To write	Wrote, have written	Writing	Will write

Practice

Choose the correct form of the irregular verb. Look for the helping verb if you get confused.

1. Many wild animals *have drunk/dranks* at the watering hole.

2. My uncle *has grew/grown* oranges for 10 years.

3. The chorus *sang/sung* songs at the concert.

4. The catcher *threw/thrown* out the runner at second.

5. She *has swam/swum* in the Olympic trials.

Answers

1. Have drunk

2. Has grown

3. Sang

4. Threw

5. Has swum

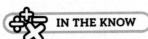 **IN THE KNOW**

Verbs like *to drink* and *to swim* are often misused. Knowing the correct way to form their tenses shows that you have a good understanding of verb usage, so expect to see those tricky examples on the test.

The Many Forms of *to Be*

The verb *to be* has quite a few forms, and none bear any real semblance to another, as you can see when you consider that *am, are, is, was, were, have been, will have been, will be,* and *have been* are all forms of *to be*. *To be* is one of the English language's most-used verbs and is used to show a state of being. It will definitely appear multiple times on the GED, so be sure you are comfortable with it.

The Four Purposes of *to Be* in a Sentence

First, *to be* can be, and most often is, a *linking verb*, as in the following examples:

I *am playing* the piano.

The dog *was running* through the water.

As a linking verb, the forms of *to be* provide support for the main verb.

Second, *to be* can stand on its own and simply state the existence of something:

> I am, I said.

> You are?

> They will be.

Third, *to be* can act as a *subject complement*, which means it simply provides a link between the subject of a sentence and further information about the subject:

> Diane *is* the boss.

> The trucks *were* all Fords from the 1950s.

In the first example Diane is the subject, and the verb *is* acts as a subject complement to give us further information about her. In the second example, the trucks are the subject, and the verb *were* acts as a subject complement to fill us in on what type of trucks they were.

Fourth, *to be* can be an *adjective complement*. In this case, the verb provides a link between the subject and some kind of modifying adjectives:

> Reba *is* very successful.

This sentence gives us more information about Reba, using an adjective and an adverb.

For the GED, you need to know how *to be* can work in a sentence so you can spot any errors—although, as always, you don't have to name the grammatical rule or verb tense in play. It's easy to get tripped up by the different forms of *to be*. Studying this section just before taking the GED will help keep you on the right path.

Present, Past, and Future of *to Be*

No matter how *to be* is used in a sentence, it will fall into one of the tenses and forms shown in the following table.

	Present	Past	Future
I	Am	Was	Will be
You	Are	Were	Will be
He/she/it	Is	Was	Will be
They	Are	Were	Will be

In some regions of the United States, it's common to change the usage of *to be*. For example, some people are used to saying "You was …" for the past tense instead of "You were …." Some people also say "They was …" instead of "They were …." These regionalisms are technically incorrect, and you should be ready to fix them on the GED. Be particularly wary of any sentence using *You*, which is always matched with the plural form of the verb. It's never *You was* and is always *You were.*

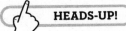   **HEADS-UP!**

You is always considered plural, even if you are writing about only one person. In other words, there is never a time when *you was* will be correct in formal English.

Problem Areas with *to Be*

To be is a vital verb, but it can easily lead you into trouble. Let's look at a few problems to watch out for.

First, there is no such word as *ain't*, at least not in formal English. If you're writing a song, a play, or quoting someone who speaks with this regionalism, you can get away with using *ain't*. Otherwise, don't use it on the GED, including in the essay section!

Not only is *ain't* always wrong, but it also often tends to turn up in sentences with double negatives, such as *We ain't never going to believe that guy.* Double negatives are always wrong, too. It's much simpler to write *We don't believe that guy.*

Sometimes *to be* is used when it's not really necessary. When you're writing, it's worth taking a minute to review your words and see if you can take out any forms of *to be*. For example, if you look carefully at the sentence *Everyone who is willing to participate will get an A*, you'll notice that you don't need "who is." It can just read *Everyone willing to participate will get an A.*

Another way *to be* is unnecessary is when an action verb could take its place. Action verbs are always more enticing to readers. For example, instead of writing *Béyonce was influential in my decision to become a singer*, you could write *Béyonce influenced my decision to become a singer.* That's much more direct.

Practice

Read the following sentences and fix the *to be* usages if needed.

1. It were the only way to find out what had happened.

2. We were all in agreement.

3. All five of us will have taken part.

Answers

1. *It* is singular, but *were* is plural. Change *were* to *was*.

2. You could just write *We agreed*. The form of *to be* isn't needed.

3. No mistakes.

Subject and Verb Agreement

Ensuring your subjects and verbs agree is of utmost importance if you want your writing to be clear and professional. When you're writing, it's easy to mismatch your verb and subject, and readers are quick to spot such mistakes. You need to be sure you understand the rules of subject and verb agreement, especially for the Extended Response portion of the GED. We gave you an overview of subject and verb agreement in Chapter 1. In this section, we look at more specific tips for subject-verb agreement.

Special Forms of Several Linking Verbs

When looking for errors in verb usage, pay attention to linking verbs. It's crucial that you remember which linking verbs are singular and which are plural. If your subject is singular, your linking verb must be as well, and the same is true for plural subjects and linking verbs. Be sure they match. Singular linking verbs include *is, was, has,* and *does*. Plural linking verbs include *are, were, have,* and *do*.

Does Is Singular, but *Do* Is Plural

It might be easiest to show examples for this one instead of try to explain. *She has three sisters* is correct. (*She* is singular, and so is *has*.) *She do the dishes* is not correct. (*She* is singular, but *do* is the plural form of that verb.)

Watch Out for Phrases

A *prepositional phrase* is a series of words that begins with a preposition and is inserted into a sentence. The phrase may modify the subject or the verb, but it never *contains* the subject or verb.

Remember, on the GED you won't need to diagram a sentence, so you don't need to be able to label a prepositional phrase. However, you do need to recognize when a sentence contains one so you don't allow it to affect your verb choice.

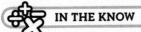 **IN THE KNOW**

Common prepositions include *to, of, by, in, around, above, below, at, until, like,* and *for.* A prepositional phrase usually begins with a preposition and contains its object and any modifiers (adjectives or adverbs) of the object. For example, in the prepositional phrase *below the garage, below* is a preposition, and the *garage* is the object. In the phrase *in the city park,* the preposition is *in,* and the object is *park. City* modifies *park.*

Let's look at two examples:

One of the plates *was/were* smashed.

The president, in addition to his staff members, *is/are* here.

Which form would you use? The correct answers are, respectively, *was* and *is.* Why? Although *plates* and *members* are plural, they are part of prepositional phrases—*of the plates* and *in addition to his staff members*—so they cannot be the subject. The true subjects of both sentences, *One* and *The president,* are both singular.

If you find this confusing, remember that a prepositional phrase can always be removed from a sentence, and the sentence will still be complete and make sense:

One was smashed. (We may not know what exactly was smashed, but the sentence is still a sentence.)

The president is here.

Matching Verbs with Compound Subjects

Sentences with compound subjects—or when the subject is more than one noun—also should put you on alert. The question of whether to use a singular or plural verb comes down to how the compound subject is constructed. Here are two rules:

- A compound subject that contains the conjunction *and* is plural. Use a plural verb.

- With a compound subject that contains the conjunctions *or* or *nor,* match the verb to the subject nearest to it.

That's right—one of the rules is based on proximity. Still, it works. For example, look at this sentence:

The orchestra and the singer *is/are* performing tonight.

Look to the conjunction. It's *and,* so the case is closed. The verb is plural, just like its compound subject: *The orchestra and the singer are performing tonight.*

Here's another example:

> George or the cowboys *were/was* the first choice.

Look to the conjunction. It's *or*, so you know you must look to the subject closest to the verb. In this sentence, that's *the cowboys*, so *George or the cowboys were the first choice* is correct.

Verbs in Inverted Sentences

An *inverted sentence* is just a fancy name for a sentence in which the verb comes before the subject. For example:

> In the garden is a beautiful rose.

The typical way of writing that sentence is *A beautiful rose is in the garden*, but the inverted way is also correct. You just need to be sure you still match the verb and subject. What would you do for this sentence?

> Through the stadium *stream/streams* a thousand fans.

Not sure which to choose? Reorder the sentence:

> A thousand fans *stream/streams* through the stadium.

With the reordering, it's clear that the subject, *fans*, is plural, so the verb *stream* should be as well.

Verbs with *There*

Many English sentences use *there* where a subject is expected, but *there* isn't the subject, usually. Look farther along in the sentence, and you'll often see the subject. Yet *there* must match the accompanying verb, so we need to figure out if it is singular or plural:

> There *are/is* all of my friends.

Here, the trick is to look ahead for the subject. In this sentence, it is *all* (*of my friends* is a prepositional phrase), and *all* is plural. So:

> There *are* all of my friends.

Balance Between Verb Tense and Subject

Take a look at this sentence:

> The closer to the edge Sheila walked, the farther away Amanda moved.

It's a nicely balanced sentence, comparing what Sheila did (walk closer) and how Amanda responded (moved farther way).

Now look at this example:

> The closer to the edge Sheila walked, Amanda moves away.

See the lack of balance in that sentence? The verb changed in the second part: *moved* became *moves* in the present tense. Because *walked* is in the past tense, the parallel verb should be, too.

You also want to balance sentences that begin with *The more* or *The less*. For example:

> The more he talked, the more I wanted to listen.

Or:

> The less interested he looked, the less enthusiastic Bob was in talking to him.

Practice

In the following paragraphs, spot and correct the errors in verb usage for each labeled sentence.

1. (A) Most of our films have been distributed. (B) We have been waiting for all of the contracts to be signed and returned. (C) Fortunately, there is no festivals we want to enter them in this year. (D) Festivals in New York, Chicago, and Berlin is of interest to us, however. (E) The film or prints of it has to be sent. (F) The longer we wait, I get weary.

2. (A) There are several different routes to becoming a doctor. (B) Doesn't they all seem to be difficult? (C) More and more people are choosing to major in a field other than pre-med. (D) For example, Lenora do want to become a doctor, but she's majoring in accounting so that she can work first. (E) An internship or volunteer work is her next step in getting more experience. (F) The more she studies, the more excited she is about becoming a doctor!

Answers

1. (A) Correct. Remember, ignore the prepositional phrase *of our films*, and look at the subject, which is the plural *Most*. (B) Correct. (C) *is* should be *are*. Take a look at the rest of the sentence to see whether *there* is plural or singular. Because it's tied to *festivals*, it is plural. (D) It's the same mistake: *is* should be *are*, because *festivals* is plural. Check and you'll see that *in New York, Chicago, or Berlin* is a prepositional phrase. (E) *Has* should be

have. In this sentence, a compound subject is joined by *or.* That means you look at the subject closest to the verb and match the verb to it. (And ignore the prepositional phrase, *of it.*) (F) Try "the wearier I get" instead, so the verbs match in parallel construction.

2. (A) Correct. (B) *Doesn't* should be *Don't.* If you're not sure why, remember to change the question to a statement. (C) Correct. It has a compound subject that's joined by *and,* so the plural verb is correct. (D) *Lenora does,* not *Lenora do.* (E) Correct. It doesn't seem like it's correct, does it? But if you look at the sentence, it has a compound subject, joined by *or.* So look to the subject closest to the verb, which is *volunteer work,* and see that it is singular, so a singular verb is used. (F) Correct.

Tricky Parts of Speech

In this chapter, we review some of the grammatical rules that are most likely to cause you to slip up on the Language portion of the Reasoning Through Language Arts Test. The bulk of this chapter is spent on tricky pronouns, but we also take a look at adjectives, adverbs, and especially the comparison of adjectives, a very dicey area in grammar. Don't worry, though—by the end of this chapter, you'll be able to deploy the correct grammar rules that will help you in the Language portion of the test as well as in the Extended Response.

In This Chapter

- The correct way to use confusing parts of speech
- Sample GED®-style questions to practice the skills on which you'll be tested
- Answers and explanations for all questions

Using the Correct Pronoun

A pronoun is a word used in place of a noun. Pronouns can be subjects, objects, or possessives. Nouns don't change, even if they're used differently in a sentence, but pronouns change depending on what role they take in the sentence. Let's look at all three.

Subject

Subject forms of pronouns are used as the subject in a sentence. They're not difficult to remember: *he, she, it,* and *they.* For example:

> Sue ran = she ran. *Sue* is the subject in the sentence, and *she* is the subject form of the pronoun.

> The bike crashed = It crashed. *The bike* is the subject, and *it* is the subject form of the pronoun.

 HEADS-UP!

Don't confuse *pronouns* with *proper nouns.* Pronouns replace a noun, but proper nouns are the name given to a particular noun. For example, you can talk about a rock singer (a noun) or Bono (a proper noun). The pronoun form would be *he, him,* or *his.*

One use of subject forms of pronouns that might trip you up is when they are used as *predicate pronouns.* A predicate pronoun is a pronoun that follows a linking verb and is linked by the verb to a subject. Remember, a linking verb shows a state of being. Here's an example:

> The students were she and I.

In this sentence, *she* and *I* are the pronouns. They are used in the subject form because *were* is a linking verb. Are you wondering why it wouldn't be *The students were her and me?* That's a common confusion. A simple tip is to flip the sentence's predicate and subject. You would end up with this:

> She and I were the students.

Her and me were the students doesn't sound right at all, so you know *she* is correct.

Object

The object of a sentence is the noun or pronoun receiving the action of the verb. In the sentence *Ted saw Dwight, Ted* is the subject and *Dwight* is the object because he's the receiver of the action of seeing. The usage of pronouns is instinctual here. We know what sounds right. If we change *Dwight* to the correct pronoun, we know we would write *Ted saw him,* not *Ted saw he* or *Ted saw his.*

The only exception to this rule is *you,* which is the same in both subject and object form: *You are going to the store* or *I saw you.* If you haven't guessed by now, here's a reminder: always be extra alert when *you* is involved in the answer choices on the GED.

By the way, one of the most common mistakes in the English language is trying to determine the difference between subject and object pronouns. Let's say you wanted to talk about your all-female book club and the trip you took together. Do you say *We girls went on vacation* or *Us girls went on vacation?* Neither one really sounds great, but you can find the correct choice by trying the pronoun alone in the sentence: *We went on vacation* or *Us went on vacation.* That helps you realize the first one is correct. If you get confused, take out the extra parts of the sentence to focus on the word in question. You'd write *We went on vacation.*

Possessive

Possessive forms of pronouns show ownership by the pronoun. They are *my/mine, our/ours, your/yours, his/her/hers/its,* and *their/theirs.*

Note these don't use apostrophes. The possessive form of *it,* which is *its,* has no apostrophe. Therefore, you write *The horse turned its head* because the head belongs to it (the horse).

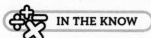 **IN THE KNOW**

Only use *it's,* with the apostrophe, when you can substitute *it is* into the sentence and have it make sense.

Antecedents are the nouns replaced by the pronouns. For example, in the sentence *Mel came by today and brought his payment, Mel* is the antecedent, and *his* is the pronoun that replaces it.

Antecedents may seem obvious—and they are—but they become more important when you're dealing with singular and plural nouns. You replace a singular noun, which deals with one thing, with a singular pronoun. You replace a plural noun, which deals with more than one thing, with a plural pronoun. For example:

The *actor* learned *his* lines.

The *girls* learned *their* harmonies.

When you get confused about whether to use a singular or a plural pronoun, look to the antecedent.

Other Types of Pronouns

You should be aware of a few more particular kinds of pronouns. Here's a quick review.

Compound personal pronouns are pronouns that have *-self* or *-selves* added to the end for emphasis. For example:

We always do the cooking *ourselves.*

Demonstrative pronouns are used to point out which persons or things are referred to. They are *this, that, these,* and *those. This* and *these* refer to persons or things close by. *That* and *those* refer to persons or things farther away:

> *That* is the lighthouse we could see from the house.

> *This* is my aunt.

Interrogative pronouns ask questions. They are *who, whose, whom, which,* and *what*.

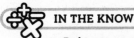 **IN THE KNOW**

Did you just panic at the thought of trying to decide between *who* and *whom?* Don't worry! You can tell the difference easily by remembering that *who* is the subject form of the pronoun and *whom* is the object form. So you'd write *Who is coming today?* and *Whom did Lori call?*

Indefinite pronouns do not refer to a particular person or people. That's why they're called indefinite—who they're referring to is not definite!

Singular indefinite pronouns include *anybody, anyone, anything, each, everybody, everyone, everything, neither, nobody, no one, somebody,* and *someone*. When you use these words in a sentence, if you want to show their possession, you must use singular possessive pronouns, such as *his, her,* and *its*. For example:

> Everybody took his turn.

> Something left its tracks here.

When a singular pronoun must refer to both males and females, the English language defaults to the awkward *his or her*. So you would write:

> Someone left his or her skates.

 HEADS-UP!

The way we commonly talk is not always the same as formal written English. Many of us say *their* instead of *his or her*, as in: *Someone left their skates*. That's not correct, even though it's very common. Don't let that mistake slip by you on the GED!

There are a few plural indefinite pronouns: *both, few, many,* and *several*. Use the plural form of the pronoun with them:

> Both watched their pets.

There are four indefinite pronouns that are tricky enough to sometimes be singular and sometimes be plural: *all, any, none,* and *some.* You'll need to look at the context of the rest of the sentence to see which they are. In this sentence, for example, *all* is singular:

> All of the cake was eaten.

Here, it's plural:

> All of the seats were empty.

Writers get in trouble using pronouns when they don't pay attention to (or don't know) which type of pronoun they should use: subject, object, or possessive. If you get confused, figure out what role in the sentence the pronoun plays and then remember this handy table.

	Subject	**Object**	**Possessive**
Singular	I You She, he, it	Me You Him, her, it	My, mine Your, yours Her, hers, his, its
Plural	We You They	Us You Them	Our, ours Your, yours Their, theirs

Practice

For each sentence, choose the correct pronoun.

1. *We/Us* and the book club had dinner.

2. The magician balanced *him/himself* on the pedestal.

3. *Who/Whom* made this CD?

4. Will somebody loan me *his or her/their* pocketknife?

5. All of the snakes shed *its/their* skin.

6. The spider spun *its/it's* delicate web.

Answers

1. We (Take *and the book club* out, if needed.)

2. Himself (To make it clear he balanced his own body.)

3. Who (Because it's used as the subject of the sentence.)

4. His or her (Even though it's awkward.)

5. Their (In this usage, *all* refers to more than one.)

6. Its (Remember, *it's* is only for *it is,* and *The spider spun it is delicate web* doesn't make sense.)

Understanding Adjectives and Adverbs

Adjectives and *adverbs* play similar roles in sentences, helping you describe what's around you, and it's easy to confuse them. However, you can't just substitute one for the other, so it's a good idea to be clear on which is which before you take the Reasoning Through Language Arts Test.

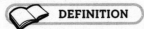 **DEFINITION**

Adjectives modify nouns. **Adverbs** modify verbs, adjectives, and other adverbs.

Adjectives

Adjectives help you describe what you've seen and heard by *modifying* (that is, changing the meaning of another word by making it more precise) nouns. For example, the word *sky* is a noun. By adding adjectives, you can modify the meaning and make it more clear:

a *blue* sky   a *darkening* sky   a *rose-tinged* sky

a *low* sky   a *threatening* sky   a *damp* sky

Adverbs

Adverbs, on the other hand, modify much more than nouns. Adjectives describe, but adverbs answer *how, when, where,* or *to what extent.* Adverbs can modify verbs, adjectives, and even other adverbs. Let's look at a few examples.

Adverbs modify verbs in the sentence *I walked:*

I walked *slowly.*

I walked *recently.*

I walked *outside.*

Adverbs modify adjectives in the sentence *It was a nice day.* (Did you notice that *nice* is an adjective, describing *day?*)

> It was a *fairly* nice day.
>
> It was a *surprisingly* nice day.
>
> It was a *very* nice day.

In all of these examples, the italicized words are adverbs modifying an adjective to tell readers more about what kind of nice day it was.

Adverbs even can modify other adverbs, as in the sentence *Andrew danced well.* Here, the first adverb is *well*, which describes how Andrew danced. If we add in more adverbs:

> Andrew danced *very* well.
>
> Andrew danced *really very* well.

The adverbs modify *well*, making it more clear just how well Andrew danced.

Many adverbs are formed by adding *-ly* to an adjective, as shown in the following table.

Adjective	Adverb
Plain	Plainly
Brave	Bravely
Noisy	Noisily
Large	Largely

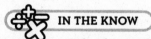 **IN THE KNOW**

Only a few words in the English language end in *-ly* but are not adverbs. *Lovely* and *lonely*, for example, are adjectives. However, you're usually pretty safe guessing that if a word ends in *-ly*, it's an adverb.

Good Versus *Well*

A pitfall in grammar and writing is not knowing when to use *good* and when to use *well*. It's actually quite simple: use *good* as an adjective and *well* as an adverb unless you're talking about someone's health. For example:

> He plays tennis well. (*Well* modifies the verb *plays*, so it's an adverb.)
>
> That book was good. (*Good* modifies the noun *book*, so it's an adjective.)

Practice

Choose the adjective or adverb form of the word to complete the sentence.

1. Our team won *easy/easily.*

2. Keisha plays the piano *good/well.*

3. John felt *bad/badly* about the accident.

Answers

1. Easily (Use the adverb form because you're describing the verb *won.*)

2. Well (Remember, *good* is used as an adjective only to modify nouns and pronouns; the adverb form is always *well.*)

3. Badly (Use the adverb form because you're describing the verb *felt.*)

Making Comparisons with Adjectives

Adjectives are useful in so many ways, especially when making comparisons. Yet the rules for making comparisons are not widely employed. Here's how to do it, and how to catch and fix errors in comparisons on the GED.

You'll need to know two forms of adjectives: *comparative* and *superlative.* The comparative form is used when you compare one thing or person with another. The superlative form is used when you compare a thing or person with more than one other of its kind. This might seem overly picky, but we bet at least one question on the test will require you to know this.

For example, if I want to compare the cleanliness of two rooms, I might write: *This room is cleaner than the living room. Cleaner* is the comparative form, which is correct because I'm comparing the room to only one other. However, if I wanted to say that *This room is the cleanest in the house,* I'm correct in using the superlative form, *cleanest,* because I'm comparing the room to all of the other rooms in the house.

The Comparative Form

You can form the comparative version of an adjective in two ways. For a short adjective like *slow* or *clean*, simply add *-er:*

Clean + -er = cleaner

Slow + -er = slower

Happy + -er = happier (Note that the spelling changed, too.)

For longer adjectives, like *delicious* or *selfish*, add the word *more* or *less* in front:

The food was more delicious than I remember.

Her uncle was less selfish than I remember.

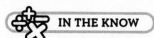 **IN THE KNOW**

Some adjectives—generally those that are one or two syllables long—can be used in the comparative form by adding -er or using *more*. For example, *soft* can be *more soft* or *softer*. It's really the writer's preference.

The Superlative Form

Remember, the superlative form is only used when making a comparison between more than two things. Again, you can do this two ways. For adjectives to which you added *-er* to make the comparative form, now add *-est* to make the superlative form. On the other hand, if you made the adjective into the comparative form by adding the word *more* before it, to make the superlative, you'll want to add *most* before it.

The following table offers a few examples.

Adjective	Comparative	Superlative
Full	Fuller	Fullest
Dim	Dimmer	Dimmest
Annoying	More annoying	Most annoying
Courageous	More courageous	Most courageous

Tips for Using Comparative and Superlative Forms

When deciding between comparative and superlative forms, look for how many things or people are being compared. That will tell you which form to use:

> That kitten is the cutest of the two.

Sounds right, doesn't it? Nope! You've only got two kittens, so the one can only be *cuter*, not the *cutest*.

Also, remember not to leave out the word *other* when you're comparing something with everything else of its kind. Therefore, you wouldn't write:

> That kitten is cuter than any animal.

That makes it seem like the kitten is not an animal. Instead, write:

> That kitten is cuter than any other animal.

Written this way, it's clear that the kitten is an animal, and that you're comparing it to one, other, unspecified animal.

Avoid using both *-er* and *more* or *-est* and *most* in the same sentence. *Wool is more harsher than cotton,* for example, is incorrect.

Finally, you need to be aware of a few irregular comparisons. They don't follow the rules, so you'll just have to know them. Study the following table.

Adjective	Comparison	Superlative
Good	Better	Best
Well	Better	Best
Bad	Worse	Worst
Little	Less or lesser	Least
Much	More	Most
Many	More	Most
Far	Farther	Farthest

Practice

Find the pronoun, adjective, and adverb faults in the paragraphs, and decide how to fix them.

1. (A) We guys were late for the meeting. (B) We were held up by a truck that had jack-knifed, blocking it's lane of traffic. (C) Joel called the office, but the reception was poorer. (D) We ended up walking fast back to the nearest exit.

2. (A) Sam was feeling poorly. (B) His sister was ill, too, but Sam felt worst. (C) He wanted a new medicine and asked if the doctor would bring them. (D) Before too long, he was fastly asleep.

Answers

1. (A) The usage of *we guys* sounds a little off, but it's actually correct. If you drop *guys*, it's easy to see that *We were late …* is right. (B) That's the wrong form of *its*. It doesn't need the apostrophe because it's showing possession, not substituting for *it is*. (We review possessives in the next chapter, so if you're confused, don't worry.) (C) *Poorer* is incorrect because there's no comparison in the sentence. (D) *Fast* is incorrect because it is an adjective and being used to modify a verb, not a noun. The adverb form, by the way, would be *quickly*. By the way, *nearest* is okay, too, because the sentence compares that exit to all of the other exits in the world.

2. (A) It might sound like a regionalism, but *poorly* is correct in this sentence. (B) Sam is compared to only one other person, so you'd write *worse*, not *worst*. (C) Remember the antecedent rule: *a new medicine* is singular, so you should use *it*, not *them*. (D) *Fast*, not *fastly*, because *asleep* is an adjective. Don't overthink your answers.

Punctuation and More

Punctuation marks are the street signs on the highway of reading and writing, guiding you toward your destination: a correct understanding of what the words are trying to convey. When you, as a writer, know what you're doing with commas, semicolons, quotation marks, and other punctuation, your reader has a smooth ride ahead. The same is true with capitalization. However, whenever the rules are not properly followed, readers will be slowed down and potentially confused. An understanding of how to use punctuation and capitalization correctly is a must for anyone who writes in any way in his or her career.

In this chapter, we review the basics of punctuation and capitalization and practice spotting the types of punctuation errors you'll see on the Language portion of the Reasoning Through Language Arts Test.

In This Chapter

- Overview of punctuation
- Tips on when to capitalize and when not to
- Sample GED®-style questions to practice the skills on which you'll be tested
- Answers and explanations for all questions

Correct Usage of End Marks

End marks do two things: they alert your reader that your sentence is over, and they indicate the tone of the sentence. There are three types of end marks:

- Period (.)

- Question mark (?)

- Exclamation point (!)

The period closes a declarative sentence, which makes a statement:

> The car is red.

A period also can end an imperative sentence, which requires or tells someone to do something:

> Please open the window.

A question mark goes at the end of an interrogative sentence, which asks a question:

> Has anyone seen my ferret?

 HEADS-UP!

Do not use a question mark with an indirect question, which is part of a statement that tells what someone has asked without giving the exact words. For example:

Incorrect: Micah asked if anyone had seen his ferret?

Correct: Micah asked if anyone had seen his ferret.

An exclamation point is used at the end of an exclamatory sentence, which expresses strong feeling:

> That was a great game!

Exclamation points also are used after interjections or any exclamatory expression:

> Oh boy!

In addition, exclamation points are used at the end of imperative sentences that express excitement or emotion:

> Close that window, now!

It's easy to get confused about whether to end an imperative sentence with an exclamation point or a period. When in doubt, consider whether the sentence is meant to convey *strong* feeling. Keep in mind, you are unlikely to face a question that requires this level of judgment on the GED.

Practice

Choose the end mark for each of the following sentences.

1. Do you know the way to San Jose

2. That's the ferret he lost

3. Help

4. Takeysha was asking everyone if they had seen the movie yet

Answers

1. ?

2. .

3. !

4. . (Remember, indirect questions do not end with question marks.)

The Many Purposes of the Comma

Think of commas (,) as the breaths, or pauses, in a sentence, giving both you and your reader a quick moment to relax or blink your eyes before moving on to the rest of the statement. When you read the sentence to yourself, the moments where you naturally pause in your speaking are often where a comma should be used.

Here are the comma's major uses:

- To avoid confusion
- To indicate a series
- After introductory words
- With multiple adjectives
- With *interrupters*
- With names in direct address

- With *appositives*

- With quotations

- In compound sentences

- In dates, locations, and addresses

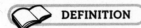 **DEFINITION**

Interrupters are words or phrases that disturb the flow of a sentence. The most common interrupter is when you add the name of the person you're speaking to in the middle of the sentence: I asked him, Laurence, but he said no. **Appositives** are words placed immediately after other words to clarify meaning or define who or what is meant. (Interrupters and appositives are discussed in more detail later in the chapter.)

That list might look overwhelming, but most comma usage is instinctual and simple to understand. Let's take a closer look at the rules.

To Avoid Confusion

Use a comma where necessary to avoid confusion. For example:

After eating my grandma takes a nap.

The sentence is much more clear with a well-placed comma:

After eating, my grandma takes a nap.

To Indicate a Series

In a series, a comma should be used after every item except the last:

We ate, packed, and departed an hour later.

Sheila, Danielle, and Erica were the first to arrive.

It was getting cold, the wind picked up, and Carlos began to worry about getting home safely.

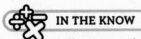 **IN THE KNOW**

The comma placed after the next-to-the-last item in the list is called the serial comma in the United States. It is the American version of the Oxford comma, common in the United Kingdom.

After Introductory Words

Commas should be used after introductory words, such as in this sentence:

> Then, Shelby demanded a ride home.

With Multiple Adjectives

Commas also should appear in lists of two or more adjectives, except before the last item in the list (remember, adjectives modify nouns):

> It was a great, big, wild party.

> I love how a bright, sunny, brisk day makes everything better.

Watch out, though. If two adjectives are used together to express a single idea of closely related thoughts, don't use a comma:

> The little old woman lived in a shoe.

> The big red truck thrilled the little boy.

Practice

Let's pause for some practice. Where should the commas go in these sentences?

1. It was the best nicest most amazing gift ever.
2. Also I'm tired of waiting for you.
3. When we entered the room was empty.
4. It's nice to see a sweet old couple taking a walk together.

Answers

1. It was the best, nicest, most amazing gift ever. (Rule: series of adjectives.)
2. Also, I'm tired of waiting for you. (Rule: introductory word.)
3. When we entered, the room was empty. (Rule: to avoid confusion.)
4. No commas needed because the adjectives are closely linked.

With Interrupters

Commas are used with interrupters, which pop up in the middle of a sentence, as their name suggests:

> This ferret, however, is not the one we lost.

> The true story, it seems, will never be known.

With Names in Direct Address

Commas are used to set off nouns of direct address:

> Call me later, Steve.

> Did she ask you, Jane, if you would go?

With Appositives

Commas are used with appositives, which are most often seen in conversations about people. The comma should appear on either side of the appositive, unless it's at the end of a sentence:

> My teacher, Mr. Smith, is not returning to our school.

> Andrew, the boy in the flannel shirt, is my best friend.

Practice

Take a moment now for some more comma practice. Where should the commas go in these sentences?

1. Yes Justin is my brother.

2. Give me a kiss Kryz.

3. She is the best person for the role I guess.

4. The minister Reverend Hale is late.

Answers

1. Yes, Justin is my brother. (Rule: introductory word.)

2. Give me a kiss, Kryz. (Rule: direct address.)

3. She is the best person for the role, I guess. (Rule: interrupter.)

4. The minister, Reverend Hale, is late. (Rule: appositive.)

With Quotations

We cover quotation marks later in this chapter. For now, let's review how commas are used with quotations. Commas should be used in quotations to set off the explanatory words of a direct quotation, which tell you who is speaking. For example, consider the following sentence:

Amir said, "Let's get some ice cream."

Amir said are the explanatory words. They're followed by a comma to help set up the quotation better.

Explanatory words can come at the end of a quotation sentence, too, such as:

"I like the penguins best," said the girl.

In sentences like this, the comma is placed after the last word of the spoken (quoted) sentence but before the explanatory words.

Explanatory words also can be placed in the middle of a sentence. This is called a *divided quotation*. A comma is used after the last word of the first part and again after the last explanatory word:

"We can see the penguins," said her brother, "but then let's get ice cream."

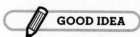 **GOOD IDEA**

> Rules for commas can be confusing. Remember that you don't have to explain the rules for comma usage on the GED; you only have to be able to identify how they should be used in a sentence.

In Compound Sentences

Commas are used in compound sentences, in which two or more simple sentences are joined together with an independent conjunction: *and, but, or, yet, for, nor,* and *so.* For example, we can join together the two simple sentences *Sue got back from her trip* and *Now, Sue is sleeping* like this:

Sue got back from her trip, and now she's sleeping.

We insert a comma after the first simple sentence and before the conjunction.

In Dates, Locations, and Addresses

Include commas in dates, locations, and addresses. Commas go between the parts of a date (except between the month and date), between the name of a city or town and the name of its state or country, and between the parts of an address (except between a street number and street name and a state and a zip code). Therefore, we write:

> May 25, 2012
>
> New York, New York
>
> Auckland, New Zealand
>
> 1231 Mitchell Dr., Des Moines, Iowa

In Letter Greetings

One final spot where commas are needed is after the introductory greeting in informal letters. (Note this differs from formal business letters, which take a colon, as discussed later.) Place a comma after the opening salutation:

> Dear friend,
>
> Dear Alice,

Practice

Add commas where they are needed in the following sentences.

1. We were sad but we weren't very surprised.

2. I'm having trouble finding information for what happened on June 18 1889.

3. "If it rains" Joe said "we'll have to cancel."

4. We started our honeymoon in Sydney Australia.

Answers

1. We were sad, but we weren't very surprised. (Rule: compound sentences.)

2. I'm having trouble finding information for what happened on June 18, 1889. (Rule: date.)

3. "If it rains," Joe said, "we'll have to cancel." (Rule: divided quotation.)

4. We started our honeymoon in Sydney, Australia. (Rule: location.)

Semicolons and Colons

In contrast to the comma's many usages and rules, the semicolon and colon are much simpler. The semicolon looks like a period over a comma (;), and a colon looks like two stacked dots (:). On the GED, you only need to know one way the semicolon will be used, and that's to join the parts of a compound sentence together when no conjunction is used.

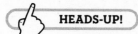 **HEADS-UP!**

Remember, the independent conjunctions are *and, but, or, yet, for, nor,* and *so.* If you see one of them, do not use a semicolon.

For example, look at this sentence:

Mother threw the frying pan away it was worn out.

Inserting a semicolon corrects the sentence and keeps it from being a run-on:

Mother threw the frying pan away; it was worn out.

Colons have three uses as far as the GED is concerned. They follow the greeting of a business letter (more formal than a conversational letter, for which a comma is used, as discussed earlier):

Dear Sir or Madam:

To Whom It May Concern:

They separate numbers indicating hours and minutes:

11:11 A.M.

9:30 P.M.

They are used to introduce a list of items:

I gave Michael a list of what he needed to bring: firewood, marshmallows, graham crackers, and chocolate.

 **GOOD IDEA**

The GED often presents a business letter or email and asks you to locate and fix any errors. Colon and semicolon errors are often included in those sections. Keep your eyes peeled for them!

Practice

Add semicolons and colons where they are needed in the following sentences.

1. I bought my aunt a new blouse it is red, her favorite color.

2. She liked it but she said it was too small.

3. When the store opens at 1000 A.M., Mother wants me to buy the following for our ski trip gloves, a hat, warm socks, a scarf, and snow boots.

Answers

1. I bought my aunt a new blouse; it is red, her favorite color.

2. Trick question! You need to add a comma, not a semicolon: She liked it, but she said it was too small.

3. When the store opens at 10:00 A.M., Mother wants me to buy the following for our ski trip: gloves, a hat, warm socks, a scarf, and snow boots.

Quotation Marks

Quotation marks (" ") may well be the most abused form of punctuation, but the rules for how to use them are actually quite simple. Just be sure you know them before you take the GED, and you'll be fine.

Quotation marks enclose the exact words of a speaker or writer:

"Now is the time," he yelled.

"To be or not to be" is a famous quote from Richard Shakespeare's *Hamlet.*

Quotation marks are used only for the exact words of another speaker or writer. Indirect quotations and paraphrases—when one is definitely not using the writer or speaker's exact words—do not need quotation marks:

She asked if we were from around here.

Quotation Marks with Commas

We already know from looking at commas earlier in the chapter that the explanatory words around a quotation require commas, whether they are at the beginning, middle, or end of a sentence. Just remember that the explanatory words at the beginning of a sentence are followed by a comma outside the quotation marks, but the punctuation at the end of a sentence is usually placed inside the quotation marks:

> Her daughter responded, "I did well on the test."

When explanatory words arrive at the end of the sentence, the quoted words earlier in the sentence are followed by a comma inside the quotation marks:

> "I'll text you when I'm home," I said.

For divided quotations, the first part of a divided quotation is followed by a comma that is placed inside the quotation marks. Then, remember, the explanatory words get a comma *before* the second part of the quotation's marks. The punctuation at the end of the sentence is still included in the quotation marks:

> "Of course," he said, "you can go."

 **IN THE KNOW**

The first letter of the first word of the second part of a divided quotation is not capitalized unless it is a proper noun or starts a new sentence.

Practice

Add quotation marks where they are needed in the following sentences.

1. If you like, we will stay, she said.

2. Gina said, I will bring the sauce.

3. I guess I can go, said Rafael, but I want to bring something.

Answers

1. "If you like, we will stay," she said.

2. Gina said, "I will bring the sauce."

3. "I guess I can go," said Rafael, "but I want to bring something."

Quotation Marks with Question Marks and Exclamation Points

Don't be confused about the end punctuation in a quotation if it's a question mark or exclamation point. If they're a part of the original quotation, include them inside the quotation marks:

> Kim asked John, "Did you finish the dishes?"

> "Look out!" Miguel shouted.

If not, place them outside the quotation marks and don't include a period:

> Did Rachel say, "I'll meet you at 5"?

> My boss said, "I'll give you a raise"!

Practice

Add quotation marks where they are needed in the following sentences.

1. The woman screamed, Stop that thief!

2. Would you ask her, Which way is it to Edgeware Road?

3. Do you think Bev said, That's my first choice?

Answers

1. The woman screamed, "Stop that thief!"

2. Would you ask her, "Which way is it to Edgeware Road?"

3. Do you think Bev said, "That's my first choice"?

Apostrophes

The apostrophe (') has two basic usages. First, it shows *possession*. To show possession of a singular noun, add an apostrophe and an *s:*

> The bike belongs to the girl. It is the girl's bike.

> That is the lunch Renee brought. It is Renee's lunch.

 **DEFINITION**

Possession means that a noun owns something, whether it's an object, quality, or idea.

To form a possessive of a plural noun that ends in *s*, add only an apostrophe:

> These are my friends' designs.

> There are the countries' flags.

To form the possessive of a plural noun that does not end in *s*, add an apostrophe and an *s*:

> The women's department is through that door.

> I thought the mice's cage was larger than the hamsters'.

To form the possessive of a singular noun that ends in *s*, add an apostrophe:

> I found Travis' shoes by the door.

> We studied Jesus' teachings at church.

Apostrophes are used in contractions as well. The apostrophe simply replaces one or more omitted letters from the two words joined together to make the contraction. Here's a list of some common contractions:

- Cannot = can't
- Here is = here's
- I would = I'd
- She is = she's
- They are = they're
- Was not = wasn't
- We are = we're
- We will = we'll
- Will not = won't
- Would not = wouldn't

Watch out, though, for *it's* and *its!* Remember the rule:

> *It's* (with an apostrophe) means *It is* or *It has*.

> *Its* (without an apostrophe) is the possessive of *It*.

For example:

> It's time for the bird to have its dinner.

Practice

Insert the apostrophes in the following sentences.

1. Its late. Are you done?

2. That wasnt what I expected.

3. The childrens gifts are hidden.

4. Watch out for its bite.

Answers

1. It's late. Are you done? (Remember, you can substitute *It is* for that *Its,* so it needs an apostrophe.)

2. That wasn't what I expected.

3. The children's gifts are hidden.

4. No change needed because you can't substitute *it is* or *it has* for the *its.*

The Rules of Capitalization

Quite a few rules cover capitalization, so for clarity's sake, we break them down into two categories: when to capitalize and when *not* to capitalize.

When to Capitalize

Sometimes capital letters are there to make reading easier. For example, they signal the beginning of a sentence and the first and main words in a title:

Tina loved reading *The Catcher in the Rye.*

We also capitalize the following:

- **Proper nouns:** John, Paris, Sweden, Ohio, Congress

- **Adjectives made from proper nouns:** Parisian, Swedish, Congressional

- **Initials and titles in a name:** Reverend Sheila A. Miller, Dr. M. J. Byre

- **Titles of high-ranking offices, monarchy, and groups:** the Office of the President of the United States, the Queen of England

- **Family relationships when they are used as names:** Hi, Mom! Is Dad home yet? Aunt Christine is here!

- **The pronoun *I*:** She and I went outside.

- **All words referring to God and religious scriptures:** We read the Gospel of St. John from the Bible, and a passage from the Koran.

- **Geographical names, whether continents, bodies of water, landforms, states, public areas, or roads:** North America, Lake Erie, the Rocky Mountains, Pennsylvania, Mount Rushmore, Route 66

- **Sections of the country:** the American South, the Pacific Northwest

- **Names of organizations and institutions:** Windber Hospital, Starbucks, Inc.

- **Proper adjectives derived from names of sections of the country:** a Western painting

- **Names of events, documents, and periods of time:** World War II, the Magna Carta, the Middle Ages

- **Months, days, and holidays:** May, Sunday, Christmas

- **Languages, races, nationalities, and religions:** French language, African American, Irish linen, Lutheranism

- **Ships, trains, airplanes, and automobiles:** the *Titanic,* a Mustang

- **Abbreviations and acronyms:** B.C.E., A.M., SCUBA

- **The first word of a letter or email and the first word of the closing:** Dear Cynthia, Yours truly,

- **The first word of a quotation:** Shakespeare wrote, "To thine own self be true."

When Not to Capitalize

Don't capitalize the following:

- **Common nouns:** woman, nation, government

- **Lower-ranking titles that don't precede a name:** the PTA president

- **Family relationships when they are not used as names (usually preceded by *a, the, my, your*, etc.):** Say hello to your mom for me; I saw my dad at the gas station

- **Directions on the compass:** We drove north through the rain and hail; I like to fly south for the winter

- **Words such as** *church, college, school,* **and** *hospital* **when not used in titles:** Did you go to church? I left school at 16

- **School subjects (unless they are course names followed by a number or are a language):** I studied math; she practiced for her Italian test; I like Astronomy 101 so far

There! Now you've thoroughly reviewed punctuation and capitalization. Let's take the rest of the chapter to practice using these rules as you may need to apply them on the GED. The practice paragraphs that follow specifically focus on punctuation errors.

Practice

Insert or correct the punctuation as needed in the following sentences.

1. (A) Sues car won't start. (B) She's frustrated that its happening again. (C) Her husband not a great mechanic himself couldn't get it to work either. (D) He tried turning over the engine, looking in the manual, putting the car into neutral and kicking the tires.

2. (A) We were the first to arrive at the park; and we were the last to leave. (B) While other people stayed for only a few minutes, we couldn't stop staring at the view, (C) "I've never seen anything like this", my wife said. (D) I couldnt help but agree.

Answers

1. (A) is missing an apostrophe: *Sue's* is possessive. (B) is also missing an apostrophe: *it's* stands in for *it is* so one is needed. (C) You need a comma after *husband* and again after *mechanic* to set apart that descriptive phrase. (D) Remember the serial comma! It should appear in the sentence after *neutral:* He tried turning over the engine, looking in the manual, putting the car into neutral, and kicking the tires.

2. (A) Either the semicolon or the *and* needs to come out because they serve the same purpose and are redundant together. (B) Watch that end punctuation! You need a period, not a comma. (C) The comma should go inside the quotation marks: "I've never seen anything like this," my wife said. (D) Put an apostrophe in *couldn't.*

Reading Quickly and Well

We all need to read. You might read work communications, directions, announcements, instruction manuals, and more. Or you may be in school, where reading in different subject areas is a daily necessity. If you're lucky, you have time to read for pleasure—stories, current information, biographies, and so on. All of your daily reading is good background experience for future learning or for test-taking—including the GED tests.

In this chapter, we review good practices for successful reading and look at the seven types of reading tasks the GED might test you on in this portion of the exam.

Secrets of the Successful Reader

Many people feel panicky about the reading portion of the GED, worrying that they're not fast enough readers, or that the literature passages will prove too difficult. The best way to become a faster reader is to practice, so we advise trying to read something—anything—on a daily basis before taking the GED. If you're especially concerned about understanding a poem on the GED (a common apprehension), don't worry. We give you pointers on how to understand the literature passages in Chapter 7.

In This Chapter

- Tips for reading well
- Types of questions on the Reasoning Through Language Arts Test
- Sample GED®-style questions to practice the skills on which you'll be tested
- Answers and explanations for all questions

The most important thing to remember is that the test is not actually measuring how good or fast or impressive a reader you are; instead, it's measuring how well you can answer questions about what you've read. That means you can use all the tricks we teach you in these chapters to do well on the test.

The first trick? Warming up before diving into a reading passage. Great athletes would never start a game or event without a warm-up. They know that a warm-up prevents injuries and ensures a better performance. Readers, too, need to warm up before jumping into reading passages.

What do we mean by a reading warm-up? Before you begin to read, scan the passage. Read the title, and look for any subtitles. Identify what kind of passage it is—first, nonfiction or literary? Then, if it's factual, what kind of nonfiction is it—an email, a report, or something else? Or what kind of literature is the passage—a short story, a poem, or perhaps an excerpt from a play? Notice if an author is listed, if there's further publication information, and how long the passage is. These questions get your mind thinking about the subject at hand.

Now that you've warmed up, you're ready to practice a bit. Skim the passage and, if you're able, the questions provided about it. Don't worry about understanding everything the passage says or answering the questions. Just skim it for an overview for now. Try to get a sense of what the passage will be about.

You've warmed up and practiced, so now it's time to play: read the entire passage. As you read, you can ask yourself what the main idea of the passage is, because you are sure to be asked that. Another way to think of this is to ask yourself, "What is the topic sentence for this entire passage?" or, "If someone asked me to summarize this passage in one sentence, what would I say?"

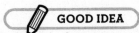 **GOOD IDEA**

Titles often supply the answer to questions about the topic or main idea of a passage. If a title in your ordinary reading isn't a question, turn it into one. Then, keep looking for the answer to the question as you read.

Last step: you're ready to answer the test questions. As always, read them carefully, eliminate answer choices you're sure are incorrect, choose the best answer, and move on. Don't be afraid to look back at the passage for help answering questions; that's what it's there for.

The Seven Types of Reading Tasks

The next tip to help you do well on the Reasoning Through Language Arts: Reading Test is to understand what types of questions you'll be asked. Just as in the Language section of the test, where you could anticipate that every question would involve choosing the best answer to complete the sentence correctly from four drop-down answer choices, you should know what types of questions will be on this section. Nearly every question on the Reading portion of the Reasoning Through Literary Arts Test asks you to evaluate the passage and consider one of the following:

- The main idea

- Vocabulary

- The structure of the passage

- The author's development of the passage

- The author's argument and how successful it is

- The author's purpose

- Comparisons

The questions can be in drop-down fill-in-the-blank or multiple-choice formats, but they'll almost always ask you to identify one of these. Let's look at each.

Main Idea

As stated earlier, you need to be able to figure out the main idea for every passage, almost without exception, on the test. Here, you need to step back and consider the passage as a whole—not on a sentence level, but as a whole—and choose what its overall idea is. The test often asks you to do something with the main idea after finding it, such as find the sentences that support it. That's why it's helpful to not only decide what the main idea is, but be able to figure out *how* you know that.

Vocabulary

Don't panic! You don't need to study dozens of SAT-level words for the GED. But some questions do ask you to figure out what a word means from the context of the sentence it's in. Read the sentence carefully and consider the way the word is used, and you should be able to find the correct answer in the definitions provided.

Structure of the Passage

This type of question asks you to show your understanding of how the passages work. You might be asked to explain why the author chose to use a phrase like "on the other hand," or why there's an example that proves the main idea in the second paragraph. Skimming the passage and then reading it more closely should help you see how it's structured. This type of question isn't about the meaning or the purpose, but about how the passages are constructed.

Development

Very similarly to the structure questions, development questions ask you to figure out how the author shaped his or her passage. You might be asked how the author reaches a conclusion at the end of the paragraph, for example, or why a character is needed in the passage. These questions aren't structural but rather about showing how the author makes his or her case.

Assessment of Author's Successful Argument

Occasionally on the Reasoning Through Language Arts Test, you're asked whether you think the author has been successful in a passage. Has she persuaded you in an op-ed passage that might have been written for a newspaper? Is the logic of a politician's speech as airtight as he presents it? This is not merely an opinion question about whether you agree or disagree with the author. Rather, you have to examine the passage to see if it makes logical sense.

Author's Purpose, or Why?

Here, you need to figure out why the author wrote the passage. What was his purpose or her intent? This is similar to a main idea, but shows the author's hand more. This type of question is easy to overthink, so keep in mind that the GED isn't asking you to read the author's mind. Instead, you must simply think through the author's likely purpose or audience

Comparisons

This is the least-common form of question on the test, but we wanted to mention it. You occasionally are given several shorter passages and asked to compare them in some way. Generally, you need to find the main idea in each passage and compare the two.

Practice

Use the prereading skills discussed earlier in this chapter to answer the following questions, which are typical of GED style.

Before the space shuttle *Endeavor* returned to Earth, many articles about it appeared in magazines and newspapers. The following is an example of one.

The *Endeavor* Is Finished, but the International Space Station Continues On

On May 29, 2011, the space shuttle *Endeavor* crew said a last goodbye to the astronauts on the International Space Station (ISS) and began their journey earthbound. Although another crew will stay on the space station, *Endeavor* made its final trip. On this final mission, *Endeavor*'s crew installed equipment that will allow the ISS to send huge amounts of data to Earth. Researchers around the world will gather the information and analyze it. Scientists have NASA's last crewed flight to look forward to when the space shuttle *Atlantis* is launched.

1. A main idea in this paragraph is that the International Space Station:

   (1) Will continue to send information to Earth even though the *Endeavor* crew has left.

   (2) Has never had anyone onboard to fix equipment or install equipment.

   (3) Has requested that *Atlantis* not launch.

   (4) Is uninhabited; no people reside there.

2. The author implies that NASA:

   (1) Will sink into a depression over the end of the space program.

   (2) Will turn its attention to the launching of the space shuttle *Atlantis*.

   (3) Should attempt to build a space station of its own.

   (4) Should not have grounded *Endeavor*.

3. The author indicates that the researchers from around the world will do what with the data:

   (1) Revise it.

   (2) Recall it.

   (3) Study it.

   (4) Upload it.

Answers

1. **(1)** An important idea in the paragraph is that, although *Endeavor* made its final trip, the crew of the ISS prepared the space station to do much more work in the future. The only choice that makes this statement is (1). The title, which you should have noticed in your prereading practice, helps point you in the right direction. It states that the ISS has a purpose that extends beyond the life of the *Endeavor*.

2. **(2)** The final sentence in the paragraph implies that NASA will move on from the end of the *Endeavor* because it needs to focus on launching the *Atlantis*. Avoid choosing answers like (1), which encourage you to read into a passage more than is justified. There's no sense that the entire space program will "sink into a depression."

3. **(3)** The question is a vocabulary question, asking you to find the synonym for *analyze* as it is used in the paragraph. The best answer is *study*.

Reading Informational Passages

As mentioned earlier, the bulk of the passages in the Reading portion of the Reasoning Through Language Arts Test are taken from nonfiction sources (75 percent, actually). The good news is that you probably are reading a lot of nonfiction already. After all, it's rare for a day to go by without reading some kind of factual writing, such as a bus schedule, a TV listing, a map, or a restaurant menu. Of course, the vast majority of us principally read nonfiction at work, whether we review an email, check the stock market reports online, read a memo from a colleague, or take an online course to learn about a new kind of software. Nonfiction fills our lives, so it makes sense that the GED wants to be sure you understand how to read and interpret it.

The Reasoning Through Language Arts: Reading Test is aptly named. It does not pose questions that are merely factual, in which you need to read the passage and find a simple answer. Instead, the test asks you to *reason* your way through the reading passages and then answer multiple-choice or drop-down fill-in-the-blank questions about what you've read.

What will you be reading? The passages could be taken from any kind of material you might see at work: a letter or ad for customers, say, or policy statements from a company. You could read a speech from an executive or an announcement

In This Chapter

- Overview of nonfiction reading, including articles, books, workplace writings, legal documents, biographies and autobiographies, and more
- Sample GED®-style questions to practice the skills on which you'll be tested
- Answers and explanations for all questions

about a company initiative. Academic materials, such as journal articles, also might be included, and they will likely be on topics taken from scientific materials or those that look at history in some way. Another significant source for passages on the test are historical materials, such as the U.S. Constitution.

Because so many of the questions ask you about the author's purpose or point of view, the nonfiction passages often are written from a particular viewpoint, such as an editorial from a newspaper. You won't find strictly factual information (such as a Wikipedia entry) on the GED Reading test.

In this chapter, we review some of the ways you can improve your ability to read and interpret nonfiction passages, building on the ideas we presented in the previous chapter.

Looking for the Main Idea and Details as You Read Nonfiction

Every kind of reading requires that you read for the main idea and important details, but that's particularly true in the type of nonfiction included on the GED, where literary elements such as tone, mood, character, and voice often aren't present. We look specifically at several different types of nonfiction in this chapter, but finding the main idea is key for all types.

The question is, how do you find the main idea in nonfictional materials? The answer starts with what you already learned in Chapter 5: before you read, you need to warm up your brain. Begin by considering the format of the document in front of you: is it a memo? An email? A report? Each of these looks different and clues you in to what you can expect to find in the passage.

In the following sections, we share tips on reading a variety of types of passages, including articles; other kinds of nonfiction; workplace documents; consumer ads, letters, and documents; autobiographies, biographies, and memoirs; op-eds (or opinion-editorials); and historical documents.

Reading Articles

You're very likely to be asked to read several passages from nonfiction articles on the test. The passages often are about a page long, and sometimes are taken from historical documents, which could make them seem a bit flowery compared to how we write and speak today.

To begin, examine the structure of the passage so you can see what type of article it is—perhaps an excerpt from a speech or something taken from an academic journal? Look at the title of the article as well as any subtitles, and ask yourself what those mean to you. Skim the entire passage to get an idea of its scope and shape. Now read the first paragraph or introduction as well as the last paragraph or summary. At this point, you should have a better idea of what the article is about. You can then read the entire passage and, if you can, the questions asked about it.

You'll almost always need to find the main idea of the passage in order to answer the GED questions correctly. To do so, it's helpful to read the first and last sentences of every paragraph, where main ideas are often placed. The sentence that holds the main idea is called the *topic sentence*. If the main idea comes first, the rest of the paragraph adds details to support it. If the main idea comes last, the supporting details appear first and then are summarized in the topic sentence. It's rare that a nonfiction passage doesn't include at least one clear topic sentence.

Supporting details give you information that backs up the main idea. To find those supporting details, it's helpful to turn the title of the article into a question. Then, actually give yourself the task of finding the answer to the question as you read. For example, given the following title:

Happy Families Have Certain Characteristics

How can you turn this into a question that leads you to the main idea and details? Try the following:

What characteristics do happy families have?

Look for the main idea and supporting details as you read the following passage.

Happy Families Have Certain Characteristics

If you read 10 articles written by experts in family happiness, at least five of them will contain this quote from a famous book, *Anna Karenina*, by Tolstoy:

"All happy families are alike; each unhappy family is unhappy in its own way."

What does that mean? Perhaps there are discernible patterns in happy families. If so, what defining features make up the pattern? The experts seem to agree on at least four characteristics. Here are four that appear over and over again.

Communication

Happy families seem to enjoy talking to each other. Although it's difficult for today's busy families to enforce a rule about having dinner together every night, it is one of the ways that families gather to talk. Not all of the conversation may be about happy moments in the family's life. Parents may want to ask about what happened that day that was happy, but just as important about something that was unhappy or disappointing. Then, at least, there is the possibility of getting the conversation and the path to solutions going. One good rule: you can keep conversations going if you stay away from questions that require only one-word answers. Stay away from, "How was school today?" The answer is undoubtedly going to be, "Fine" or "Okay." If your question is, "What was the worst (or best) thing that happened in school today?" you are likely to start a conversation.

Activities for Mom and Dad

A mom and dad or single parent should try to maintain a few activities that they love. Kids don't want to give up soccer or baseball, so why should parents give up everything they love? Parents should plan for an activity that provides exercise as well as fun. Fun activities make for happier parents. Happy parents are likely to bring home a smile and positive outlook.

A Few Good Rules

Happy families have rules by which they live. Many say that the simpler they keep the rules, the better. For example, one family chose to follow a broad rule, such as showing respect for everyone in their circle. Their circle includes children, parents, grandparents, friends, and teachers. However, this family's rule included the children showing respect for each other. You don't need very many rules if the guiding rule is respect for each other.

Commitment

Happy families are committed to each other in good times and in difficult times. Happy families tend to pull inward to rally around an adult or child in trouble. This is simply putting the family first. It is also a commitment to help each individual in the family become all that he or she can be. To accomplish this, a parent or child may have to give up an immediate desire in order to help the family member who needs special help or attention.

Practice

1. Which answer best states the main idea of this passage?

    (1) Only parents can make a family happy, healthy, and committed to each other.

    (2) Happy families have certain characteristics in common, such as enjoying each other and being committed to the family.

    (3) Only families who have many strict rules are happy.

    (4) Happy families don't need any rules; good behavior comes naturally.

2. In the paragraph under "Commitment," which of these sentences carries the main idea?

    (1) This is simply putting the family first.

    (2) It is also a commitment to help each individual in the family become all that he or she can be.

    (3) Happy families are committed to each other in good times and in difficult times.

    (4) A parent or child may have to give up an immediate desire.

3. In the paragraph under "A Few Good Rules," which of the following statements is a main idea you can infer from reading all of the details?

(1) Happy families seem to allow for Mom and Dad to do fun activities together as a couple or alone.

(2) Without the children, no activities are fun.

(3) Emergencies always stand in the way of parents' activities.

(4) Kids always want to give up soccer or baseball, so why shouldn't parents give up everything they love?

Answers

1. **(2)** This answer is reflected in the title as well. Answers (1), (3), and (4) are all incorrect details and opposite to what the passage states.

2. **(3)** Answers (1), (2), and (4) state only a small portion of the main idea.

3. **(1)** Answer (2) is the opposite of the paragraph's main idea. Answer (3) is incorrect because it is an exaggeration. Answer (4) is an incorrect detail.

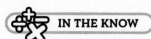 **IN THE KNOW**

Occasionally a writer does not include a main idea or topic sentence in a paragraph. As a reader, being able to infer the main idea is a useful skill. You need to figure out the main idea by "adding up" all the clues in the paragraph.

Reading Other Kinds of Nonfiction

After practicing looking for a main idea in an article, let's review some of the specific types of nonfiction passages you may encounter on the test. Each presents a slightly different type of writing and must be considered as representative of its type.

For all nonfiction passages, it will be helpful to think about the five types of questions you could be asked, besides a main idea question (and a comparison question). Pay attention to the author's purpose—why do you think he or she wrote this piece? In the case of a newspaper op-ed, does the author want to convince readers of some new idea, for example? If you are presented with an op-ed, you can almost bet you'll be asked to find the author's purpose or point of view.

Consider, too, the structure of a passage. A biography is put together quite differently than, say, a contract. The logic used in a passage might be evident, as in a warranty, or might need to be thoughtfully analyzed, as in an article. The same is true in the way the author develops a passage.

Many works of nonfiction don't have much development—a memo about conserving water in an office, for example, rarely needs to build momentum. Finally, what kind of vocabulary does the author use? It would be strange to find words like *ethereal* or *gloaming* in an email about parking passes.

Reading Workplace Documents

As mentioned, one of the most common types of nonfiction passages you'll encounter on the GED are workplace documents. In fact, these are the most common after articles. Workplace documents contain important information for employees. They often are written in a dry and dull way, but they contain information that all employees should be able to read and understand.

When reading a workplace document, it's helpful to imagine that you are an employee of the company and the information presented is vital to you. You should think about what the author of the document is trying to convey: what is your take-away after reading the document? You are less likely to be asked about the author's tone or bias here, but you might be asked about assumptions contained within the piece. In workplace documents, it is very common for the point of the document to be clear from the first or last sentence; you can often find the topic sentence/ main idea that way.

Take a look at the following passage, which is a portion of a federal law, presented to the employees of the XYZ Clothing Company:

What Does the FMLA (Family Medical Leave Act) Entitle Employees To?

The XYZ Clothing Company follows FMLA provisions with its employees. Please read this document carefully and refer to it whenever you face a family medical emergency. If you have questions related to this policy, please visit the personnel department and we will make every effort to clarify the following.

Basic Provisions/Requirements

The FMLA, a federal law passed in 1993, entitles eligible employees of covered employers to take job-protected, unpaid leave for specified family and medical reasons. Eligible employees are entitled to the following.

- Twelve workweeks of leave in any 12-month period for:

  - Birth and care of the employee's child, within 1 year of birth

  - Placement with the employee of a child for adoption or foster care, within 1 year of the placement

  - Care of an immediate family member (spouse, child, parent) who has a serious health condition

- For the employee's own serious health condition that makes the employee unable to perform the essential functions of his or her job

- Any qualifying *exigency* [a need or emergency] arising out of the fact that the employee's spouse, son, daughter, or parent is on active duty or has been notified of an impending call or order to active duty in the U.S. National Guard or Reserves in support of a contingency operation

- Twenty-six workweeks of leave during a single 12-month period to care for a covered service member with a serious injury or illness if the employee is the spouse, son, daughter, parent, or next of kin of the service member (Military Caregiver Leave)

If an employee was receiving group health benefits when leave began, an employer must maintain them at the same level and in the same manner during periods of FMLA leave as if the employee had continued to work. An employee may elect (or the employer may require) the substitution of any accrued paid leave (vacation, sick, personal, etc.) for periods of unpaid FMLA leave ....

Employees may take FMLA leave intermittently or on a reduced leave schedule (that is, in blocks of time less than the full amount of the entitlement) when medically necessary or when the leave is due to a qualifying exigency ....

When the need for leave is foreseeable, an employee must give the employer at least 30 days' notice, or as much notice as is practicable. When the leave is not foreseeable, the employee must provide notice as soon as practicable in the particular circumstances. An employee must comply with the employer's usual and customary notice and procedural requirements ....

An employee who returns from FMLA leave is entitled to be restored to the same or an equivalent job with equivalent pay, benefits, and other terms and conditions of employment ....

Practice

1. The main idea of this statement is that:

   (1) Employees may take leave of 12 unpaid workweeks in any 2-year period for family and medical reasons.

   (2) Employees may take job-protected leave for the care of a child but not for a spouse.

   (3) Employees are entitled to take unpaid leave for specified family and medical reasons.

   (4) Employees are not entitled to take unpaid leave for medical care of family or spouse until the employee has worked for the company for 3 years.

2. Because the XYZ Clothing Company provides group health benefits, you can conclude that:

   (1) On medical leave, employees will lose benefits until they return to work.

   (2) The employee on leave will maintain health benefits for 12 weeks.

   (3) The employee on leave will regain health benefits 1 year after returning to work.

   (4) The employee will maintain health benefits during and after the leave.

3. Based on the information in this passage, which of the following statements is true?

   (1) It is never necessary to give notice of a leave.

   (2) An employee may take leave when a spouse returns to active military duty.

   (3) Intermittent leave is never an option.

   (4) An employee may not expect paid leave for the adoption of a child.

4. Why does the author of the passage include a list of what the 12 workweeks of leave in any 12-month period can be used for?

   (1) To provide clarification about a policy that may initially cause confusion for employees.

   (2) To warn employees not to take too many days off.

   (3) To explain that the adoption of a child is just as important as the birth of a child.

   (4) To allow employees to petition the company for more time off.

Answers

1. **(3)** All other answers contain incorrect facts.

2. **(4)** All other answers contain incorrect facts.

3. **(2)** Answers (1), (3), and (4) are opposite to what is stated.

4. **(1)** We don't know enough about the company to guess answer (2). Answers (3) and (4) are not justified by the text.

Reading Consumer Ads, Letters, and Documents

In the same way that the GED test may include a workplace document or two, it would not be unusual for you to be asked to read and answer questions about a document meant for consumers. This could take the form of an advertisement that might run in a newspaper; a letter from a car dealership to buyers; or another kind of document, such as a warranty. Like workplace documents, consumer materials are usually fairly direct and easy to understand. In an advertisement, you may see the author's bias (usually toward the company sending the advertisement). In a workplace document, you are unlikely to see a distinctive tone or bias.

Let's take a look at a contract and answer a few practice questions about it. The contract should provide a clear idea of the responsibilities of both the buyer and the seller.

Contract for Purchase of a Car

Buyer's name: _____

Address: _____ Phone: _____

Seller's name: _____

Address: _____ Phone: _____

The Seller hereby conveys to the Buyer full ownership and title to the motor vehicle described below:

Description of motor vehicle sold:

Year: _____   Make: _____   Model: _____   VIN: _____

The Buyer hereby agrees to pay the Seller $X on MM/DD/YY, and $Y on the Nth day of each month beginning MM/DD/YY, until all payments made to the Seller total $X.

If the Buyer fails to make a payment on or before its due date, a late fee of $X shall be added to the balance due and shall be payable immediately.

Both parties hereby agree that this is an "as-is" sale, with no warranties of any kind expressed or implied.

This agreement shall be governed by the laws of the State of _____ and the County of _____ and any applicable U.S. laws.

The parties hereby signify their agreement to the terms above by their signatures affixed below:

Buyer's signature, date: _____

Seller's signature, date: _____

Practice

1. Which statement summarizes the content or main idea of this contract?

   (1) A buyer and seller are still discussing the price of the car.

   (2) The buyer will fill out the contract because all the responsibility is with him or her.

   (3) The buyer and seller agree to terms of the sale and promise to abide by them.

   (4) A buyer agrees to buy and a seller agrees to sell a car for a stated amount of money to be paid in a certain amount of time.

2. You can conclude from this contract that the buyer:

   (1) Needs to decide if the color is really right for him or her.

   (2) Is the only one governed by the state's laws.

   (3) Needs to check the car carefully because it is an "as-is" sale.

   (4) Does not need anything more than a check to pick up the car.

3. If you compare the buyer and seller responsibilities in this contract, you see that:

   (1) The buyer only has to say he or she wants the car, while the seller has to deliver it in good shape.

   (2) The seller only has to agree to sell the car at some date in the future.

   (3) The seller promises to fix all dents, bring a car in perfect condition to the sale, and offer later dates for payments.

   (4) The seller gives ownership to the buyer, while the buyer makes payments on a schedule, is penalized for late payment, and agrees that it is an "as-is" sale.

Answers

1. **(4)** This is the only answer that includes all the main idea elements. Answer (1) is incorrect because you sign a contract only after the details (including the price) have been decided, while answer (2) is an incorrect detail. Answer (3) is correct as far as it goes, but it is not the complete main idea.

2. **(3)** The other answers are incorrect details.

3. **(4)** The other answers are incorrect details.

Reading Autobiographies, Biographies, and Memoirs

Another type of passage you may see on the Reasoning Through Language Arts: Reading Test is a selection from an autobiography, biography, or memoir. A biography tells the story of someone's life, an autobiography tells the story of the author's own life, and a memoir is a type of autobiography in which the focus is on a smaller portion of the author's life. For example, in a memoir, a soldier might write about a specific tour of duty she completed.

This form of nonfiction is interesting for GED test-makers because it combines the factual information of an article with the opportunities not often found in articles for questioning readers about the author's attitude toward some aspect of the person they're writing about. What clues can you look for to identify the author's viewpoint? Consider the author's vocabulary, the details he or she chooses to reveal, and the author's own background.

In the following biography of Bill Gates, you'll learn some important details about his life, his education, and his personality. Look for the sentences in which the author reveals his viewpoint of Gates' achievements.

Bill Gates and the History of Great Inventions

Frequently in history, there have been men and women who profited from new inventions. In the late 1800s and early 1900s, new inventions turned up regularly. The typewriter, the telephone, and the internal combustion engine gave forward thinking businessmen reasons to cheer. Alexander Graham Bell (telephone), Thomas Edison (the incandescent lightbulb), Andrew Carnegie (innovations in the steel industry), to name just a few, saw the opportunities that important discoveries provided. These people were made enormously wealthy by the discoveries of the industrial age.

Many years later, Bill Gates, now the chairman and CEO of Microsoft, followed that model. When Gates was born in 1955, no one owned a personal computer. You couldn't buy one and carry it home. Yet after being introduced to the enormous computers that were mostly contained in scientific research labs and government offices at that time, he immediately understood that everyone would want and need a personal computer.

As a youngster, Bill Gates was fun-loving and attention-seeking, so much so that his parents transferred him to an academically demanding school in hopes of focusing his energy. There he excelled in reading, math, and science. Doing well in this difficult school got him positive attention. While Gates was at Lakeside School, a Seattle computer company offered to provide computer time for the students. The school purchased a teletype terminal for students to use. Gates became totally absorbed in learning what a computer could do. At 13 years old, he began programming computers. He spent much of his free time working on the terminal. Some of that time was spent writing a tic-tac-toe program in BASIC computer language, which allowed users to play against the computer.

While using an existing computer, Gates honed his programming skills and developed his new ideas. At Lakeside School, Bill met Paul Allen, who was 2 years older. Both boys had such enthusiasm for the computer that they became great friends. However, they were two very different people. Allen was more reserved and shy. Bill was energetic and at times aggressive. Nonetheless, the two spent much of their free time together working on programs. Later, Gates left Harvard University to form Microsoft, the most successful software company in the world, with Allen.

Practice

1. The author's opening paragraph leads the reader to view Bill Gates as:

   (1) A rowdy but brilliant school boy.

   (2) One of the most successful businessmen in American history, a descendant of the men mentioned.

   (3) A great inventor but terrible a businessman.

   (4) The inventor of the telephone and telegraph.

2. You can infer that Bill Gates was very intelligent, but he:

   (1) Needed to be left alone to do what he liked.

   (2) Was prohibitively shy.

   (3) Clearly enjoyed recess more than class.

   (4) Needed the right school environment to build on his intelligence.

3. Considering the overall themes of the biography, why does the author bring Paul Allen into the passage?

   (1) To establish that Bill Gates did not do everything on his own.

   (2) To show contrast Bill Gates' outgoing nature with the more shy Paul Allen.

   (3) To wrap up the passage with an interesting fact.

   (4) To point to what would be Gates' most remarkable achievement: the development of Microsoft.

Answers

1. **(2)** By starting the article with information about American tycoons, the author places Gates in their company. All other answers are incorrect details.

2. **(4)** Answer (1) is the exact opposite of what the passage proves: Gates needed more structure, not less. Answer (2) is an incorrect detail. Answer (3) is not proven in the passage, but (4) is an inference that makes logical sense. We are never told that Gates needed a different environment, but it is strongly implied.

3. **(4)** This is a question about how the author developed the themes of the passage, which we've established to be about Gates' place in the pantheon of great American tycoons. Only answer (4) ties back to that idea, and so it is correct.

Reading Op-Eds

It's typical for the Reasoning Through Language Arts: Reading section of the GED to present an op-ed for you to read and interpret. Short for *opinion-editorial,* op-ed refers to the section of a newspaper (or magazine or website) where writers share their opinions in editorials about current topics in hopes of informing and influencing their readers. Due to their nature, op-eds present the author's bias, so you can expect questions about that. Op-eds also provide opportunities to ask about how the author structures and develops his or her arguments.

You can tell the difference between an op-ed and an article by looking for the author's opinion and what he or she is trying to convince you of. This is often found right in the title. Remember to preread op-eds as you would other passages. Let's take a look at an op-ed:

Downin Park Needs More Trees

Since the early 1800s, Downin Park has provided our town with a place to enjoy nature with our family and friends. Many residents use the park for biking, hiking, picnicking, and sunbathing. But in the last few years, development of residential apartment blocks to the west of the park has led to the removal of many trees in that area. Downin Park no longer provides the deep shade it once did. We need to fix this!

As a lifelong resident of this town, I'm disappointed that the Town Council has allowed development to occur so close to the park. We don't have need for expensive apartment housing like that being constructed. Nevertheless, the developers and the Council could help by replacing the lost trees cut down to make way for the new apartment buildings. Trees should be planted on the other side of the park fence, and the sooner the better.

It's alarming to realize that it will still take decades for Downin Park to recover the shade it once offered, but that's no reason to put off planting the trees. Even if the people of my generation are not here to see the trees at their full beauty, our children will be.

Isn't that the most generous act of all, to undertake work that we may not see the results of ourselves?

I hope with all my heart that the Town Council and the developers will listen to reason and plant trees in Downin Park. Let's save the park!

Practice

1. The author's use of the word *alarming* most closely means:

   (1) A loud, ringing bell

   (2) Upsetting

   (3) Unalarming

   (4) Disgusting

2. The author wrote and published this op-ed because:

   (1) She wanted to see her name in the paper.

   (2) She believes the new apartment developments are ugly and should not be built.

   (3) She wants the people in her town to stop cutting down trees.

   (4) She wants to draw attention to the need to plant more trees in Downin Park.

Answers

1. **(2)** Answer (3) is just the opposite of the word in question. Answer (1) refers to a different kind of alarm. Answer (2) is the best substitute for *alarming*.

2. **(4)** Answer (1) isn't proven by the passage, and answer (2) is about a smaller point in the passage. The main point is in answer (4).

Reading Historical Documents

The final major category of nonfiction reading you may be asked to do on the Reasoning Through Language Arts: Reading section of the GED is to read an interpret a historical document. This could be anything from a section of the Declaration of Independence to a speech given by the Reverend Martin Luther King Jr. Although you cannot predict what kind of historical document you'll get, you can know what to expect: the language probably will be flowery, even ornate, and you can be sure the piece will contain a strong point of view from the author. You also should know that you will not be asked factual questions about the historical importance of the document. That's for another GED test. Here, you're only asked to read and interpret what's in front of you. Be sure to preread so you'll know you're reading a historical document. Let's take a look at the first two amendments in the Bill of Rights.

The Bill of Rights

Amendment I

Congress shall make no law respecting an establishment of religion, or prohibiting the free exercise thereof; or abridging the freedom of speech, or of the press; or the right of the people peaceably to assemble, and to petition the government for a redress of grievances.

Amendment II

A well regulated militia, being necessary to the security of a free state, the right of the people to keep and bear arms, shall not be infringed.

Practice

1. In the second amendment, what does the word *infringed* mean?

   (1) Insisted upon

   (2) Repeated

   (3) Violated

   (4) Helped

2. The first amendment protects rights in regards to which of the following?

   (1) The free practice of religion

   (2) The right of women to vote

   (3) The right to drive a car

   (4) The rules for jailing a criminal

Answers

1. **(3)** Answer (3) is the only choice that makes sense when substituted into the amendment. Even if you do not know what *infringed* means here, you can see that *violated* makes the most sense.

2. **(1)** Answer (1) is the only answer supported by the facts. The first amendment is best known for protecting free speech, but remember that you must base your answer on the passage, not any outside information you might know.

Literary Passages

As you know from Chapter 6, you have fewer literary passages to read on the GED test compared to nonfiction passages. In fact, you may end up having only one literary passage to read and interpret. Literary passages come from three main types of literature: most will be fiction (an excerpt from a short story or a novel), one might be a poem, or, much more rarely, you may be asked to read an excerpt from a drama. We go over what to look for in each of these three types in this chapter. As with nonfiction, the literary passages could be from an old book or a modern poem. The passages could be as short as 450 words or as long as 900 words.

The biggest difference between literary passages and nonfiction passages is the emphasis placed on the author's mood and tone, as well as on literary terms. We review those at the beginning of this chapter because you might see them in any of the forms of literature on the test.

Don't forget to preread. Simply put, everything you learned about main ideas, details, and vocabulary in earlier chapters applies here as well. The type of reading you do might change, but the basic skills you need do not.

In This Chapter

- Overview of fiction, poetry, and drama
- Sample GED®-style questions to practice the skills on which you'll be tested
- Answers and explanations for all questions

A Brief Review of Literary Terms

The literary terms defined in this section are good to keep in mind. They may be included on the test in the questions (as in "What is the main plot of this story?") or in the answers (such as when you're asked which literary elements a certain line in a poem displays).

Fiction   Stories made up by an author. They can be based on real or imaginary events.

Poem   Writing that makes use of distinctive formatting, verse, figurative language, and descriptive words to evoke emotion. Sometimes, poetry rhymes or is written in a specific format or structure.

Drama   A story told by actors on a stage. It is usually fictional as well.

Conflict   A component in stories and dramas, as well as some poems. It's the problem that drives the story forward and involves the protagonist.

Protagonist   The main character of the story or play who wants something.

Antagonist   The character (or characters) who oppose the protagonist and keep him or her from getting what he or she wants.

Plot   The series of events that make up the story and help the conflict build. Plots usually have a beginning, middle, and end.

Characters   The people (or, sometimes, beings who are not people) in the story.

Setting   The place or places where the story unfolds.

Time period   The time in history during which the story unfolds.

Alliteration   A technique in poetry wherein repeating initial consonant sounds are used to create an effect ("Peter Piper picked a peck of pickled peppers …").

Analogy   A comparison of two things that have similar features ("A gas pump works in a similar way to a straw").

Hyperbole   A type of figurative language; overexaggerating for effect, as when a character says, "I was so embarrassed I could die!"

Metaphor   A type of figurative language; the description of something by saying it is the same as something else ("The snowstorm was a blanket over the town").

Simile   Similar to metaphor, but the comparison is made using *like* or *as* ("The snowstorm was like a blanket over the town"). Also a type of figurative language.

Symbolism   The author's use of an object, person, or place in a story or drama to stand in for something else.

Theme   An idea that the writer wants to explore in the work.

Reading Fiction

Now that we've briefly reviewed the literary terms you need to know for this part of the test, let's dig in to learn how to use them in fiction. We'll spend the most time on fiction because you can be sure you'll be asked to read it on the test.

Plot

First, we focus on plot, or the events of the story. The plot of a fictional piece almost always involves a main character who wants something very badly. The character pursues what he or she wants despite opposition and struggles. In the end, he or she either wins or loses.

From the very first sentence of Edgar Allan Poe's famous short story, "The Cask of Amontillado," you know the plot is built upon something the narrator wants badly—*retribution*. This is another way to say he wants revenge, vengeance, or payback. In the second paragraph, the narrator smiles at the thought of Fortunato's *immolation*. This word means killing someone as a ritual sacrifice. This is a scary thought—perfect for a scary story.

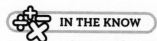 **IN THE KNOW**

Just as with some nonfiction passages, the literary passages on the test may be from older works like this one. You can see that here with the strange punctuation and flowery language Poe used. Also, keep in mind that although we're focusing on fiction in this section, plot is also an element in drama and even in some poems.

Read this small portion of the story and find the lines that push the plot forward. What happens first, second, third, …? What horrible deed does the narrator have planned?

"The Cask of Amontillado"

THE thousand injuries of Fortunato I had borne as I best could, but when he ventured upon insult, I vowed revenge. You, who so well know the nature of my soul, will not suppose, however, that I gave utterance to a threat. AT LENGTH I would be avenged; this was a point definitively settled—but the very definitiveness with which it was resolved precluded the idea of risk. I must not only punish, but punish with impunity. A wrong is unredressed when retribution overtakes its redresser. It is equally unredressed when the avenger fails to make himself felt as such to him who has done the wrong.

It must be understood that neither by word nor deed had I given Fortunato cause to doubt my good will. I continued as was my wont, to smile in his face, and he did not perceive that my smile NOW was at the thought of his immolation.

He had a weak point—this Fortunato—although in other regards he was a man to be respected and even feared. He prided himself on his connoisseurship in wine. Few Italians have the true virtuoso spirit. For the most part their enthusiasm is adopted to suit the time and opportunity to practise imposture upon the British and Austrian MILLIONAIRES. In painting and gemmary, Fortunato, like his countrymen, was a quack, but in the matter of old wines he was sincere. In this respect I did not differ from him materially; I was skillful in the Italian vintages myself, and bought largely whenever I could.

It was about dusk, one evening during the supreme madness of the carnival season, that I encountered my friend. He accosted me with excessive warmth, for he had been drinking much. The man wore motley. He had on a tight-fitting parti-striped dress and his head was surmounted by the conical cap and bells. I was so pleased to see him that I thought I should never have done wringing his hand.

I said to him—"My dear Fortunato, you are luckily met. How remarkably well you are looking to-day! But I have received a pipe of what passes for Amontillado, and I have my doubts."

"How?" said he, "Amontillado? A pipe? Impossible? And in the middle of the carnival?"

"I have my doubts," I replied; "and I was silly enough to pay the full Amontillado price without consulting you in the matter. You were not to be found, and I was fearful of losing a bargain."

"Amontillado!"

"I have my doubts."

"Amontillado!"

"And I must satisfy them."

"Amontillado!"

"As you are engaged, I am on my way to Luchesi. If any one has a critical turn, it is he. He will tell me"—

"Luchesi cannot tell Amontillado from Sherry."

"And yet some fools will have it that his taste is a match for your own."

"Come let us go."

"Whither?"

"To your vaults."

Practice

1. Poe immediately engages you in the plot by declaring:

    (1) "I have my doubts."

    (2) "… this was a point not definitively settled."

    (3) "… neither by word nor deed had I given Fortunato cause to doubt my good will."

    (4) "I vowed revenge."

2. In a short story, the plot needs a main or central character, called the protagonist (the narrator here), but the protagonist needs someone to oppose, the antagonist. Who or what is the antagonist in this story?

    (1) Fortunato

    (2) Motley

    (3) Luchesi

    (4) Amontillado

Answers

1. **(4)** Poe has a plan for the plot, and that is revenge. Plot means the action you can expect. None of the other answers engage you in the plot. Answer (3) describes Fortunato, not the plot. Answer (2) is an incorrect version of the sentence. Answer (1) is a word play the narrator uses to entice Fortunato.

2. **(1)** Whom does the narrator oppose: the antagonist? The answer is clearly Fortunato, who is responsible for the "thousand injuries" the narrator has borne. None of the other answers is an antagonist. Answer (2) is simply a description of his brightly colored outfit. Answer (3) is a harmless character whose name is used to infuriate Fortunato. Answer (4), Amontillado, is important to the action, but it's still just the wine.

Setting

As mentioned earlier, the setting is the place or places where the story takes place. In the story you just read, the setting is clear … but also contradictory.

The main characters meet at a carnival filled with fun and brightly dressed people. But Poe's story develops into a dark plot. His theme or main idea for the story is that the narrator seeks revenge. This gives the setting a very dark and mysterious feel. Early on you learn that the narrator wants revenge, and you get the distinct feeling that it will take place in the vaults—a very dark thought.

What contradiction between dark and light does Poe set up early in the story in order to set the scene?

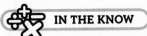 **IN THE KNOW**

Dramas and poems frequently have a distinct setting as well.

Practice

1. Poe sets the scene by contrasting:

   (1) Happy people in motley with dark thoughts of revenge

   (2) Good wine with Amontillado

   (3) Sunny weather with the storms the revelers are experiencing

   (4) The perfectly quiet Fortunato with the narrator

Answer

1. **(1)** The other answers are either opposite to the truth or inaccurate.

Using Context Clues

No matter what kind of fiction you're studying, as readers, you're often faced with vocabulary you might not be familiar with. It's typical for the GED to focus on those words in questions. The best way to handle questions like these is to use context clues, drawing a conclusion about the meaning of a word by considering the *context* in which it's used. There even may be a synonym for the word you know.

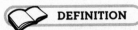 **DEFINITION**

Context includes all the words and sentences around the unknown word. In these sentences, you'll find hints to the meaning of the unknown word.

Look at the third paragraph in "The Cask of Amontillado." What does *connoisseurship* mean? Study the entire paragraph for clues to its meaning.

Practice

1. As used in the third paragraph of "The Cask of Amontillado," *connoisseurship* means:

    (1) Tricking someone

    (2) Owning a wine shop

    (3) Expert opinion

    (4) Being a good friend

Answer

1. **(3)** The narrator says Fortunato is not an expert (a synonym for *connoisseurship*) in art, but he is in wine. There is no mention of tricking (1), owning a wine shop (2), or being a friend (4).

Characters

As you've learned, the protagonist in a story is a central character, a leading figure who wants something and has a problem to solve. That is certainly true of Della in the excerpt from a story you are about to read. However, in this excerpt, who is the antagonist—the person or thing who opposes Della? Is it Della's husband, or is it someone or something else entirely that Della must oppose?

American writer O. Henry (1862–1910) published "The Gift of the Magi" in 1906. Here are some things to think about as you read the story:

*   What is the setting? Is it set in modern times?

*   Who are the main characters?

*   What is the main problem to be solved in the course of the plot?

*   Which words didn't you know? How did the context help you to figure them out?

*   What makes this young wife cry?

"The Gift of the Magi"

One dollar and eighty-seven cents. That was all. And sixty cents of it was in pennies. Pennies saved one and two at a time by bulldozing the grocer and the vegetable man and the butcher until one's cheeks burned with the silent imputation of parsimony that such close dealing implied. Three times Della counted it. One dollar and eighty-seven cents. And the next day would be Christmas.

There was clearly nothing left to do but flop down on the shabby little couch and howl. So Della did it. Which instigates the moral reflection that life is made up of sobs, sniffles, and smiles, with sniffles predominating.

While the mistress of the home is gradually subsiding from the first stage to the second, take a look at the home. A furnished flat at $8 per week. It did not exactly beggar description, but it certainly had that word on the look-out for the mendicancy squad.

Della finished her cry and attended to her cheeks with the powder rag. She stood by the window and looked out dully at a grey cat walking a grey fence in a grey backyard. Tomorrow would be Christmas Day, and she had only $1.87 with which to buy Jim a present. She had been saving every penny she could for months, with this result. Twenty dollars a week doesn't go far. Expenses had been greater than she had calculated. They always are. Only $1.87 to buy a present for Jim. Her Jim. Many a happy hour she had spent planning for something nice for him. Something fine and rare and sterling—something just a little bit near to being worthy of the honor of being owned by Jim ….

Suddenly she whirled from the window and stood before the glass. Her eyes were shining brilliantly, but her face had lost its color within twenty seconds. Rapidly she pulled down her hair and let it fall to its full length.

Now, there were two possessions of the James Dillingham Youngs in which they both took a mighty pride. One was Jim's gold watch that had been his father's and his grandfather's. The other was Della's hair. Had the Queen of Sheba lived in the flat across the airshaft, Della would have let her hair hang out of the window some day to dry just to depreciate Her Majesty's jewels and gifts. Had King Solomon been the janitor, with all his treasures piled up in the basement, Jim would have pulled out his watch every time he passed, just to see him pluck at his beard from envy.

So now Della's beautiful hair fell about her, rippling and shining like a cascade of brown waters. It reached below her knee and made itself almost a garment for her. And then she did it up again nervously and quickly. Once she faltered for a minute and stood still while a tear or two splashed on the worn red carpet.

On went her old brown jacket; on went her old brown hat. With a whirl of skirts and with the brilliant sparkle still in her eyes, she cluttered out of the door and down the stairs to the street.

Where she stopped the sign read: "Mme Sofronie. Hair Goods of All Kinds." Della ran up the steps to the shop and collected herself, panting.

"Will you buy my hair?" asked Della.

Practice

1. You can tell that Della and Jim's relationship is:

   (1) Caring and loving

   (2) Good when they give each other presents

   (3) Thoughtless

   (4) One of protagonist and antagonist

2. What is the meaning of *parsimony* in paragraph 1?

   (1) Generosity

   (2) Thriftiness

   (3) Happiness

   (4) Emotional

Answers

1. **(1)** The other answers are not true of the couple. The couple are not protagonist and antagonist (4) because we see that they care deeply for each other. If anything, the only protagonist—or force—in the story is the fact that they are poor.

2. **(2)** Della has to be thrifty to make her small amount of money last. *Parsimony* makes her cheeks burn. She's not happy (3) about it, but neither does she show the tradesmen that she's overly emotional (4). You can't substitute the word *generosity* (1) for *parsimony:* you can't be broke and generous, at least not with money.

Conflict

There may be no outright fighting in a story, yet still there is conflict. A good story—and for that matter, a good drama—always has conflict. Sometimes poems do, too. It's for you, the reader, to figure out what the main characters want or yearn for and what is standing in the way of their achieving it. The conflict may be literally one person against another, a person against himself, or a person against outside forces.

In the story you just read, Della is clearly struggling against forces outside her marriage. She loves her husband and wants so badly to give him a Christmas gift, but circumstances didn't allow her to.

Reading Poetry

Poetry makes many people uneasy. If you are one of them, it might be helpful to recollect that the literary passages on the Reasoning Through Language Arts: Reading Test are only 25 percent of the passages. Statistically, you are unlikely to encounter a poem or a drama. But just in case you do, let's briefly review some major ideas about poetry you'll want to keep in mind.

Many of the questions about poetry make use of the concepts we covered when discussing fiction: plot, character, and so on. So here, we focus on the difference between poetry and fiction and nonfiction. Both are prose, a straightforward writing style. Poetry, however, uses figurative language and descriptive language that often appeals to your senses.

The following example makes comparison of poetry to prose clear and dramatic. The descriptive poetry is from William Wordsworth's (1770–1850) poem "I Wandered Lonely as a Cloud," often referred to as "Daffodils":

> I wandered lonely as a cloud
> That floats on high o'er vales and hills,
> When all at once I saw a crowd,
> A host of golden daffodils;
> Beside the lake, beneath the trees,
> Fluttering and dancing in the breeze …

Here is the same thought in straightforward prose:

> I was walking one day when I saw a large number of yellow daffodils swaying in the breeze.

A poem is simply an idea the writer communicates by representing one thing in terms of another. In the previous example, the poet uses language in a special way to compare himself to a cloud ("I wandered lonely as a cloud"). This representation (man/cloud) allows you to experience, to see everything, as a cloud would from above.

Finding the Meaning

What can you, the reader, do to start the process of deriving meaning from a poem? Of course, you should begin by prereading, as we've discussed before. But we also suggest reading the poem out loud or at least mouthing the words if you can't actually speak during the test.

When you read out loud, you pay attention to the flow of ideas. You also are more likely to pay attention to the poem's punctuation, and that is crucial for meaning. Remember to pause at a comma, stop briefly at a semicolon, and make a full stop at a period. Carefully observing the punctuation will make a big difference in how well and how quickly you understand the poem.

Figurative Language

Have you ever said something you didn't mean literally, or factually, even though what you said expressed an idea perfectly because it created a picture? For example, after being outside with the children in the snow, Amelia said, "My feet are blocks of ice!" We know Amelia's feet have not turned to blocks of ice, but, if she wants sympathy, the image is perfect—blocks of ice represent her feet. That is figurative language. Figurative language includes metaphors, similes, and hyperbole, all of which were mentioned at the beginning of this chapter.

One of the great American poets, Carl Sandburg (1878–1967) was a genius with figurative language. Read his poem, "Fog," and ask yourself how Sandburg represents fog in the poem:

> **"Fog"**
>
> The fog comes
> on little cat feet.
>
> It sits looking
> over harbor and city
> on silent haunches
> and then moves on.

This poem is more than a comparison: the fog becomes a cat. By bringing these two figures together, Sandburg painted a perfect picture of fog creeping in, sitting a while, and then moving on. Six lines say it all, and that is the power of figurative language.

Different figures of speech are used to accomplish different effects. In "Fog," the poet uses a figure of speech called a metaphor in which two unlike things—living cat and inanimate, or nonliving, fog—are shown to have something in common. The poem is a powerful example of a technique called *personification*. The poet gives living qualities to something that is not alive—such as the fog.

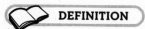 **DEFINITION**

Personification attributes a human quality to an object.

Ralph Waldo Emerson (1803–1882) wrote "The Concord Hymn" in 1836 for the dedication of the *Obelisk*, a monument built in Concord, Massachusetts. The monument commemorates the men who died in the Battle of Lexington and Concord (April 19, 1775), the first battle of the American Revolution. Following is the first *stanza* of the hymn. Can you identify an example of hyperbole in this stanza?

By the rude bridge that arched the flood,
Their flag to April's breeze unfurled,
Here once the embattled farmers stood,
And fired the shot heard round the world.

Although the sounds of war are loud, "the shot heard round the world" is obviously an exaggeration, or hyperbole.

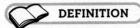 **DEFINITION**

> A **stanza** is a number of lines of verse that form a unit within the poem. In many poems, each stanza has the same number of lines and the same rhythm and rhyme scheme.

Now read the poem "Taxi," by Amy Lowell, with an eye out for figurative language. As you read, ask yourself what human qualities the taxi ride has.

"Taxi"

When I go away from you
The world beats dead
Like a slackened drum.
I call out for you against the jutted stars
And shout into the ridges of the wind.
Streets coming fast,
One after the other,
Wedge you away from me,
And the lamps of the city prick my eyes
So that I can no longer see your face.
Why should I leave you,
To wound myself upon the sharp edges of the night?

Practice

1. The main idea of "Taxi" is that:

   (1) The poet and her friend do not get along.

   (2) The poet has been wounded by glass.

   (3) This is going to be the shortest taxi ride she's ever taken.

   (4) Leaving the one she loves is as painful as if she had been wounded.

2. Which one of these phrases is an example of personification?

    (1) One after the other

    (2) I call out for you

    (3) Streets coming fast

    (4) Why should I leave you?

Answers

1. **(4)** The entire poem talks about the pain of leaving someone and likens the pain to being wounded. Answer (1) is the opposite of the truth. Answers (2) and (3) are facts not found in the poem.

2. **(3)** This is the only answer that assigns a living quality—the ability to move fast—to a nonliving thing—streets. Answers (1), (2), and (4) are all details in the poem.

Imagery

In poetry, *imagery* is what the words make you "see" in your imagination as you read the poem. Imagery consists of the colors, sounds, and sometimes feelings evoked by the poem. You are drawn into the poem because it speaks of images you already know. If you have had the same experience—seen, smelled, touched, felt—that experience always intensifies your reading.

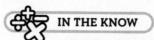 **IN THE KNOW**

Imagery provides the mental pictures that open your mind to the meaning of poems. Similes and metaphors are two techniques that add imagery to poetry—and prose as well.

Wordsworth's poem contains great examples of imagery. For example, the poet's open mind is touched by the picture of a thousand yellow daffodils swaying in the breeze (visual) against the background of waves breaking on the rocks (auditory), and he conveys that vivid image to the reader. He gives us a word of caution as well: we should slow down enough and seek solitude (internal state), in order to see something very, very special in our wanderings. We can easily relate to what the poet sees, hears, and feels.

Historical Poems

To give you a chance to practice looking for imagery, let's turn to one of the most moving poems to come out of World War I. If you do need to work with a poem on the GED, it's likely to be something like this one: older and on a historical topic. The author, a Canadian doctor named Colonel John McCrae (1872–1918), wrote "In Flanders Fields" in May 1915. He had just spent more than 2 weeks treating severely wounded and dying soldiers in World War I, and, exhausted, he sat down near a field and wrote this poem.

"In Flanders Fields"

In Flanders fields the poppies blow
Between the crosses, row on row,
That mark our place; and in the sky
The larks, still bravely singing, fly
Scarce heard amid the guns below.

We are the Dead. Short days ago
We lived, felt dawn, saw sunset glow,
Loved, and were loved, and now we lie
In Flanders fields.

Take up our quarrel with the foe:
To you from failing hands we throw
The torch; be yours to hold it high.
If ye break faith with us who die
We shall not sleep, though poppies grow
In Flanders fields.

Practice

1. The poem is written through the voice of:

    (1) The poet, John McCrae

    (2) The dead soldiers

    (3) Colonel McCrae's staff

    (4) The priest

2. The main idea of the poem is:

   (1) These dead soldiers who "lived, felt dawn … loved, and were loved" should never be forgotten.

   (2) Everyone knows the war will soon be forgotten.

   (3) The doctor was about to take up arms.

   (4) The fight took place in Flanders Field.

3. You can infer from this poem that poppies were the poet's choice of flowers because:

   (1) Poppies are red, the color of blood on the battlefield.

   (2) Poppies grow in broken or uprooted soil, such as a battlefield.

   (3) Poppies are a sign that this troop of men wanted to retreat.

   (4) Answers (1) and (2).

Answers

1. **(2)** The second and third verses both say the soldiers are dead, yet they speak to the living. Answers (1), (3), and (4) all contradict the evidence that the dead soldiers are speaking.

2. **(1)** The soldiers ask to be remembered and implore the reader to take up the fight. There is no proof that answers (2) and (3) are true. Answer (4) is a correct detail, not a main idea.

3. **(4)** If you know anything about growing flowers, you know that poppy seeds can lie in the ground for years and sprout only when someone uproots the soil. Also, poppies are red, the color associated with blood and war. Answer (3) is an incorrect detail.

Reading Drama

Having to read and interpret a piece from a play on the Reading portion of the Reasoning Through Language Arts Test is even more unlikely than having to work with a poem. Just in case, though, we'll briefly review reading a drama, with a focus on theme.

Of course, everything covered so far still holds true: you should preread, looking for the distinctive formatting of the dialogue that lets you know you're going to read an excerpt from a play. Everything we covered about fiction has a place here, too, because dramas also have characters (including a protagonist and an antagonist), conflict, setting, and so on.

If you are asked to work with a selection from a play on the test, you'll likely be asked about the *theme* of the play, which we have not yet covered. A theme is a main idea the writer wants to explore in his or her work. Themes occur in poetry and fiction, too, of course. If you reread the poem "In Flanders Fields" from earlier in this chapter, you'll see that a main theme might be the author's frustration over the great loss that occurs in a war.

The following play, "The Wave" by Michael Diamond (1939–), has only two characters: a husband and wife, Harold and Mary. Think about their relationship as you read. What words would you use to describe how they relate to each other? What is the wave that Harold experiences?

"The Wave"

(Harold and Mary, a married couple who appear to be in their 60s, have just exited an office building and are walking through a small park that is dotted with shade trees and benches.)

HAROLD

You know, you're supposed to feel better after you sign one of those things.

MARY

The living will?

HAROLD

The living will. (He pauses.) I don't feel better.

MARY

Forget about it. We go on with our lives. Believe me, in a week or two you won't even remember what you signed or what you said in that office.

HAROLD

I'll remember. I said not to bother too much keeping me alive. If it looks like I'm cooked ….

MARY

Cooked? That's funny. (Mary laughs and kisses Harold on the cheek. She holds his arm as they walk.)

HAROLD

… Then, pull the plug. Rip out the tubes. Nothing to eat or drink. In a couple of days, I'm on my way to a refrigerator with a tag on my big toe that says "Harold Macy was here." But he's not here anymore.

MARY

Harold, that's awful. Why are you making such a big deal now?

HAROLD

Because I never really thought about it before. If I'm not here—and that's what it's gonna say on my big toe—then, where the hell am I?

MARY

Harold, you're sixty-seven years old. Don't tell me you never thought about death before. I heard you myself say it, many times, that you'll meet your father and your brother, Eddie, when you die. Oh, yeah and you'll meet your first wife, too. You weren't going to talk to her up there. And you always said that you looked forward to pulling up a cloud and sitting down for a long talk with your father, the kind of talk he didn't have time for when he was alive. You said all that, didn't you?

HAROLD

(Pauses to think.) I said it.

MARY

So, I'm not making this up, right? You remember?

HAROLD

Yes.

MARY

Okay. That's what happens. Nice. You'll like seeing Eddie again. You'll snub Vivian. Your pop will be glad to see you. You'll tell him that the Red Sox won the World Series. He'll say, "Why the hell did I have to die so soon?" And then you'll tell him which of those men hit home runs and ...

HAROLD

Quit it, Mary. I never meant any of that. I never imagined an end. It was talk—talk to take up time.

(Harold sits on a bench. Mary sits next to him.)

HAROLD

You know how we sometimes say that we're doing things to take up the time? You know, so that life doesn't drag on too much? We do the crossword puzzle. You talk to your sister. We take a walk, and all of a sudden, it's time for lunch. And that's how we took the time up. Well, that's what my talking about death was about. A little noise to fill the time. And it made me feel smart. But I never imagined ....

MARY

So, now that you see an actual ending to the life of Harold A. Macy, where do you think what's left of him might go after the refrigerator door closes on his torso that's covered by a sheet?

HAROLD

He goes …

MARY

He goes …

HAROLD

Jesus, Mary, all I have him doing is looking at the top of the inside of a refrigerator. It's a stainless-steel drawer. And he's saying get me the hell out of here.

MARY

Okay. So death is the end. There is nothing else. Done. Gone. Harold used to be, and then he wasn't any more.

HAROLD

That's why you put down for them to use every means? No tubes are too many. "Keep me alive for as long as there are trees." That's exactly what you said. The lawyer laughed. He asked you to add that sentence at the end of the will in your own handwriting.

MARY

Well, I know there's nothing else. Once the door is closed on life, that's it. Candle out. Done. And we're all yesterday's sushi that gets thrown out with the trash.

HAROLD

But what if there's more?

MARY

Time to go. I didn't call my sister yet today.

HAROLD

Really. What if there's more? And what if the people on the other side know all about us? Mary, at the end, I don't think they'll ask you whether you thought to call your sister, that day.

MARY

Cut it out, Harold. You don't understand what you're talking about. For all you know, it could be that there's a spirit up there, and he'll tell me to get right back into my life so that I can call Helen.

HAROLD

I can't imagine an angel giving you a special pass to call her. All she does is gossip. And when she's not gossiping, she's telling you how much she weighs and whether her ass looks fat that day.

MARY

All of a sudden, you're on some high horse? Better than Helen? And what the hell made you so superior? The fact that you can see the inside of a refrigerator. Go ahead, shoot for sainthood. Picture what it must look like inside a box that's deep in the ground. (She gets up.) Are you coming?

HAROLD

Wait a minute … a wave. Did you feel it? I just felt it. Eddie and Pop must have moved, like in a pool, and I felt the ripple. Mary.

MARY

Harold, this is ridiculous. That was me standing up. What you felt was …

HAROLD

Please. Something happened. I don't know what to say or how to say it. Something … (long pause) … like what we live for.

MARY

Children feel things that go bump in the night.

HAROLD

Yes. They can feel God, but they don't have the words to talk about it. And if they say something that doesn't sound real, we tell them they're wrong. We tell them they imagined their bumps in the night.

MARY

I never heard you talk like this.

HAROLD

And I never … (Looks into the distance. Begins to talk. Says nothing.)

MARY

Harold.

HAROLD

I made the right choice. There's nothing to be afraid about. Only …

MARY

Only?

HAROLD

They'll ask us what we've done.

MARY

You mean? …

HAROLD

Not if we rooted for the Red Sox.

MARY

What do you know? Here I am, taking your junky talk seriously. You said yourself that you only jabbered on to fill the time. This is no different. It's just a new patter, a new little dance routine, as you say, to while away the time.

(He rises. They walk a little, arm-in-arm.)

HAROLD

I don't think I'll ever use those words again: "filling up the time."

MARY

Harold, when we get older, we sometimes begin to get a little strange. Those around us are supposed to tolerate us, even though we're strange. That's what I'm doing now.

HAROLD

One day, Mary, you'll feel a presence. Like nothing you've ever experienced.

And everything will …

MARY

There's a game on tonight. I'll make corned beef, the way you like it. (Pause.) You know, sometimes I call my sister, and I hold the phone up so she can hear the noises that come out of you when you watch the game: yips and atta-boys and a lot of goddamnits. She laughs and I laugh. I never told you.

HAROLD

… everything will sort of go through you, like a wave. Mary, I never …

MARY

I'll turn the game on.

HAROLD

I don't think so. Maybe some other night.

(They walk off the stage together.)

© 2005 by Michael Diamond

Practice

1. What is the meaning of *wave* in the title?

   (1) We ride the wave of sadness.

   (2) Mary and Harold are happier living near the water.

   (3) A felt experience that goes beyond our everyday lives.

   (4) We make our own happiness.

2. In the play, Harold, the protagonist, seems disturbed by the experience with the living will, while Mary:

   (1) Is even more upset than Harold and spends the time crying

   (2) Accepts that signing the living will is just another event in her life

   (3) Only wants to go home and plan their funerals

   (4) Is more concerned about her sister than she is about Harold

3. You can conclude from the dialogue that regardless of their very different reactions to the living will, Harold and Mary are obviously:

   (1) A well-suited, happily married couple

   (2) A recently divorced couple

   (3) A severely depressed couple

   (4) At odds over every aspect of their lives

Answers

1. **(3)** The wave is never identified as happy or sad. Answers (1), (2), and (4) are not correct because they do not deal with what appears beyond the surface of our lives.

2. **(2)** Answers (1), (3), and (4) are all incorrect details.

3. **(1)** Answers (2), (3), and (4) are incorrect details.

The Extended Response

It's possible that no section of the GED tests will give you as much anxiety as the Extended Response question on the Reasoning Through Language Arts Test. Many people find writing essays stressful, and having a time limit doesn't help. We can't eliminate the Extended Response portion of the test for you, but we can give you our best advice about how to write it well.

As a reminder, the Extended Response is the final portion of this GED test, and you're given 45 minutes to complete it. You'll be typing it directly into the computer you're using, and those 45 minutes begin after a 10-minute break following the Language and Reading section. Take advantage of those 10 minutes to try to relax as much as you can. Don't fret over missed answers, but use the facilities, get a drink of water, walk around for a bit, and do whatever you can to prepare for the final portion of this test.

The Extended Response: An Overview

More good news: you do not need to come up with an essay topic on the GED. Instead, you are given a rather complicated task: you need to read two passages arguing two sides of a

In This Chapter

- What to expect in the Extended Response
- Tips on reading and interpreting the Extended Response question prompt
- How the GED® Extended Response is graded

real-life issue. It's likely to be an issue that has strong beliefs on either side, but not something so polarizing that you already have an unchangeable opinion about it. The passages are generally in different formats, not that dissimilar to the types of writing you saw in the informational passages on the Reading part of the test. In your essay, you'll need to choose one of the two passages and write a convincing piece that shows how it supports the viewpoint it favors better than the other passage.

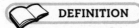 **DEFINITION**

An **essay topic** is an essay prompt. It is the subject (topic) you are being prompted to write about.

To be clear, the passages will be roughly equivalent—they each may contain some logical flaws or strong supports. The idea isn't that you are to pick the correct passage, but instead, to choose one or the other and show which you feel is better supported.

To be extra clear, you are not writing your opinion about the issue. You're analyzing the passages to prove why you feel one is the better supported piece of writing. You'll use evidence from both sources to support your argument. In fact, the prompt asks you to use specific and relevant evidence from the passages to do so.

It's a different and more complicated essay than what you may be used to, but the good news is that you're analyzing existent pieces of writing, not trying to develop your own argument. In many ways, that's much simpler.

Remember that many people from different backgrounds take the GED. Therefore, the Extended Response topics cover ideas that every GED candidate will be able to say something about.

Reading and Understanding the Extended Response Prompt

As you know, you will have 45 minutes to write your essay. Don't panic—that's more than enough time. The first thing you want to do is to read the Extended Response prompt. This should only take about 5 to 7 minutes of your 45 minutes, so having an understanding of what you're going to be looking at is key.

When you first look the Extended Response question on a computer screen, you might feel overwhelmed. You'll see both passages, one after the other, on the left side of the screen. Instead of beginning there (which is a natural instinct), take a look at the right column. That's where you'll find a brief introduction to the passages as well as the prompt for the essay itself. The prompt will be something like, "In your response, analyze both [passage 1] and [passage 2] to determine which position is best supported. Use relevant and specific evidence from both sources to support your argument."

Below the essay prompt, you'll see a text box where you can write your essay. You should be aware of a few things about that box:

- It will grow as you write, so don't attempt to write an essay that fits into that rather small box.

- You are not able to cut and paste from the passages into the box. You'll have to type in anything you want to quote. However, you can cut and paste *within* the text box, which is helpful if you decide to make your second paragraph your third, or something like that.

- There's no spell check for the text you type in the box. You have to find and correct your spelling and grammar mistakes on your own.

Now that you know how the screen is set up, where should you begin? As always, we suggest a little prereading. Begin with the brief introduction to the two passages, which will let you know what topic they address. Then scroll through the passages, taking note of their format (are they an op-ed and a letter from a high school principal? an article and an email?) and who wrote them. Check out the titles and subtitles, too. We also suggest reading the prompt *before* the passages to remind yourself of what you're looking to do in the Extended Response, especially if the topic is one you immediately have strong feelings about. Then read the passages themselves, making mental notes about which evidence you find most convincing and where you see flaws in the arguments. Don't worry about getting this all worked out on the first read-through. You'll be able to go back and gather evidence again.

Having read the passages, you need to make a quick decision about which side you want to argue is better supported. Here, since you can't research the topic, you'll need to go with your gut. Remember that both passages will be about equal in how well they are supported, so choose the one you feel is slightly stronger. It does not have to be the side that you personally agree with, so if you feel that the argument for your side is deeply flawed, choose the other side. (We discuss how to begin planning for your essay in the next chapter.)

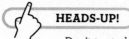 **HEADS-UP!**

> Don't try to have it both ways and argue that both sides are supported well. That might well be true, but it's not what the essay question is asking you to do. Choose, and move on.

Remember, limit your reading to 5 to 7 minutes maximum. You need to have enough time left over to write your essay.

How the Extended Response Is Graded

Before we move on to the next chapter and review how to plan, write, and proofread your Extended Response, we want to explain how the Extended Response is graded. Every other question on the Reasoning Through Language Arts Test is multiple-choice and, therefore, graded by computer.

Perhaps surprisingly, the Extended Response is graded by a computer as well. Whether you find that unnerving or not, knowing that it's true does provide some helpful guidance for you. The computer is trained to look for particular word patterns and typical essay structures, both of which you can be sure to use in your essay.

The good news about having a computer grade your essay is that you get your score much faster than if it had to be sent to a human grader.

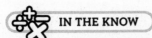 **IN THE KNOW**

If there is something very unusual about your Extended Response—if you leave it blank, write in a language other than English, or use a lot of fancy words, for example—the computer will flag it and it will be sent to a human grader.

Planning, Writing, and Editing Your Extended Response

Now that you've reviewed how to preread, read, and consider the passages presented to you as part of the Extended Response, the next step is to plan what you'll write in your essay. It's tempting to skip this step, especially when you feel pressed for time, and start immediately writing, but organizing your thoughts into an outline is just as important as the actual writing. Don't forget to edit your essay after you've drafted it, too. Let's review how to accomplish these tasks.

Taking Notes

In the preceding chapter, we reviewed what the Extended Response portion of the test looks like. Now let's plan how you should prepare to write it.

By now, you've decided which of the two passages you want to argue is better supported. The next step is to gather evidence to use in your essay.

In the Extended Response prompt you're asked to "use relevant and specific evidence from both passages to support your argument." You need to reread both passages to find that evidence. For the passage you find to be superior, look for places where the author does a great job of supporting her thesis. For the passage you find to be inferior, look for places

In This Chapter

- Organizing your thoughts
- Writing your Extended Response
- Finalizing your work for submission
- A sample GED®-style Extended Response question to help you practice

where the author has not sufficiently supported his thesis. We suggest using your note-taking tools to do this; it's too stressful to try to keep it all in your head. Every paragraph of the passages will be numbered, so you should be able to write very short notes to keep track of what you would like to use, jotting down notes like "2—evidence quote."

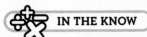

IN THE KNOW

If this is the first GED test you've taken, you might not know that scrap paper and pencils aren't always allowed. Instead, you'll be able to use an erasable note board and dry-erase marker. That's something you'll want to keep in mind as you think about organizing your Extended Response.

What should you look for? Here are some suggestions:

- Moments in the superior passage where the author uses specific and strong evidence to support her thesis. Look for statistics and fact-based evidence.

- Moments in the inferior passage where the author makes a broad assertion without evidence to support it.

- The actual structure of the passages. The superior passage might make only one claim but offer four pieces of evidence to assert it, while the inferior passage might make four claims but offer only scattered evidence to support them.

- Logical fallacies. These are moments (which you'll look for in the inferior passage) where the author uses faulty logic. You don't have to explain what kind of logical fallacy is employed (although if you can do that, go for it!), but merely that the logic doesn't hold true. By the way, you may see these in the argument you find superior, but don't point them out. Remember, both arguments will be flawed. Don't switch sides in the middle of your planning or, worse yet, in the middle of the essay itself.

- Assumptions on the part of the writers. You might find an assumption to be valid (such as assuming that many American high school students plan to go to college), or you may feel it's a stereotype or bad assumption. For the argument you find superior, you want to look for valid assumptions. For the other side, you want to find flawed assumptions.

- The author of the passages. If one passage about vaccinations is written by a concerned dad with no medical training and the other by a pediatrician, you most likely will give more weight to the pediatrician, right?

You might have noticed that this task involves looking very closely at the passages again. Yes, for sure, you should plan to spend another 5 to 7 minutes closely looking at the passages. Scroll through them, jot down important parts of the passages, and collect the evidence that builds your case. Simply moving on to writing at this stage is not a good idea.

Creating Your Thesis

Before you begin outlining your essay, take a minute—really, at this point, you should only need a minute—to state your *thesis*. We suggest writing it down so you don't lose track of it. At this stage, it should be something simple, along the lines of, "Passage 1 is the superior passage because it is written by a professional in the field and makes use of extensive statistics from the field." This most likely isn't going to be the exact thesis you'll use in the essay, but it's good enough to start with.

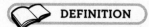 **DEFINITION**

A **thesis** is the critical sentence in your introduction that expresses the controlling idea of your paper. It tells your readers what your essay is about and outlines what they will find in the following paragraphs.

If you find that you can't put together your thesis yet, you need to step back and ask yourself why. Are you trying to write about both passages? Have you failed to choose one as superior to the other? Are you finding writing against your actual opinion to be problematic? Have you tried to read too quickly? Whatever the problem is, stop, take a couple deep breaths, and reengage. You have plenty of time left to write.

Outlining Your Extended Response

This is a good moment to assure you that there is no set minimum or limit for your essay's length and no expected format. Many people will end up writing the classic five-paragraph essay they've encountered so often in high school, but there's no reason why you must extend or shorten your essay to be five paragraphs. If you find that you have one strong point to make, write a three-paragraph essay (a one point paragraph plus an introduction and a conclusion). If you truly feel you have four strong points to make, write a six-paragraph essay (four point paragraphs plus an introduction and a conclusion). We do strongly advocate for a clear introduction and conclusion, but beyond that, whatever works best for you is fine. Don't adjust to meet some standard you aren't asked to follow, but don't write too short or too long because you feel you have too little or too much time.

With your notes in hand, you're ready to begin outlining your Extended Response.

 **GOOD IDEA**

Remember the goal of your essay: you want to prove why you feel one of the passages better supports the position it presents than the other.

Your rough outline might look something like the following:

Introduction/thesis: If you've jotted down your thesis already, you can use it here. If not, it's time to decide which of the passages is the one you want to argue better supports the position it presents. You also might note how you'll get your readers' attention with a strong opening (such as a question or quotation from the passage). Finally, you'll want to close with an overview of everything you're going to point out in the supporting paragraphs.

Body paragraphs: Remember, you can have one body paragraph or as many as you prefer. It depends on what you feel your strongest supporting points are. For now, simply note which supporting point you're going to make in each paragraph. You also might note why or how it proves your thesis and the evidence (in the form of quotations from the paragraph) you intend to use.

Conclusion: Here, you want to reassert your opening thesis. Don't just rewrite it in the exact same words, though. If you happen to have personal experience that's relevant, it's fine to include that here. Or you can make a point of dismissing the other argument. However you close, be thoughtful about how to conclude your essay clearly and vigorously so it leaves a strong impression.

This is a very general outline. You can include as many specifics as you want in your outline, but you must remember that your time is very short, so jot down the basics. If you find that you're ready to write, it's okay to stop outlining and move on to typing.

Time Is of the Essence

The time element is important, of course. You need to keep track of how much time you have left as you approach each part of the writing process. Here's a rough guide on how you might divide your time:

- Brainstorming and creating a rough outline: 5 to 7 minutes
- Writing the introduction and conclusion: 10 minutes
- Writing the body paragraphs: 20 minutes
- Proofreading and editing: 5 to 8 minutes (or more if you have it)
- Doing a final read of your essay: 1 to 3 minutes

These suggestions are only a guideline to help keep you on track. The important point is that you have a total of 45 minutes, no matter how you decide to use it.

GOOD IDEA

When you go to take your test, be sure you have a watch with you to help you schedule your writing time. Cell phones are not allowed at your computer station.

Writing Your Extended Response

You've preread the passages, taken notes on them, and sketched an outline. There's nothing left to do but write your essay. Here are some points to keep in mind:

- Remember, the Extended Response is graded by a computer, so don't try to dazzle. Instead, write clearly and at a steady pace, varying your sentence length and style.

- Take time to transcribe quotations from the passage correctly.

- Keep an eye out for troublesome words like *their/they're/there*.

- Most importantly, make your points as clearly as you can. (We give you a good example of this at the end of this chapter.)

Editing Your Essay

You did it! You wrote a whole draft! Congratulations! In the few minutes that remain, you'll want to take the time to proofread (reading for errors) and edit (correcting errors) your Extended Response. Although your time will be limited for this effort, you must give the essay the thorough going-over it needs. Resist the urge to just hit Submit and be done with it. Almost every Extended Response can be improved. Just don't make the mistake of cutting entire paragraphs without being sure you have enough time to redo them.

Next to writing your essay, the most important thing you can do is carefully proofread what you've written and make any necessary adjustments to the text. To stay focused, it might be helpful to read your essay out loud (or at least mouth it, if speaking would be disruptive).

You need to look at your essay's basic structure and how well you have used transitions to make it flow and allow the reader to follow your logical thinking patterns. Have you avoided trite, overused expressions? You also need to check that you avoided homonym mistakes, your spelling is correct, and your vocabulary is appropriate to the occasion. Let's dig in.

Check Your Structure

Look at your written essay, and ask yourself the following questions:

- Does it have a beginning, a middle, and an end?

- Does your first paragraph clearly introduce the main idea of your essay?

- Do your body paragraphs fully develop your main point?

- Does the final paragraph bring everything to a conclusion and provide a sense of closure?

Check for Transitions

To improve your writing, you need to be sure your ideas, both in sentences and paragraphs, have coherence and that you've bridged the gap between ideas smoothly. Transitional words and phrases help do this. The more cues you give your reader about your reasons or your attitude toward your topic, the better.

 **IN THE KNOW**

The computer program that evaluates your essay is trained to look for transitions in your writing, so be sure to provide a few of these transition guideposts for readers to follow.

You don't need to use many transition words in your essay. Just pick out a few from the following list and remember them while you write and when you proofread your essay.

- **To show cause or additional information:** consequently, clearly, then, furthermore, additionally, in addition, moreover, because, similarly, besides that, in the same way, since

- **To change the line of reasoning (contrast):** however, on the other hand, but, yet, nevertheless, on the contrary, although

- **To open a paragraph or begin a new idea:** admittedly, assuredly, certainly, obviously, of course, true, unquestionably, in general, in this situation

- **For the final points of a paragraph or essay or to signal a conclusion:** finally, lastly, therefore, in conclusion

- **To restate a point within a paragraph in another way or more precisely:** in other words, in fact, specifically, to illustrate

- **To indicate sequence or time:** after, during, as soon as, at first, at last, before, finally, in the meantime, later, meanwhile, next, soon, first … second … third

Check Your Sentence Length

Try to keep your sentences varied. A long series of short sentences can be grueling to read and shows a lack of sophistication in your writing. Instead, use phrases and clauses, separated by commas, to keep your writing lively. Look at this example:

> Melody enjoys singing. She has taken lessons for several years. She hopes to continue to study it in college.

There's nothing technically wrong with it, except it's dull writing because each sentence is nearly the same length and structure. Here, using a more complicated construction, we can jazz it up a bit:

> Melody, who enjoys singing, has taken lessons for several years and hopes to continue to study it in college.

As you proofread your Extended Response, look for opportunities to vary your sentence length and structure.

Check Your Vocabulary

Because a passing score on the GED earns you a high school graduation equivalency diploma, it's reasonable to expect that you have a vocabulary reflecting a certain level of knowledge.

The internet offers a number of resources for learning vocabulary words. The College Board website (collegeboard.com) has a program that will send you a new word to learn every day, and it can provide you with lists of vocabulary words. The editors of the American Heritage Dictionaries publish a book called *100 Words Every High School Graduate Should Know*. Every source is going to offer slightly different lists, but many of the words are the same among all the vocabulary word sources.

Check Your Grammar

Don't overlook your grammar when writing and proofreading your essay. Be sure to correct any grammar errors that have made their way into your essay.

- **Subject-verb agreement:** A singular subject takes the singular verb form; a plural subject takes the plural verb form. The *child stands/children stand* at attention.

- **Subject-object pronouns:** Subject pronouns can perform action within a sentence, while object pronouns are receivers of an action. Subject pronouns include *I, you, he, she,* and *it;* object pronouns include *me, you, him, her,* and *they. She and I* (subject) are taking *them* (object) to the mall.

- **Pronoun agreement:** Singular pronouns match with singulars; plurals with plurals. Remember that some pronouns sound plural—*everybody, everyone, nobody, somebody*—but they are really singular. *Everyone* takes out *his* or *her* homework from last night (not *your* homework).

- **Adjectives versus adverbs:** Adjectives modify (describe) nouns; adverbs modify mostly verbs but also adjectives and even other adverbs. The *extremely* (adverb) *humid* (adjective) night air *suddenly* (adverb) erupted into a *noisy* (adjective) thunderstorm.

Check Your Usage

The English language is often confusing, even for those of us who have been speaking it all our lives. Here are a few English usage rules that need to be followed when you write and review your essay:

- **Avoid double negatives:** Some words like *barely, scarcely,* and *hardly* are already negative, so don't use another negative with them. For example, *I hardly have none* shows incorrect usage. *Barely any, scarcely any,* or *hardly any* shows correct usage.

- **Avoid sexist references:** Rather than *waiter* or *waitress,* use *server;* instead of *steward* or *stewardess,* use *flight attendant.* The use of *he or she* is preferred if a singular pronoun is needed and you mean both.

Check Your Sentence Structure

A sentence needs a subject and a verb and forms a complete thought. This is called an *independent clause.*

Two sentences (independent clauses) can be joined together with either a semicolon or a comma and an independent conjunction: *and, but, or, yet, for, nor, so.*

Besides independent clauses (a subject and a verb forming a complete thought), we have *dependent clauses* that usually have a subject and a verb with an incomplete thought.

Independent clauses and dependent clauses can be joined together, usually by dependent conjunctions such as *because, after, as, as soon as, before, when, whenever, while, where, wherever, who, whoever, although, though, since, which,* or *that.*

Check Your Punctuation

All sentences begin with a capital letter and end with a period, question mark, or exclamation point.

Two independent clauses are joined by either a comma and an independent conjunction or a semicolon.

When combining a dependent and independent clause, if the dependent clause comes first, it is followed by a comma; if it comes second, no comma is needed.

Check Your Verb-Preposition Combinations

Sometimes we use verb-preposition combinations incorrectly when we slip into local, regional, or informal speech patterns. The following list reviews the correct combination of words:

- You *agree on* a thing; you *agree with* a person.

- You are *angry about* or *at* a thing; you are *angry with* a person.

- You *argue about* a thing; you *argue with* a person.

- You are *concerned with* a problem; you are *concerned for* a person.

- You *escape from* a bad situation; you *escape to* another place.

- You *wait for* a thing or person; you *wait on* a customer; and you *wait with* someone else.

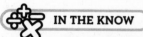 **IN THE KNOW**

It is not unusual for people to use informal language around friends and family. Also, certain areas of our cities and various regions of our country sometimes have unusual ways of using language. However, the GED uses Edited American English (EAE), which is the kind of English a school textbook would use.

Check for Trite Expressions

This isn't the most important concept for the Extended Response, but if you have time, you can try to eliminate overused expressions. We call such expressions *trite*—they're stale and worn out. If you find any trite expressions while proofreading your essay, remove them and say something in your own words instead. Being able to express your thoughts in a unique or unusual way is a sign of a good writer.

This list is just a sampling of boring, trite, overused expressions. You can find more examples online. Change these expressions if you find them in your essays:

- At that/this point in time
- At the present time
- At this time and place
- Better than ever
- Contrary to popular opinion/according to popular opinion
- Due to the fact that
- Easier said than done
- Few and far between
- From the beginning of time/since the beginning of time
- In today's world/in the world today
- Last but not least
- Over and above
- When all is said and done

Check for Commonly Confused Words

Some words are easily mixed up. *Homonyms,* for instance, are words that sound alike but mean different things (*see* and *sea,* for example). Although these confusing words might seem obvious while you're looking at them in this book, they can be easy to mix up when you're composing an essay quickly. Be on the lookout for them when you proofread your essay.

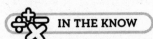 **IN THE KNOW**

If you listen closely, even professional news reporters and politicians fall victim to these confusing word demons. Don't let them hide in your essay.

Check out this list of some commonly confused words:

- **A lot/allot:** *A lot* (two words; *alot* is not a word) refers to many; *allot* (one word) refers to putting something aside. Because many people do not *allot* much of their income into savings, they do not have *a lot* to fall back on when times get tough.

- **Accept/except:** *Accept* is a verb meaning to agree; *except* is a preposition that suggests exclusion or rejection. All the guests had *accept*ed the dinner invitation *except* Duane.

- **Affect/effect:** *Affect* (verb) means to act upon something else; *effect* (noun) is a result. The *effects* of a long time with no sunshine often *affects* people's spirits. (Less commonly, *effect* also can be used as a verb meaning "to bring about": The hot and muggy weather *effected* severe thunderstorms.)

- **All together/altogether:** *All* is a pronoun; *together* is an adjective or adverb. During the holidays, families are *all together* for an *altogether* good time.

- **Among/between:** *Between* implies two; *among* implies more than two. *Among* all the brothers and sisters, Jada was the one who settled disagreements *between* their mom and stepdad.

- **Amount/number of:** An *amount* refers to a mass of something; *number of* refers to the number of somethings. Before you can form a *number of* snowballs, you have to have a certain *amount of* snow.

- **Coarse/course:** *Coarse* refers to something rough, as in *coarse* sandpaper; *course* refers to a subject or a path one follows. Miguel's *course* in life was a *coarse* one: he suffered many setbacks before he made his fortune.

- **Disinterested/uninterested:** *Disinterested* refers to a neutral state of mind; *uninterested* means you don't care. Marcel was glad he had a *disinterested* government teacher who would listen to both sides of an argument rather than an *uninterested* one who didn't care what anyone said.

- **Fewer/less:** *Fewer* you can count; *less* you have to measure. When choosing foods that are good for you, look for those with *fewer* calories and *less* fat.

- **Irregardless/regardless:** There is no such word as *irregardless*. *Regardless* of the fact people do use the word, *irregardless* is not a word.

- **Its/it's:** As you learned in previous chapters, *its* shows possession; *it's* is a contraction for *it is*. *It's* funny to watch my dog trying to catch *its* own tail.

- **Loose/lose:** *Loose* means roomy, plenty of slack; *lose* means to fail to win or to misplace. Granmama always *loses* her false teeth because they are too *loose*.

- **Personnel/personal:** *Personnel* refers to a group of people; *personal* means belonging to an individual. *Personnel* offices are now referred to as HR or human resources to give the department a more *personal* touch.

- **Quiet/quite/quit:** *Quiet* means calm, serene, or silent; *quite* is an adverb meaning very or a lot. The *quiet* of a school at night is *quite* a contrast to its daytime clamor. *Quit* means to free oneself from something, to leave or depart from. She *quit* the school play.

- **There/their/they're:** *There* is an adverb referring to place or position; *their* is a possessive adjective; *they're* is a contraction for the words *they are*. *They're* convinced it is *their* destiny to move *there* before they die.

- **Thorough/through/threw:** *Thorough* means complete or careful; *through* is a verb indicating direction; *threw* is a verb form of *to throw*. The pitcher *threw* the ball directly *through* the strike zone, which *thoroughly* surprised the batter.

- **To/too/two:** *To* is a preposition showing direction or the word preceding a verb; *too* is an adverb meaning also; *two* is the number following one. The *two* young goblins were *too* excited *to* say "Trick or treat!"

- **Whose/who's:** *Who's* is a contraction of the two words *who is*; *whose* is a possessive pronoun showing ownership. *Whose* turn is it to see *who's* ringing the doorbell?

- **Your/you're:** *Your* is a possessive pronoun showing ownership; *you're* is a contraction of the words *you are*. *You're* very quick to show off *your* new car.

Remember, there's no spellcheck on your GED computer so you have to find these errors yourself!

Practice

Now that we've thoroughly reviewed all you need to do on the Extended Response, it's time to practice writing one. We give you an Extended Response prompt and the two passages you need to read for it. Then, in the Answers section, we show you what a well-written essay could look like. Please keep in mind that there are dozens of ways to write this essay well, and this is just one example. Before you begin, set an alarm for 45 minutes so you're aware of how much time you have left.

First, read the Extended Response summary, which tells you about the passages you're going to read:

> While a popular local gym is encouraging people to skip breakfast, a consortium of local doctors warns that doing so is dangerous and ineffective.

Second, remind yourself of the task at hand by rereading the prompt:

> In your response, analyze both the gym's email to patrons and the consortium's letter to its patients to determine which position is better supported. Use relevant and specific evidence from both sources to support your argument.

> Type your response in the box below [in this case, type it on a computer to practice]. This task may require approximately 45 minutes to complete.

Now, preread and read the passages, taking notes as you go if you like. When you're done reading the passages, you should be ready to put together a thesis.

Passage 1:

Subject Line: Why Isn't the Weight Coming Off? Have Your Tried Morning Fasts?

Hey Tough Talk Gym members, we hear you—you're frustrated that you work out regularly with us and yet do not see the weight coming off the way you would like. We're writing today to suggest you join us in trying a simple and effective way to lose extra weight without fuss: morning fasts!

What Is a Morning Fast?

Pretty much just what it sounds like: you refrain from eating until noon. It's okay to drink water and other beverages (although we always advise against drinking alcohol and sugary soda drinks!), but no food should pass your lips until the clock strikes 12 times!

The concept is simple: by depriving your body of fresh nutrients during the morning, you force it to burn reserves (also known as *fat!*), and that causes weight loss. When you fast in the morning, you're adding more hours without food to those you've already slept through, making the fasting more likely to succeed.

Why Is Fasting Safe?

Fasting is an ancient idea. Most major religions practice some form of fasting, continuing traditions that started thousands of years ago. You read the papers and keep on top of the news, so you know that millions of people have fasted throughout history without any sort of major health issues.

Science backs us up on this. In a 1995 study of 14 participants, those who fasted through noon every day lost an average of 5 pounds after 2 weeks on the program. That's the kind of weight loss that a little discomfort is worth, right?

As great as the weight loss is, though, the real benefit of fasting is the mental clarity you gain from doing it. When your body is relying on extra reserves of fat, it's burning through the weight that's been holding you back. You will feel lighter, physically and mentally, and you'll see a sharpened awareness for the beauty of the world around you.

Are you ready to try fasting?

Join us for a free webinar to:

- Learn from our head trainer, Daniel Hudson, as he explains why fasting may be right for you

- Watch Daniel talk with several gym members who have switched to fasting

- Download a free plan for easing into fasting

Point your browser to ToughTalkGym.net on Thursday night at 6:30 P.M. to watch live. You also can access the webinar on our webpage after it has completed.

Passage 2:

Dear Friends:

There's no other way to say it except clearly: fasting is not a healthy choice.

We, the doctors of the Bonneville Medical Consortium, are moved to write to you after receiving numerous requests to sign "Physician's Permission Forms" for you, asking us to sign off on trying Tough Talk Gym's new morning fasting program. We love Tough Talk Gym—it's great to have a full-scale gymnasium with a caring, committed staff of trainers in a town of our size—but we cannot condone this new program. It is unsafe, but, more importantly, it will not get you the results you want.

We know that Tough Talk has made several claims about fasting, so we want to clearly explain why they are not true.

First, Tough Talk points to the tradition of religious fasting and claims that it has never resulted in harm to any who practice it. That's not true. A 2012 study of over 1,000 people who fast as part of their religious practice shows that they are more likely to faint, cause vehicular accidents because of muddled thinking, and make poor safety choices by a ratio of nearly 3 to 1, when compared to those who are not fasting. You should also keep in mind that fasting for religious observations generally means avoiding food for a day, week, or month, not a continuous program of skipping all food before noon for years.

Secondly, fasting can lead to nutritional imbalances. What often happens is that the person fasting is so ravenous by the time they can eat again, they eat too much food—far in excess of what they would normally eat over the course of breakfast and lunch. People who are hungry will naturally reach for high-fat, high-sugar foods, as well, and often allow themselves to overindulge in them, because they think, "Well, I didn't eat any breakfast."

Finally, and perhaps most dishearteningly, fasting often backfires as a weight loss technique. Besides the problem with overeating, as mentioned above, fasting does not always force the body to burn extra reserves of fat, as Tough Talk claims. Instead, the body's metabolism is likely to slow, burning less fat in order to protect it. This is because our bodies may react to fasting as a stressor and could shift into survival mode to help us endure when not much food is coming in. Thus, weight loss may not increase at all.

While we understand the desire to regain a healthy weight, as well as the constant hope that some sort of fad diet will make doing so easier, the only real way to lose weight is through a healthy diet and an exercise plan. We stand by ready to help you put that together—and to cheer you on as you lose those extra pounds! Just give us a call!

Yours in good health,

The Doctors of the Belleville Consortium

Having read both passages, go with your gut and choose which one you feel is better supported. Write a thesis based on your choice. After that, collect the evidence you'll use to prove your point. Where do you see flaws in the arguments? What is left unsaid, or implied, but not proven? Refine your thesis, ensuring you're as clear about your opinion as possible. Then, draft your essay, being sure you're not using more than the time you have left. Take the time to proofread and edit next. Finally, compare your essay to the sample one we've included in the following section.

Answer

To fast or not to fast? That is the question. A local Bonneville business, Tough Talk Gym, advocated for its patrons to try fasting, while a group of local doctors feels moved to release a statement to their patients advising against fasting. The gym's lure of rapid, painless weight loss is compelling, but ultimately, the doctors have logic, science, and common sense on their side, making the more powerful argument.

To look at Tough Talk's view first, notice the claim, "In a study of 14 participants, those who fasted through noon every day lost an average of 5 pounds after 2 weeks on the program." Although at first this sounds very convincing indeed, a moment's consideration reveals that this is a very small study—only 14 people!—covering a very short time—only 2 weeks! In contrast, the doctors, who are scientists after all, note that "Instead, the body's metabolism is likely to slow, burning less fat in order to protect it. This is because our bodies may react to fasting as a stressor, and could shift into survival mode to help us endure when not much food is coming in." It's telling that this does not actually contradict the small study presented by the gym, but merely shows that when long-term fasting (of more than 2 weeks) sets in as a pattern, weight loss is likely to decline as the body goes into survival mode. Thus, the purpose of fasting as presented by the gym, which is to lose weight, will not be sustainable.

Additionally, the doctors' consortium makes a better case against fasting for reasons beyond weight loss. Although the gym offers assurances that fasting will create some sort of "mental clarity," the consortium offers a much more realistic bit of common sense. They note that "A 2012 study of over 1,000 people who fast as part of their religious practice shows that they are more likely to faint, cause vehicular accidents because of muddled thinking, and make poor choices by a ratio of nearly 3 to 1, when compared to those who are not fasting." You can't argue with that evidence, especially when the doctors also note that religious fasting is a temporary and often very brief practice.

All in all, it's clear that Tough Talk genuinely may be trying to aid its patrons, but with the suggestion of fasting, is actually promoting a harmful practice. They offer no convincing proof of the claims they've made, and even their head trainer, who is to lead the webinar on fasting as a practice, is not promoted as having a license or medical training. The gym's claims are vague or easily disproven. The consortium clearly has a superior case to make, and does so by marshalling facts, scientific proof, and common sense in a way that is ultimately convincing.

CHAPTER 10

Reasoning Through Language Arts Practice Test

Are you ready for some serious practice? The Reasoning Through Language Arts practice test is comprised of 50 questions, which you have 150 minutes to complete. You need to time yourself for this test in order to have an accurate understanding of what taking the real thing is like. Just as on the GED®, you'll begin with a 95-minute section in which you'll be asked to complete both Reading and Language multiple-choice questions of various types. Then, you'll give yourself a 10-minute break before returning to spend 45 minutes on the Extended Response. Note that as on the real GED test, you'll spend the bulk of that first 95-minute period (75 percent of it) on the Reading section and only 25 percent of your time on the Language section.

Instructions

You should allot yourself 150 minutes to complete the 50 multiple-choice questions and Extended Response essay on this practice test. Work carefully, but don't spend too much time on any one question. If you are having trouble with a question, make the best guess you can and move on. Your score is based on the number of correct answers; there is no penalty for guessing.

When taking the practice test, try to simulate actual test conditions as much as possible. Go to a place where you won't be interrupted, and follow test instructions. Start the timer after you've read the instructions and are ready to begin the first question.

As you check your answers, you might want to go back over the appropriate parts of Chapters 1 through 9 of this book to review the material on any questions you answered incorrectly. This way you are focusing your attention only on the areas you need to.

Go on to the next page when you are ready to begin.

Questions 1 through 6 refer to the following passage:

From *The Scarlet Letter* by Nathaniel Hawthorne (1850)

After her return to the prison, Hester Prynne was found to be in a state of nervous excitement that demanded constant watchfulness, lest she should perpetrate violence on herself, or do some half-frenzied mischief to the poor babe. As night approached, it proving impossible to quell her insubordination by rebuke or threats of punishment, Master Brackett, the jailer, thought fit to introduce a physician. He described him as a man of skill in all Christian modes of physical science, and likewise familiar with whatever the savage people could teach, in respect to medicinal herbs and roots that grew in the forest. To say the truth, there was much need of professional assistance, not merely for Hester herself, but still more urgently for the child; who, drawing its sustenance from the maternal bosom, seemed to have drank in with it all the turmoil, the anguish, and despair, which pervaded the mother's system. It now writhed in convulsions of pain, and was a forcible type, in its little frame, of the moral agony which Hester Prynne had borne throughout the day.

1. Based on the passage, one could predict that Hester and her child needed medical attention because:

   (1) They were having trouble sleeping.

   (2) Hester might hurt herself and the child.

   (3) The jailer had a friend who was a physician.

   (4) The child was suffering due to its mother's immorality.

2. On the actual test, you would be asked to "drag and drop the events into the chart to show the order in which they occur in the excerpt." For this practice test, simply write the event letters in the correct order:

   (1) Night approached.

   (2) Hester's baby writhed in agony.

   (3) Hester was found to be in a state of nervous excitement.

   (4) The jailer saw fit to call a physician.

3. Which definition best matches the use of the word *medicinal* in the passage?

   (1) Tasty

   (2) Having healing properties

   (3) Unpleasant

   (4) Illegal

4. Read the following sentence from the passage:

"To say the truth, there was much need of professional assistance, not merely for Hester herself, but still more urgently for the child; who, drawing its sustenance from the maternal bosom, seemed to have drank in with it all the turmoil, the anguish, and despair, which pervaded the mother's system."

The description of the baby's illness enhances the story by:

(1) Revealing that the baby was born ill.

(2) Explaining the medical condition of the baby was tied to the mother's nervous state.

(3) Sharing with readers a physical description of the mother and baby.

(4) Connecting an old-fashioned belief in evil to a modern-day understanding of what medicine can accomplish.

5. In the passage, which characteristic is revealed about Hester as she nurses her baby?

(1) Reluctance

(2) Corruption

(3) Nervous excitement

(4) Evil

6. On the actual test, you would be asked to "drag and drop each word that describes Hester into the character web." For the practice test, simply write or circle each word that should go into the web:

(1) Upset

(2) Anguished

(3) Placid

(4) Amiable

(5) Resentful

Questions 7 through 12 refer to the following passage:

Workplace Smoking Policy

Introduction

Secondhand smoke—breathing in other people's tobacco smoke—has now been shown to cause lung cancer, heart disease, and many other illnesses in nonsmokers.

Section 2 (2) (e) of the Health and Safety at Work Etc. Act 1974 places a duty on employers to provide a working environment for employees that is: safe, without risk to health, and adequate with regards to facilities and arrangements for their welfare at work.

The Health Act 2006 requires workplaces to be smoke-free by the end of May 2007. Smoking rooms will no longer be allowed. The employer acknowledges that breathing other people's tobacco smoke is both a public hazard and a welfare issue. Therefore the following policy has been adopted concerning smoking in this organization.

General Principles

This smoking policy seeks to guarantee nonsmokers the right to work in air free of tobacco smoke, while taking account of the health needs of those who smoke.

All premises will be designated smoke-free from this day forward. Smoking will only be permitted at designated smoking areas outside the buildings.

Smoking while on duty will only be allowed during official break periods.

7. The main concern of this policy is:

    (1) Secondhand smoke is harmful to all.

    (2) Smoking will still be allowed outside.

    (3) Smoking is allowed only on breaks.

    (4) Employers need to provide smoking rooms.

8. The policy appears to be:

    (1) Complied with on a voluntary basis only

    (2) A punishment for smokers

    (3) Harmful to those who choose to smoke inside

    (4) Meant to keep all workers safe and healthy

9. For employees, the organization is showing it is:

    (1) Concerned about their well-being and health

    (2) Afraid of getting sued

    (3) Worried about hurting smokers' feelings

    (4) Overreacting to research on smoking

10. How do the "General Principles," laid out at the end of the passage, relate to the "Introduction" to the passage?

    (1) The "General Principles" shows how the ideas from the policy explained in the "Introduction" will be put into effect at the workplace.

    (2) The "General Principles" section shows the same information as the "Introduction" but in shorter sentences.

    (3) The "Introduction" introduces the main ideas of the passage, while the "General Principles" explains the general principles of the passage.

    (4) The "Introduction" section shows the scientific proof that secondhand smoke is dangerous, while the "General Principles" explains the way scientific proof is obtained.

11. In the passage, what is the effect of the word *hazard* in the third paragraph?

    (1) It reminds the reader that smoking is a kind of blinking light.

    (2) It informs the reader that smoking in public is frowned upon.

    (3) It advises the reader that the employer sees smoking as actively dangerous to other people besides the smoker.

    (4) It cautions the reader not to assume the employer is against smoking.

12. Which idea about the effect of smoking on health is included in the passage?

    (1) Smoking is no longer acceptable in the eyes of most Americans.

    (2) Aiding employees in quitting smoking is an important goal for this company.

    (3) Smoking on duty is only allowed during break periods.

    (4) Secondhand smoke is proven to contribute to a number of serious illnesses, including cancer.

For questions 13 through 16, the following passage is incomplete. On the actual test, you would be asked to choose the option that correctly completes the sentence from a drop-down menu. For this practice test, you can circle your selection.

Mr. Harry Stockwell, Manager, Complaint Department
ABC Small Appliances
267 Main Road
Wilmington, DE 11234

January 10, 2012

Dear Mr. Stockwell,

I visited ABC Appliances on November 20th and purchased a Doe toaster oven. I was pleased for about a week with the way it cooked, toasted,

13. *Select ...*

(1) and broiled food however in the second week,

(2) and broiled food and however in the second week,

(3) and broiled food. However, in the second week,

(4) and broiled food. however in the second week,

the broiler burst into flames, scorching my countertop.

14. *Select ...*

(1) the sight of my countertop in flames is one I will forget not soon.

(2) the sight, in flames, of my countertop is one I will not soon forget.

(3) The sight of my countertop in flames is one I will not forget soon.

(4) The sight I will not forget, soon of my countertop in flames

It was a shocking sight, and one that has stayed with me for days. The smell of smoke and the damage to my countertop are constant reminders of what happened.

15. *Select …*

    (1) I know you will want to replace the toaster oven we have to discuss replacing the countertop.

    (2) I know you will want to replace the toaster oven, we have to discuss replacing the countertop.

    (3) I know you will want to replace the toaster oven, however we have to discuss replacing the countertop.

    (4) I know you will want to replace the toaster oven; we have to discuss replacing the countertop.

    Please let me know when you are available to meet with me. Alternatively, if you prefer, you may simply mail me a check for the amount mentioned in the contractor's estimate I am including with this letter. Make it payable to "Perry Webb" and mail

16. *Select …*

    (1) her

    (2) one

    (3) that

    (4) it

    to the address listed below. I look forward to hearing from you. Thank you.

    Sincerely,

    Perry Webb
    103 Mitchell Drive
    Saparila, MN 89456

Questions 17 through 20 refer to the following passage:

From *Emma Goldman—Biographical Sketch* by Charles A. Madison (1960) (Project Gutenberg)

In the meantime, discouraged and lonely, she had welcomed a fellow worker's show of affection. She felt no love for him and, as a result of an attempted rape at the age of fifteen, she still experienced a "violent repulsion" in the presence of men, but she had not the strength to refuse his urgent proposal of marriage. She soon learned to her dismay that her husband was impotent and not at all as congenial as she had thought.

However, the very suggestion of a separation enraged her father, who had recently come to Rochester. After months of aggravation she did go through the then rare and reprehensible rite of Orthodox divorce, but she had to leave town to avoid social ostracism. When she returned some months later, her former husband again pursued her, and his threat of suicide frightened her into remarrying him.

17. When Emma discovered her husband's impotence, she:

    (1) Developed a revulsion toward men.

    (2) Called her father to come to Rochester.

    (3) Threatened suicide.

    (4) Suggested a separation.

18. What does the last sentence in the passage suggest about why Emma Goldman remarried?

    (1) Her father insisted she do so.

    (2) She no longer loved her ex-husband.

    (3) She remarried her ex-husband at least partly because she was afraid he would kill himself if she did not.

    (4) She felt marriage was a trap.

19. Why does the author use the phrase *social ostracism* in the passage?

    (1) To make clear how difficult getting a divorce made Emma's life.

    (2) To draw a connection between Emma's state of mind and her husband's mental illness.

    (3) To paint a portrait of Emma's father as a selfish and uncaring man.

    (4) To show how far we've come as a society in recognizing divorce as a reasonable option.

20. Read this sentence:

"In the meantime, discouraged and lonely, she had welcomed a fellow worker's show of affection."

Why does the author begin the excerpt with this sentence?

(1) To tell readers about Emma's birth and young childhood.

(2) To show readers how Emma became a feminist and social justice pioneer.

(3) To remind readers that Emma was not always strong and independent; she made poor decisions.

(4) To make it clear that Emma's husband was a con artist.

Questions 21 through 28 refer to the following passage:

U.S. Department of Labor's Disability Employment Policy

I. ADA BASICS

What is the ADA?

The ADA is a federal civil rights law that was passed in 1990 and went into effect beginning in 1992. Its purpose is to protect people with disabilities from discrimination in employment, in the programs and activities offered by state and local governments, and in accessing the goods and services offered in places like stores, hotels, restaurants, football stadiums, doctors' offices, beauty parlors, and so on. The focus of this guide is Title I of the ADA, which prohibits discrimination in employment and requires employers to provide reasonable accommodations for employees with disabilities.

Who must comply with Title I of the ADA?

Only "covered entities" must comply with Title I of the ADA. The term "covered entities" includes employers with 15 or more employees, employment agencies, labor organizations, and joint labor-management committees. For simplicity, this guide will refer to covered entities as "employers."

For more information about covered entities, see www.eeoc.gov/policy/docs/threshold .html#2-III-B.

Who is protected by Title I of the ADA?

Title I protects "qualified employees with disabilities." The term "qualified" means that the individual satisfies the skill, experience, education, and other job-related requirements of the position sought or held, and can perform the essential job functions of the position, with or without reasonable accommodations.

For additional information about the definition of qualified, see http://askjan.org/links/ADAtam1.html#II.

The term "employee" means "an individual employed by an employer." The question of whether an employer-employee relationship exists is fact-specific and depends on whether the employer controls the means and manner of the worker's work performance.

21. This policy is meant to protect:

    (1) All workers in the organization

    (2) Employers who employ the disabled

    (3) Workers with disabilities

    (4) Employees

22. The policy contains information on:

    (1) Who can be sued for noncompliance

    (2) What the ADA is

    (3) Who must comply and who is protected

    (4) Both (2) and (3)

23. The ADA's purpose is to:

    (1) Ensure disabled workers can get high-paying jobs

    (2) Allow disabled people to gain access to football games, hotels, and restaurants

    (3) Get jobs for workers with disabilities

    (4) Protect workers with disabilities from discrimination on the job

24. The author's tone toward the reader is one of:

    (1) Condescension

    (2) Factual reporting

    (3) Intimidation

    (4) Reassurance

25. In the passage, the author includes a link to a web page. What effect does the addition of that website's address have on the passage?

    (1) It proves the author is hiding something by not giving all of the available information.

    (2) It shows that the passage's topic is complex enough to require additional reading.

    (3) It allow readers to skip over information that they may otherwise find boring.

    (4) It provides an opportunity for readers who are particularly interested in the definition of "qualified" to read further on it.

26. What definition best matches the use of the word *reasonable* in the first paragraph?

    (1) Above and beyond

    (2) Comprehensive

    (3) Feasible

    (4) Token

27. Read this sentence from the second complete paragraph:

    The term "covered entities" includes employers with 15 or more employees, employment agencies, labor organizations, and joint labor-management committees.

    What can be inferred about *covered entities* from this sentence?

    (1) Businesses with 14 or fewer employees do not have to follow the ADA.

    (2) Businesses with 14 or fewer employees are not considered "covered entities" under the ADA.

    (3) "Covered entities" are considered to be any kind of business, no matter how many employees work there.

    (4) All "covered entities" are also businesses.

28. The author of the passage notes that "qualified" employees with disabilities must have several characteristics to meet that definition. Circle the characteristics mentioned below that help an employee be classified as "qualified."

    (1) Can perform the essential characteristics of the job description

    (2) Has the appropriate education for the job

    (3) Has the appropriate training for the job

    (4) Has held the job in another capacity (e.g., for another company) before

    (5) Has at least 2 years of experience in the job

The following passage is incomplete. On the actual test, you would be asked to choose the option that correctly completes the sentence from a drop down menu. For this practice test, you may circle your selection.

Job Posting

The XYZ store is looking for sales associates for immediate hire. If you meet the minimum qualifications, please forward your résumé and a letter of application to J. D. Ducklemeyer at Suite 2020, 1400 Thurston Street, Applegate, MD 45545 by November 30, 2012.

Qualifications

The perfect candidate will have previous sales experience

29. *Select …*

(1) in childrens clothing, televisions, small appliances, or pet supplies.

(2) in childrens' clothing, televisions, small appliances, or pet supplies.

(3) in children's clothing, televisions, small appliances, or pet supplies.

(4) in childrens clothing, televisions, small appliances, or pet supplies.

Please be sure to list which area you have experience in on your letter of application.

30. *Select …*

(1) Experience in all of these areas are a plus but not necessary.

(2) Experience in all of them areas is a plus but not necessary.

(3) Experience in all of these areas is a plus to you but not necessary.

(4) Experience in all of these areas is a plus but not necessary.

We're interested in hiring someone who can work both weekend and night-time hours, on a flexible schedule. Schedules are made on a monthly basis.

31. *Select …*

    (1) Additionally, candidates who speak a second language such as spanish or portuguese would be highly desirable.

    (2) Additionally, candidates who speak a second language such as Spanish or portuguese would be highly desirable.

    (3) Additionally, candidates whom speak a second language such as Spanish or Portuguese would be highly desirable.

    (4) Additionally, candidates who speak a second language such as Spanish or Portuguese would be highly desirable.

    A salary commensurate with experience will be negotiated with the successful candidate, as well as benefits and employee discounts.

32. *Select …*

    (1) Bonuses will be offered to those meeting certain sales goals on a quarterly basis.

    (2) Meeting certain sales goals, bonuses will be offered to those.

    (3) Goals on a quarterly basis should be met for a bonus.

    (4) Those meeting certain sales goals on a quarterly basis will be offered bonuses.

    Must be outgoing and comfortable with a variety of products. High school diploma or GED required. Don't delay! Send in your information as soon as possible. We plan to fill these positions as soon as qualified candidates are available.

Questions 33 through 40 refer to the following passage:

From "The Raven" by Edgar Allen Poe (1845)

Once upon a midnight dreary, while I pondered, weak and weary,
Over many a quaint and curious volume of forgotten lore,
While I nodded, nearly napping, suddenly there came a tapping,
As of some one gently rapping, rapping at my chamber door.
"'Tis some visitor," I muttered, "tapping at my chamber door—
Only this, and nothing more."

Ah, distinctly I remember it was in the bleak December,
And each separate dying ember wrought its ghost upon the floor.
Eagerly I wished the morrow;—vainly I had tried to borrow
From my books surcease of sorrow—sorrow for the lost Lenore—
For the rare and radiant maiden whom the angels name Lenore—
Nameless here for evermore.

And the silken sad uncertain rustling of each purple curtain
Thrilled me—filled me with fantastic terrors never felt before;
So that now, to still the beating of my heart, I stood repeating
"'Tis some visitor entreating entrance at my chamber door—
Some late visitor entreating entrance at my chamber door;—
This it is, and nothing more."

Presently my soul grew stronger; hesitating then no longer,
"Sir," said I, "or Madam, truly your forgiveness I implore;
But the fact is I was napping, and so gently you came rapping,
And so faintly you came tapping, tapping at my chamber door,
That I scarce was sure I heard you"—here I opened wide the door;—
Darkness there, and nothing more.

Deep into that darkness peering, long I stood there wondering, fearing,
Doubting, dreaming dreams no mortal ever dared to dream before;
But the silence was unbroken, and the darkness gave no token,
And the only word there spoken was the whispered word, "Lenore!"
This *I* whispered, and an echo murmured back the word, "Lenore!"
Merely this, and nothing more.

Back into the chamber turning, all my soul within me burning,
Soon again I heard a tapping, somewhat louder than before.
"Surely," said I, "surely that is something at my window lattice;
Let me see, then, what thereat is, and this mystery explore—
Let my heart be still a moment and this mystery explore;—
'Tis the wind and nothing more!"

Open here I flung the shutter, when, with many a flirt and flutter,
In there stepped a stately Raven of the saintly days of yore.
Not the least obeisance made he; not a minute stopped or stayed he;
But, with mien of lord or lady, perched above my chamber door—
Perched upon a bust of Pallas just above my chamber door—

Perched, and sat, and nothing more.

33. In the second stanza, the line "And each separate dying ember wrought its ghost upon the floor" refers to:

    (1) A shadow from the fire seen on the floor

    (2) An ember falling to the floor

    (3) A fire in a fireplace

    (4) A ghost in the room

34. Drag two ways the author portrays the main character in the poem into the boxes below. (For this practice test, circle the correct answers.)

    (1) Afraid of his/her shadow

    (2) In an upbeat, happy mood

    (3) Expecting a visitor

    (4) Half-asleep

    (5) Someone who is hearing things

35. What was the main character doing before the knock came to the door?

    (1) Reading

    (2) Sleeping

    (3) Falling asleep while reading

    (4) Waiting for a visitor

36. What can the reader infer from the references to "Lenore" in this poem?

    (1) Lenore is the raven.

    (2) Lenore is the reason for the main character's sadness and despair.

    (3) Lenore is related to the main character by blood.

    (4) Lenore was not important to the main character.

37. The author's use of the word *curious* in the second line is most similar to which of the following?

    (1) Strange

    (2) Common

    (3) Irreplaceable

    (4) Shiny

38. Read the following section of the poem:

Open here I flung the shutter, when, with many a flirt and flutter,
In there stepped a stately Raven of the saintly days of yore.
Not the least obeisance made he; not a minute stopped or stayed he;
But, with mien of lord or lady, perched above my chamber door—
Perched upon a bust of Pallas just above my chamber door—

Perched, and sat, and nothing more.

This section of the poem indicates that the raven is most likely a symbol of:

(1) The author's mental breakdown

(2) The author's grief over the loss of Lenore

(3) The author's belief in a higher power

(4) The author's desire to move away from such sad memories

39. Based on the details in the poem, in what month does it take place?

(1) December

(2) January

(3) September

(4) May

40. Which of the following descriptions best captures the tone of the poem:

(1) Cheerful

(2) Studious

(3) Outraged

(4) Gloomy

Questions 41 through 50 refer to the following passage, a speech given by Susan B. Anthony after her arrest for casting an illegal vote in the presidential election of 1872. At that time, women were not allowed to vote.

Friends and fellow citizens: I stand before you tonight under indictment for the alleged crime of having voted at the last presidential election, without having a lawful right to vote. It shall be my work this evening to prove to you that in thus voting, I not only committed no crime, but, instead, simply exercised my citizen's rights, guaranteed to me and all United States citizens by the National Constitution, beyond the power of any state to deny.

The preamble of the Federal Constitution says:

"We, the people of the United States, in order to form a more perfect union, establish justice, insure domestic tranquillity, provide for the common defense, promote the general welfare, and secure the blessings of liberty to ourselves and our posterity, do ordain and establish this Constitution for the United States of America."

It was we, the people; not we, the white male citizens; nor yet we, the male citizens; but we, the whole people, who formed the Union. And we formed it, not to give the blessings of liberty, but to secure them; not to the half of ourselves and the half of our posterity, but to the whole people—women as well as men. And it is a downright mockery to talk to women of their enjoyment of the blessings of liberty while they are denied the use of the only means of securing them provided by this democratic-republican government—the ballot.

For any state to make sex a qualification that must ever result in the disfranchisement of one entire half of the people, is to pass a bill of attainder, or, an ex post facto law, and is therefore a violation of the supreme law of the land. By it the blessings of liberty are forever withheld from women and their female posterity.

To them this government has no just powers derived from the consent of the governed. To them this government is not a democracy. It is not a republic. It is an odious aristocracy; a hateful oligarchy of sex; the most hateful aristocracy ever established on the face of the globe; an oligarchy of wealth, where the rich govern the poor. An oligarchy of learning, where the educated govern the ignorant, might be endured; but this oligarchy of sex, which makes father, brothers, husband, sons, the oligarchs over the mother and sisters, the wife and daughters, of every household—which ordains all men sovereigns, all women subjects, carries dissension, discord, and rebellion into every home of the nation.

Webster, Worcester, and Bouvier all define a citizen to be a person in the United States, entitled to vote and hold office.

The only question left to be settled now is: Are women persons? And I hardly believe any of our opponents will have the hardihood to say they are not. Being persons, then, women are citizens; and no state has a right to make any law, or to enforce any old law, that shall abridge their privileges or immunities. Hence, every discrimination against women in the constitutions and laws of the several states is today null and void, precisely as is every one against Negroes.

Susan B. Anthony—1873

41. What is the likely reason Anthony includes a long quotation from the Constitution in her speech?

    (1) To use the words of a man to bolster her claim that women deserve voting rights

    (2) To remind listeners that the Constitution is not perfect

    (3) To tie her quest to secure voting rights for women to the very beginning of the American ideal

    (4) To fill space in her essay

42. On the actual test, you would be asked to drag and drop the words that describe Anthony's tone in this speech. For this practice test, circle the words that are correct.

    (1) Determined

    (2) Reluctant

    (3) Reasoned

    (4) Wealthy

    (5) Inspiring

43. In paragraph 6, Anthony repeatedly used the word *oligarchy*. What effect does this repetition have?

    (1) It is numbing for the listener because words should not be repeated so often.

    (2) It hammers home the point that she is making.

    (3) It proves that Anthony's vocabulary is very limited.

    (4) It provokes her listeners into researching what an oligarchy is.

44. Based on her speech, what is Anthony's attitude toward voting rights for African Americans?

    (1) She is in favor of all people having the right to vote.

    (2) She is in favor of women getting the right to vote before African Americans.

    (3) She believes that only white citizens should be allowed to vote.

    (4) She is silent on the issue.

45. Anthony's tone toward her listeners is one of:

    (1) Condescension

    (2) Intimidation

    (3) Reassurance

    (4) Impassioned reason

46. Which definition best matches the use of *abridge* in the last paragraph?

    (1) A constructed device that crosses a gap and joins two sides

    (2) To make longer

    (3) To weave two wholes together

    (4) To shorten

47. Who does Anthony claim make up the "whole people" of the United States?

    (1) All men

    (2) All white people

    (3) All people

    (4) Landowners

48. What can we infer about "Webster, Worcester, and Bouvier" from Anthony's reference to them in her speech?

    (1) They are all friends of Anthony.

    (2) They are all authorities on the American Constitution.

    (3) They all agree with Anthony on every point she has made.

    (4) They are all supporters of voting rights for women.

49. What can the reader infer about the speech's intended audience?

    (1) The speech is written to convince a group of men who are adamantly against women's voting rights.

    (2) The speech is written to help women learn what next steps they can take to gain voting rights.

    (3) The speech is written to convince people who may be moved by a logical look at the historical precedent for women's rights.

    (4) The speech is intended to influence the group of people who will decide whether Anthony should be imprisoned for breaking the law.

50. Anthony claims that individual states may not make a law against allowing women to vote for what reason?

    (1) It would contradict the supreme law of the country.

    (2) It would be a traitorous act.

    (3) Women should be allowed to vote.

    (4) Most people favor her side of the issue.

Extended Response

The following press release and letter to the editor present opposing sides to a debate about whether to allow off-leash (also called "leash-free") zones for dogs in a town's park. Proponents and critics disagree about the merits of off-leash areas.

In your response, analyze both positions presented to determine which is best supported. Use relevant and specific evidence from the article to support your response. You are allotted 45 minutes to complete this task.

Press Release: Boyertown Park to Become Leash-Free

At noon today, Mayor Sandy Nelson will hold a press conference to announce that Boyertown Park will become a Leash-Free zone for dogs between 11 A.M. and 3 P.M., and then again after 9 P.M.

Here is the text of Mayor Nelson's remarks:

I'm pleased to announce that Boyertown Park will become a Leash-Free zone! At last, our town park will be a place of freedom and frolic for our four-legged doggie friends as well as for humans!

As many Boyertown residents know, the Town Council undertook a study of the feasibility of a Leash-Free zone over the last few weeks. Together, we visited Downinville and Morsoraburg to review the policies they had in place for their parks' Leash-Free zones. We discovered that both villages have had overwhelmingly positive experiences in creating Leash-Free zones. They report that their residents have been over the moon about the Leash-Free zones, which have been in place for 3 months in Downinville and 2 months in Morsoraburg. No incidents have been reported to their local police: no biting or fighting!

We were able to tour the Downinville dog park, which is Leash-Free, and saw that it was clean and well-maintained. There was no odor. While it's true that Downinville's Leash-Free zone is enclosed, the size of the dog park is roughly equivalent to the size of Boyertown Park. Thus, we anticipate that our Leash-Free zone will work equally well.

It's also worth noting that both Downinville and Morsoraburg report an increase in home prices in their municipalities. A Leash-Free park is just one of the amenities they offer, of course, but I'm sure that many dog owners are thrilled to learn that they live in an area where their pets' freedom is a top priority. As home prices continue to fall in Boyertown, we should keep that in mind.

The Town Council and I have decided to limit Leash-Free hours to between 11 A.M. and 3 P.M. and after 9 P.M. We've made this decision because Boyertown Park is widely used by runners, including our local high school's track and cross-country teams, before 11 A.M. and between 3 and 9 P.M. That should keep any of our doggie friends from chasing!

We're eager to get started, so join us next Monday for our first Leash-Free zone dog party! We'll have doggie treats and free bottled water; you should just bring your doggie friends—Leash-Free, of course!

Letter to the Editor

To Whom It May Concern:

I'm writing to firmly protest the Mayor's foolish decision to institute a so-called "Leash-Free" zone in our town's beautiful park. Allowing unleashed dogs to run free all over the park will present a real danger to all park visitors and destroy the park's beauty. I can't imagine what the Mayor and her Council were thinking!

When I was a child, a free-roaming dog bit my leg so badly that I was hospitalized for several weeks. Thankfully, I fully recovered. But I'll never forget what that dog's owner said to my parents: "He's never bitten anyone before!" It is the nature of dogs to bite when they feel aggressive. Allowing dogs to run amok winds them up. They will feel aggressive. They will bite. Every resident of Boyertown should be deeply concerned about having dogs running free in the park for this reason.

The Mayor points out that nearby towns are giving off-leash areas a chance. I can agree that a leash-free area, enclosed with a strong fence, is a nice amenity for dog owners. However, that's not what the Mayor is implementing in Boyertown. Instead, she says that dogs will be allowed to roam all over the park! This unbelievable. Will dogs be allowed to rampage through the beautiful ornamental garden that our Garden Club spends many hours working on? How about in the children's play areas, including the sandboxes? Or over the baseball fields? During the game? Will there be no end to the destruction dogs can cause?

It will be madness. I deeply hope that the Mayor and the Town Council will rethink this insane plan. I'm no dog-hater. In fact, I have a beloved dog of my own, Buddy, who I'd love to allow to run free all the time. But I recognize that isn't safe for Buddy or for others. Limiting the hours when dogs can be off-leash is a good beginning, but there's much more to do! Building a specially fenced area for a dog park is the better plan. I hope the Mayor sees sense soon!

Yours,
Bernice McGregory

Answers and Explanations

1. **(2)** Hester might hurt herself and the child is the best answer because of the passage, "lest she should perpetrate violence on herself, or do some half-frenzied mischief to the poor babe."

2. **(3, 1, 2, 4)** This type of question, in which you are asked to correctly order the events of a passage, is quite common on the GED Reasoning Through Language Arts Test. Here, the only tricky part is to recognize that the jailer calls for a doctor (4) because the baby is writhing in agony (3).

3. **(2)** In this passage the word *medicinal* is used to mean "having healing properties." The physician is said to collect roots and other plants that will help heal.

4. **(2)** The sentence from the passage enhances the story by connecting the mother's agitated state to the baby's illness. Whether you believe that is scientifically possible or not is not important. Remember, in a passage from an older work, like this one, you will not always find modern ideas.

5. **(3)** This is the only answer supported by the passage, which explicitly states that Hester shows "nervous excitement."

6. **(1, 2)** If you have read *The Scarlet Letter*, you may feel justified in choosing other words as well as these two, but the question refers only to the passage, and only answers (1) and (2) are justified.

7. **(1)** This passage provides the foundation for the smoking policy, making answer (1) correct: "The employer acknowledges that breathing other people's tobacco smoke is both a public hazard and a welfare issue. Therefore the following policy has been adopted …."

8. **(4)** The passage "This smoking policy seeks to guarantee nonsmokers the right to work in air free of tobacco smoke, while taking account of the health needs of those who smoke" makes (4) the correct answer.

9. **(1)** The policy refers to health concerns of both smokers and nonsmokers, making (1) the correct answer.

10. **(1)** Answer (2) merely restates the obvious relationship between the two sections of the passage. The GED wants something more thoughtful, as in answer (1).

11. **(3)** In this case, *hazard* is used as to mean "a likely danger."

12. **(4)** This fact is taken directly from the first sentence of the passage. Note that answer (3) is from the passage as well but does not align with the rest of the question, which asks for an idea about smoking's effect on health.

13. **(3)** This fixes the run-on sentence and capitalizes the first word of the new sentence (*However*) correctly.

14. **(3)** The sentence is a confusing run of prepositional phrases. Answer (3) puts them in the correct order and does not commit any punctuation errors in the process.

15. **(4)** The sentence, as presented, is a run-on. Answer (4) inserts a semicolon to correctly join the two independent clauses together as linked in thought.

16. **(4)** The correct answer is *it* in this question that asks you to work with pronouns correctly. *It* refers to the check, which cannot be anything else.

17. **(4)** This question is a simplified version of the type in which you are asked to reorder events in a passage. Here, you're simply asked to choose what happened next.

18. **(3)** The trick here is to be sure you determine which answer is justified by the last sentence in the passage. Only answer (3) is.

19. **(1)** The phrase *social ostracism* is used to show how much getting a divorce changed Emma Goldman's life. She had to leave her community after obtaining one.

20. **(3)** The opening makes it clear that Emma was human and had times of difficulty and self-doubt.

21. **(3)** This sentence clearly states the intent of the policy: "Title I protects 'qualified employees with disabilities.'"

22. **(4)** Information about the ADA as well as who must comply and who is protected is provided in the policy.

23. **(4)** The sentence "Its purpose is to protect people with disabilities from discrimination in employment …" makes (4) correct.

24. **(2)** You might be thinking this passage doesn't have a tone at all. It's dry and factual, which makes answer (2) the best choice. All writing has a tone, but sometimes that tone is only about reporting the facts.

25. **(4)** The inclusion of a web address is introduced with the phrase, "For additional information about the definition of qualified …."

26. **(3)** The author uses *reasonable* to mean changes that can be made without excessive effort. *Feasible* is the best synonym for that.

27. **(2)** It's tempting to guess one of the other answer choices, but only answer (2) is proven by rereading the passage.

28. **(1, 2, 3)** The first three answer choices are listed in the passage; answers (4) and (5) are not.

29. **(3)** Answer (3) forms the possessive of *children* correctly.

30. **(4)** Answer (4) fixes the subject/verb agreement problem (*Experience … is …*) and doesn't add unneeded words.

31. **(4)** The errors in the sentence are not about the use of *who* or *whom* but about the lack of capitalization for the words *Spanish* and *Portuguese*.

32. **(4)** The rewritten sentence in answer (4) puts the phrases in the best order to be the most clear.

33. **(1)** The ember's shadow is referred to as a "ghost" because they flit and disappear like ghosts.

34. **(4, 5)** The poem shows that the narrator is uneasy and sleepy.

35. **(3)** The narrator of the poem is shown to be reading, but "napping" while he tries to do so.

36. **(2)** Lenore is repeatedly evoked in the poem as the reason for the main character's despair. We can infer that she had died and he misses her.

37. **(1)** In this usage, the word *curious* could be replaced best out of the answer choices by "strange."

38. **(2)** It's clear from the way the raven arrives, calmly, and does not leave that it is most like a symbol of the narrator's grief over losing Lenore.

39. **(1)** The poem clearly states that it takes place in the month of December.

40. **(4)** The tone is best described, out of the choices offered, as "gloomy." Even if you are not sure what tone is, you should be able to make a reasonable guess based on your reading of the poem.

41. **(3)** Anthony seeks to show that America's founders always intended for all people to have voting rights. Her long quote of the Constitution is her proof of that idea.

42. **(1, 3, 5)** It's clear that Anthony is reluctant to speak, and "wealthy" isn't a tone at all.

43. **(2)** The repetition is a deliberate attempt to tie the word *oligarchy* with the United States. Remember that you can assume all authors quoted on the GED are making deliberate choices about literary techniques they use.

44. **(2)** It is clear from the last paragraph of the passage that Anthony believed the argument against African Americans voting is as invalid as the argument against women voting.

45. **(4)** Of the answer choices, only answer (4) could be correct: Anthony's argument is very logical, but she also is clearly passionate about what she's saying.

46. **(4)** ~~familiar~~ with the word *abridge,* the context clues should help you det____ ____ makes sense.

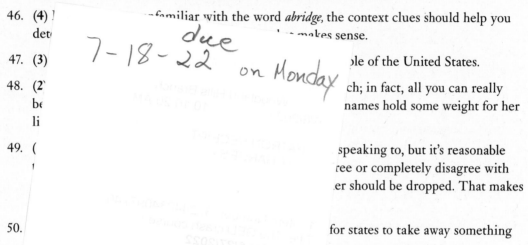

47. **(3)** ____ ____le of the United States.

48. **(2)** ____ch; in fact, all you can really be____ names hold some weight for her li____

49. **(** ____speaking to, but it's reasonable ____ree or completely disagree with ____er should be dropped. That makes

50. ____for states to take away something

Exter

You ____ ____nse in many ways. The sample essay we p____ ____ver, it does do the following: the auth____ ____rted; the author presents evidence from ____ ____er than the other; the essay uses transitions and varied sentence ____ ____clear introduction and conclusion; and the essay is grammatically correct.

Sample essay:

> The issue of creating a leash-free zone in a local park is a delicate one. On one hand, most would agree that it's a lovely benefit for dogs and their owners, and that getting enough exercise is important for dogs' good health. On the other hand, most people wince at the idea of large packs of dogs allowed to run free over public property, potentially destroying beautiful areas and terrifying people as they rampage. Ultimately, the letter to the editor makes a better case, for McGregory is able to find a middle ground: allow dogs to run free, but only in specifically designated, enclosed areas.

To begin with, we must look at the mayor's speech. At first, it seems that she has made a good case. She mentions a period of research, as well as data from nearby towns that have instituted dog-free zones. They have proven successful, although they haven't been in place for very long (three months, tops!). However, she then extends the limited information she's provided far beyond what it can safely encompass. For example, she notes that Downinville's dog park is nearly the same size as Boyertown Park, but skips past the fact that Downinville's dog run is enclosed. It's false to make the entirety of Boyertown Park—unfenced, we assume—the equivalent of Downinville's fenced dog run.

Bernice McGregory, the author of the letter to the editor, makes a stronger case. She mentions that as a dog owner herself, she is not against leash-free zones, but merely wants the mayor and Town Council to think through what it means to allow dogs to run free throughout the entire park. She points out the beautiful gardens in the park—wouldn't the dogs, even sweet dogs, ruin them? No doubt. She strikes a much more reasonable note by suggesting that Boyertown embrace all the advantages of having an off-leash zone while also making it safer and more likely to be successful than the plan the Mayor has put forth.

In short, it's easy to see that McGregory has thought through the issue of off-leash zones better than the mayor and the Town Council. Perhaps this is because of the injury she sustained from a dog when she was a child. Boyertown should be grateful to have such a thoughtful, concerned citizen who spoke up before the mayor's plan ended in disaster.

Social Studies Test

Each of the five review chapters in Part 2 provides an overview of one of the subject areas on the Social Studies Test along with GED®-style practice questions. Chapter 11 focuses on U.S. government and civics, on which 50 percent of the test questions are based; Chapter 12 discusses U.S. history, which comprises 20 percent of the test; Chapter 13 reviews basic concepts of economics, which accounts for 15 percent of the test questions; Chapter 14 deals with world history, which amounts to 7.5 percent of the test questions; and Chapter 15 provides concepts of geography, which are 7.5 percent of the test questions.

In Chapter 16 you can take a realistic social studies practice test, which is half the length of the real GED version. On the practice test, a reading and/or visual item such as a graph, cartoon, map, photo, or table is followed by questions. You won't need to memorize dates and facts; rather, you'll be tested on your skill in comprehending, interpreting, analyzing, or applying the information you are given.

U.S. Government and Civics

U.S. government and civics—the study of the rights and duties of citizens and of how government works—comprise the largest number of questions on the GED Social Studies Test. You can expect about 25 of the 50 questions to be based on U.S. government and the rights and duties of citizenship content.

You won't be required to memorize facts like the names of government agencies, presidents, or Supreme Court decisions to ace the test. Most of the facts you need to know will be given to you in the reading passages or the visuals, such as graphs, maps, and tables, included with the test questions. The test focuses on your skills in understanding, analyzing, and applying the information presented to you. Still, a good background in U.S. government and politics helps you understand the readings and work through the questions quickly.

This chapter provides an overview of the fundamentals of U.S. government and civics that will almost certainly be included in some way on the test. Following each overview of a key subject, you'll find GED-style questions that help prepare you for the types of skill-based questions you'll get on the real test. Don't forget to read the explanations—not just for the questions you missed, but for all the questions and answer choices you did not completely understand.

In This Chapter

- Overviews of key areas of U.S. government and civics
- Sample GED®-style questions to practice the skills on which you'll be tested
- Answers and explanations for all questions

The Framework of U.S. Government

One of the most basic ideas or principles of American government is the idea that government is limited to the powers that have been granted it by the people. This principle is known as *limited government* or *constitutionalism*. The U.S. Constitution defines what powers are granted to the U.S. government and sets up the framework of government.

Another fundamental principle of American government is *federalism*. Federalism is the coexistence of independent state and federal governments. State governments have their own constitutions that define and limit their governments. Under the U.S. Constitution, some powers are given to both state and national governments (taxation and public works, for example), while some powers are given only to the national government (printing money, controlling interstate commerce), and other powers have traditionally been reserved for the states (education). Increasingly, state and federal governments work together on all types of problems, from education to health care to transportation.

The U.S. Constitution sets up three separate, independent branches of government—the legislative branch, executive branch, and judicial branch, summarized in the following table. This is called the *separation of powers*. Congress, the legislative branch, makes the laws. The president heads the executive branch, which carries out the laws. The executive branch includes most agencies (offices) of the federal government, from the Department of Defense to the Environmental Protection Agency to the Social Security Administration—all of which carry out laws passed by Congress. The agencies of the federal government—including the 2 million people who work there—are known as the *federal bureaucracy*. The Supreme Court and the federal court system make up the judicial branch, whose role is to settle disputes about the law.

Branches of the U.S. Government

Branch	Comprised Of	Purpose
Legislative	Congress (the Senate and House of Representatives)	Makes laws
Executive	President and the federal bureaucracy	Carries out laws
Judicial	Supreme Court	Settles disputes about the law

Contained within the Constitution is a *system of checks and balances*—another basic principle of American government. Although each branch of government operates independently, the Constitution provides ways each branch can block or "check" the other branches. For example, the president can check the power of Congress by vetoing proposed legislation passed by Congress. Congress can check the president's power by overriding the president's veto by a two-thirds majority. Congress also can check the power of the president and the federal bureaucracy through its control of the federal budget. The Supreme Court can check Congress and the president by declaring a law or presidential order unconstitutional and thereby invalidating it. Congress can check the power of the Supreme Court by passing a new law using different language or proposing a constitutional amendment. The system of checks and balances prevents any one branch of government from becoming too powerful and dictatorial.

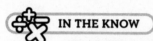 **IN THE KNOW**

> The Constitution sets up the framework of the American government; however, much of the way our government operates is not in the Constitution but has developed over time through practice. For example, the idea that the Supreme Court can declare a law unconstitutional is not in the Constitution but is a widely accepted principle today.

Following are the chief roles or powers of each of the three branches of the federal government:

The president:

- Heads the executive branch (the federal bureaucracy)

- Commands the armed forces

- Signs or vetoes laws (Congress can pass a law over the president's veto if it passes in both the Senate and House by a two-thirds majority.)

- Conducts foreign policy

- Nominates federal officials and Supreme Court justices

Congress (the Senate and the House of Representatives):

- Makes laws

- Determines the federal budget (how much and for what purposes money will be spent by the federal government)

- Conducts investigations of the executive branch

- Approves or disapproves the president's nominees for federal officials and Supreme Court justices (Senate)

- Ratifies (approves) treaties (Senate)

The Supreme Court:

- Settles disputes about the meaning of federal laws

- Interprets the Constitution, determining if laws passed by Congress or orders given by the president are constitutional

Practice

Questions 1 and 2 refer to the previous lists.

1. Who has the most power in determining how much money the government spends on farm programs?

   (1) The president

   (2) Congress

   (3) The Senate

   (4) The federal bureaucracy

   (5) State governments

2. Which statement best describes the process by which Supreme Court justices are chosen?

   (1) They are selected by the president.

   (2) They are selected by the Senate but must be approved by the president.

   (3) They run for office, and the American people elect them.

   (4) They are selected by the president but must be approved by the Senate.

   (5) They are selected by the president but must be approved by the House of Representatives and the Senate.

Question 3 is based on the following reading:

What Is a Filibuster?

The *filibuster* refers to continuing debate endlessly to prevent a vote on a proposed law that is likely to pass. The rules of the House of Representatives do not allow a filibuster, but in the Senate, a minority of the senators can block a vote on a proposed law that has majority support. Sixty percent of senators must vote to end debate (cloture) before a vote on the proposed law can be taken. Nowadays, the Senate usually moves on to other business until a sufficient number of senators can be convinced to support cloture rather than wasting time with endless debate.

3. The filibuster is an example of:

   (1) Federalism

   (2) Checks and balances

   (3) Limitations on the power of the majority

   (4) Separation of powers

   (5) Constitutionalism

Answers

1. **(2)** Although the president (1) makes a budget request, it's Congress that writes the final budget and determines how much is spent on each federal program. The president can veto an appropriations bill (legislation that provides money to the federal government), but this would be risky and could result in the president getting a bill that is even less favorable to him or her or getting no bill at all (and thus no money to spend on federal programs). The Senate (3) can't act on its own; for an appropriations bill to pass, both the House and the Senate must approve it. The federal bureaucracy (4) and state governments (5) are directly affected by the federal budget and try to influence the result, but they are not the decision-makers.

2. **(4)** The president selects Supreme Court justices, but they then must be approved by a majority vote of the Senate, not the reverse (2). Answer (1) does not describe the whole process, and the House of Representatives (5) plays no role in the process.

3. **(3)** The filibuster limits the power of the majority to take action. For a new law to pass, a supermajority (60 percent) is needed. The filibuster is a rule of the Senate and not part of the Constitution. Because filibustering is an action within one branch of government, checks and balances (2) and the separation of powers (4) are not involved. Filibustering is unrelated to federalism (1), which involves the division of power between state and federal governments. Filibustering is also not related to the principle of constitutionalism (5), which is the idea that government is limited to the powers the people have granted it.

Elections and Political Parties

Democracy is rule by the majority; this is another fundamental principle of American government. However, this wasn't always the case. At the time the U.S. Constitution was written (1787), only white males who owned land could vote. By the time of the Civil War (1861), all white males—even those who did not own property—could vote. The Fifteenth Amendment (1870) extended the right to vote to African American males in all states. Women won the right to vote in all states with the passage of the Nineteenth Amendment (1920). The Twenty-Sixth Amendment (1971) lowered the minimum voting age to 18 from 21 in most states. Thus, over the years, the right to vote has been broadened to allow voting by nearly all adults, establishing the principle of rule by the majority or democracy.

Democracy is characterized by elections. In indirect democracy, elections are held to elect representatives who then make the laws. In direct democracy, elections are held on laws themselves—if a majority approves a measure, it becomes a law. Both state and federal governments in the United States are characterized by representative government (indirect democracy). Some states, however, have provisions that allow votes by the people on laws themselves by referendum or initiative (direct democracy).

Political parties are not mentioned in the Constitution, but they play a vital role in the American political system. Political parties in the United States select the candidates and then try to get their candidates elected to office. The United States is characterized by a two-party system. Today the two parties are the Democratic Party (symbolized by a donkey) and the Republican Party (symbolized by an elephant). Many minor parties, or *third* parties, also exist, but they seldom have enough support to get their candidates elected. An *independent* is a person who does not identify with any political party.

Two basic types of elections are held in the United States. In the primary election, each political party selects its candidate. The primary election is followed by the general election, in which the final winner is chosen from the candidates who were victorious in the primary election.

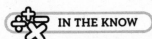 **IN THE KNOW**

Although it is a right and a duty, there is no requirement in the United States that people vote. In the last 30 years, voter turnout for presidential elections has ranged from 50 to 57 percent of eligible voters. Even fewer people—sometimes as low as 33 percent—vote for congressional candidates. Therefore, winning an election is often more about motivating your supporters to vote than about gaining the support of a majority of the people.

State legislators, state governors, and U.S. senators and representatives all are elected by votes of the people in general elections. The president, however, is not elected by the people, but by specially chosen persons called electors. When a presidential candidate wins the election in a state, a group of electors pledged to the winning candidate are chosen. The number of electors each state gets equals their number of senators and representatives in Congress. The electors then cast their votes for president a few weeks following the general election. If no candidate gets more than half of the electoral votes (for example, if a third candidate wins some states), then the president is selected by the House of Representatives, with each state getting one vote.

In this electoral system, the states with the most people get many electoral votes—California, for example, gets 55 votes—and the least-populous states such as Alaska, Delaware, Montana, North Dakota, South Dakota, Vermont, and Wyoming get only 3. Each state's votes are cast as a block (exceptions to this rule: Maine and Nebraska). So even if a candidate gets only one more individual's vote than his opponent, *all* the state's electoral votes go to the winning candidate. This winner-take-all system has the following effects:

- The electors sometimes select a president who did not get the most votes in the general election (as happened in 2016 when Hillary Clinton won the popular vote by 2.1 million votes but Donald Trump became president by winning 304 electoral votes to Clinton's 227).

- Candidates focus on the big states; for example, only five states (California, Texas, New York, Florida, and Pennsylvania) account for 171 of the 270 electoral votes needed to win.

- Candidates focus on "swing" states, where the election is close and the swing of a few votes could move the entire block of the state's electors from one candidate to another.

 **IN THE KNOW**

Maine and Nebraska are exceptions to the block voting rule. These two states sometimes divide their small block of votes, and electoral votes are awarded on the basis of which candidate won in each congressional district of the state.

Practice

Question 1 refers to the following political cartoon:

Courtesy of William S. Wiist.

1. What is the main point the cartoonist is making in this cartoon?

   (1) Politicians in both parties admire Abraham Lincoln.

   (2) Government officials will do anything for money.

   (3) Money plays too large a role in American elections.

   (4) Lincoln was able to provide real leadership and get both parties to support him.

   (5) Politicians are responsive to the people in their state or district.

Question 2 refers to the following map:

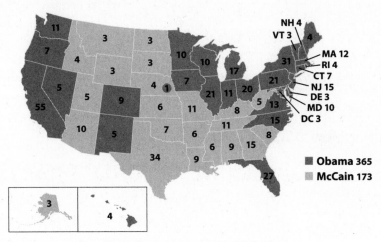

Electoral votes: 2008 presidential election.

2. Based on the information shown on the map, which one of the following statements is correct?

   (1) Smaller states have no say in selecting a president.

   (2) In awarding electoral votes to states, population is not important.

   (3) The states with the smallest population get only one electoral vote.

   (4) The number of electoral votes each state gets is based on how big the state is in land area.

   (5) In the presidential electoral system, virtually all states cast their electoral votes as a block for the same candidate.

Answers

1. **(3)** The main idea of this cartoon is that money plays too important a role in American elections. The donkey (a symbol of the Democratic Party) and the elephant (a symbol of the Republican Party) are both bowing down in homage, not to President Lincoln, but to the money his image appears on. The cartoon does not show government officials, but political parties, so answer (2) is not the best choice. The cartoon does not say anything about Lincoln (1 and 4) nor how responsive politicians are to the people they represent (5).

2. **(5)** The map shows how virtually all states cast their electoral votes as a block for the candidate who wins in each state. Answer (1) is incorrect because small states do have a say in selecting a president, and occasionally the swing of one small state to the other side changes the election. (This last happened in 2000.) In fact, small states actually have a larger share of the electoral vote than their population would warrant because the minimum is three votes, making answer (3) incorrect. Population is the primary basis on which electoral votes are allocated to states (2), not land area (4). In fact, Alaska, the largest state in land area, gets only three electoral votes.

Interest Groups and the Political Process

Interest groups are a key part of the American political process. In fact, a common way of viewing the American political system is one in which competing interests struggle to determine public policy. The view that good government comes out of the compromises made by a multitude of competing interests is called *pluralism*.

Interest groups are numerous voters organized in support of a particular set of political goals. Unlike political parties, they do not field candidates for office, but they often do endorse and raise money for candidates who support their political goals. Examples of interest groups include automakers, environmentalists, antiabortion groups, gun dealers, teachers, automobile owners, airline pilots, veterans, truck drivers, retired people, dairy farmers, and coal mine owners, to name just a few, and all have common interests and want to see certain types of laws passed. Interest groups may represent large groups like retired people (AARP) or automobile owners (American Automobile Association), or small special-interest groups like the oil companies (Petroleum Institute).

Hundreds of interest groups exist in the United States, and the most powerful are the ones with lots of members or lots of money (for contributions to election campaigns). Interest groups not only try to get candidates who support their goals elected, they also try to influence officials after they're in office. They try to affect both the law-making process of Congress and the administration of the law by the federal bureaucracy. This is called *lobbying*. Lobbying includes providing information favorable to their cause, mobilizing members to speak out and contact lawmakers, promising support (or opposition) in the next election, and conducting media campaigns to sway public opinion.

Both political parties and interest groups play important roles in American democracy. In some ways, they are similar: both are organized groups of people working to accomplish their goals, and both support political candidates and raise money to fund their objectives. In the United States, however, the two groups serve different purposes as outlined in the following table.

Political Parties and Interest Groups Compared

	Political Parties	**Interest Groups**
Number	Two important parties	Hundreds of important interest groups
Goal	Get their candidates elected	Advance their political agenda
Focus	Elections	Policy-making
Role in elections	Select candidates and help their candidates win by raising money and providing other types of support	Endorse individual candidates (usually from both parties) and raise money for their campaigns
Role in government	None—once elected, officials act on their own, not on behalf of the party	Influence congressmen and federal officials in making laws and formulating policies

Practice

1. Both interest groups and political parties are likely to:

    (1) Raise money for candidates running for office

    (2) Try to get all the candidates from one political party elected

    (3) Try to influence the policy-making process of the federal government

    (4) Recruit candidates to run for office

    (5) Make compromises with opponents

2. Which statement correctly contrasts political parties and interest groups?

    (1) Interest groups are not involved in elections, while political parties are.

    (2) Political parties need money and members to be effective, but interest groups do not.

    (3) Many powerful interest groups exist but only two main political parties.

    (4) Political parties usually work with other political parties, while interest groups do not.

    (5) Interest groups do not have a formal organizational structure, while political parties are highly organized at federal, state, and local levels.

Answers

1. **(1)** Both political parties and interest groups raise money for candidates running for office. Political parties try to get all their candidates elected (2), but interest groups only help candidates (from either party) who support their political goals. Only interest groups try to influence the policy-making process of the federal government (3) and make compromises with opponents (5). Only political parties take an active role in recruiting candidates to run for office (4).

2. **(3)** Powerful interest groups number in the hundreds, but we have just two important parties in the United States. Both political parties and interest groups get involved in elections (1); interest groups endorse and raise money for candidates. Both interest groups and political parties need money and members to be effective (2). Political parties do not work with other parties—they run against them—but interest groups often work with other interest groups when their interests overlap (4). Both interest groups and political parties need to be well organized at federal, state, and local levels to maximize their effect (5).

Constitutional Rights

Another key idea in understanding American government is the concept of individual rights. Shortly after the Constitution went into effect, 10 amendments called the Bill of Rights (1791) were added to the Constitution to specifically list limitations on the power of government and, thereby, establish individual rights. Later, the Fourteenth Amendment (1868) was interpreted by the Supreme Court to expand these limitations on the power of government to state governments as well as Congress and the federal government.

The basic rights necessary to an effective democratic government are stated in the First Amendment to the U.S. Constitution. The text of this amendment prohibits the government from limiting freedom of speech, freedom of the press, freedom to peacefully protest, and freedom of religion. This last one involves two separate prohibitions: the government cannot make a law "respecting the establishment of a religion" or one "prohibiting the free exercise" of religion. The prohibition of government establishment of a religion, which has been interpreted as prohibiting government-sponsored prayer in public schools and the display of religious symbols by the government, has been the most controversial part of this amendment.

Other rights contained in the Bill of Rights include the prohibition of "cruel and unusual punishment," guarantees on the right to a fair trial, and freedom from unreasonable searches and seizures of persons or property. Recently, the Supreme Court has interpreted the Second Amendment to guarantee a right to gun ownership. The Ninth Amendment states that an individual's rights are not limited to those specifically stated in the Constitution, and the Supreme Court has recognized rights implied in the Constitution, such as the right to privacy.

Often the extent of individual rights is subject to interpretation. What, for example, is "cruel and unusual" punishment? What exactly are "unreasonable" searches and seizures? And how far does the right of privacy go—does it include a woman's right to terminate a pregnancy? The Supreme Court must answer these questions through the individual cases appealed to the Court. Its decisions in these areas are often controversial.

Often, too, individual rights may conflict. For example, when a parent's religious belief not to seek medical treatment for a child could cause the child's death, does the parent's right to the free exercise of religion win out over the child's right to life? The courts must answer these questions as well through the individual cases they hear.

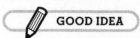 **GOOD IDEA**

You don't need to know what each amendment of the Bill of Rights does. But the Social Studies Test will have an excerpt from the U.S. Constitution, Bill of Rights, or Declaration of Independence that you have to read, interpret, and answer questions about. Before the test, it's a good idea to read and try to understand the first few paragraphs of the Constitution and Declaration of Independence and the entire Bill of Rights so you have some familiarity with them.

Practice

Questions 1 and 2 refer to the following text of the Sixth Amendment:

Amendment VI

In all criminal prosecutions, the accused shall enjoy the right to a speedy and public trial by an impartial jury ... and to be informed of the nature and cause of the accusation, to be confronted with the witnesses against him, to have compulsory process for obtaining witnesses in his favor, and to have the assistance of counsel for his defense.

1. Which right is granted by the Sixth Amendment to persons accused of a crime?

   (1) The right not to be tried twice for the same crime.

   (2) The right not to answer questions in court or in a police interrogation.

   (3) The right to a lawyer.

   (4) The right to be released on bail.

   (5) The right not to appear in court.

2. Which statement best summarizes the Sixth Amendment?

   (1) The Sixth Amendment is part of the Bill of Rights.

   (2) The Sixth Amendment lists various rights of citizens.

   (3) The Sixth Amendment lists *all* of the rights of persons accused of a crime.

   (4) The Sixth Amendment lists rights of persons accused of a crime.

   (5) The Sixth Amendment makes it too easy for criminals to get off free because of the rights it gives them.

Answers

1. **(3)** The last phrase of the Sixth Amendment grants a person accused of a crime the right to a lawyer ("counsel for his defense"). Answers (1) and (2) are constitutional rights of accused persons, too, but these rights are not contained in the Sixth Amendment; they appear in the Fifth Amendment. Answer (4) is also a general right of the accused (provided there's no evidence to suggest the person accused might flee); this right is contained in the Eighth Amendment. No right allows accused persons to avoid appearing in court (5).

2. **(4)** The Sixth Amendment does list rights of persons accused of a crime. Answer (3) is virtually the same except the word *all* has been added. Be sure to read carefully, and don't jump to conclusions! The Sixth Amendment does not have *all* of the rights of persons accused of a crime; other rights of the accused are in the Fifth and Eighth Amendments. Answer (1) is a correct statement but not a summary of the amendment. Answer (2) is not as descriptive nor as specific as the correct answer, which better summarizes the amendment. Answer (5) is not a summary of the amendment but an opinion about the effect of the amendment.

U.S. History

U.S. history comprises 20 percent of the questions on the Social Studies Test. You can expect about 10 of the 50 questions to be based on U.S. history content.

You won't be required to memorize dates and facts to ace the test. Most of the facts you need to know are given in the reading passages or the visuals included with the test questions. The test focuses on your skills in understanding, analyzing, and applying the information presented to you. Still, you do need to have a good understanding of U.S. history to put the readings and visuals into their historical context and work through the questions quickly.

This chapter provides overviews of important areas of U.S. history that will almost certainly be included in some way on the test. Following these overviews are GED-style questions that help prepare you for the types of skill-based questions you'll confront on the real test. Be sure to read the explanations for all the questions you missed or did not completely understand.

In This Chapter

- Overviews of key periods and developments in U.S. history
- Sample GED®-style questions to practice the skills on which you'll be tested
- Answers and explanations for all questions

The Establishment of the United States

The Eastern Seaboard of North America was one of the last areas of the New World to be colonized by Europeans. The Spanish already controlled Mexico, Central America, and much of South America. The Portuguese had colonized Brazil; the French had settled in Quebec; and the British, French, Dutch, and Spanish had established sugar plantations throughout the West Indies. No obvious source of wealth was found along the Eastern Seaboard of North America. Many of the British colonies established along the North American coast in the 1600s were founded by people seeking not wealth, but religious freedom (the Puritans in New England, Quakers in Pennsylvania, and Catholics in Maryland, for example). Of course, many early settlers also came for economic opportunity, a possibility that became more likely after a demand for tobacco, grown in Virginia, developed in Europe in the 1600s.

The British colonies along the Eastern Seaboard grew and prospered, but by the mid-1770s, many colonists wanted greater self-government and resented not having representation in the British Parliament. The Boston Tea Party (1774) is an example of American revolt against the distant British government. "No taxation without representation" became the American slogan, and tea with a tax imposed by the British Parliament was dumped into Boston Harbor. The government in Britain seemed remote and deaf to colonial views. Other disputes developed, and skirmishes with British troops caused reactions that drove the sides farther apart. The result: in 1776, the 13 colonies united for the purpose of gaining their independence from Britain.

The Declaration of Independence was written to justify the American rebellion. Based on the ideas of French and British Enlightenment thinkers, among the revolutionary ideas it contained was that governments derive their powers from the consent of the governed (rather than from the divine right of kings). It also stated the revolutionary idea that people have natural, God-given rights to life, liberty, and the pursuit of happiness. It went on to say that government's role is to protect these rights and, when it does not, the people have the right to rebel.

 **IN THE KNOW**

Historians estimate that 15 to 20 percent of Americans remained loyal to Britain during the American Revolution. Sometimes even families were divided. For example, William Franklin, son of Benjamin Franklin, remained loyal to Britain, and the two never reconciled their differences. After the war, loyalists found themselves citizens of the new United States; some moved to England and Canada to remain British.

A rudimentary national government was formed—the Continental Congress—and George Washington formed a national army to fight the British. At first the effort to defeat the army of what was then the world's most powerful nation seemed almost hopeless, but the Americans enjoyed some advantages, such as popular support and familiarity with the land. Finally, with the support of the French military and assistance from other European nations who had a score to settle with Britain, the Americans prevailed, the British army surrendered, and Britain granted independence to its colonies.

It wasn't until almost 10 years later, however, that the Americans established a unified nation and an effective national government. The U.S. Constitution that went into effect in 1789 was a bundle of political compromises among competing interests.

One key compromise ended a bitter dispute between the larger, more populous states and the smaller ones. It established a bicameral legislature (Congress) in which all states, large and small, had equal representation in one house (the Senate), while representation in the other (the House of Representatives) was based on the state's population. It also spelled out that to become law, a proposed bill had to be passed by both houses of Congress.

Other difficult compromises had to be worked out between slave states (the six Southern states) and the states that had already outlawed slavery (the seven Northern states). Among these were agreements not to limit the importation of African slaves for at least 20 years and to count slaves as three fifths of a person for purposes of taxation and representation.

Another compromise agreed to by the supporters of the proposed Constitution (the Federalists) in order to gain the votes of states needed to ratify the document was the addition of a "bill of rights" specifically stating limitations on the power of government. As a result, shortly after ratification of the new constitution, 10 amendments, known today as the Bill of Rights, were added.

 GOOD IDEA

> You can expect the Social Studies Test to have at least one question based on an excerpt from the Constitution or Declaration of Independence. Understanding these documents is doubly important, considering that they are key parts of two subject areas covered on the test: U.S. history and U.S. government. Chapter 11 has more information about the Constitution and the government it established.

Practice

Questions 1 and 2 refer to the following passage from the beginning of the Declaration of Independence:

> When in the course of human events it becomes necessary for one people to dissolve the political bands which have connected them with another … a decent respect for the opinions of mankind requires that they should declare the causes which impel them to the separation.

We hold these truths to be self-evident, that all men are created equal, that they are endowed by their Creator with certain unalienable Rights, that among these are Life, Liberty and the pursuit of Happiness. That to secure these rights, Governments are instituted among Men, deriving their just powers from the consent of the governed ….

1. The primary reason this passage was written was to:

   (1) Make the case that people have God-given rights

   (2) Reform the British government

   (3) State new theories developed by American philosophers on the nature of government

   (4) Justify the position of the colonists that they need to set up their own independent government

   (5) End the British royalty and replace it with a government elected by the people

2. The existence of slavery in the United States is inconsistent with which of the following ideas stated in the Declaration of Independence?

   (1) One reason for the existence of governments is to protect rights, including property rights.

   (2) The Americans and British need to go their separate ways.

   (3) All men are created equal and have a right to life, liberty, and the pursuit of happiness.

   (4) The government's powers are derived from the consent of the governed.

   (5) The British government has abused its power and not respected the rights of Americans.

Question 3 relates to the following political cartoon that was first published in 1754 and is attributed to Benjamin Franklin:

3. What opinion is the cartoonist expressing?

(1) The large states can "go it alone" and do not need to join the United States.

(2) Compromise is necessary if the Constitution is to be ratified.

(3) Human beings need to stop acting like snakes if they are to succeed.

(4) Transportation routes between the colonies need to be improved to better connect the colonies.

(5) The colonies need to unite in order to maximize their power and stand up to Britain.

Answers

1. **(4)** The first sentence states the purpose of the document: to explain why the colonists are revolting and want to set up their own country. The document does state the belief in God-given rights (1), but this is only in the context of explaining why they are revolting. At this point, they are not trying to reform the British government (2) but establish their right to create an independent government (5). The ideas contained in the Declaration of Independence (3) came from European theorists (chiefly John Locke), not Americans.

2. **(3)** The existence of slavery in the American colonies is completely inconsistent with the idea that all men are created equally and endowed with a right to liberty. The ideas that Americans and Brits should go their separate ways (2) and that the British government has abused its power (5) had little or nothing to do with slavery. Answers (1) and (4) do not directly contradict the existence of slavery; slave owners regarded owning slaves as a property right, and the majority of the governed in slave states might support the existence of slavery.

3. **(5)** In this famous cartoon, Franklin was urging the colonies to unite. A snake cut up will not survive, but it can be ferocious if it's in one piece. No distinction is made between the larger colonies (1) like New York (N.Y.), Pennsylvania (P), and Virginia (V) and the smaller ones like New Jersey (N.J.) and North Carolina (N.C.). Nothing in the cartoon indicates Franklin was talking about how humans behave (3), trade routes (4), or the Constitution (2), which, by the way, wasn't written until 30 years later.

The Growth of the United States

At the time of American independence, all states bordered the Atlantic Ocean, and the American settlement ended at the Appalachian Mountains only a couple hundred miles inland. Scarcely 65 years later (1848), the land of the United States stretched 2,500 miles across the continent to California and Oregon on the Pacific Ocean. Territory was added to the United States by purchases (the Louisiana Purchase from France and Florida from Spain), by military conquest (California and the Southwest from Mexico), and by boundary negotiations (Oregon Country south of the 49th parallel in an agreement with Britain). Texas was a unique case: Americans settled in Mexican-controlled Texas in great numbers, came to outnumber Mexicans living there, fought for and gained their independence from Mexico, and finally joined the United States.

Large numbers of Native Americans were wiped out by diseases, mostly European diseases to which they had no built-up natural immunity. Remaining Native Americans were pushed westward, defeated militarily, and eventually forced onto unproductive reservations, where many more died from disease and starvation. The U.S. Army established bases throughout the West to subdue Native American people and make the land "safe" for settlement.

Most settlers moved westward in search of new farmland, but gold rushes in the California and the Rocky Mountains also were instrumental in pulling settlers to the western frontier. Settlers moved westward via canals (especially the Erie Canal), rivers (especially the Ohio, Mississippi, and Missouri), and rudimentary roads (the most famous is the Oregon Trail). As the nation developed industrially, railroads were built across the continent—the first transcontinental railroad was completed in 1867—and these became the primary means of westward settlement.

Westward movement was fueled partly by the arrival of thousands of new immigrants each year. Successive waves of immigrants came first from Britain, then Ireland and northern Europe, then southern Europe and Asia, and finally today, from Latin America. As a result, the United States grew rapidly in population as well as land area. The United States is still a nation where most people are either immigrants themselves or can trace their family background to immigrant parents, grandparents, or great-grandparents.

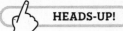 **HEADS-UP!**

Don't confuse immigrant with emigrant. An *immigrant* is a person who comes to a new country to live there, while an *emigrant* is a person who leaves a country to live in a different one. Each immigrant is also an emigrant; which word is used depends on the perspective of the speaker. A person moving from Italy to the United States would be an immigrant to Americans but an emigrant to Italians.

Although a nation of immigrants, many Americans have typically feared that later waves of immigration would change the character of the United States and threaten their dominance. For example, in the 1850s the Know Nothings, a secretive organization formed to oppose the immigration of Catholics, became one of the largest political parties in the United States, scoring victories in gubernatorial, congressional, and mayoral elections across the country. From the mid-nineteenth century to the mid-twentieth century, Asian immigrants in particular faced anti-immigrant sentiment and many discriminatory laws. But immigrant energy, derived from a strong desire to work hard and create a better life for immigrants and their children, has fueled American economic development and created one of the world's most dynamic economies.

Not only were the land area and population of the United States rapidly expanding, so was industry. As industry developed in the Northeast and Midwest, rather than settling on the Western frontier, immigrants increasingly moved to impoverished ethnic enclaves in the cities, where they provided labor for factories. By the end of the nineteenth century, the United States was the world's leading industrial power.

But industrial strength and wealth had been achieved partly through the exploitation of labor. In the early twentieth century, in what is called the Progressive Era, government began to step in to protect worker rights, outlaw child labor, set minimum wages, limit working hours, establish safety regulations, and break up business monopolies. This economic system of capitalism, with some government intervention and regulation, defines the American economy today.

Practice

Question 1 refers to the following map:

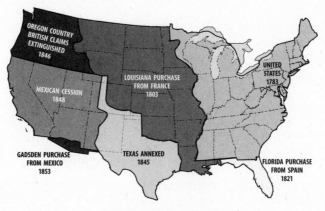

U.S. territorial acquisitions.

1. According to the map, from what country did the United States first acquire land for expansion?

    (1) France

    (2) Mexico

    (3) Spain

    (4) Britain

    (5) Texas

Questions 2 and 3 refer to data presented in the following table:

States with the Highest Percentages of Immigrants (2009)

State	Total Population	Foreign-Born Population
California	36.3 million	26.8%
New York	19.4 million	21.3%
New Jersey	8.7 million	19.7%
Nevada	2.6 million	18.7%
Florida	18.2 million	18.7%
Texas	23.8 million	15.8%

U.S. Census Bureau.

2. In 2009, in which state(s) were more than one out of five residents immigrants to the United States?

   (1) California only

   (2) California and New York

   (3) California, New York, and New Jersey

   (4) All of the states listed

   (5) None of the states listed

3. Which states had a larger number of foreign-born residents than Nevada?

   (1) California, New York, and New Jersey

   (2) California, New York, and New Jersey had more, and Florida had the same number as Nevada

   (3) Florida and Texas

   (4) All of the other five states

   (5) None of the other five states

Answers

1. **(1)** The earliest acquisition shown on the map was the 1803 Louisiana Purchase, which doubled the size of the original United States. (1783 was the date of the Treaty of Paris, which officially granted American independence.)

2. **(2)** Twenty percent is equivalent to one out of five. In two states, immigrants comprised more than 20 percent of the population in 2009. A basic understanding of percents is important to understanding data presented on the Social Studies Test.

3. **(4)** This question is asking for numbers, not percentages. Numbers of foreign-born residents are not given on the table, but you don't really need to do any math to see that Nevada's foreign-born population is much smaller than any of the other states in the table. Doing the math, Nevada's 18.7 percent of 2.6 million (486,000) is much smaller than even Texas's 15.8 percent of 23.8 million (3,998,000).

The Civil War, Reconstruction, and the Civil Rights Movement

Sectional issues divided the United States for four decades before war broke out between the states in 1861. Two conflicting social and economic systems were developing in the country: an industrial, more egalitarian North (where slavery was illegal) and an agrarian, hierarchical South (where slavery formed a vital part of the plantation economy). Irresolvable conflicts arose over issues like whether slavery should be allowed to spread into Western territories, whether taxes on imports (tariffs) should be levied to help Northern manufacturers, and whether runaway slaves who made it to the North had to be returned. Compromises were hammered out in Congress.

For example, from 1820 until 1850, states joined the Union in pairs (a slave state and a free state) so there was always the same number of slave and free states and the Senate was equally divided between North and South. But antislavery sentiment was building in the North, and the South was feeling more vulnerable as the North became increasingly more populous, more industrial, and more technologically advanced than the South.

When the Republican Party, which wanted to stop the expansion of slavery to new territories, won the presidency with the election of Abraham Lincoln in 1860, 11 Southern states declared they were leaving the United States and setting up a new country, the Confederate States of America. Technically, the issue the Civil War was fought over was whether or not a state that had decided to join the United States could secede (leave the Union) if it later wanted to. The South argued in favor of states' rights, while from the Northern perspective, the states' rights issue was just a cover for the real issue dividing the North and South: slavery.

IN THE KNOW

Eleven states formed the Confederate States of America, also known as the Confederacy, or the South. Twenty-two states remained in the United States, also known as the Union, or the North. The Union included four "border states" (Missouri, Kentucky, Maryland, and Delaware) that continued to allow slavery but for various reasons did not leave the Union. The terms *North, South,* and *border states* are still used in discussing regional differences within the United States.

To be victorious, the South only had to keep the Union army out of its territory or inflict enough casualties to cause the North to give up and let the South go its own way. The South almost succeeded. For the North to be victorious, the Union army had to defeat and occupy the South. The North, which had an enormous advantage in manpower, industrial capacity, and transportation systems, accomplished that goal after 4 years of war.

The Civil War was by far the United States' most deadly and destructive war. More than 1 million Americans died, including 620,000 soldiers. The North succeeded because it destroyed not only the South's army but also its economy, which had provided food and supplies to the soldiers. At the end of the war, the South was in ruins.

The Civil War was followed by a period called Reconstruction, a time of reform imposed by the North on the South. The Thirteenth Amendment (1865) freed the slaves, the Fourteenth Amendment (1868) required state governments to treat all their citizens equally regardless of race, and the Fifteenth Amendment (1870) gave voting rights to former slaves.

The election of Rutherford Hays as president in 1870 ended Reconstruction, and control of the state governments of the South reverted to the same interests, classes, and race that controlled them before the Civil War. African Americans were effectively denied the right to vote by literacy tests and poll taxes. Races were segregated (separated) so African Americans could not attend the same schools, ride in the same railroad cars, or eat at the same lunch counters as whites. In the end, most African Americans were not in much better situations than before the war. As a result, a century-long migration of African Americans to Northern cities began.

About a hundred years after Reconstruction, a second reconstruction known as the civil rights movement occurred. This period of reconstruction differed in that it was led by African Americans, who demanded equal rights in nonviolent protests. Dr. Martin Luther King Jr. became the best-known leader of the civil rights movement, which was characterized by peaceful protest marches and sit-ins that called attention to injustice and succeeded in bringing far-reaching change.

Some of the key achievements of the civil rights movement are summarized as follows:

1948: President Harry Truman desegregated the armed forces, allowing blacks and whites to serve in the same units.

1954: In *Brown* v. *Board of Education of Topeka,* the Supreme Court ruled that segregation of public schools by race was inherently unequal and, thus, unconstitutional under the Fourteenth Amendment.

1957: President Eisenhower ordered federal troops to Arkansas to force the state government to allow African Americans to enroll at Little Rock's all-white Central High School.

1964: In *Loving* v. *Virginia,* the Supreme Court ruled that states cannot prohibit interracial marriage.

1964: Congress passed the Civil Rights Act that ended racial segregation and discrimination in public accommodations such as restaurants, stores, buses, and parks.

1964: The Twenty-Second Amendment outlawed the poll tax, a tax on voting used to keep poor people, especially African Americans, from voting.

1965: Congress passed the Voting Rights Act, which ended literacy tests and required state governments to take action to encourage minorities to register and vote.

Practice

1. According to the preceding list, milestones of the civil rights movement included all of the following types of governmental actions *except:*

   (1) Laws passed by state governments

   (2) Supreme Court decisions

   (3) A constitutional amendment

   (4) Laws passed by Congress

   (5) Presidential orders

Question 2 refers to the following bar graph:

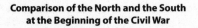

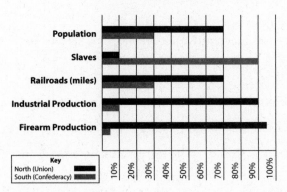

2. Which statement is supported by the information shown in the graph?

    (1) At the beginning of the Civil War, the North and South each had about the same population.

    (2) Having more slaves gave the South an advantage in the Civil War.

    (3) At the beginning of the Civil War, the South had slaves and the North did not.

    (4) At the beginning of the Civil War, nearly all firearms manufactured in the United States were produced in the North.

    (5) The North's railroads were the key factor that helped it win the war.

Question 3 refers to the following passage, which contains excerpts from the 1858 Lincoln-Douglas debates between Abraham Lincoln and Stephen A. Douglas, both campaigning to become a senator from Illinois in the U.S. Congress. Note that at this time, the United States contained states and territories on the Western frontier under federal control that did not yet have enough population for statehood.

> **Lincoln (a member of the Republican Party):** "The Republican Party looks upon slavery as a moral, social, and political wrong …. [We] nevertheless have due regard for its actual existence among us and the difficulties of getting rid of it in any satisfactory way …. Yet having a due regard for these …, [we] insist that it should be treated as a wrong and one of the methods of treating it as a wrong is to make provision that is shall spread no further …. [I am in favor of] restricting the spread of [slavery] and not allowing it to go into territories where it has not already existed."

Douglas (a member of the Democratic Party): "Mr. Lincoln tries to avoid the main issue by attacking the truth of my proposition that our fathers made this government divided into free and slave states, recognizing the right of each state to decide all its local questions for itself [including whether or not to permit slavery]. I assert that this country can exist as they made it, divided into free and slave states, as long as any state chooses to retain slavery …. I assert that the people of a territory, as well as those of a state, have the right to decide for themselves whether slavery can or cannot exist in such territory."

3. Lincoln and Douglas would probably agree that:

   (1) Slavery is wrong.

   (2) States and new territories should decide for themselves whether or not they want to permit slavery.

   (3) Slavery should not be allowed to spread to new territories within the United States.

   (4) Nothing should be done immediately to end slavery in the states where it already exists, and most people favor it.

   (5) It would be easy to simply abolish slavery in the United States.

Answers

1. **(1)** Most state governments in the South strongly resisted the civil rights movement, and a number of Southern governors tried to block desegregation. All of the milestones were actions of the U.S. government, including the Supreme Court, the Congress, and the president, as well as an amendment to the U.S. Constitution.

2. **(4)** The bar graph shows that at the beginning of the Civil War, 95 percent of firearms manufactured in the United States were produced in the North. Answers (1) and (3) are contradicted by the information shown in the graph. Answer (2) correctly states that the South had more slaves, but no information in the graph indicates this was an advantage for the South. In fact, slavery didn't help the South's war effort; slaves could not be relied upon to fight for the South, and many ran away and joined the Union army. The bar graph contains no information indicating how important railroads were in causing the North's victory (5); in fact, the North's advantage in railroads was just one of a number of advantages that helped it win the Civil War.

3. **(4)** Both Lincoln and Douglas would agree that nothing should be done immediately to end slavery in the states where it already exists. Answer (1) is Lincoln's position, but not that of Douglas, who believes it should exist as long as the people in a state want it. Answer (2) is Douglas's position, which contrasts with Lincoln's position in answer (3). Both Lincoln and Douglas would disagree that slavery can be ended easily.

The United States as a World Power

Until the twentieth century, the United States was absorbed with internal affairs such as westward expansion, economic growth, and the conflict between the North and South. The United States had only a small army, stayed out of foreign alliances, and did not get involved much in world affairs. In the twentieth century, however, this changed dramatically as the United States increased the size of its armed forces, became involved in wars around the world, established alliances, joined international organizations, and became a leader in world affairs.

As a result of a victory in a war with Spain (1898), the United States suddenly found itself an imperialistic power—a country with an empire containing distant lands and peoples. Americans took control of Puerto Rico (which is still a commonwealth today) and the Philippines (a country it controlled until 1946).

These events changed Americans' view of themselves and their role in world affairs. Business interests began promoting American intervention in world affairs as a way of promoting U.S. economic interests around the world. The United States annexed Hawaii, an independent nation (1898), and took control of land in Panama (1903) for the building of the Panama Canal.

Then, in 1917, Americans, for the first time, entered a European war that did not directly involve the United States. Involvement was driven in part by commercial interests but also by an idealistic view that this war (called the "Great War" at the time but today known as World War I) would be "the war to end all wars," as President Woodrow Wilson described it. He envisioned American leadership in a new international order that included the League of Nations, an international organization whose purpose was to help peacefully resolve international disputes. In World War I, American forces ended a military stalemate and brought victory to France, Britain, Russia, and Italy against Germany and Austria-Hungary, gaining the United States international recognition as a world power. But Wilson's vision of a new global political order in which the United States would play an important role ended when American isolationists in the U.S. Senate blocked the United States from joining the League of Nations and playing a leadership role in world affairs.

Only two decades later, an even larger war broke out in Europe and Asia between the Axis Powers (Germany, Italy, and Japan) and the Allied Powers (Britain, France, the Soviet Union or Russia, and China). The United States, which opposed the Nazism of Germany and the imperialism of Japan, supported the Allied Powers but did not actually join the war until Japan attacked the U.S. naval base at Pearl Harbor, Hawaii, in 1941. World War II (1939–1946), the first truly global conflict, involved most of the world's nations and more than 100 million troops. It brought death to more than 70 million people and total destruction to large areas of Japan, Germany, Russia, China, and other countries. It also brought the Holocaust, an effort by the German Nazis to destroy the Jewish people during which 6 million Jews were systematically killed. Finally, the Allies achieved victory in 1945, first in Europe and a few months later in Asia after the United States used nuclear weapons against Japan.

After the war, peace did not result; instead, two of the victorious Allied Powers—the United States and the Soviet Union—immediately squared off against each other in the Cold War. Largely due to the threat of mutual nuclear annihilation, the Cold War (1946–1991) between the two nuclear superpowers did not actually involve direct fighting between American and Soviet troops. Instead, it was fought through a continuing series of *proxy wars* (national and regional wars in which the Soviet Union supported one side and the United States the other). The most significant of these wars were in China, Korea, Cuba, Vietnam, and Afghanistan. The Cold War also included direct confrontations between the United States and the Soviet Union (the Berlin airlift and the Cuban missile crisis) that stopped just short of direct warfare between the two nuclear superpowers. In the Cold War, the Soviet Union and its allies sought to expand throughout the world through its system of totalitarian government and communism, while the United States and its allies tried to contain communism and Soviet expansion simultaneously promoting the systems of democratic government and capitalism. The Cold War came to an end in 1991 when the Soviet Union collapsed under the weight of its own inefficient economy and government. The Soviet Union broke up into 15 separate countries, of which Russia is the largest one.

Since the 2001 terrorist attacks on the World Trade Center and Pentagon, U.S. foreign policy has focused on a *war on terror* in which the enemy is not a foreign nation but small extremist terrorist groups operating on their own in the international arena. Today, the conduct of international affairs no longer involves only the governments of countries interacting with each other. Many other actors are wielding power on the international stage, including international terrorist groups; multinational corporations (global banks and companies); and international organizations such as the United Nations (UN), the International Monetary Fund (IMF), the European Union (EU), and the North Atlantic Treaty Organization (NATO).

 **GOOD IDEA**

Understanding World Wars I and II and the Cold War could be especially helpful on the GED because both U.S. history and world history questions can focus on these events.

Practice

Question 1 refers to the following map:

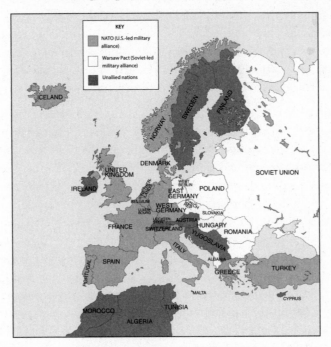

Division of Europe during the Cold War.

1. Which statement best summarizes the information shown on the map?

   (1) All the European nations along the border of the Soviet Union were allied with the Soviet Union.

   (2) Alliances such as NATO and the Warsaw Pact dangerously divide the world and encourage war.

   (3) During the Cold War, most nations of Eastern Europe were allied with the Soviet Union, while most nations of Western Europe joined the United States in opposing the Soviet Union.

   (4) The Soviet Union controlled most of Europe, while the United States had relatively little power there.

   (5) All of Europe would be communist if the United States had not stood up to the Soviet Union.

Question 2 refers to the following bar graph:

World War II Deaths
(in millions)

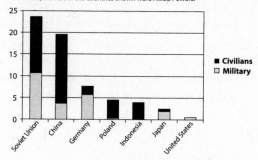

The chart below shows the six countries with the highest number of deaths in World War II.
For comparison the United States has been added to the chart. Germany and Japan were
Axis Powers; the rest of the countries shown were Allied Powers.

2. Which statement is supported by the information presented in the bar graph?

(1) Most of the dead in World War II were citizens of the Soviet Union.

(2) In World War II, the Soviet Union lost a higher percentage of its people than any other country.

(3) The overwhelming majority of Soviet deaths in World War II were civilians.

(4) More civilians were killed in China than in any other country.

(5) Germany and Japan, who lost World War II, had the highest numbers of military deaths in the war.

Answers

1. **(3)** Not all European nations along the Soviet border (1) aligned themselves with the Soviet Union (Finland, for example, did not). There is no information on the map about whether alliances threaten the world or promote peace (2); more information would be needed to research this question. The Soviet Union, which itself makes up about half of Europe, did control more land area of Europe (4), but the map offers no information about the power of the United States in Europe. The United States in fact had considerable power in Europe due to many American military bases there, a strong U.S. navy presence, and a strong NATO alliance. Answer (5) is an opinion; no evidence on the map supports or rejects this opinion.

2. (**4**) The bar graph shows that China had the most civilian deaths of any country in World War II. (The dark portion of China's bar on the graph is the biggest.) The Soviet Union had more deaths than any other country, but you cannot say that most of all the deaths in World War II were in the Soviet Union (1). No one country accounted for most of the dead. The map does not show percentages (2); to figure percentages, you would need to know the populations of each country. In actuality, Poland lost the highest percentage of its people in World War II. Answer (3) is contradicted by the graph, which shows about an equal number of the dead in the Soviet Union between civilians and military personnel. Although they lost World War II, Germany and Japan did not suffer nearly as many deaths as the Soviet Union and China, which were on the winning side.

CHAPTER 13

Economics

Economics accounts for 15 percent of the questions on the Social Studies Test. You can expect 6 to 8 of the 50 questions to be based on graphs, charts, and reading passages about economics.

Similar to the other subject areas of the Social Studies Test, you won't be required to memorize facts and formulas or know the definitions of technical terms to do well on the economics questions. Facts and definitions are given in the reading passages, graphs, and charts included with the test questions. The test focuses on your skills in understanding, analyzing, and applying the information presented to you.

Don't let economics scare you. Even if you've never taken a class in economics or think you know nothing about it, you probably won't have too much trouble understanding the basic economics presented on the GED. However, an understanding of key economic concepts is helpful. Understanding these concepts familiarizes you with how economists think and helps you analyze and interpret the economics content on the test.

This chapter focuses on basic concepts of economics. The concepts probably seem fairly simple—they're based on common sense—but it's in the application of these concepts

In This Chapter

- Overviews of important economic concepts

- Sample GED®-style questions to practice the skills on which you'll be tested

- Answers and explanations for all questions

that you'll likely be challenged. The GED-style practice questions in this chapter help you prepare for the types of skill-based questions you'll see on the real test.

Basic Concepts of Economics

Economics is the study of the *production* and *consumption* of goods and services. *Goods* are products, from milk to automobiles. *Services* are products, too, but intangible ones, like a haircut, a hotel stay, a checking account, or police protection. People are consumers of goods and services and, in their roles at work, produce goods and services.

Economic systems arise because of *scarcity*—the supplies of goods and services are limited. If something is not scarce, like air, it is not bought and sold and, therefore, not part of our economy. The price of a good or service is determined by how scarce it is—the *supply*—and by how many people want it—the *demand*. Prices fluctuate based on supply and demand. For example, if half of Florida's orange crop is destroyed by frost (the supply decreases), the price of orange juice goes up. With that price increase, consumption declines until supply and demand are back in balance. What would happen to the price of juice if the supply increases due to importation of orange juice from Brazil? The price of orange juice will fall until the cheap price encourages more people to drink juice and supply and demand are back in balance. Perhaps the most basic concept of economics is the relationship between supply and demand: the price of a product tends to move toward the price at which the supply equals the demand.

 HEADS-UP!

The law of supply and demand is a commonsense concept, but people often get tripped up when applying the concept to actual circumstances. Keep in mind the following:

The price of a good or service tends to go up if demand is greater than supply.

The price of a good or service tends to go *down* if supply is greater than demand.

Currency (money) was invented in ancient civilizations to facilitate trade. *Money economies* have pretty much replaced *barter economies,* in which people trade goods and services directly. The value of money is determined by how many goods and services it can buy. If prices, in general, are going up, *inflation* is occurring and the currency is losing value. This happens when people have money to spend but the supply of goods and services is limited. If prices are generally going down, *deflation* is occurring. This happens when consumers don't have a lot of money while unsold goods and services are plentiful.

Gross domestic product (*GDP*) is a measure of the monetary value of all the goods and services produced by a country in a year—it measures the size of a nation's economy. However, if GDP is not adjusted for inflation, it is difficult to compare GDP from one year to another. A rising GDP could mean more goods and services are being produced, or it could just mean prices are going up. Thus, economists use the concept of *real GDP* to adjust for price changes (inflation or deflation), allowing them to compare the size of the economy from one year to another year and determine economic growth or decline. To do this, economists use *constant dollars;* they pick a year (for example, 2010) and measure each years' production of goods and services in 2010 dollars. In other words, they use the prices of goods and services in 2010 to measure production in all years.

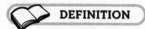 **DEFINITION**

> Economists use the term **real GDP** to indicate that inflation/deflation have been adjusted for. They talk about real growth, real incomes, and real costs. To arrive at real amounts, they measure prices in **constant dollars,** whose value does not change over the years. If a chart or graph says "in 2000 dollars," you know the amounts for all years are being measured using 2000 prices and that the figures are "real."

A decline of real GDP for at least 6 months is defined as a *recession*. In a recession, consumer spending, investment, business profits, and production all decline while unemployment rises. A *depression* is a more severe and sustained drop in GDP that usually involves deflation and financial crisis due to the failure of banks and other financial institutions.

In the United States, privately owned businesses produce most of the nation's goods and services. Businesses can be structured in different formats; the most common of these are individual proprietorships (single owner), partnerships (two or more joint owners), and corporations. In a partnership, the owners make decisions jointly and share in the profits. Corporations have many owners, and each owner's share of ownership is determined by the amount of the company's stock owned. Stockholders elect the company's directors, who manage the company and distribute profits back to the stockholders based on the amount of stock each owns.

Businesses have both inputs (factors of production) and outputs (goods or services). The *factors of production* are divided into three groups: raw materials, labor, and capital. *Raw materials* (iron ore, unrefined petroleum, soil, water, etc.) and *labor* (workers) are self-explanatory. *Capital* refers to any item used to produce other goods or services, including a bank's computers, a car manufacturer's robot welders, and a farmer's tractor. All three factors of production are necessary to produce goods and services.

Practice

Question 1 refers to the following graph:

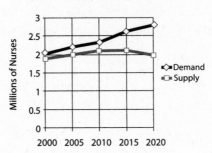

1. Which statement best states what can be predicted to happen to the wages of nurses and why?

   (1) Wages will decline because the supply of nurses is growing.

   (2) Wages will rise because demand for nurses is declining.

   (3) Wages will rise because the demand for nurses exceeds the supply of nurses.

   (4) Wages will rise because the supply of nurses is growing.

   (5) Wages for nurses will not change much because hospitals can't afford to pay more to nurses.

Question 2 refers to the following graph:

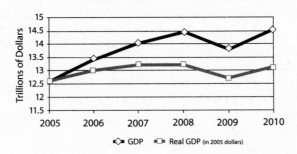

2. Which statement best explains how unadjusted GDP could grow between 2007 and 2008 while real GDP remains stable?

   (1) Deflation was occurring with prices dropping.

   (2) Supply and demand were out of balance.

   (3) Unadjusted GDP increases when production of goods and services increases.

   (4) A recession was beginning.

   (5) The increase in unadjusted GDP was due to price increases, not increases in production.

Answers

1. **(3)** The concept of supply and demand applies to wages as well as products. Wages for nurses tend to keep rising until supply equals demand. An increase in supply (1) would produce a decline in wages only if supply rises above demand. Answer (2) is inaccurate because wages rise when the demand increases, not declines. A growing demand for nurses won't necessarily lead to wage increases; that happens only if demand exceeds supply. Wages are rising (4), but that's not because supply is rising; a rising supply of nurses tends to bring down wages. Answer (5) doesn't relate to supply and demand and, therefore, isn't a basis on which predictions of wages can be made. Hospitals that cannot afford to pay nurses competitive rates won't have nurses and would have to close or make some kind of alternative arrangement in which nurses weren't needed.

2. **(5)** In this graph, the real GDP line shows the total value of goods and services produced for all years using 2005 prices. Thus, the real GDP line only measures production changes, while unadjusted GDP measures changes in both prices and production together. Because we know that production (real GDP) was flat between 2007 and 2008, we also know the increase in unadjusted GDP was entirely due to inflation. A period of price increases is inflation, not deflation (1). The concept of GDP has little to do with the concept of supply and demand (2). Answer (3) is only a half-truth because unadjusted GDP measures both changes in production and prices together. A recession could be beginning (4), but that doesn't explain the difference between real GDP and unadjusted GDP.

Economic Systems

Different countries have different economic systems—in fact, each country's system is at least a little different from that of any other country. The chief difference is in the role the government plays in the economy.

In pure *capitalism,* the government plays only a minimal role. It does not own factories, control prices, or regulate business. Businesses are privately owned, and the owners (capitalists) are free to operate how they want. But even in pure capitalism, the government still plays a vital economic role in printing money, settling disputes, enforcing contracts, protecting property, setting standards of weights and measures, etc. Another term for a capitalistic economic system is a *free enterprise system.* The term *market economy* is used as well because prices and production are determined by free markets (supply and demand) rather than by the government.

On the other side of the spectrum is pure *socialism,* in which the government controls the economy. Under socialism, the means of production (mines, factories, land, businesses, etc.) are owned by the people as a whole through the government. The government decides what to produce and sets the prices at which products will be sold. Communism is a form of socialism in which a dictatorial government makes economic decisions and all private enterprise is suppressed. Under democratic socialism, there is more freedom, but the elected government still owns and runs at least the largest mines, factories, and businesses.

Since the fall of the Soviet Union, nearly all countries have some form of market economy, in which prices, wages, and production are largely determined by free markets (supply and demand) rather than the government. However, even in the United States, which prides itself on its free enterprise system, the government often gets involved rather than letting privately owned businesses determine all economic decisions. An example of this is minimum-wage laws in which the federal and state governments set minimum wages, rather than allowing businesses to pay what they want. Today, nearly all countries, including the United States, have mixed economies, with a degree of government involvement and control somewhere between pure socialism and pure capitalism.

Practice

1. Which statement correctly compares capitalism and socialism?

   (1) In both economic systems, the government plays a role in the successful operation of the system.

   (2) In both economic systems, the law of supply and demand determines prices.

   (3) In both economic systems, business enterprises are owned by private citizens who are motivated by profits.

   (4) Both economic systems allow wealth to accumulate in the hands of a few individuals.

   (5) In both economic systems, the government performs essentially the same role.

Questions 2 and 3 refer to the following reading passage:

Socialism was in decline even before the breakup of the Soviet Union in 1992 brought an end to its government-run economy. Well before that event, China, the world's most populous socialist country, started economic reforms that broke up communal farms and encouraged free enterprise. And after the free market economies of four "Asian Tigers" (South Korea, Taiwan, Singapore, and Hong Kong) demonstrated "miracle" economic growth (1960–1990), most of the developing world started emulating them rather than socialist models. Even Western European countries have backed away from socialism and returned many government-run industries to private ownership. Today, only a handful of countries remain deeply committed to socialism and opposed to capitalism.

But should socialism die? If you value economic growth, capitalism wins hands down. But if you value an equitable distribution of wealth, the revival of a more socialistic approach with more government involvement may be a better alternative.

The situation in which the rich get richer and the poor remain poor now characterizes most market economies, from Russia to India to the United States. In the United States, the median family income level was in decline for years even before the real estate bubble burst and recession set in. Workers in the United States earn lower wages, have less job security, work longer hours, and have less health coverage than before. Allowing the economy to operate without government controls serves the rich but not the majority of the people. At some point, the government should step in to the economic system to ensure the benefits flow not just to business owners but to the workers as well.

2. Which statement best summarizes the author's argument?

   (1) Socialism should replace capitalism so wealth is more equitably distributed.

   (2) Capitalism is better than socialism because it's better at generating economic growth.

   (3) Capitalism is good for economic growth, but the government should intervene to ensure wealth is distributed fairly.

   (4) Both capitalism and socialism should be replaced with a better system.

   (5) Some countries should continue to be socialistic so socialism doesn't die out.

3. Which statement is a fact the author uses to support her argument?

   (1) Socialism is in decline.

   (2) The government-controlled economy of the Soviet Union was a failure and collapsed.

   (3) Capitalism is an efficient system for economic growth.

   (4) The average American worker's salary and benefits are declining, while the rich get richer.

   (5) The gap between rich and poor in the United States is narrowing.

Answers

1. **(1)** In both systems, the government plays an important role. Under capitalism, the government builds infrastructure like roads, prints money, protects private property, establishes courts to settle disputes and enforce contracts, etc. Furthermore, even the most extreme proponents of capitalism usually agree that some services, like police protection, are best provided by the government rather than private enterprise. Under socialism, the government gets even more involved in the economy by owning businesses, setting prices, and making production decisions. Free markets governed by the law of supply and demand (2), business enterprises owned by private citizens (3), and the accumulation of wealth in the hands of a few people (4) are all characteristic of capitalism, but not socialism. Government plays a role in both systems but not the same role (5). The government is much more involved in economic decisions under socialism.

2. **(3)** Answers (2) through (4) require you to analyze an argument. The best summary of the position the author is taking is (3). Answer (1) goes further than the author, who says only that the government should intervene to regulate a capitalistic system so the wealth doesn't disproportionately go to the rich. Answers (2), (4), and (5) do not accurately reflect the argument the author is making.

3. **(4)** The author uses the fact that the average American worker's salary and benefits are declining while the rich get richer to make her case that the government should intervene to ensure that workers get their fair share of the wealth. The facts in (1) and (2) provide background information but are basically unrelated to the author's position on the role of government. The author agrees with (3), but this statement isn't used to support her main argument that government should intervene in the economy. The author says the gap between rich and poor is widening, not narrowing (5), and uses this fact to support her argument.

U.S. Economic Goals and Policies

The two most important goals of the U.S. government regarding the economy are promoting economic growth and controlling inflation. However, these two goals are often contradictory: promoting growth usually increases inflation, and reining in inflation usually slows economic growth. Generally, the government must decide what the priority is at any given time. To accomplish its economic objectives, the government can use fiscal policy and/or monetary policy.

Fiscal policy refers to government's actions on taxation and spending. To promote economic growth, the government can do the following:

- **Decrease taxes:** Decreasing taxes has the effect of increasing individual incomes, allowing people to buy more products, thus encouraging business profits and expansion, increasing employment, and growing the economy.

- **Increase government spending:** With this option, the government spends more to purchase products like weapons systems and roads or provide services like small business loans and medical care for the poor. Increasing government spending has the same effect of encouraging business profits and expansion, increasing employment, and growing the economy.

However, either decreasing taxes or increasing government spending has the negative effects of encouraging inflation and increasing the budget deficit. The *federal deficit,* the gap between what the government gets in taxes and fees and what it spends, must be covered by borrowing. The fact that the federal government often runs a deficit has increased the national debt to more than $19 trillion today (excluding debt one branch of the U.S. government owes another branch) or about 126 percent of the GDP. Economists are in disagreement over the long-term effects of an ongoing federal deficit.

On the other hand, if the government's main economic goal is to control inflation or reduce the deficit, it can decrease government spending or increase taxes. However, these steps have the negative effect of slowing economic growth.

Monetary policy refers to the ways the government can influence the supply of money and interest rates. An easy-money policy is one that promotes low interest rates that encourage lending. The result is an increase in the supply of money in play in the economy. An easy-money policy promotes economic growth but also encourages inflation and a decline in the value of the dollar. On the other hand, a tight-money policy promotes high interest rates that discourage borrowing, thus reducing the supply of money and slowing economic growth. A tight-money policy slows inflation and increases the value of the dollar.

In the U.S. economy, the money supply is influenced by the Federal Reserve Bank (often called "the Fed"), an independent government agency not directly under the control of either Congress or the president. Its Board of Governors can move interest rates upward by charging banks more to borrow money from the U.S. government. At the time of this writing in 2017, the Federal Reserve Bank was following an easy-money policy with very low interest rates to try to encourage economic growth.

In today's global economy, an increase in the value of the Chinese currency, a loan default by a Western European government, the collapse of a bank in Japan, or a drop in wages in India would all directly affect the U.S. economy. Global economic interdependence means that events far beyond a nation's borders (and generally beyond its control) often influence a nation's potential for economic growth. The power of individual national governments to control their own economies through both fiscal and monetary policies has become more limited.

 **IN THE KNOW**

In economics, any action always has both positive and negative effects. For example, lowering interest rates encourages investment and results in economic growth, but low interest rates also lead to inflation and a decline in the value of the dollar. Even a decline in the value of the dollar has both positive and negative effects: a lower dollar means imports become more expensive for Americans, but U.S. exports increase and spur economic growth (with a lower dollar, American products become cheaper for other countries to buy). Policy-makers always must make guesses as to whether positive effects will outweigh negative effects for any proposed action.

Practice

Questions 1 and 2 refer to the following pie charts and accompanying text:

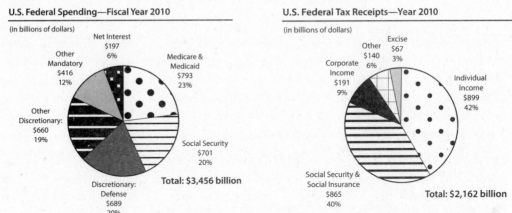

The *federal budget* is a complicated document thousands of pages long. It includes interest payments on the national debt, mandatory spending, and discretionary spending. *Mandatory spending* is spending required by law, including Social Security, Medicare, and veterans benefits. After both interest on the national debt and mandatory spending are paid, everything left is called *discretionary spending.* Discretionary spending includes spending on defense, education, transportation, homeland security, welfare programs, disaster relief, national parks, agricultural subsidies, etc. The programs that receive funding and the amount they get each year is determined by Congress.

1. About how much was the federal deficit in fiscal year 2010?

   (1) $1,294 billion

   (2) $2,162 billion

   (3) $3,456 billion

   (4) $5,618 billion

   (5) Can't be determined from the information given

2. According to the first pie chart, about what percentage of the federal budget involves discretionary spending?

   (1) 19 percent

   (2) 20 percent

   (3) 39 percent

   (4) 45 percent

   (5) 62 percent

3. If Social Security payments were increased without any change in taxes or in other federal spending, which one of the following would be expected as a result?

   (1) Unemployment would increase.

   (2) Prices would move downward.

   (3) Production would increase, and the economy would grow.

   (4) Consumer spending would drop.

   (5) The federal deficit would decline.

Answers

1. **(1)** To compute the federal deficit, you subtract the amount of money the federal government takes in ($2,162 billion) from the amount it spends ($3,256 billion). The federal deficit for fiscal year 2010 was $1,294 billion, or about $1.3 trillion.

2. **(3)** Discretionary spending is what's left after interest on the national debt and mandatory spending is taken out. Programs like Social Security and Medicare involve mandatory spending because these payments to individuals are required by law. Using the pie chart, you would add defense spending and other discretionary spending to get 39 percent.

3. **(3)** Increasing Social Security payments would give more money to seniors and other Social Security recipients. This would increase consumer spending, which would have the effect of encouraging businesses to hire more people to produce more goods and services to meet the increased demand. This would increase production, and the economy would grow. Thus, answers (1) and (4) are incorrect. The increased consumer spending would increase the demand for goods and services and push prices upward rather than downward (2). Increasing government spending without increasing taxes would have the effect of increasing the federal deficit (5). But note that this increase would be offset in part by the increased taxes the government would get from the growth in business profits and from the income taxes generated by higher employment levels.

World History

World history accounts for about 7 or 8 percent of the questions on the Social Studies Test. You can expect 3 or 4 of the 50 questions to be based on world history content.

Similar to the other subjects covered on the Social Studies Test, you aren't required to memorize any dates or facts to ace the questions on world history. Most of the facts you need to know are given in the reading passages or the visuals included with the test questions. The test focuses on your skills in understanding, analyzing, and applying the information presented to you. Still, a good understanding of world history is useful for putting the readings and visuals into their historical context and working through the questions quickly.

The subject area of world history is broad; it covers developments around the world since the beginning of history. It is impossible to provide even a sketchy review of all of the subjects that might appear on the Social Studies Test. Instead, this chapter summarizes a few key developments in world history and offers some GED-style questions that will help prepare you for the types of skill-based questions you will see on the real test.

In This Chapter

- Overviews of important developments in world history
- Sample GED®-style questions to practice the skills on which you'll be tested
- Answers and explanations for all questions

Classical Civilizations

A classical *civilization* is one that endures for a long period of time, develops new social and political institutions, and has a lasting influence on the world. In this section we briefly review five classical civilizations that have changed the world.

 **DEFINITION**

Civilization refers to a society with a relatively high level of cultural and technological development. World history is the study of the rise and fall of civilizations.

Western Civilization (Classical Greece and Rome)

Ancient Greek civilization is regarded as the beginning of western civilization. Greece was divided into many city-states (small countries around a single city) that never united to form a unified country. The most influential city-state was Athens. In the classical period (750–400 B.C.E.), the Greeks, especially the Athenians, valued the individual and had a high regard for the potential of individuals to learn, achieve, and govern themselves. The Greeks sought to develop the person's mind and body; even Greek gods looked like humans and had human personalities. Thus, western civilization places a high value on the worth and freedom of the individual.

The Romans adopted Greek ideas, including the worth of the individual, and built one of the largest and most influential of the world's civilizations. They established control over Italy about 300 B.C.E. and expanded until their empire stretched from Egypt to Britain and included all the lands around the Mediterranean Sea. The Romans brought security and the rule of law that resulted in prosperity across the region. Their roads and sea routes carried trade, and many cities thrived. It was in the Roman Empire that Christianity was born; it spread rapidly and eventually became the official religion of the empire.

The western part of the Roman Empire collapsed as barbarian tribes from the north and east invaded. The fall of Rome (476 C.E.) brought a collapse of security and order, bringing an end to most trade. This was the beginning of the Middle Ages, also called the Dark Ages. However, the eastern part of the Roman Empire survived another thousand years. As Western Europe emerged from the Middle Ages centuries after the fall of Rome, people looked back to classical Greece and Rome for inspiration. This was the Renaissance (French for "rebirth") of western civilization.

The institutions and culture of classical Greece and Rome have deeply influenced not only the culture and institutions of Europe, but also, through the global spread of European culture, the entire modern world. The Greek and Latin (Roman) languages form the basis for many European languages, including English. Our alphabet is the Roman alphabet. The civilization of ancient Greece and Rome has influenced our beliefs, political system, sports (including the Olympics), art, and architecture. Our legal system, science, mathematics, and medicine all have foundations in ancient Greece and Rome.

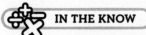

IN THE KNOW

Because there is no set year at which history began, years in history must be dated forward and backward from some arbitrary point in time. That point for Westerners was the birth of Jesus, and this system of numbering years is now used worldwide. For many years, B.C. and A.D. were used in our system of dating events in history. B.C. means Before Christ and A.D. is an abbreviation for *Anno Domini,* a Latin term referring to the birth of Jesus. Today, B.C.E. (Before the Common Era) and C.E. (Common Era) are often used for a more religion-neutral designation of years, although the birth of Jesus is still the point in time used as the basis for numbering years.

Chinese Civilization

China was one of the earliest centers of human civilization. In contrast to the Greco-Roman emphasis on individual worth, Chinese culture developed around the idea of faithfulness to family and society, taught by China's most influential philosopher, Confucius. The first Chinese empire was established in 221 B.C.E., bringing under its control a large area of current-day China and completing the Great Wall of China to protect China's northern frontier from invasion by barbarian tribes. For the next 2,000 years, the Chinese system of government remained basically the same. It is defined by the dynasties (royal families) who ruled China as emperors under what was believed to be a mandate from Heaven.

Under the Han Dynasty (206–220 C.E.), China achieved an advanced civilization, rivaling the achievements, wealth, and power of the Roman Empire, which existed at roughly the same time. In fact, trade routes were opened that connected China and the Roman Empire, bringing silk to Europe and warhorses to China. An efficient government was created for the Chinese Empire, with officials hired on the basis of merit using an objective written test. Trade and commerce flourished, and a money economy was established. Advancements were made in science and mathematics, including the use of negative numbers. Paper was invented, and scholars established the currently used system of Chinese characters for writing.

During this period China created institutions and a culture that have had a lasting influence on China and neighboring Korea, Japan, and the countries of Southeast Asia. To this day, Chinese written characters are called Han characters, and the majority ethnic group of China is called the Han Chinese. Later dynasties borrowed from or built upon the achievements of the Han Dynasty. Although China was conquered several times by less-civilized outsiders from the north and west, the invaders were usually quickly absorbed into Chinese culture and civilization.

Civilization of India

India was also an early center of civilization, the birthplace of both Hinduism, the oldest of the religions of our world today and, later, Buddhism. Through Indian trade, Hinduism and then Buddhism spread from India to Southeast Asia. Buddhism also spread to China, Korea, and Japan.

India was first united under a single empire in the third century B.C.E., but for most of Indian history, India has been divided among a number of smaller states ruled by princes. During the Gupta Empire (320–535 C.E.), much of present-day India and Pakistan were again united. The peace and prosperity created under the Gupta Empire produced a golden age of Indian art, literature, science, and mathematics. During this time, the codes of law that defined the caste system were created. This system defined four castes (priests, warriors, peasants and artisans, and slaves or "untouchables"); people were born into castes and could not change their status.

One of the most influential achievements of the Gupta Empire was its mathematics, including the invention of the decimal system and the number zero. This system spread from India to the Arab Empire in the Middle East to Europe, and today it is used worldwide. In India, the influence of the Gupta Empire today is seen in its art, religions, and the caste system, which, although outlawed, continues to influence modern society.

Arab Civilization

Shortly after the death of Mohammed, the founder of Islam, in 632 C.E., Arab armies swept out of Arabia, quickly conquering the area from Egypt to Persia (Iran). In this area they established the religion of Islam as well as Arab language and culture. By 711, this empire had expanded across North Africa and conquered Spain, further spreading Arab religion and culture. In the east, Muslim armies swept into northern India, bringing Islam to the Indian subcontinent, where it spread to Southeast Asia (Malaysia and Indonesia).

Following this expansion came what is known as the Islamic Golden Age under the Arab Abbasid Dynasty (750–1258). The Arabs learned the art of papermaking from China, and they brought the Gupta decimal numerical system from India. In the great cities of the empire—Baghdad, Damascus, Cairo, and Cordova (Spain)—science and mathematics flourished along with trade and commerce. From here, new ideas in math and science—including the art of making paper and books—spread to medieval Europe. The influence of the Arab empire is seen today in the wide extent of Arab language and culture, which is the dominant language and culture in the area from Morocco to Iraq. Its legacy also is seen in the spread of Islam to this area and beyond.

Mayan Civilization

One of the earliest advanced civilizations in the Americas was the Mayan civilization, whose classical period began around 250 C.E. Centered in Guatemala and the Yucatan Peninsula of Mexico, it is believed to have been a collection of city-states rather than a centralized empire. The Maya developed trade routes and invented a system of writing. Their study of astronomy was more advanced than any other classical civilization, and they created a highly accurate calendar. The Maya built great religious-political centers but are not believed to have built large cities.

Mayan civilization collapsed about 900 for unknown reasons, but its influence can be seen in later civilizations in the region. However, the Spanish, who conquered Mexico and Central America in the 1500s, tried to eradicate the indigenous (native) civilizations. During hundreds of years of colonial rule, they imposed the Spanish language, culture, and religion. Thus, today, the influence of the classical Mayan civilization is not as obvious as the other civilizations discussed in this chapter. However, some traditions and beliefs of Mayan civilization have survived in Mexico and Central America and, in some of the less-modernized areas of this region, the Mayan language is still the spoken language.

Practice

Question 1 refers to the previous sections on classical civilizations.

1. What was one way the civilizations of classical China and classical Greece and Rome differed from each other?

   (1) Greeks and Romans built great cities, but the Chinese did not.

   (2) Chinese civilization was threatened by less-civilized warlike tribes from the north, but Greece and Rome were not.

   (3) Greece and Rome made trade among different regions an important part of their civilization, but China did not.

   (4) Greece and Rome built great stone structures (aqueducts, bridges, and temples), but the Chinese did not.

   (5) They had different ideas about the role of the individual in society.

Question 2 refers to the following photo:

2. Identify the influences of classical civilizations in this photo taken in Times Square in 2011.

    (1) The high-rise architecture was influenced by the towering jungle temples of the Mayan civilization, and the decimal numeric system is from the Greek and Roman civilization.

    (2) The decimal numeric system shown on the sign is from the Chinese Empire of India, and the alphabet is from the Roman Empire.

    (3) The alphabet shown on the sign is from Greek civilization, and the decimal numeric system is from Chinese civilization.

    (4) The decimal numeric system shown on the sign is from the Gupta Empire, and the alphabet is from the Roman Empire.

    (5) The decimal numeric system shown on the sign is from the Arab Empire, and the high-rise architecture is from the Chinese Empire.

Question 3 refers to the following world map:

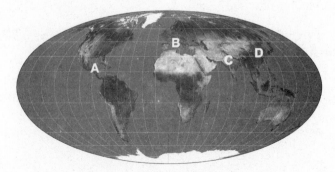

3. Identify the correct location of classical civilizations on the world map.

   (1) A is the Gupta Empire, B is the Roman Empire, and D is China.

   (2) B is the Arab Empire, C is the Gupta Empire, and D is China.

   (3) A is the Mayan civilization, B is the Roman Empire, and D is China.

   (4) A is the Mayan civilization, C is the Arab Empire, and D is the Gupta Empire.

   (5) B is the Roman Empire, C is China, and D is the Gupta Empire.

Answers

1. **(5)** In classical western civilization (Greece and Rome), a high value was accorded the individual, while in classical China, faithfulness to family and society were valued more. Both classical China and classical Greece and Rome built large cities (1) and conducted trade among different regions (3). Both the Roman Empire and the Chinese Empire were threatened by invasion from barbarian tribes to the north (2). China built the Great Wall to keep them out, and, for the same purpose, Rome established garrisons along border rivers (the Rhine and Danube) as well as a wall across Britain. Both civilizations built great structures of stone (4); the Great Wall of China remains the world's largest stone structure.

2. **(4)** The decimal numeric system was invented by mathematicians in the Gupta Empire of India, and the alphabet is the Roman (Latin) alphabet.

3. **(3)** Mayan civilization was based in Guatemala and Mexico (A), the Roman Empire extended around the Mediterranean Sea (B), and the Chinese Empire, of course, was in China (D). Only answer (3) places these in the correct locations. The Gupta Empire was in India (C). The Arab Empire was centered in the Middle East (approximately midway between B and C).

The Global Expansion of Europe

The period from the late 1400s to the middle of the twentieth century was characterized by the spread of western civilization from Europe to all parts of the world. European civilization expanded through trade, *colonization*, and conquest.

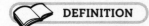 **DEFINITION**

Colonization is the establishment of new settlements (colonies) in a distant land. During the Age of Discovery, European countries established colonies in the new lands they discovered, such as the 13 British colonies that eventually became the United States. The colonies were under the control of the colonizing country (or mother country).

The Age of Discovery

At the end of the Middle Ages, trade and commerce reappeared in Europe as governments became stronger and better able to guarantee security. As Europe began to prosper, the demand grew for products from the Far East, including silk, spices, porcelain, and tea. The Italian city of Venice became wealthy by controlling the final Mediterranean portion of a long overland route across Asia to China, but this route was slow, dangerous, and unreliable. The emerging European nations began looking for an alternative sea route to India, China, and the Indies (today's Indonesia). Thus began the Age of Discovery.

During this period the European nations discovered and colonized "new" lands previously unknown to them, such as North and South America. Europeans also discovered new sea trade routes that allowed them to establish and dominate world trade. For the first time, the world's continents—and economies—were linked by maritime trade. Making this possible were new European scientific advancements in navigation, the construction of better ships, and improvements in European firearms. The Chinese invented gunpowder (which they used for fireworks), but it was the Europeans who developed guns and cannons.

Portugal, one of the first modern nation-states in Europe, led the way. After discovering the sea route from Europe around Africa to Asia, this small European nation on the Atlantic Ocean was able to dominate trade on the Indian Ocean nearly halfway around the world for more than 100 years.

Spain, another of the first modern nations to emerge in Europe, took a bold move to counter Portugal by sending an expedition to reach the Far East by sailing not east but west around the world. When Christopher Columbus reached the Caribbean Islands in 1492, he thought he had reached the Indies. However, before long, Europeans realized Columbus had instead discovered a new continent, which they called the New World. After conquering the New World empires of the Aztecs and the Inca, Spain appropriated vast quantities of gold and silver, making it the wealthiest and most powerful country in the world.

In the 1500s, Spain and Portugal divided the world in half, each taking one side for expansion and, thus, avoiding war. However, in the 1600s Britain, France, and the Netherlands also began overseas expansions, bringing an almost continuous state of war, especially between archrivals Britain and France. Britain and France began by establishing colonies in the Caribbean and North America but later extended their empires around the world.

Changes in the New World

In the 1600s, another source of wealth from overseas colonies developed: the production of crops that couldn't be grown in Europe. Sugar, especially, was in great demand in Europe. It replaced honey as the common sweetener and is the raw material used to make rum, which was widely consumed. To produce sugar cane, Britain, France, and the Netherlands took control of various Caribbean islands while Portugal focused on Brazil.

To provide the labor needed for the sugar-plantation economy, Western Europeans (and their American colonists) forcibly took large numbers of people from West Africa and transported them to the New World as slaves. Slavery also provided workers for tobacco, rice, and cotton plantations. The legacy of slavery includes human suffering, civil wars, and racial tensions. Today the descendants of slaves throughout the Americas often still have less economic and political power than the descendants of slave owners.

The British colonies in North America rebelled against British rule in 1776—the first modern successful rebellion of colonies against their mother country to obtain independence. This inspired Latin American colonies to revolt against Spain. By 1830, most of North and South America was composed of independent nations. However, these rebellions were carried out not by Native Americans but by the descendants of European settlers. Even after independence, the nations of the Americas remained examples of the spread of European civilization and culture.

The Age of Imperialism

During the Age of *Imperialism* (from the mid-1800s until the mid-1900s), European culture and civilization continued to expand around the world. But instead of colonizing newly discovered lands, Europeans focused on conquering the peoples of Africa and Asia.

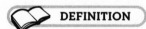 **DEFINITION**

Imperialism involves extending the power of one nation over the land and people of another nation. During the Age of Imperialism, European nations sought to conquer other peoples to form great empires. Some nineteenth-century European empires (such as Russia and Austria-Hungary) controlled neighboring peoples; others (such as Britain and France) extended their empires to include lands around the world.

In spite of the colonial rebellions in the Americas, the European expansion continued, but with the attention shifted to Asia. The British conquered India; the French, Southeast Asia (Indochina); and the Dutch, the East Indies (Indonesia). Russia, Britain, France, and Germany carved out spheres of influence in China; the Chinese emperor remained on the throne but had little power. Finally, in the last half of the 1800s, Europe divided Africa, with Britain and France getting the largest shares but with huge tracts of land also going to Italy, Germany, Portugal, and even tiny Belgium.

After World War II, with Europe in ruins, the worldwide empires of European nations finally began to crumble. India, the largest and most populous of the European colonies, gained independence from Britain (1947) after a nonviolent struggle led by Mahatma Gandhi. In most colonies, independence came fairly peaceably, but in some countries, such as Vietnam, Algeria, and Angola, independence was won only after long, brutal wars against the ruling European country. By 1960, Europe had lost all its major colonies in Asia, and by 1975, Africa also was free from European rule. As a result, the number of nations in the world increased from about 50 in 1945 to about 165 in 1975. Today, only a few small colonies remain, and most of them have chosen this status in free elections.

As a result of the global expansion of Europe from the Age of Discovery to the Age of Imperialism, the influence of western civilization has spread around the world. Europe brought modern technology, government, and education systems to the rest of the world. On the other hand, European expansion subjugated native peoples—killing or enslaving many of them. Paradoxically, it also brought the western ideals of democracy and the rights of individuals. Hundreds of revolutions—some to gain independence and others to simply gain a more democratic government—have been inspired by these western ideals, beginning with the American Revolution in 1776 and continuing today with the 2011 "Arab Spring" in the Middle East and North Africa.

Practice

Question 1 refers to the following map:

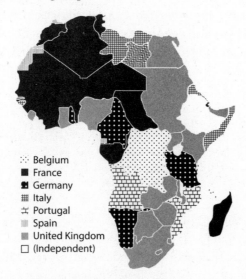

European Empires in Africa, 1914.

1. What statement best summarizes the information shown on this map?

    (1) European domination of Africa was immoral because it violated the principle of self-determination.

    (2) Europeans took African lands to gain access to the slaves they needed in the New World.

    (3) Britain and France got more than their fair share of Africa.

    (4) Belgium controlled the Congo, an area 90 times Belgium's size.

    (5) European countries divided nearly all of Africa and made these regions colonies in their empires.

Question 2 refers to the previous map of Africa and the following text of a United Nations treaty (1966) signed by nearly all the world's nations:

    All people have the right to self-determination. By virtue of that right, they freely determine their political status.

    —International Covenant on Civil and Political Rights

2. Which of the following would be the result of the application of self-determination in Africa?

    (1) The people of each European nation would vote to determine whether or not they wanted to give independence to their colonies in Africa.

    (2) The people of each empire (the mother country and the colonies) would vote to determine whether or not the colonies should be granted independence.

    (3) The people of Africa would vote to choose their status—whether or not they wanted to remain a colony or become an independent country.

    (4) The United Nations would vote to decide what the status of African colonies should be.

    (5) The people of Africa would vote on whether or not they wanted to become members of the United Nations.

Answers

1. **(5)** The map shows the facts of how the Europeans divided Africa. Because only facts are presented, you can eliminate (1) and (3), which contain value judgments about morality and fairness. Nothing on the map makes any reference to slavery (2). In fact, by 1914, the slave trade and slavery had ended; Brazil was the last country to free its slaves (1888). Answer (4) is a true statement, but it refers to only one fact and is not a summary of the whole.

2. **(3)** Self-determination is the right of a people to determine their own future and not have it imposed by a foreign country or people. Answer (3) is what actually happened in most African colonies after World War II. All African colonies chose independence rather than remaining a colony in a European empire, and since 1975, the map of Africa has shown only independent countries. In most cases, independence was granted peaceably, but in a few cases (for example, Algeria and Angola), it was achieved only after a long war with the European country controlling it.

CHAPTER 15

Geography

Geography accounts for 7 or 8 percent of the questions on the Social Studies Test. You can expect 3 or 4 of the 50 questions to be based on maps and other geography content.

Similar to the other subjects covered on the Social Studies Test, you won't be required to memorize any facts or identify specific places on a map to ace the questions on geography. Most of the facts you need to know are given in the reading passages or the visuals included with the test questions. The test focuses on your skills in understanding, analyzing, and applying the information presented to you. Still, a good background in geography is useful in understanding the maps and reading passages, as well as helping you work through the questions quickly.

You already have practiced a basic skill of geography—interpreting maps—in Chapters 11, 12, and 14. But keep in mind that the subject area of geography covers more than maps. Geography also includes topics such as climates, regions, oceans, and the interaction of humans with their environment. Included in this chapter are GED-style geography questions that help prepare you for the types of skill-based questions you'll find on the real test.

In This Chapter

- Overviews of important concepts in geography
- Sample GED®-style questions to practice the skills on which you'll be tested
- Answers and explanations for all questions

Basic Concepts of Geography

Physical geography involves the study of physical features of the world, like glaciers, oceans, rivers, and landmasses, and includes the study of natural systems like climates and ocean currents. Physical geography focuses on the natural environment of Earth, rather than the cultural or "built environment" of human geography.

Human geography is the study of human interaction with the environment. Topics of human geography include population, economic development, land usage, urbanization, agricultural development, and cultural change. Human geography overlaps with other social sciences, while physical geography overlaps with the natural sciences—however, in the study of geography, the emphasis is on the spatial dimension.

A central concept of geography is *location*. A standard system of identifying location on Earth has been developed using latitude and longitude. Latitude is based on imaginary east-west parallel lines wrapping around the earth parallel to the equator. Longitude refers to imaginary north-south lines that intersect at the north and south poles. The equator, a line around the earth equidistant from the north and south poles, is latitude 0°; the north pole is 90° north, and the south pole is 90° south. The prime meridian is longitude 0°, an arbitrary line near London drawn through the site of what was once one of the world's leading observatories. Longitudinal lines are numbered in degrees east and west from the prime meridian. All places on Earth can be located by their coordinates, their degrees north or south of the equator and their degrees east and west of the prime meridian. Washington, D.C., for example, is 38.9072° N, 77.0369° W.

Another central concept of geography is *region*. Identifying, defining, and understanding regions are basic to both physical and human geography. Physical geography focuses on natural regions (for example, the Amazon Basin, the Gobi Desert, or the continent of Australia), while human geography looks at man-made regions. These can be well-defined regions with marked borders, like the country of Spain, or regions that are not well demarcated, like the French-speaking region of Belgium. They also can be functional regions, like the regional management structure of a large corporation or the different interrelated systems of a metropolitan area. They even can be perceptual regions with only vague borders, like the Bible Belt or an ethnic neighborhood in a city.

Maps are a common tool geographers use to provide information. Maps can show physical features and/or man-made features. Maps usually include a scale that relates the size of the map to the size of the actual area shown on the map, depicted as an equation (1 inch = 100 miles) or a ratio (1:100,000). Most maps also include a key or legend that explains the markings on the map. However, one problem with maps, especially those showing a large region or the entire world, is distortion. Any projection of the curved surface of Earth onto a flat map is not entirely accurate. To combat this, geographers have developed a number of different methods for projecting the curved surface of Earth onto a flat map.

 **GOOD IDEA**

When taking the GED, you won't have to locate places like Nebraska or Paris on a map, but you might be required to recognize the continents. The question won't focus on simply naming continents, but this knowledge could be a basic requirement to interpreting information on a map. It's also a good idea to know on which continents major countries like India, Brazil, China, Australia, and Canada are located.

Practice

Question 1 refers to the following two world maps:

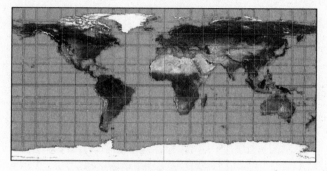

World Map A: Equirectangular projection.

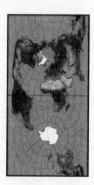

World Map B: Cassini projection.

1. Which statement correctly describes the two maps?

    (1) Map A shows an accurate view of the world while Map B distorts reality.

    (2) Map B shows an accurate view of the world while Map A distorts reality.

    (3) Map A would be of greater use to a pilot trying to fly from Alaska to Europe than Map B.

    (4) Both maps distort the size, shape, and location of the continents.

    (5) Map B provides a less-accurate view of the shape of Antarctica than Map A.

Question 2 refers to the following table:

The World's Largest Deserts*

Desert	Location	Size (Square Miles)	Selected Facts
Antarctic	The continent of Antarctica	5.4 million	With average annual precipitation of only 2 to 8 inches, Antarctica is the world's driest continent; paradoxically, it contains most of the world's supply of fresh water.
Sahara	Northern Africa	3.3 million	Most of the Sahara, where the world's hottest temperature has been recorded, gets less than 1 inch of rainfall annually, but its Nile River Valley is lush and green year-round.
Arabian	Arabian Peninsula	900,000	Although the Arabian Desert is one of the hottest and driest areas of the planet, oases (sites naturally supplied with underground water) make it an important producer of dates.
Gobi	China and Mongolia	500,000	Snowfall accounts for most of the precipitation in the Gobi Desert, where temperatures can drop to −40°F in the winter.
Kalahari	Southern Africa	300,000	Although it only gets 3 to 7.5 inches of rainfall annually, areas of the Kalahari support an abundance of desert plants and wildlife.

Deserts are areas that get less than 10 inches of annual precipitation (rain, snow, hail).

2. Which statement provides the best general conclusion that can be made from the table as a whole?

   (1) Deserts are always sparsely populated areas.

   (2) Deserts around the world look about the same.

   (3) Most of the world's deserts are in Africa.

   (4) Not all deserts have the same climate.

   (5) South America doesn't have any deserts.

Answers

1. **(4)** Any projection of the world's curved surface onto a flat map distorts the size and shape of the continents. In this case, the amount of distortion on the two maps happens to be the same because both use the same method of projection. The only difference is that the equirectangular projection is centered on the equator (which runs horizontally across the center of the map), while the Cassini projection centers on the prime meridian (which runs vertically through the center of the map). Both are equally accurate and correct, even though Map A looks more like the world maps we are used to. Because the earth is a ball in space, there is no fixed up or down or direction it must be put in. The equirectangular projection shows the area around the equator more accurately but distorts the polar regions, while the Cassini projection does the opposite. Thus, Map B would be of greater use to a pilot flying across the polar region (3) and also provides a better view of Antarctica (5).

2. **(4)** You can conclude from the table that not all deserts have the same climate; in fact, the difference in climate between Antarctica, the coldest continent, and the Sahara, where the world's hottest temperatures have been recorded, is stunning. This contrast makes answer (2) incorrect. The table does not have information on population density, so it would not be logical to draw the conclusion that deserts are sparsely populated (1) based on this table. In fact, some areas of deserts, like the Nile River Valley, are among the most densely populated areas of the world. The table has information about five deserts (two of which are in Africa), but not about *most* of the world's deserts (3), so it is impossible to make conclusions about most deserts from this table. Similarly, the fact the table has no information about deserts in South America (5) does not mean they do not exist; they are simply not among the five largest deserts.

HEADS-UP!

Be careful whenever a question asks for the "best" answer or conclusion. This is
a dead giveaway that you need to read all answer choices and use the process of
elimination to compare choices. Throw out all the "worst" choices until you have only
the "best" left.

World Population

The study of population is an important branch of human geography called *demography*. One
important topic in this field is population growth. Demographers study population statistics
(along with economic development, government policies, societal norms, and cultural values) to
understand population growth and predict what will happen in individual cities, countries, and
on the planet as a whole. This topic is one of many geography topics that could appear on the
test.

In 1800, the world's population was 1 billion; by 1927, it had reached 2 billion; by 1974, it was
4 billion; and in 2017, it reached 7.5 billion. This increase has been caused not by an increase
in birth rates (which have actually declined during this period), but by a marked decrease in
death rates, especially infant mortality rates. In the early 1800s, British scholar Thomas Robert
Malthus posited that human population would grow faster than technology could increase Earth's
carrying capacity (the number of people Earth can support on a sustainable basis). Whether this
will ultimately prove true and lead to overpopulation—along with economic and environmental
disaster—remains an unanswered question.

There's a direct relationship between economic development and fertility rates (the number of
children, on the average, a woman has during her lifetime). As nations develop economically,
generally their fertility rates decline. The reasons for this include decreased infant mortality,
greater economic security, and a better-educated public. Countries with rapidly developing
economies have seen large declines in fertility rates in recent years. For example, in Brazil, where
the standard of living has risen significantly, the fertility rate declined from 6.2 in 1950 to 1.76 in
2016.

In some of the world's advanced industrial economies, fertility rates are now below the replacement level (the level needed for zero population growth). As a result, the populations of Japan, Russia, and Germany are declining. Due to falling fertility rates, Western Europe, Japan, and, to a lesser degree, the United States face a new and different kind of population problem: a large aging population that must be supported by a decreasing number of younger workers. In the United States, the fertility rate as of 2015 (1.84 children per woman) is near the replacement level, but population growth continues due to emigration from other countries.

In any given period, a nation's population growth can be expressed as follows:

$$\text{Population growth} = \text{births} - \text{deaths} + \text{immigrants} - \text{emigrants}$$

Along with population growth, geographers study *population density*. Seventy-five percent of the world's population lives on only 5 percent of the earth's surface. Most of the growth in the world's population is occurring in places where people are already thickly settled. Large cities, especially those in Asia, Africa, and Latin America, are getting much larger as a result of both natural population growth and migration from rural areas. The planet's human settlement pattern in the twenty-first century will be characterized by a growing number of densely populated cities, many with more than 10, or even 20, million people.

 **DEFINITION**

Population density (the average number of people per square mile or square kilometer) is used to describe how thickly settled a region is. Singapore, a small island nation in Southeast Asia, has a population density of 18,645 people per square mile, while Mongolia, composed mostly of the Gobi Desert, has a population density of fewer than 3 people per square mile.

Practice

Questions 1 and 2 refer to the following line graphs:

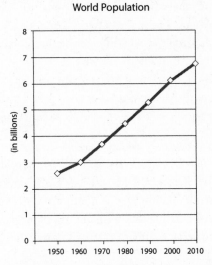

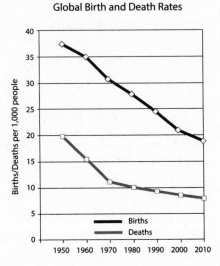

1. Which one of the following trends is *not* consistent with the information shown on the graphs?

   (1) The world population is increasing.

   (2) The global birth rate is falling.

   (3) The global death rate is falling.

   (4) The global birth rate is higher than the global death rate.

   (5) The world population is increasing at a faster rate today than it was 20 years ago.

2. What best explains the cause of the rapid growth in the world's population even though the birth rate is falling?

   (1) Both a falling death and a falling birth rate have the effect of causing the world's population to grow.

   (2) As long as the birth rate is above zero, the world's population will grow.

   (3) Seventy-five percent of the world's people live on 5 percent of the earth's surface.

   (4) A birth rate higher than the death rate causes world population to grow.

   (5) Immigration can cause the population of a country to grow even though its birth rate is low.

Questions 3 and 4 refer to the following passage:

Population Density and the Rise of Early Civilizations

For civilization to arise, a certain population density needed to be reached. Roaming tribes of hunters and gatherers or even scattered agricultural villages did not have the critical mass necessary to develop an advanced civilization. That critical mass was achieved through irrigation.

The agricultural surplus produced by the irrigation of crops made population growth possible and allowed many workers to specialize in jobs other than growing food. Cities came into existence, filled with craftsmen, merchants and traders, construction workers, and religious and governmental officials, etc.

In the valley of the Tigris and Euphrates, the Sumerians are usually credited with creating the earliest civilization about 5,000 years ago. Besides extensive irrigation systems, they developed the first system of writing, the earliest cities, the calendar (on which ours today is based), and the first written code of law. Other locations where the development of irrigation led to the rise of early civilizations were the Nile River Valley in Egypt, the Yellow River in China, and the Indus River Valley in Pakistan.

3. Which statement best states the main idea of the passage?

(1) Early civilizations developed along rivers, which served as a source of irrigation water and a highway for trade.

(2) The rise of civilization about 5,000 years ago is a relatively recent event in the time span of human existence.

(3) Early civilizations developed in the valley of the Tigris and Euphrates and in the valleys of the Nile, Indus, and Yellow Rivers.

(4) The birth of agriculture led to the development of civilization.

(5) Irrigation produced the population growth and population density needed for civilization to develop.

4. An implication is something not stated that can be reasonably concluded from what is stated. The author of the passage implies that:

   (1) The development of irrigation systems is related to the development of civilizations.

   (2) The rivers along which early civilization developed provided the source of water for irrigation systems.

   (3) Irrigation produced the population density needed for civilization to develop.

   (4) The Sumerians were the first to develop civilization because they had two rivers in their valley (the Tigris and Euphrates).

   (5) An agricultural surplus allows some people to do jobs other than raising food.

Answers

1. **(5)** No evidence in the graphs shows that world population is growing at a faster rate today than 20 years ago. The growth rate has not changed much since 1960. If anything, the growth rate has started to level off a bit. All other answer choices state trends shown in the graphs.

2. **(4)** World population growth is caused by the fact that the world's birth rate is higher than its death rate. Be careful with questions that ask for a cause. Just because the birth rate is falling while population is increasing doesn't mean there's a causal relationship between the two trends. A falling birth rate has the effect of reducing population growth, making answer (1) incorrect. In this case, that downward pressure on population growth is offset by a falling death rate, which is keeping the gap between the birth rate and the death rate about the same. It's impossible for a birth rate near zero (meaning almost no births) to produce population growth unless, somehow, death has been eliminated (2). Answer (3) is a correct factual statement, but one that does not explain why the world's population is increasing. Immigration (5) plays a role in an individual country's population growth rate but not in the global growth rate because there is no immigration from outer space to Earth.

3. **(5)** The last answer best describes the main idea of the passage. You can eliminate (1) and (2) because these introduce new ideas (the time span of human existence and trade) not covered in the passage. Answer (3) is true but simply restates examples from the last paragraph and misses the main point—the relationship between irrigation, population density, and civilization. Although it's true that the birth of agriculture (4) was a prerequisite to the development of irrigation and, thus, also an important step in the rise of civilization, this passage doesn't mention that.

4. **(2)** All these early civilizations with irrigation systems probably didn't just happen to arise alongside rivers. The rivers, the author implies, were the source of water for the irrigation system of each civilization. An implication is something not stated, so eliminate all the statements that *are* explicitly stated in the passage. This includes (1), (3), and (5), which were explicitly stated in different wording. Answer (4) doesn't seem to be something the author is implying because there's no development of—or apparent reason for—the idea that two rivers are better than one.

Social Studies Practice Test

Taking a practice test is the most important part of your GED® test preparation plan. The practice test in this chapter allows you to review the content and skills you'll be tested on; become more familiar with the type of questions you'll encounter; and most importantly, practice test-taking strategies, including pacing. Taking a practice test also helps you build confidence and control your stress.

No matter how much you've studied and reviewed, you can expect that some of the content presented on the Social Studies Test will be new to you. Therefore, some of the questions on this practice test are based on new content rather than the material you reviewed in the five preceding chapters. Don't worry—most of what you need to know to answer each question is given. You only need to demonstrate your ability to work with the information using the skills you've been practicing.

The actual Social Studies Test contains 50 questions, and you have 70 minutes to complete it. The practice test contains 25 questions, so you should give yourself 35 minutes to complete it. Although this practice test is only half the length of the actual test, it contains the same mix of question types, subject areas, and skills tested that you'll encounter on the real test.

If, after taking the test provided here, you feel you need more practice and want to take another simulated test, several websites offer free GED practice tests. One site we recommend is PBS Literacy Link (litlink.ket.org), which offers two free half-length practice Social Studies Tests.

Instructions

The Social Studies Test is designed to measure your understanding of general social studies skills and concepts. Each question is based on a short reading or on a map, table, cartoon, graph, or photo. Use the information provided to answer the question(s) that follow. You can refer to the information as often as you want when answering the question(s).

You have 35 minutes to complete the 25 questions on this practice test. Work carefully, but don't spend too much time on any one question. If you're having trouble with a question, make the best guess you can and move on. Your score is based on the number of correct answers; there is no penalty for guessing.

When taking the practice test, try to simulate actual test conditions. Get a timing device of some sort and a couple No. 2 pencils with good erasers. Go to a place where you won't be interrupted, and follow test instructions. Start the timer after you've read the instructions and are ready to proceed to the first question.

Go on to the next page when you are ready to begin.

Question 1 refers to the following passage:

The development of trade was an important factor that helped advance and spread early civilizations. Besides providing products a region may not have access to itself, trade allows regions to specialize in products they can produce best, thus increasing overall production.

Minoan civilization, centered in Crete, was the earliest civilization based on trade rather than agriculture. Unlike other early civilizations, the Minoans did not have an agricultural surplus produced by irrigation. Instead, Minoan cities were supported by trade conducted by ships that carried cargo on the Mediterranean Sea.

1. The author of this passage implies that:

    (1) Minoans developed wine-making rather than the production of food crops.

    (2) Trade allows countries to specialize in the products they can produce best.

    (3) Minoans did not eat as well as other early civilizations.

    (4) Trade allows countries to obtain products they otherwise would not have access to.

    (5) Minoans obtained at least some of their food from trade rather than growing it all themselves.

Questions 2 and 3 refer to the following political cartoon:

Courtesy of William S. Wiist.

2. What assumption is the cartoonist making?

   (1) Readers already know the elephant stands for the president and the donkey for Congress.

   (2) Readers already know the elephant stands for the Republican Party and the donkey for the Democratic Party.

   (3) Readers already know the economy is sinking.

   (4) Readers already know the human hand stands for the economy.

   (5) Readers already know the water stands for the Potomac River.

3. What is the main point the cartoonist is trying to make?

   (1) Republicans and Democrats are working together to help the economy.

   (2) Elections determine which party—Democratic or Republican—decides how to rescue the economy.

   (3) Republicans and Democrats are fighting with each other for political advantage rather than working together to help the economy.

   (4) The political process in a democracy is at its best when the two parties keep each other in check.

   (5) A third party should arise to save the economy while the Democrats and Republicans bicker.

Question 4 refers to the following passage from the U.S. Declaration of Independence:

> We, therefore, the Representatives of the United States of America, in General Congress Assembled, appealing to the Supreme Judge of the world for the rectitude of our intentions, do, in the Name, and by Authority of the good People of these Colonies, solemnly publish and declare that these United Colonies are, and of Right ought to be Free and Independent States ….

4. Based on this passage, what value did the authors of the Declaration share?

   (1) A desire to maintain peace

   (2) A belief in inalienable rights

   (3) A belief in Christianity

   (4) A belief in national self-determination

   (5) A desire to be loyal to authority

Question 5 refers to the following paragraph:

> According to the economic law of supply and demand, prices fluctuate based on supply and demand. The price of a good or service goes up if demand is greater than supply. Or if supply is greater than demand, the price goes down.

5. According to the economics of supply and demand, what is most likely to happen if the Brazilian soybean crop is one of the best ever?

    (1) The demand for soybeans will fall in Brazil.

    (2) Brazilian farmers will earn more money.

    (3) Brazilian farmers will earn less money.

    (4) The price of soybeans will go down in Brazil.

    (5) Demand for soybeans will grow as the world's population grows.

Question 6 refers to the following photo:

A Roman temple built 1,800 years ago in Heliopolis, a city located in Asia a short distance inland from the eastern shore of the Mediterranean Sea (present-day Lebanon).

6. Which statement can be rejected using evidence in the photo?

    (1) Romans were master builders of great public buildings.

    (2) The Romans built great buildings only in and around their capital of Rome.

    (3) Roman influence and control spread to all the lands around the Mediterranean Sea.

    (4) The Romans honored their gods by building large temples.

    (5) Heliopolis was an important religious center in Roman times.

Question 7 refers to the following graph:

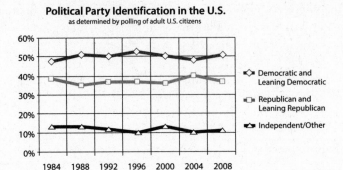

Political Party Identification in the U.S.
as determined by polling of adult U.S. citizens

7. Which conclusion is supported by information presented in the graph?

(1) Most independents usually vote for Republican candidates, giving Democrats and Republicans about an equal chance of winning.

(2) The breakdown of Americans who identify with each political party did not change much between 1984 and 2008.

(3) Independents comprise less than 10 percent of American voters.

(4) The Democratic Party is about the same size as the Republican Party.

(5) The U.S. political system is characterized by three main parties.

Questions 8 and 9 refer to the following paragraph and table:

It is difficult to compare how well off the people in one country are compared to the people in another. One simple way of making a rough comparison is by using gross domestic product (GDP) per capita. GDP is the value of all the goods and services produced in a country in 1 year. However, GDP by itself doesn't tell us how well off individuals in a country are because some countries have large populations and others do not. Per capita GDP divides the GDP by the number of people in the country to arrive at an average GDP per person.

GDPs of Selected Countries (2010)

Country	GDP (in US$)	Rank	GDP per Capita (in US$)	Rank
United States	$14.5 trillion	1	$46,860	10
China	$5.9 trillion	2	$4,382	91
Germany	$3.2 trillion	4	$40,274	19
Brazil	$2.1 trillion	7	$10,816	54
India	$1.6 trillion	9	$1,371	133
Russia	$1.5 trillion	11	$10,856	57
Australia	$1.2 trillion	13	$55,672	7
Mexico	$1.0 trillion	14	$9,522	61
Switzerland	$500 billion	19	$67,779	4
Norway	$400 billion	25	$84,144	2

8. In which countries shown in the table are the people on average better off economically than Americans?

   (1) China

   (2) Norway

   (3) Norway and Switzerland

   (4) Norway, Switzerland, and Australia

   (5) No countries; the United States is highest

9. What is the best explanation why India has the world's ninth-biggest economy but ranks so low in how well off its people are?

   (1) India's people are not well educated.

   (2) India has a lot of people.

   (3) Wages are very low in India.

   (4) Workers put in long hours without overtime pay.

   (5) The table doesn't give this information.

Questions 10 and 11 refer to the following passage:

Napoleon, emperor of France (1804–1814), and Hitler, dictator of Germany (1934–1945), both led their countries in wartime to conquer nearly all of Europe. But neither was able to end British naval dominance or completely defeat the Russian army. Both Hitler and Napoleon made the mistake of invading Russia. Although they won victories and reached or occupied Moscow, both lost most of their armies due to the vicious fighting and harsh Russian winter. Napoleon was finally defeated in 1815 and exiled to a remote Atlantic island where he died. Hitler committed suicide in 1945 as the Russian army entered Berlin.

Napoleon is honored in France and regarded everywhere as one of the world's great political and military leaders, but Hitler is almost universally associated with absolute evil. Hitler is known for the Holocaust, the mass murder of 11 to 14 million people, including two thirds of Europe's Jews as well as large numbers of Poles, political opponents, homosexuals, and others. Napoleon, on the other hand, is honored both for his military genius and helping lead Europe into the modern age. He freed serfs; spread the idea of nationalism; and established a fair, written code of law (the Napoleonic Code), which still forms the basic law for about a quarter of the world's nations.

10. What major contrast between Hitler and Napoleon is made in the passage?

    (1) One succeeded in conquering Europe while the other did not.

    (2) One was a dictator; the other, an emperor.

    (3) One is regarded as a hero and the other as one of the world's most evil villains.

    (4) One committed suicide, and the other died of natural causes.

    (5) One was able to defeat the British navy; the other was not.

11. According to the passage, what was a major cause of both Napoleon's and Hitler's eventual downfalls?

    (1) Neither Hitler nor Napoleon was well educated.

    (2) They were both excellent military strategists.

    (3) Both Hitler and Napoleon wanted to end British naval dominance.

    (4) Both Hitler and Napoleon had absolute power in their countries.

    (5) Both Hitler and Napoleon decided to invade Russia.

Questions 12 and 13 refer to the following paragraph and map:

Presidents in the United States are not chosen directly by a vote of the people but by an electoral vote system. The number of electoral votes each state gets to cast is equal to the total number of representatives and senators it is allocated in Congress. The more populous states get more electoral votes because the number of representatives a state has in the House of Representatives depends on the state's population. Generally, a state's electoral votes all go to the candidate who wins the popular vote in that state. If a candidate wins more than half of the electoral vote, that candidate becomes president. If no candidate gets a majority of the electoral votes, the president is chosen by the House of Representatives.

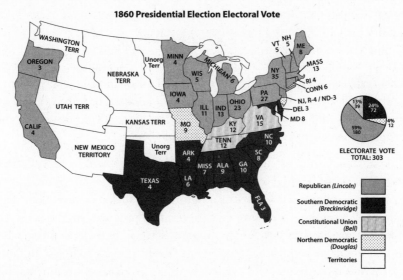

12. Which factor best explains why Lincoln won the presidency in 1860?

(1) Lincoln carried more than half of the 33 states.

(2) More than half the people voted for Lincoln.

(3) Lincoln won a majority of the electoral vote.

(4) Lincoln carried the Northern states that stayed in the Union.

(5) The states that didn't vote for Lincoln weren't united and divided their electoral votes among three other candidates.

13. Which of the following states an assumption that can be accurately made based on the information presented earlier?

    (1) Both states and territories participated in presidential elections.

    (2) According to the most recent official U.S. census of the day, more people lived in Vermont than in California.

    (3) Many states split their electoral votes to represent the voting pattern in their state.

    (4) The Civil War could have been avoided if the Southern states had been given more electoral votes.

    (5) The West was the key to Abraham Lincoln's victory.

Questions 14 and 15 refer to the following passage:

Vertical farming could revolutionize our concept of where food should be grown. Soon a farm inside an abandoned eight-story office building in Manchester, England, will join vertical farms already operating in Kyoto, Seoul, Chicago, and Seattle. The produce market at street level will be filled with lettuce, tomatoes, strawberries, and other fruits and vegetables grown year-round on the floors above.

While organic farming strives to take agriculture backward in time, vertical farming attempts to adapt farming to the modern urbanized world. Crops are grown in a nutrient-rich solution under artificial lighting in a sealed environment that requires no pesticides. Using these methods, vertical farming produces six times the yield as the same crops grown outdoors. Furthermore, while half of fruits and vegetables grown outdoors are never eaten (due to droughts, floods, insects, spoilage, shipping damage, etc.), there is no such loss with vertical farming. From an environmental perspective, vertical farming ends the toxic runoff of pesticides and fertilizers, eliminates transportation costs and pollution, reduces pressure on world water supplies, and slows deforestation. Increasingly, vertical farming is being viewed as part of the solution for feeding the planet's growing population.

14. Which statement best states the main point of the passage?

(1) An alternative is needed to organic farming, which takes agriculture backward in time.

(2) Vertical farming causes less harm to the environment than our current system of growing fruits and vegetables.

(3) Vertical farming provides fresher fruits and vegetables to urban residents than organic farming.

(4) Vertical farming can efficiently provide fresh fruits and vegetables to urban residents while reducing damage to the environment.

(5) Traditional farming in outdoor fields should be cut back or stopped.

15. Which of the following is an effect of vertical farming?

(1) Increased use of pesticides

(2) Fresher fruits and vegetables year-round in cities

(3) Increased transportation costs

(4) Lower yields than when food is grown using natural sunlight

(5) Increased water pollution

Question 16 refers to the following table:

Education and Participation in Presidential Elections

	Percentage of Voting-Age Population Reporting That They Voted		
School Years Completed	**2000**	**2004**	**2008**
8 or fewer years	26.8	23.6	23.4
Some high school but no diploma	33.6	34.6	33.7
High school graduate or GED	49.4	52.4	50.9
Some college or Associate's degree	60.3	66.1	65.0
College Bachelor's or advanced degree	72.0	74.2	73.3

16. What conclusion can clearly be drawn from the data in the table?

(1) The more education a person has, the more likely the person is to vote in a U.S. presidential election.

(2) Most voters in U.S. presidential elections have some college or a college degree.

(3) More people with college degrees are voting in U.S. presidential elections than people with only high school (or GED) diplomas are voting.

(4) People who have more education are smarter and better able to get involved in democratic government.

(5) People with less education shouldn't vote because they are less likely to understand the candidates and issues.

Questions 17 and 18 refer to the following map:

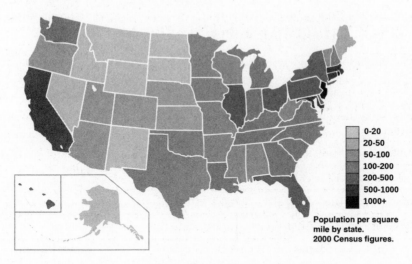

U.S. population density.

17. Based on the information in the map, which statement most accurately compares the Western states with the Eastern states?

    (1) The states with the largest populations are in the East while the states with the smallest populations are in the West.

    (2) The Western states generally have a lower population density than the Eastern states.

    (3) States that cover a large area have lower population densities than states that cover a small area.

    (4) Western states are generally larger in territory and have larger populations than the Eastern states.

    (5) Except for California, the Western states have higher population densities than the Eastern states.

18. What is the best explanation why Texas ranks second in population, but 25 states have a higher population density?

    (1) Many people in Texas are illegal aliens and not counted in the census.

    (2) Many people in Texas have moved there from other states.

    (3) Texas is one of the largest states in land area.

    (4) Texas's cities are spread out without a high population density.

    (5) Population density is lower in farming states than in urbanized states.

Questions 19 and 20 refer to the following paragraph:

Following the Supreme Court's ruling in *Brown* v. *Board of Education* (1954), 96 congressmen from the South signed the following declaration:

We regard the decision of the Supreme Court in the school cases as clear abuse of judicial power. It climaxes a trend in the Federal judiciary undertaking to legislate, in derogation of the authority of Congress, and to encroach upon the reserved rights of the states and the people. The original Constitution does not mention education. Neither does the Fourteenth Amendment nor any other amendment. The debates preceding the submission of the Fourteenth Amendment clearly show that there was no intent that it should affect the systems of education maintained by the states.

19. Which statement correctly states the main point of the argument made by the 96 congressmen?

    (1) The racial integration of schools is not required by the Constitution.

    (2) States should disobey the Supreme Court decision because it violates the Constitution.

    (3) The Fourteenth Amendment should be repealed.

    (4) The federal government does not have the power to get involved in education, which is a matter the Constitution leaves to the states.

    (5) State governments should not encroach on the authority of Congress to make laws regarding education.

20. Applying this argument to today's issues, which one of the following measures would this argument support?

    (1) Increasing federal loans to college students

    (2) Reduction of the federal deficit

    (3) Passage of a law by Congress to reform the health-care delivery system in the United States

    (4) Strengthening federal laws regarding pollution

    (5) The elimination of the federal Department of Education

Questions 21 and 22 refer to the following passage and bar graph:

Imports are goods and services purchased from other countries, and exports are goods and services sold to other countries. Together imports and exports constitute international trade. The balance of trade shows the net effect of imports and exports on a country's economy.

Balance of trade = exports − imports (computed for a 1-year period)

If the balance of trade is favorable (a positive number), a country has balance of trade surplus. If the balance of trade is unfavorable (a negative number), the country has a balance of trade deficit. A country with a balance of trade surplus accumulates foreign currency, which it can keep in reserve, loan to other countries, or invest in other countries. A country with a balance of trade deficit usually must borrow money from other countries to finance its deficit.

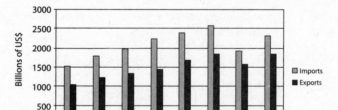

U.S. International Trade, 2003-2010

21. Which statement is best supported by the evidence in the graph?

(1) The United States had a balance of trade surplus in all years shown in the graph.

(2) With the recession in 2009, the U.S. balance of trade deficit increased.

(3) U.S. international trade increased every year between 2003 and 2010.

(4) For the time period shown in the graph, the balance of trade deficit was the smallest in 2009.

(5) Imports and exports were in balance in 2003.

22. Adding together all countries' imports and all countries' exports, which statement best describes the global balance of trade?

(1) The global balance of trade is always zero (neither a surplus nor a deficit).

(2) The global balance of trade is the total value of all countries' imports and exports added together.

(3) There generally would be a global balance of trade deficit.

(4) There generally would be a global balance of trade surplus.

(5) The global balance of trade cannot be determined.

Questions 23 and 24 refer to the following political cartoon published in 1778 by a British newspaper during the American Revolution:

THE HORSE AMERICA, throwing his Master.

23. In the cartoon, who or what does the rider of the horse stand for?

(1) The 13 colonies in rebellion against the British king

(2) George Washington

(3) The British government

(4) The Americans as a whole

(5) The Continental Congress

24. Which of the following is a statement of fact rather than an opinion or value judgment?

    (1) America is like an unruly horse that doesn't obey its master and needs to be disciplined.

    (2) The British army found it difficult to subdue the American colonies and end the rebellion.

    (3) The British government should have given the colonies more freedom.

    (4) The American colonies were rebelling against an unjust British government that denied them their rights.

    (5) King George V was not a good ruler.

Question 25 refers to the following passage from Article I of the U.S. Constitution:

Section 1: All legislative powers herein granted shall be vested in a Congress of the United States, which shall consist of a Senate and House of Representatives.

Section 2: The House of Representatives shall be composed of members chosen every second year by the people of the several States ….

Section 3: The Senate of the United States shall be composed of two Senators from each state, chosen by the legislature thereof for six years ….

25. Which statement is not consistent with Article I of the U.S. Constitution?

    (1) Representatives and senators are to be chosen by the people of each state.

    (2) Representatives are elected for 2 years and senators for 6 years.

    (3) There are to be two senators from each state.

    (4) Law-making authority is given to Congress.

    (5) There are to be two chambers of Congress.

Answers and Explanations

1. **(5)** Something implied is something not specifically stated but strongly suggested by what the author does state. Because the author says Minoan civilization was based on trade rather than agriculture, the implication is that at least some of their food was obtained through trade. The author doesn't imply anything about wine-making (1) because it was a subject not addressed in the passage. Answers (2) and (4) are specifically stated rather than implied. The author doesn't seem to be suggesting that the Minoans

didn't eat well (3); in fact, because of their trade, they may have had access to more different types of foods than other early civilizations.

2. (**2**) The cartoonist assumes readers know that the elephant and donkey stand for the Democratic and Republican parties. The parties are pulling in opposite directions rather than working together (1). The cartoonist explains answers (3) and (4) in the cartoon rather than assuming readers already know this. The water does not stand for any particular body of water (5).

3. (**3**) Answers (1) and (4) state viewpoints contrary to the cartoonist's opinion. The cartoon doesn't contain anything about a third party (5) or elections (2).

4. (**4**) A value is a deeply held belief that forms part of the basis for a person's views and outlook. All the authors shared and were motivated by a strong belief in national self-determination, the idea that people have the right to determine their own system of government rather than having it imposed by an outside power. By signing the Declaration of Independence, the authors knew they were disloyal to the established authority (5) and taking an action that would lead to war, not peace (1). This passage mentions nothing about Christianity (3) or inalienable rights (2).

5. (**4**) The supply of soybeans increases (while demand stays the same) so the price goes down. Then, at the lower price, there is *increased* demand for soybeans (1). There is not enough information to determine if Brazilian farmers will earn more (2) or less (3) money. That depends on how much the price falls. Answer (5) is true, but not a result of the size of the Brazilian soybean crop.

6. (**2**) The temple in Asia shown in the photo provides evidence that the Romans built great buildings well beyond Rome, so answer (2) can be rejected. The temple in the photo provides evidence that helps support all the other statements.

7. (**2**) The graph provides supporting evidence for the statement that the breakdown of Americans by political party did not change much. The graph doesn't give any information about how independents voted in any of these years (1). The Democratic and Republican parties are competitive despite the larger numbers of Democrats because the groups that tend to identify with the Democratic Party are groups that also tend to have lower-than-average voter turnout. Independents comprise 10 to 13 percent of the American public (3), and the Democratic Party is larger than the Republican Party (4). The United States is characterized by a two-party system (5); independents are people who do not identify with either of these two parties.

8. (**4**) According to the data, per capita GDP is higher in Norway, Switzerland, and Australia than in the United States.

9. **(2)** India produces a large number of goods and services (GDP), but with nearly 1 billion people, the average amount of goods and services per person (per capita GDP) is relatively small. Wages (3) have no influence on GDP, which only measures the value of goods and services produced. People who work long hours (4) and people with a good education (1) tend to produce more goods and services, thereby increasing GDP, but these factors play no role in explaining the gap between the ranking of India's GDP and the ranking of its per capita GDP.

10. **(3)** The reading paints a vivid contrast between how Hitler and Napoleon are regarded today. Both succeeded in conquering most of Europe (1), yet neither succeeded in conquering Britain (5). It is true that Hitler was a dictator and Napoleon an emperor (2), but there is little difference between these titles so this is actually as much a similarity as a contrast. Hitler committed suicide, but the reading doesn't provide enough information to make the contrast stated in choice (4). Some believe Napoleon had stomach cancer, but others think he was poisoned or took his own life. Regardless, this isn't a major contrast made in the reading.

11. **(5)** The armies of both Napoleon and Hitler were severely weakened by their invasions of Russia, contributing to their eventual defeats. The reading doesn't give information about their education (1). Their strengths as in military strategists (2) facilitated their conquests of most of Europe; it was not a cause of their downfalls. Both wanted to end British military superiority (and failed to achieve this goal), but trying to end British naval dominance (3) wasn't a direct cause of their downfalls. Both had absolute power (4), but this power did not directly contribute to their downfalls; both also enjoyed widespread popular support during most of their rule.

12. **(3)** A person becomes president by getting a majority of the electoral votes. The pie chart shows that Lincoln did this. He won just over half the states (1), but this doesn't make someone the president. A candidate can become president by winning the most populous states without carrying most of the states. The map and pie chart do not have information about the number of people who voted for Lincoln (2); in fact, only about 40 percent voted for Lincoln. The country didn't split until after Lincoln was elected, so the breakup of the Union didn't affect the election (4). The fact that the opposition to Lincoln was not united had little effect on the election because even a total of all the other candidates' electoral votes would not have been enough to defeat Lincoln (5).

13. **(2)** Based on the information on the map, Vermont (VT) had five electoral votes and California (CA) had only four. Therefore, we can assume that Vermont had more people at the time of the most recent official census. From the information given, we can assume that the territories did *not* participate in the presidential election (1) because they had no electoral votes allocated to them. From the map, we can assume that states rarely split their electoral votes (3); only New Jersey did so in 1860. We can't jump to

the conclusion that the Civil War could have been avoided if the South had had more electoral votes (more people); there's not nearly enough information to make such an assumption (4). The West, with only seven electoral votes, was not an important factor (5) in the election; Lincoln would have still won easily if he had not carried the West.

14. **(4)** Answer (4) provides a good summary of the entire passage. You can immediately eliminate (1) and (5) because they don't mention vertical farming, the subject of this passage. The passage is not about traditional farming (5) or finding an alternative to organic farming (1). Answer (2) makes a point not brought up until near the end of the last paragraph, so this choice also can be eliminated. Answer (3) makes a comparison not even made in the passage.

15. **(2)** Vertical farming would result in fresher fruits and vegetables in cities year-round. Vertical farming, compared to traditional farming, would decrease the use of pesticides (1), decrease transportation costs (3), increase yields (4), and reduce water pollution (5).

16. **(1)** The table shows that people with more education are more likely to vote. We can't make any comparisons involving numbers of people voting in each group (2 and 3) because the table doesn't give these numbers. For example, 26.8 percent of the people with only an eighth-grade education voted in 2000, not 26.8 percent of the people who voted had an eighth-grade education. Answers (4) and (5) involve opinions not supported by the data.

17. **(2)** In general, the map shows that Western states have lower population densities than Eastern states. The map only has information about population densities, not populations. Therefore, it contains no evidence that most-populous states are in the East (1) or West (4). In fact, the states with the largest populations—California and Texas—are in the West, but most of the other more-populous states are in the East. Answer (3) is not always true; California is a large state but also has one of the highest population densities. Furthermore, answer (3) makes no comparison between Eastern and Western states as required by the question. Western states generally have lower, not higher, population densities than Eastern states (5).

18. **(3)** The reason that Texas has a large population but a low population density is simply that Texas is a large state in land area. Illegal aliens (1) and where people came from (2) have nothing to do with population density. Answers (4) and (5) are true statements in general but do not completely explain why Texas is one of the most populous states yet has a relatively low population density.

19. **(4)** Their argument is one of states' rights that holds that the federal government has no authority to get involved in education. Although *Brown* v. *Board of Education* required public school integration, the 96 congressmen avoid arguing the case for or against racial integration (1) much as Southerners during the Civil War period tried to make states'

rights the issue rather than slavery. The congressmen do not go so far as to say states should disobey the Supreme Court decision (2) or that the Fourteenth Amendment should be repealed (3). The congressmen are making the argument that the federal government should not encroach on the power of state governments, rather than vice versa (5).

20. **(5)** This question requires you to apply the argument the Southern congressmen made in 1954 to today's issues. Because they argue the federal government should not be involved in education, they would have to support the elimination of the federal Department of Education. Their argument also would support the elimination of federal loans for college (1). They argue the case for states' rights, so they would probably take the position that the federal government should not be involved in health care (3) or pollution control (4), as these areas also are ones not mentioned in the Constitution. Based on their 1954 statement, we don't know how these congressmen would feel about the federal deficit (2) because the states' rights argument doesn't apply to the federal deficit and the Constitution clearly gives the federal government the power to borrow money.

21. **(4)** According to the graph, there was a balance of trade deficit in all years, making answers (1) and (5) incorrect. The gap between imports and exports was smallest in 2009, making answer (4) correct and (2) incorrect. International trade is the sum of imports and exports. In general, international trade increased during the time period shown in the graph, but in 2009 it decreased, making answer (3) incorrect.

22. **(1)** This question requires you to apply the concept of balance of trade to the global economy. One country's exports become another country's imports, so imports and exports are always in balance when considered on a global scale. The only way the global balance of trade would not be zero is if there were imports or exports to/from another planet. The world's total international trade is described in answer (2), but don't confuse this with the balance of trade.

23. **(3)** The American colonies (the horse) were rebelling to try to throw off their master, which was the British government.

24. **(2)** It is a factual statement that the British found it difficult to end the American rebellion. Words such as *should* (3), *unjust* (4), and *good* (5) imply value judgments or opinions. Answer (1) is also an opinion or value judgment regarding what should be done, rather than a statement of fact.

25. **(1)** According to the Constitution, senators were to be chosen by the state legislatures, not the people of each state. This was changed in 1913 with the passage of the Sixteenth Amendment. All the other choices correctly restate provisions of Article I of the U.S. Constitution.

Science Test

The six review chapters in Part 3 give you overviews of broad subject areas that are likely to be included on the Science Test. Each overview is followed by GED®-style questions to give you practice with the types of skills you're required to use on the real test. Then, the practice test in Chapter 23 allows you to test your understanding of what you've learned.

The Science Test is divided into three areas of study: life science (40 percent), physical science (40 percent), and earth and space science (20 percent). Approximately 50 percent of the test questions are in scenarios, in which two or three items are based on a single stimulus (textual, graphic, or a combination of both). The other 50 percent of the test questions are stand-alone questions.

CHAPTER

17

What Is Science?

Science is not only a list of facts and figures, but a way of looking at and interpreting the world around you. Scientists take the information they have and put it into precise and understandable language. For the Science Test, you need to know what method scientists use when testing and how they reach scientific conclusions—that is the basis of science.

This chapter helps you understand scientific method, data collection, and how organisms are grouped and classified. With this background, you will be able to design experiments, read graphs and charts, and understand the history of science and the scientific method.

Scientific Method and Inquiry

The scientific method is a way of asking questions about a problem, testing the questions, recording data, and forming a conclusion. Good scientific method practice also involves repeating the experiment many times to ensure the information is correct.

In This Chapter

- Overviews of key areas of science, including the scientific method, data analysis, and classification
- Sample GED®-style questions to practice the skills on which you'll be tested
- Answers and explanations for all questions

The scientific method involves six steps:

1. **Observe:** Determine what problem you are trying to solve.

2. **Research:** Do background research about the problem.

3. **Hypothesize:** Make an educated guess of what you think will solve the problem.

4. **Experiment:** Perform an experiment to test your hypothesis (your educated guess).

5. **Analyze:** Use the information from the experiment to draw conclusions.

6. **Conclude:** Report your results and decide if your hypothesis was correct.

The scientific method enables scientists to form theories and test those theories. On the Science Test, you may be asked to read a passage about a lab that was completed and answer questions about the lab. Be sure you know the six parts of the scientific method and can draw conclusions from the experiment performed and the data collected.

Two other very important parts of an experiment are the control and the variable. The *control* is the part of the experiment that is "normal" and not being tested. The *variable* is the part of the experiment that is being manipulated and tested. Variables come in two types: dependent and independent. The independent variable is the part of the experiment the scientist is manipulating, or the part he or she is changing. The dependent variable is the response to the independent variable—in other words, the effect or what happened to the independent variable.

For example, let's say a scientist is studying the amount of light a particular plant can take before it dies. If this plant normally is found outside in the sun, the control plant in this experiment would need to be outside in the sun. The experimenter then could put other plants in various amounts of light (the variable) and record the results.

An experiment can never have more than one thing being tested at a time. In the experiment with the plant and the amount of light it can take, the scientist must leave all other conditions the same. For example, he or she must water all the plants the same amount, give all the plants the same type of soil, etc. Then, the scientist can get accurate results.

If instead the scientist had left one plant outside in the sun where it got rain and good soil and took the other plants inside, didn't water them, and left them in only rocks, this would be a bad experiment. The scientist might draw the conclusion that all plants taken inside die, when in reality, the plants could have died due to lack of water and not because they were taken inside. The only type of valid science experiment is when just one thing is being tested at a time.

Practice

A scientist is conducting an experiment on how mice react to different temperatures. The scientist first makes an educated guess as to what he thinks will happen when the mice are subjected to various levels of heat and cold. Next, the temperature in the room (in Celsius) is changed, and the heart rate (beats per minute, or bpm) of the mice is recorded. The following table shows the data collected during the experiment.

Temperature in Room	Heart Rate
10°C	250 bpm
15°C	350 bpm
20°C	450 bpm
25°C	550 bpm
30°C	650 bpm
35°C	750 bpm

1. Which conclusion does the data most directly support?

    (1) The mice move around faster as the temperature in the room is increased.

    (2) The mice are unable to survive in temperatures below 10°C.

    (3) The heart rate of the mice increases exponentially with temperature increases.

    (4) The heart rate of the mice increases as the temperature in a room increases.

Answer

1. **(4)** If you picked answer (4), you noticed that the data table shows that as the temperature in the room increases, the heart rate of the mice increases by 100 beats per minute for every 5 degrees Celsius. Answer (1) is incorrect because movement of the mice is not found in the graph. Answer (2) is incorrect because the graph does not show if the mice are able to survive below 5 degrees Celsius or not. Answer (3) is not correct because the data is not exponential but rather linear.

Science and Technology

Scientists are always searching to find answers to questions. They are curious about the world around them, and by performing experiments and testing hypothesis, they have changed the way we look at our world.

Let's review a brief history of science. We focus on the major events that have changed the field of science and the people who have made those changes.

Beginning in the fifteenth century, following the Dark Ages, is the period of time known as the Renaissance, or rebirth. This was a time when many people began to question the current school of thought. For example, Copernicus said the earth revolved around the sun, which was contradictory to early thinking that the sun revolved around the earth.

Galileo, another important scientist, invented the pendulum clock and the telescope. He used the telescope to prove Copernicus's *theory* that the earth revolved around the sun. Galileo also observed the moon through his telescope.

Following the Renaissance was the Enlightenment or Age of Reason. During this period, Isaac Newton observed the *law* of gravity and helped usher in the scientific revolution.

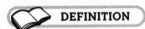 **DEFINITION**

A **theory** is something that has been shown to be true in many experiments but is unproven. A theory is valid as long as no evidence disputes it. For example, the Theory of Plate Tectonics explains how Earth's land masses went from one super continent, Pangea, to the seven continents we have today. A **law,** on the other hand, is something that has never been proven false. For example, the Law of Gravity has never been proven false and is, therefore, a law.

The modern age followed the Enlightenment. Charles Darwin (who proposed the theory of evolution by natural selection), James Watson and Francis Crick (who discovered the structure of DNA), and Albert Einstein (who made huge strides in our understanding of physics with his theory of relativity) are notable scientists from the modern age. The following table lists 10 of the most notable scientists in history.

Important Scientists in History

Scientist	Contribution
Niels Bohr	Investigated atomic structure
Marie Curie	Discovered radiation
Charles Darwin	Proposed the theory of evolution
Albert Einstein	Proposed the theory of relativity
Galileo Galilei	Observed space as an astronomer
Gregor Mendel	Studied inheritance
Dmitri Mendeleev	Developed the periodic table of elements
Isaac Newton	Described the laws of motion/gravity
Louis Pasteur	Made breakthroughs in microbiology
Anton Van Leeuwenhoek	Invented the microscope

Practice

1. Isaac Newton (1642–1727) was a physicist, mathematician, astronomer, philosopher, chemist, and theologian. One of the most important contributions Newton made to science is known as Newton's three laws of motion. The first law states that every object in motion stays in motion. The second law states that the force of an object equals its mass times its acceleration. The third law states that for every action there is an equal and opposite reaction.

   Which of the following would be the best title for this information?

   (1) "The History of Science"

   (2) "Physics Explained"

   (3) "Isaac Newton's Three Laws of Motion"

   (4) "The Life and Times of Isaac Newton"

Answer

1. **(3)** "Isaac Newton's Three Laws of Motion" summarizes what the article is about. Answer (1) is much too broad; a single article cannot include the entire history of science. Answer (2) is not what the article is about, even though Newton was a physicist. Answer (4) is partially correct, but we only read about one small part of Newton's life.

Analyzing Data

After information from an experiment has been gathered, it must be put into a clear and concise format. Information in science is known as *data,* and data is shown in a *data table* (also known as a chart) or a graph—sometimes both are used. Often this data is in the form of numbers and is gathered from an experiment. Let's look further at different types of graphs and data tables.

Assume an experiment has been completed on the effects of a particular toxin, an herbicide, on a group of pesky yard weeds. The scientist is trying to find the dose of this toxin (let's call it toxin A) necessary to successfully kill the weeds without harming the yard or the animals and microorganisms that live in the soil.

The experimenter sprays one weed with two squirts of toxin A, a second weed with four squirts of toxin A, and a third weed with six squirts of toxin A. The fourth weed is not sprayed with any toxin A and is the control. After 2 days, the experimenter comes back to count the number of dead leaves on each plant. Plant one has three dead leaves, plant two has eight dead leaves, and plant three has twenty dead leaves. Plant four, the control, has no dead leaves.

One way this information could be displayed is in a data table. Following is an example of a good data table for this experiment.

The Effects of Toxin A on Yard Plants

Number of Squirts of Toxin A	Number of Dead Leaves
2	3
4	8
6	20

By putting the information the scientist gathered into a chart, you can quickly and easily evaluate the experiment and the results.

Another way the information could be displayed is in a graph. There are many types of graphs, but the three most used in science are bar graphs, line graphs, and pie charts. A bar graph is used to compare one thing to another. A line graph is generally used to display change over time. A pie chart is another way to show comparisons, often of percentages.

The following figures show examples of a bar chart, line chart, and pie chart, respectively.

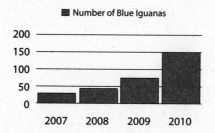

The number of blue iguanas between 2007 and 2010.

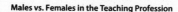

Water temperature of a lake from 2008 to 2011.

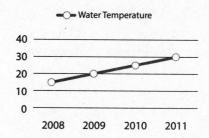

The percentage of males versus females in the teaching profession.

 **GOOD IDEA**

Notice that all three graphs include a title—this is very important. Always include a descriptive title on any graph you make. A title gives the reader an overview of what is shown in the graph.

Now it's your turn to practice. Use the information in the earlier data table ("The Effects of Toxin A on Yard Plants") to make a graph using the following blank grid.

_____

_____

_____

_____

_____

_____

So which graph would you choose to display the data from this experiment? I would use a line graph, like this:

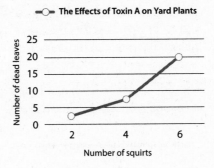

Practice

Questions 1 and 2 refer to the following graph:

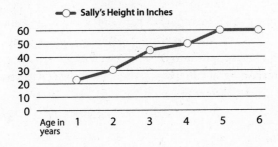

1. During which ages did Sally grow the most in height?

    (1) Ages 1 to 2

    (2) Ages 2 to 3

    (3) Ages 3 to 4

    (4) Ages 4 to 5

2. If Claire is 45 inches tall when she is 2 years old, what does the graph tell you about Claire in relation to Sally?

   (1) Claire is shorter at age 2 than Sally was at age 2.

   (2) Claire will be taller than Sally when Claire is 5.

   (3) Sally will catch up and end up taller than Claire.

   (4) Claire is 15 inches taller than Sally at age 2.

Answers

1. **(2)** Ages 2 to 3 represents the steepest part of the graph. During ages 1 to 2, Sally grew by approximately 8 inches; during ages 2 to 3, she grew by approximately 15 inches; during ages 3 to 4, she grew by approximately 5 inches; and during ages 4 to 5, she grew by approximately 10 inches. Therefore, Sally grew the most during ages 2 to 3, when she grew approximately 15 inches.

2. **(4)** To solve this problem you would need to plot Claire's growth during year 2 on the graph. Claire is 45 inches tall when she is 2, and Sally is, according to the graph, 30 inches tall when she is 2. Subtract 30 inches from 45 inches, and you come to the answer that Claire is 15 inches taller than Sally when they are 2 years old.

Classification of Organisms

Another important aspect in science is how to classify organisms, a field of science called *taxonomy*. Organisms are grouped together by a system of increasing similarity. Kingdom is the broadest classification, and there are five kingdoms: animal, plant, fungi, protist, and moneran. The kingdoms are then further split into phylum, class, order, family, genus, and finally species—the most specific classification you can give an organism. Each time you move down a step on the taxonomy scale, the organisms are more similar.

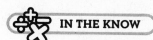 **IN THE KNOW**

> The first person to devise a system to classify organisms was Carolus Linnaeus, a Swedish doctor who published a book called *Systema Naturae,* in which he described his system of classification. This is the system still in use today.

For example, a moon jellyfish and a human are clearly different, but both would fall into the kingdom Animalia. However, that is where the similarities stop. Likewise, a dog and a wolf are both in the kingdom Animalia, but they are alike in many other ways. Both the dog and the wolf have backbones, both are mammals, and both are carnivores.

Phylum, the next classification, is less broad. For example, both dogs and wolves have backbones and are in the phylum Chordate, but a jellyfish does not have a backbone so it is not in this phylum.

In the past, organisms were classified according to their physical characteristics. Today, with our modern techniques of mapping out DNA, using genetics has become an even more precise way of classifying organisms.

Let's look at a few examples: the human compared to the moon jellyfish, and a dog compared to a wolf.

Comparison of Humans and Moon Jellyfish

Category	Human	Moon Jellyfish
Kingdom	Animalia	Animalia
Phylum	Chordata	Cnidaria
Class	Mammalia	Scyphozoa
Order	Primate	Semaestomeae
Family	Hominidae	Ulmaridae
Genus	*Homo*	*Aurelia*
Species	*Sapiens*	*Aurita*

As you can see, the similarities between the moon jellyfish and humans do not go below the kingdom category. Now let's look at two animals that are more similar, the dog and the wolf.

Comparison of Dogs and Wolves

Category	Dog	Wolf
Kingdom	Animalia	Animalia
Phylum	Chordata	Chordata
Class	Mammalia	Mammalia
Order	Carnivora	Carnivora
Family	Canidae	Canidae

Category	Dog	Wolf
Genus	*Canis*	*Canis*
Species	*Familiaris*	*Lupis*

As you can see, the wolf and dog are the same until the last category, species. Of course, the characteristics of a dog and a wolf are much closer than a human to a moon jellyfish!

Now, I'm sure you are asking yourself if you need to know the taxonomy for a moon jellyfish on the Science Test, and the answer is no. However, understanding how scientists classify organisms is important. A good way to remember the classification system is: King Phillip Cried Out For Good Soup—kingdom, phylum, class, order, family, genus, species.

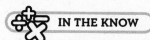 **IN THE KNOW**

All organisms are given a Latin genus and species name, and these names are always italicized. Scientists around the world follow this system of using Latin names, no matter what language they speak.

Practice

1. Which of the following statements is incorrect?

   (1) Kingdom contains a larger number of individuals than family.

   (2) Family contains fewer individuals than species.

   (3) Species is the most specific classification you can give an organism.

   (4) The broadest or largest level of classification is a kingdom.

Answer

1. (2) Answer 2 is *incorrect* because family is higher on the taxonomic chart than species and, therefore, would contain more individuals than species, not fewer. All the other answers are correct.

Health and Environment

Environmental science, also called *ecology*, is very important in the world today. Environmental science includes many other subjects and sciences such as chemistry, biology, sociology, economics, geology, and physics. When you study environmental science, you look at the relationships between what is happening in our natural world and what the human impacts have on Earth.

In this chapter, we look at the various biogeochemical cycles that are constantly changing our planet, organisms that live on our planet and their role in nature, how energy is transferred, hazards and risks we must face, and how the size of the human population has been growing exponentially.

Biogeochemical Cycles

In nature, chemicals cycle. They either change form, like from a solid to a liquid, or change composition. Five cycles might be covered on the Science Test that you should be familiar with.

In This Chapter

- Overviews of key areas of environmental science, including the major bio-geochemical cycles, ecology, energy, risks, and the human population
- Sample GED®-style questions to practice the skills on which you'll be tested
- Answers and explanations for all questions

The Water Cycle

Water is found in nature in three forms: solid, liquid, and gas. Because water is important to life on Earth, it's important to understand how water cycles. As you can see from the following figure, water can be found in oceans, underground, in the atmosphere, and on land. What's more, water can move from oceans to the atmosphere, from the atmosphere to the land, from the land to oceans, from the land to the atmosphere, and more. The water cycle explains how water can move around the earth in many forms.

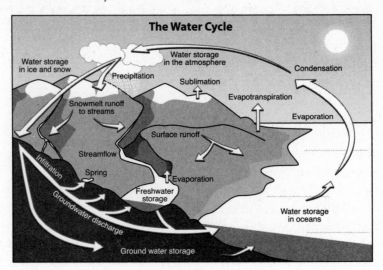

The water cycle.

Familiarize yourself with the following vocabulary terms to better understand the water cycle:

Evaporation   The conversion of liquid water into water vapor. This is how clouds form.

Precipitation   When the water molecules in the air come together, they grow and get larger. At some point they are too large to remain in the atmosphere and fall to the earth. This is precipitation—water vapor condensing and falling to the ground in the form of rain, snow, sleet, hail, or mist.

Evapotranspiration   Similar to evaporation but involving plants, evapotranspiration occurs when leaves lose water and the water becomes a vapor.

Groundwater   Water that has seeped into the soil and rocks and is stored underground. An underground water storage is known as an aquifer.

Surface water   Water stored above ground in lakes, rivers, and streams.

Condensation   Water vapor that collects, condenses, and forms droplets.

Sublimation　The conversion of water from a solid phase directly to a gaseous phase.

Infiltration　Water soaking into the soil.

Surface runoff　Water runoff, usually from rain, into rivers, lakes, streams, and ponds.

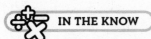 **IN THE KNOW**

The water cycle is also called the *hydrologic cycle*. If the Science Test uses that terminology, know it's referring to the water cycle.

The Nitrogen Cycle

In the nitrogen cycle, shown in the following figure, plants take nitrogen from the land and water and turn it into a form they can use. Nitrogen is a plant nutrient, and without it, most plants cannot survive. Yet plants are unable to take nitrogen directly from the soil, so they depend on bacteria to convert the nitrogen into a form they can use.

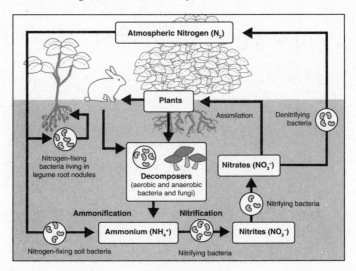

The nitrogen cycle.

Familiarize yourself with the following vocabulary terms to better understand the nitrogen cycle:

Nitrogen fixation　Occurs when bacteria convert nitrogen from the atmosphere or the soil into ammonia.

Nitrification　The conversion of the ammonia into nitrites and then nitrates.

Assimilation   The conversion of nitrates into things the plant needs, such as proteins, DNA, and amino acids.

Ammonification   The formation of ammonia due to an organism dying or excreting waste.

Denitrification   The release of nitrates back into the air as nitrogen gas.

The Carbon Cycle

Think about each time you breathe in and out. As you breathe in, you take in oxygen; when you breathe out, you release carbon in the form of carbon dioxide. Plants take in that carbon dioxide and release oxygen. The carbon cycle, shown in the following figure, is important because without it, life could not exist on Earth.

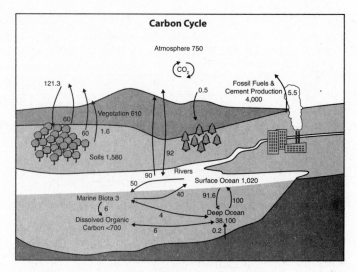

The carbon cycle.

The Phosphorous Cycle

Phosphorus is an essential nutrient for plants and animals. It's a part of DNA molecules, of molecules that store energy, and of fats of cell membranes. Phosphorus is also a building block of certain parts of human and animal bodies, such as the bones, muscles, and teeth.

In the following figure, you can see that phosphorus is taken in by plants. Then, when an animal eats the plant, the animal obtains the phosphorus from the plant. When the animal dies or excretes waste, the phosphorus is returned to the environment. Phosphorus cycles on both land and water.

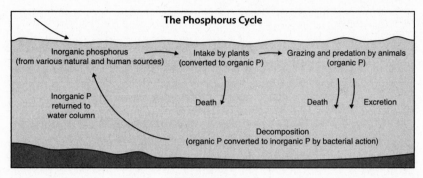

The phosphorus cycle.

The Rock Cycle

Like other elements, rocks—of which there are three kinds: igneous, sedimentary, and metamorphic—cycle, too. An example of rocks cycling would be if a volcano erupts and molten rock is thrown out onto the earth. When this rock cools, it's an igneous rock. Then, let's say the same rock ends up in a river where the water slowly breaks it down into little pieces. These small rock particles might end up getting glued together and form what's known as a sedimentary rock. Let's say this same rock gets buried and after millions of years gets squeezed due to heat and pressure. Now it's a metamorphic rock.

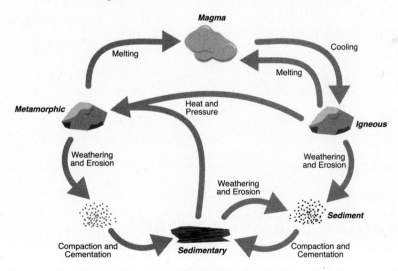

The rock cycle.

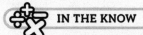 **IN THE KNOW**

The rock cycle is the slowest of all the cycles on Earth. Environmental science looks mainly at the rock cycle that's occurring at the surface of the earth.

Practice

1. According to the water cycle diagram shown earlier in this chapter, water is returned to the earth from the atmosphere by the process of:

    (1) Condensation

    (2) Precipitation

    (3) Evaporation

    (4) Evapotranspiration

2. According to the nitrogen cycle diagram shown earlier in the chapter, nitrogen cycles around the environment by all of the following except:

    (1) Decomposers adding nitrogen to the soil

    (2) Plants providing nitrogen to animals

    (3) Nitrogen-fixing bacteria returning nitrogen to plants

    (4) Precipitation providing nitrogen to denitrifying bacteria

Answers

1. (**2**) Precipitation is when water falls to the earth in the form of hail, mist, rain, sleet, or snow. This water comes from the atmosphere and ends up on the earth's surface.

2. (**4**) Nitrogen does not fall to the earth in the form of precipitation; only water does.

Ecology and the Environment

When you study the interaction between the living and nonliving world, you must look at both the biotic (living) and abiotic (nonliving) components of that ecosystem.

Plants take the sun's energy and convert it to food. *Herbivores* eat the plants, and *carnivores* eat the herbivores (or sometimes other carnivores). Some of the sun's energy is converted to heat and is unusable, so as you move through the ecosystems, less and less energy is available at each level.

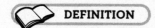 **DEFINITION**

Herbivores are animals that adapted to eat plants. **Carnivores** are animals that eat other animals. Both herbivores and carnivores must obtain their energy from something else, unlike a plant that can make its own energy.

Organisms

A living organism is known as *biotic*. Examples of biotic organisms are animals, plants, and microorganisms.

Something nonliving is *abiotic*. Examples of abiotic things are rocks, air, and chemicals.

Producers and Consumers

Producers make their own food by using the sun's energy during the process known as *photosynthesis*. Primary producers are organisms like plants and algae.

A *consumer* cannot make its own food and must consume either animals or plants to gain energy. Primary consumers would be herbivores (for example, deer) that eat plants. A secondary consumer is an animal that eats the animal that ate the plant. For example, if a mountain lion eats the deer that ate the plant, the mountain lion is the secondary consumer.

Decomposers

Decomposers break down dead or dying things and help recycle their matter and energy back into the environment. Without decomposers, animals and plants would die and never be broken down into nutrients needed in the soil. Examples of decomposers are bacteria and fungi.

Practice

1. A student is walking through the forest and observes a tree that has fallen and is covered with mushrooms, a type of fungi. The student is observing what type of organism?

   (1) Producer

   (2) Consumer

   (3) Decomposer

   (4) Autotroph

Answer

1. (**3**) A decomposer breaks down dead or dying things and helps recycle their matter and energy back into the environment. The mushrooms are breaking down the fallen tree and returning the nutrients to the environment.

Energy Transfer: Food Chains and Webs

Let's look at how energy is moved around the environment. A simple diagram of energy movement is called a *food chain* and shows how the calories move. If a grasshopper eats grass, for example, and a bird eats the grasshopper, you could show this transfer in a food chain:

$$\text{Grass} \quad \rightarrow \quad \text{grasshopper} \quad \rightarrow \quad \text{bird}$$

Notice how the arrow points from the food source to the animal eating it. Because the grasshopper eats the grass, the arrow shows the energy from the grass going into the grasshopper.

Food Webs

A food chain is usually too simple of a diagram, however. For example, what if a snake also eats the grasshopper? In nature, many food chains are occurring at the same time. A *food web* is a way to show a more complex system:

$$\begin{array}{ccc}
 & \text{Bird} & \\
 & \uparrow & \\
\text{Grass} \rightarrow & \text{grasshopper} \rightarrow & \text{snake}
\end{array}$$

A true food web is more complex than this simple one. Following is an illustration of a food web in nature. As you can see, many interactions are occurring. We see a bird eating a snake, but the same bird also is eating the rabbit. This is more real life because there are often many different food choices an animal could have.

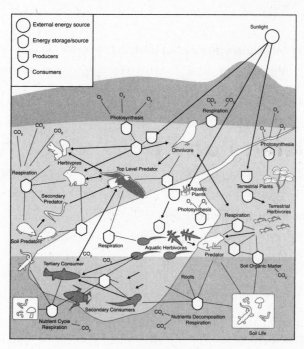

Food web.

Energy Pyramids

An *energy pyramid* shows the transfer of energy as it moves up the food chain. According to the First Law of Thermodynamics, energy cannot be created nor destroyed. However, energy can be converted to heat (the Second Law of Thermodynamics). When the grasshopper eats the grass, it uses the calories it ate to do what grasshoppers do: jump, reproduce, etc. These actions use some of the energy and transfer that energy into heat. The 10 percent rule explains this: if the grass offered the grasshopper 100 calories and the grasshopper used that energy, the grasshopper used 90 percent and stored 10 percent. Now, when the bird eats the grasshopper, it only gets the stored energy, the 10 percent that wasn't used. So the bird only gets 10 of the calories that came from the grass.

An example of this energy pyramid would look like this:

$$\text{Grass} \rightarrow \text{grasshopper} \rightarrow \text{bird}$$
$$\text{100 calories} \qquad \text{10 calories}$$

Practice

1. Which of the following statements is correct?

   (1) As energy moves through the environment, it is lost.

   (2) When energy moves through a food chain, approximately 10 percent is transferred to the next level of the chain.

   (3) Energy is stored in a food chain as heat.

   (4) When drawing a food chain, you should draw the arrow going from the animal to the plant.

2. According to the food web diagram shown earlier in the chapter, the sunlight is an example of a(n):

   (1) External energy source

   (2) Energy storage/source

   (3) Producer

   (4) Consumer

Answers

1. **(2)** According to the 10 percent rule, 90 percent of energy is used by the animal, and 10 percent moves to the next level. Answer (1) is incorrect because energy cannot be created or destroyed. Answer (3) is incorrect because energy is stored as living material, not heat. Answer (4) is incorrect because you would draw the arrow going from the plant to the animal.

2. **(1)** The sunlight is an external energy source. Notice the sunlight is designated as a circle and the key at the top left shows that a circle represents an external energy source. An external energy source comes from the sun, while an internal energy source comes from the earth itself. Energy storage would be either animals or plants; producers are plants and consumers are animals.

Toxicology: Environmental Hazards and Risks

Toxicology is the study of the adverse effects of chemical, physical, or biological agents on people, animals, and the environment. To evaluate a risk, you first need to identify the hazard and the exposure and then decide if the risk is worth it. Some risks are real, while others are perceived.

For example, many people are afraid to fly and would rather drive; however, you're actually much more likely to die in a traffic accident in the United States than in an airplane accident.

Types of Hazards

An environmental hazard is something in the environment that can potentially cause harm. There are three major types of hazards:

- **Biological:** A biological hazard would be from a bacterium, virus, insect, plant, animal, or another human. In history, we have had times when biological hazards have been extremely deadly. The bubonic plague is one example, as well as HIV/AIDS.

- **Chemical:** A chemical hazard is from a substance that causes harm to people. You are exposed to a variety of chemicals each day—pesticides, household chemicals, and pollution, for example.

- **Physical:** A physical hazard would be extreme heat, cold, noise, and ultraviolet light. Some physical hazards are weather related, such as tornadoes, hurricanes, and floods.

Acute Versus Chronic Diseases

You also should be familiar with acute versus chronic diseases. An *acute disease* rapidly attacks and affects the body. Some examples of acute diseases would be severe acute respiratory syndrome (SARS) and influenza (flu). A *chronic disease* is one that persists over a long time and slowly impairs a person. Some examples of chronic diseases are asthma, cancer, diabetes, and HIV/AIDS.

Practice

1. Air pollution coming from a coal-burning power plant would be an example of which of the following hazards?

   (1) Biological

   (2) Chemical

   (3) Physical

   (4) Seismic

Answer

1. **(2)** Air pollution is an example of a chemical hazard because it comes from a substance that harms people. Biological hazards (1) would come from something such as a bacteria. A physical hazard (3) would come from something such as a tornado. A seismic hazard (4) is a type of physical hazard.

Population Growth

The human population is growing exponentially, a faster and faster rate every year. If you graphed the growth of the human population, you'd get a result that looks like the letter J. It took thousands of years before the population began to grow like this, though.

For much of history, fewer than 1 billion people inhabited the earth. Today, there are approximately 7.5 billion people. The main reasons for such a fast growth rate are the Industrial Revolution and also modern medicine. As agriculture and sanitation improved during the Industrial Revolution, better living conditions caused death rates to fall. Modern medicine also has slowed death rates around the world. However, as death rates have decreased, birth rates continue to remain high in many countries, leading to the exponential growth of the human population.

Practice

Questions 1 and 2 refer to the following graph:

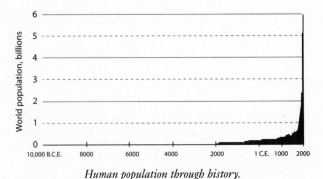

Human population through history.

1. According to the graph, approximately how many people were living in year 1000 B.C.E.?

   (1) 1 million

   (2) 5 million

   (3) 250 million

   (4) 4 billion

2. The shape of this graph is an example of what type of growth?

   (1) Linear

   (2) Exponential

   (3) Logistic

   (4) Inverse

Answers

1. **(3)** On the graph's X axis, look at 1000 B.C.E. Take your pencil and go straight up to where the black, shaded portion stops. Now, go straight across to the left to where the line hits the Y axis. Read the graph at that point, and you find the answer is approximately 250 million.

2. **(2)** This graph is an example of exponential growth. Any time you graph exponential growth, the graph will look like a letter J. Linear growth (1) will be a straight line. Logistic growth (3) will be shaped like an S. Inverse (4) is not a type of graph but means that two things are opposite.

Plants, Animals, and Human Body Systems

In this chapter, we look at biology, the study of living things. We start by exploring cells, the smallest units of life. The Science Test might ask you to know the parts of a cell and the function of each of those parts.

Because cells make up tissues, and tissues make up organs, we next review the different organ systems found in the human body. Another important part in the study of biology we cover in this chapter is how traits are passed from one generation to another—the study of genetics. Finally, we focus on evolution. Evolution is change over time, or how the species alive on the planet today have changed over millions of years.

Any student who is strong in science needs a good knowledge of the basic study of biology.

In This Chapter

- Overviews of key areas of biology, including cells, the human body, genetics, and evolution
- Sample GED®-style questions to practice the skills on which you'll be tested
- Answers and explanations for all questions

Plant and Animal Cells

As mentioned at the start of this chapter, the smallest unit of life is a cell. Cells combine to make organisms, from single-celled organisms to multicelled organisms. Cells also control the exchange of food and waste for an organism.

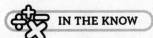 **IN THE KNOW**

Cells were first discovered in 1665 by Robert Hooke, a monk who looked at cork cells under a microscope.

The Structures of a Typical Cell

Cells are made up of many parts, each part with a special purpose. The structures (organelles) of a typical cell include the following:

Cell membrane   A protective wall found on the outside of the cell that controls what comes into and goes out of a cell. Both animal and plant cells have cell membranes.

Cell wall   Found in plant cells, the cell wall helps support the plant.

Chloroplast   Found only in plant cells, chloroplasts contain the chlorophyll plants need to photosynthesize.

Chromosomes   Chromosomes house the animal's or plant's genetic material. The chromosomes contain the DNA, or genetic code for the organism.

Cytoplasm   Found outside the nucleus, the cytoplasm is where all the plant and animal organelles are found.

Endoplasmic reticulum   The cell's highway system. The endoplasmic reticulum (ER) transports substances around the cell. Both animal and plant cells can have ER.

Golgi apparatus   The apparatus helps package the proteins and lipids for the cell. It's found in both animal and plant cells.

Lysosomes   Lysosomes help break down the waste materials of a cell. They're found in both plants and animals.

Mitochondrion   Mitochondrion help the cell obtain energy from food. Both animal and plant cells have mitochondria.

Nucleus   The brain of the cell that contains the genetic material of a cell. Both animal and plant cells have a nucleus.

Ribosomes   Help the animal or plant make protein.

Vacuoles   Large sacs in plant cells that are filled with water to help support the plant. Most animal cells do not have vacuoles.

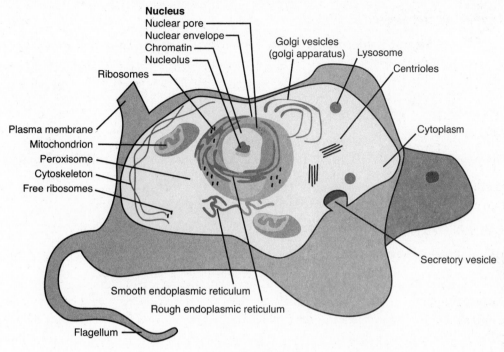

A typical animal cell.

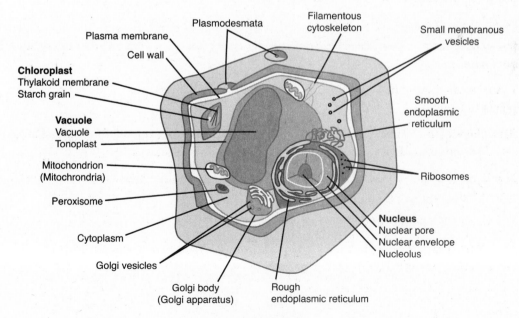

A typical plant cell.

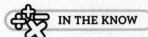 **IN THE KNOW**

Familiarize yourself with both the plant and animal cell diagrams as well as the function of each organelle. The Science Test asks you questions regarding both the names and functions of cells.

Photosynthesis

Photosynthesis is the process by which green plants and some other organisms use sunlight to synthesize food from carbon dioxide and water. The formula for cellular respiration is:

$$Carbon\ dioxide + water \rightarrow glucose + oxygen$$

Cellular Respiration

Just as you need food, air, and water to stay alive, cells also need these things to stay alive because cells are part of you. A cell cannot eat, breathe, or get rid of its waste like you and I do, so it must use its cell organelles to accomplish this and stay alive. *Cellular respiration* is the process cells use to take in oxygen to break down sugar and release energy. The formula for cellular respiration is:

$$Glucose + oxygen \rightarrow carbon\ dioxide + water$$

The reactants of photosynthesis (the left side of the arrow) are the products (the right side of the arrow) of cellular respiration and vice versa. These two reactions work together to sustain life on our planet.

Practice

1. There is a relationship between the products of photosynthesis and the reactants of cellular respiration. Which of the following statements best describes this relationship?

    (1) The products of photosynthesis do not allow the reactants in cellular respiration to occur in the presence of sunlight.

    (2) The products of cellular respiration cause a change in the reactants of photosynthesis.

    (3) The products of photosynthesis become the reactants of cellular respiration.

    (4) The products of photosynthesis cause the products of cellular respiration to shut down.

2. You are looking through a microscope at a cell. You see that the cell is square in shape, has large saclike structures inside, and contains green objects throughout. What type of cell are you observing?

   (1) Bacteria

   (2) Fungi

   (3) Plant

   (4) Animal

Answers

1. **(3)** The products of photosynthesis become the reactants of cellular respiration. If you notice, the equations are mirror images of one another because the products of one become the reactant of the other and vice versa.

2. **(3)** You are looking at a plant cell. You know this because of the presence of the "green" objects and the fact that the cell is square in shape. Both are characteristics of plant cells.

Human Body Systems

Twelve different systems are at work in the human body. Each system has a way of keeping the body in homeostasis, or balance. One system can affect another system, and all systems work together in the body.

The following table lists the systems, along with the organs and function connected to each.

Human Body Systems

System	Body Organs	Function
Integumentary	Skin	Protection
Muscular	Muscles, connective tissue	Movement
Skeletal	Bones, joints	Support, movement
Digestive	Stomach, intestines, liver, gall bladder, esophagus, mouth, colon	Digestion
Endocrine	Glands	Hormone regulation
Immune	White blood cells	Fight disease
Lymphatic	Lymph nodes, blood	Clean the blood
Nervous	Brain, spinal cord, nerves	Send information
Reproductive	Ovaries, testes, uterus, penis	Reproduction
Circulatory	Heart, blood, veins, arteries	Move blood through the body
Respiratory	Lungs, bronchi, trachea, alveoli	Help the exchange of carbon dioxide with incoming air
Excretory	Kidneys, ureter, bladder, urethra	Filter waste from the blood

The human body has a system of increasing complexity. Cells make up tissues, tissues make up organs, organs make up organ systems, and organ systems make up the human body.

Practice

1. You go to the doctor complaining of difficulty breathing and shortness of breath. What body system is the doctor going to investigate?

   (1) Circulatory

   (2) Respiratory

   (3) Integumentary

   (4) Digestive

2. A jogger goes out for his evening run. As he begins, his breathing and heart rate increase. Soon, his muscles begin to burn as they work with his bones to move his body forward. This describes the interaction between which organ systems?

   (1) Integumentary, respiratory, and lymphatic

   (2) Respiratory, circulatory, muscular, and skeletal

   (3) Excretory, reproductive, endocrine, and digestive

   (4) Muscular and circulatory only

Answers

1. **(2)** The respiratory system includes your lungs and involves oxygen exchange. Circulatory systems (1) involve the blood and heart, integumentary (3) is your skin, and digestive (4) is how your food is broken down.

2. **(2)** Respiratory, circulatory, muscular, and skeletal. The respiratory system is the runner's breathing, the circulatory is his heart rate increasing, the muscular is his muscles burning, and the skeletal is working with his muscles to move his bones.

Genetics, Mitosis, and Meiosis

Genetics is the branch of biology that deals with heredity. You probably look like your mother, father, or a mixture of both. The characteristics that you inherited from your parents are known as *traits*. The study of how these traits are passed down from parent to offspring is genetics.

Mendel's Genetic Experiment

Gregor Mendel, a monk who lived during the mid-nineteenth century, did many of the first experiments to try to figure out how traits are passed from parent to child. He experimented on pea plants, breeding one plant with a particular characteristic—say, short—with another plant that had a different characteristic—say, tall. The thinking of the day was that the offspring would "blend," and the plant would end up being medium in height, somewhere between the two parents. Mendel proved that this was incorrect.

In one of his experiments, Mendel took a tall pea plant (TT) and crossed it with a short pea plant (tt). Mendel used capital letters to show *dominant traits* and lowercase letters to show *recessive traits*. The traits that are seen (like hair color in humans and animals) are called phenotypes, and the actual genes, like TT or tt, are called genotypes. Tall pea plants were dominant, meaning that characteristic is what will be seen (phenotype).

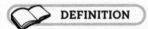 **DEFINITION**

A **dominant trait** is a trait that's "expressed" or seen. A **recessive trait** is a trait that's hidden. However, if two recessive traits are inherited, the trait will be expressed.

In the first generation of baby pea plants, all the plants were tall, but the genotype for each plant was Tt because one parent plant gave a T and the other gave a t. Each parent gives one gene to the baby, and because the tall plant had two TT, it could only give one T. Likewise, the short plant only had one t to give.

Now, these pea plant babies were crossed to create the second generation, or the grandchildren. Both plants are now Tt, so when crossed, they can give either a T or a t to the baby. It's like a flip of a coin. Mendel showed that this second generation had three tall plants and one short plant, and the genotypes were TT, Tt, Tt, and tt. In other words, if both plants gave a T, the baby would be TT (tall); if one gave a T and the other gave a t, the babies would be Tt (tall, but carrying the short gene); and if both parents gave a t, the baby would be tt (short).

Looking at Mendel's experiment, we can see that the offspring were not medium in height; he found that three of the offspring were tall and one was short. This is because the offspring always have the dominant characteristic (T) unless both parents give the recessive characteristic (t).

Mitosis and Meiosis or Cell Division

Mitosis is how cells reproduce themselves. Mitosis is important to all living things because it's how the nucleus divides to make two identical cells, called *diploid cells*. The following figure shows how mitosis occurs.

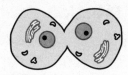

Prophase   Metaphase   Anaphase   Telophase

The stages of mitosis.

Mitosis occurs in four stages:

- **Prophase:** The genetic material inside the nucleus duplicates to form two identical chromatids, identical parts of a chromosome, and the nuclear membranes disappear.

- **Metaphase:** The chromosomes line up in the center of the cell, and spindle fibers, structures that help separate the chromosomes, attach to them. A chromosome contains all the genetic information passed from one generation to another.

- **Anaphase:** The chromatids separate and are pulled to the opposite sides of the cell by the spindle fibers.

- **Telophase:** The cell becomes two new cells with identical genetic information in each.

Meiosis is similar to mitosis, but involves sex cells. Again, we have four stages—prophase, metaphase, anaphase, and telophase—but during prophase, the two identical chromosome pairs line up and separate. One set of chromosomes goes to one side of the cell, and the other goes to the other side. This results in two cells, *haploid cells*, each with half the number of chromosomes as the parent.

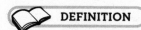 **DEFINITION**

A **haploid cell** contains half the number of chromosomes as the parent, while a **diploid cell** contains a full set of 46 chromosomes—23 from Mom and 23 from Dad. So when your mother's sex cells went through meiosis, she gave you a haploid cell, as did your father. When those cells joined, it formed a diploid cell that became you!

Practice

1. A student is trying to find a cell in which the spindle fibers have pulled the chromatids to opposite sides of the cell and now there are two cells with identical genetic information in each.

   Which cell is in the stage of mitosis the student is looking for?

   (1) Cell 1

   (2) Cell 2

   (3) Cell 3

   (4) Cell 4

2. A scientist has decided to repeat Mendel's experiment on pea plants by crossing a short pea plant (tt) with tall pea plant (TT). Which of the following would be the outcome of this experiment?

   (1) 100 percent of the offspring will be tall.

   (2) 100 percent of the offspring will be short.

   (3) 75 percent of the offspring will be tall, and 25 percent will be short.

   (4) 50 percent of the offspring will be tall, and 50 percent will be short.

Answers

1. **(4)** The final stage of mitosis is telophase, where the spindle fibers have pulled the chromatids to opposite sides of the cell and now there are two cells with identical genetic information in each.

2. **(1)** 100 percent will be tall because one parent plant gave a T and the other gave a t. Each parent will give one gene to the baby, and because the tall plant had two TT, it only could give a T. Likewise, the short plant only had one t to give. A plant with Tt will be tall because the T (tall) is dominant.

Evolution

In 1859, Charles Darwin published *On the Origin of Species,* in which he explained his theory of evolution. *Evolution* is how organisms change over time. Darwin proposed that all organisms alive today came from a single, common ancestor. He stated that through time, these organisms gradually changed to the species we have today.

The basis of Darwin's theory is known as *natural selection.* According to natural selection, organisms with characteristics that help them survive will live and produce offspring, while those organisms with characteristics that do not help them survive will not produce offspring and will die sooner. This is also known as survival of the fittest.

An example of natural selection is insects that are resistant to insecticides. If a certain insecticide is applied to a crop and 90 percent of the insects are killed but 10 percent survive because they have a characteristic that allowed them to be resistant to the pesticide, these insects will reproduce and pass on the pesticide resistance to their offspring. Over time, if these new insects with the pesticide resistance are isolated from other insects of the same species that did not come into contact with the pesticide (and, therefore, did not need this pesticide resistance), the pesticide-resistant insects could become a separate species from the original insects. This is known as *speciation.*

Evidence of evolution can be found in the fossil record and in the genetic code of organisms. Scientists look at both of these to try to find how Earth's organisms became as diverse as they are today. When a scientist finds a fossil, he can take a small amount of the remains, look at the genetic code specific to that organism, and send it to the lab to find out how old it is. This is a process known as *carbon dating* or *radioactive dating.* When the age of the fossil has been determined, the scientist can add it to the information he already has to try to see how organisms have changed over time.

Practice

1. Until the Industrial Revolution, the peppered moth was mainly white with black spots. As London's air became thick with soot from factories, the once-white trees the moths used to live on became blacker. Birds were now able to spot and eat the moths that were white on the black trees. However, some moths had more black spots than others, making them harder for the birds to spot than their whiter relatives. These moths survived and passed the genetic trait of being darker to their offspring.

   This passage describes what theory?

   (1) Theory of relativity

   (2) Theory of plate tectonics

   (3) Theory of homologous structures

   (4) Theory of natural selection

2. A student conducted an experiment wherein she applied various pesticides to mosquitoes to see which ones survived and which ones died. To ensure she used the proper scientific method, she sprayed 10 mosquitoes in each trial and recorded the ones that survived. After the first trial, she allowed the mosquitoes to reproduce and then resprayed 10 of the offspring with the pesticide. The data she collected is shown in the following table.

Pesticide	Trial 1 (# of Survivors)	Trial 2 (# of Survivors)	Trial 3 (# of Survivors)
A	9	10	10
B	2	6	9
C	5	8	10

   This data describes what phenomenon?

   (1) All the mosquitoes are dying because of exposure to all three pesticides.

   (2) All the mosquitoes are surviving due to being resistant to all three pesticides.

   (3) The mosquitoes are becoming resistant to the pesticides and passing on that resistance to their offspring who are able to survive in greater numbers.

   (4) All three pesticides have the same impact on mosquitoes during each trial and could all be assumed safe to use by the student.

Answers

1. **(4)** The moths that were darker had a better chance of surviving because they could hide from the birds. The theory of natural selection explains how organisms adapt to their environment to better survive. The theory of relativity (1) is about gravity, and the theory of plate tectonics (2) is how the earth is made of plates that move. The theory of homologous structures (4) is not a theory but the concept of two similar structures in different animals.

2. **(3)** The mosquitoes that were sprayed with the pesticides and survived were resistant to that pesticide. They passed on this resistance to their offspring, who then were able to survive in even greater numbers. The offspring that survived after being sprayed then reproduced and passed on the resistance trait to their offspring, and even more survived.

Chemistry

Chemistry is the study of atomic matter. All matter is made of atoms, and chemistry studies atoms and how they bond and react. On the Science Test, you need to understand the basics of chemistry, and often there are questions to see if you understand pH, acids, and bases. You also should be familiar with how atoms bond and what the periodic table entails. Finally, be sure you can balance chemical equations—this is an important part of chemistry!

Chemistry Basics

Let's begin by discussing the basics of chemistry.

Matter, Atoms, Molecules

Matter is anything that has mass and takes up space. Examples of matter include paper, water, air, soil—and you. *Mass* is a measure of the amount of matter an object has. Do not confuse mass and weight. *Weight* includes the gravity, but mass does not. The basic building block of matter is the *atom*. An atom contains *protons*, *neutrons*, and *electrons*.

In This Chapter

- Overviews of key areas of chemistry, including chemical formulas and reactions, density, pH, and compounds/mixtures

- Sample GED®-style questions to practice the skills on which you'll be tested

- Answers and explanations for all questions

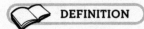

> **DEFINITION**
>
> A **proton** is a particle with a positive charge, a **neutron** is a particle that does not have a charge, and an **electron** is a particle with a negative charge.

A *molecule* is a particle that contains more than one atom. For example, the oxygen you breathe is O_2, which is a molecule, and so is carbon dioxide, CO_2.

Periodic Table

The periodic table of elements was arranged by Russian chemist and inventor Dmitri Mendeleev in the late 1800s. Mendeleev was looking for patterns within the elements and organized the elements by increasing atomic mass. Because not all elements had been discovered at this point, he left some parts of the periodic table blank.

The periodic table is arranged by column and row. All elements in a column are groups, or families, and share similar characteristics. For example, all elements in column 1 have one electron in their outer shell, and they all are extremely reactive. All elements in a row have the same number of outer rings. For example, in row 1, both hydrogen and helium have one outer ring. In row 2, lithium, beryllium, and so forth have two outer rings.

Group→	1	2	3	4	5	6	7	8	9	10	11	12	13	14	15	16	17	18
↓Period																		
1	1 H																	2 He
2	3 Li	4 Be											5 B	6 C	7 N	8 O	9 F	10 Ne
3	11 Na	12 Mg											13 Al	14 Si	15 P	16 S	17 Cl	18 Ar
4	19 K	20 Ca	21 Sc	22 Ti	23 V	24 Cr	25 Mn	26 Fe	27 Co	28 Ni	29 Cu	30 Zn	31 Ga	32 Ge	33 As	34 Se	35 Br	36 Kr
5	37 Rb	38 Cr	39 Y	40 Zr	41 Nb	42 Mo	43 Tc	44 Ru	45 Rh	46 Pd	47 Ag	48 Cd	49 In	50 Sn	51 Sb	52 Te	53 I	54 Xe
6	55 Cs	56 Ba		72 Hf	73 Ta	74 W	75 Re	76 Os	77 Ir	78 Pt	79 Au	80 Hg	81 Tl	82 Pb	83 Bi	84 Po	85 At	86 Rn
7	87 Fr	88 Ra		104 Rf	105 Db	106 Sg	107 Bh	108 Hs	109 Mt	110 Ds	111 Rg	112 Cn	113 Uut	114 Uuq	115 Uup	116 Uuh	117 Uus	118 Uuo

Lanthanides	57 La	58 Ce	59 Pr	60 Nd	61 Pm	62 Sm	63 Eu	64 Gd	65 Tb	66 Dy	67 Ho	68 Er	69 Tm	70 Yb	71 Lu
Actinides	89 Ac	90 Th	91 Pa	92 U	93 Np	94 Pu	95 Am	96 Cm	97 Bk	98 Cf	99 Es	100 Fm	101 Md	102 No	103 Lr

The periodic table of elements.

The periodic table also is grouped by metal, metalloids, and nonmetals. The nonmetals are on the right of the periodic table; the metals make up the majority of the periodic table; and the metalloids, which are elements that can behave like a metal or a nonmetal, are in the middle.

Chemical Reactions/Bonding

Each element on the periodic table has electron shells or rings. Protons and neutrons are found in the nucleus of the atom, and surrounding the nucleus are the electron rings.

The following figure illustrates the element manganese. It has four rings around it, which are the electrons in each energy level. The first ring can hold two electrons, the second ring can hold eight, and so on. As you can see, in manganese, the first ring is full, as are the second and third rings. It's the number of electrons in the outer ring that determines the chemical's properties—in this case, two.

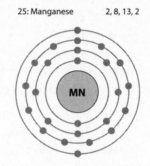

25: Manganese   2, 8, 13, 2

An atom with its electron rings.

A chemical reaction occurs when the atoms of one substance react together to form a new substance. For example, when two hydrogen atoms and one oxygen atom combine, a water molecule is formed.

An element is most stable if it has a full set of electrons in the outer ring. The first ring can hold two electrons, and the second and third rings can hold eight electrons. If an element does not have a full outer ring, the element will interact, or join together, with another element to try to fill the outer ring.

Covalent bonds are bonds where the elements share electrons. When the elements form a covalent bond, the element is more stable. In the following figure, you can see how the molecule methane contains one carbon atom and four hydrogen atoms that share electrons. The molecule is more stable now because the outer electron ring is full, with eight electrons. Before, each hydrogen atom needed another electron, and the carbon atom needed four more electrons for the outer ring to be full.

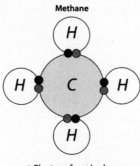

Methane

● Electron from hydrogen
● Electron from carbon

A covalent bond.

In an *ionic bond,* electrons are transferred from one element to the other. You can see how in this bond, the element on the left is transferring its electron to the element on the right.

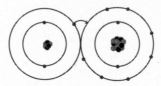

An ionic bond.

An *endothermic reaction* is when heat energy is absorbed. During an endothermic reaction, the temperature of the substance decreases. An example of an endothermic reaction is an ice cube melting. An *exothermic reaction* releases heat energy. During an exothermic reaction, the temperature of the substance increases. An example of an exothermic reaction is freezing water into an ice cube.

Physical and Chemical Changes

A *physical change* occurs when you change the physical properties of a substance. If a piece of ice melts and turns into water, a physical change has occurred. A *chemical change* occurs when you change one substance into a new substance. If I take a piece of wood and burn it, a chemical change has occurred because I no longer have a piece of wood; I now have ashes.

Practice

1. A coach takes a cold pack and pops the container inside. The following data table shows the temperature of the pack as time goes on.

Minutes	Temperature (° Celsius)
1	27°C
2	20°C
3	14°C
4	9°C
5	5°C

   This reaction is an example of what type of reaction?

   (1) Endothermic

   (2) Exothermic

   (3) Subjective

   (4) Heat of vaporization

Use the periodic table shown earlier in the chapter to answer questions 2 and 3.

2. Which of the following elements has one electron in its outer shell?

   (1) Sodium (Na)

   (2) Iron (Fe)

   (3) Carbon (C)

   (4) Aluminum (Al)

3. Which two pairs of elements would combine to create an ionic compound?

   (1) Sodium and argon

   (2) Nitrogen and chlorine

   (3) Sodium and potassium

   (4) Sodium and chlorine

Answers

1. **(1)** Endothermic reactions cause something to become cold, while exothermic reactions (2) cause something to become hot. Subjective (3) is not a reaction, and heat of vaporization (4) is when water becomes a gas.

2. **(1)** Column 1 elements have one electron in their outer ring. Sodium (Na) is found in column 1. None of the other elements are.

3. **(4)** Sodium and chlorine are correct because an ionic compound requires a metal and a nonmetal. Answer (1) is incorrect because although argon is a nonmetal, it has a full outer shell and won't react under normal conditions. Answers (2) and (3) do not contain both a metal and a nonmetal.

Interactions of Matter

Let's now discuss the interactions of matter.

Acids and Bases

The *pH* of a substance is a measure of the amount of hydrogen (H+) ions it contains. The pH is measured on the pH scale from 0 to 14.

If a substance has a pH of 7, it is considered *neutral*. A neutral substance is a combination of an acid and a base, or lacks both.

If a substance has a pH below 7, it is considered an *acid*. Acids have more H+ ions. They range from a pH of 0 to 7. The lower the pH, the more acidic the substance; the closer the pH is to 7, the weaker the acid is.

A *base* is a substance with a pH greater than 7. Bases have more hydroxide (OH−) ions. A base becomes stronger, or more basic, as you move up the pH scale, so a base with a pH of 14 is an extremely strong base, and one of just above 7 is a weak base.

A pH of 4 is 10 times more basic than a pH of 3. Similarly, a pH of 9 is 10 times more basic than a pH of 8. Each time you move up (more basic), or down (more acidic), you multiply by 10.

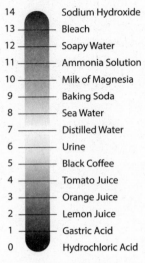

14	Sodium Hydroxide
13	Bleach
12	Soapy Water
11	Ammonia Solution
10	Milk of Magnesia
9	Baking Soda
8	Sea Water
7	Distilled Water
6	Urine
5	Black Coffee
4	Tomato Juice
3	Orange Juice
2	Lemon Juice
1	Gastric Acid
0	Hydrochloric Acid

The pH scale.

HEADS-UP!

It's easy to get confused when it comes to the strength of a substance. We have been taught that acids are very strong, so we assume they're stronger and more dangerous than a base. Not so. A base of 14 is extremely dangerous and just as strong as an acid can be. Either end of the pH scale can cause burns, react with other substances, and damage anything it comes into contact with.

Mixtures and Compounds

If you dissolve sugar in a glass of iced tea, you make a *mixture*. A mixture is two or more substances that have been combined but can be separated again. In this case, the water in the tea could be boiled out, leaving the sugar behind. A *compound*, in contrast, occurs when two or more atoms combine, like sodium and chloride combining to make salt. They cannot be separated because they are chemically combined.

Practice

Refer to the figure of the pH scale earlier in this chapter to answer the following question:

1. An acid with a pH of 3 was spilled on the floor of the laboratory. Which substance should be added to the spill to neutralize the acid?

    (1) Baking soda

    (2) Distilled water

    (3) Orange juice

    (4) Sea water

Answer

1. (**1**) Baking soda has a pH of 9, which, when added to the spill with a pH of 3, would neutralize the acid. Distilled water (2) would be adding an already neutral substance to an acid, which would raise the pH but not make it neutral. Adding orange juice (3), which has a pH of 3, to the spill would leave the pH at 3, and adding sea water (4), which has a pH of 8, would raise the pH but not to neutral.

Balancing Equations

If you need to describe a chemical reaction, you can do so with a chemical equation. An equation must be balanced to show the change that occurs when two or more substances are converted into new substances—it's a simplified way to explain a chemical reaction. For example, you might be given an unbalanced equation like the following on the Science Test and asked to balance it:

$$NaOH + H_2SO_4 \rightarrow Na_2SO_4 + H_2O$$

Start by writing down each element with the number of atoms of each, as shown in the following table. In the equation, you can see that some of the elements have a small number written next to them and some do not. Look at NaOH, for example, and you can see it has one atom of Na, one atom of O, and one atom of H. Now, if you notice, there are no small (subscript) numbers written next to the Na, the O, or the H. When there is no number, there is only one atom; there will not be a subscript 1 next to the element. However, the next molecule is H_2SO_4. The subscript numbers mean there are two hydrogens, one sulfur, and four oxygens. You need to count the total number of each element and write it next to the element's name. The arrow separates the chemical reaction into before the reaction on the left and after the reaction on the right.

Element	Number of Atoms Before Reaction	Number of Atoms After Reaction
Na	1	2
O	5	5
H	3	2
S	1	1

Next, you need to make the two sides balanced, or equal. You first need to add an Na atom to the left side. To do this, put a number 2 in front of the molecule, like this:

$$2NaOH + H_2SO_4 \rightarrow Na_2SO_4 + H_2O$$

However, this not only changed the Na, it also changed the number of Os and Hs. So you need to redo the table.

Element	Number of Atoms Before Reaction	Number of Atoms After Reaction
Na	2	2
O	6	5
H	4	2
S	1	1

You fixed the Na, but now you caused the number of Os, which were balanced before, to not be balanced any longer. So you have to fix this by adding an O to the right side:

$$2NaOH + H_2SO_4 \rightarrow Na_2SO_4 + 2H_2O$$

Again, you must redo the table due to the new changes because now not only did you change the number of oxygen atoms, you changed the number of hydrogen atoms as well.

Element	Number of Atoms Before Reaction	Number of Atoms After Reaction
Na	2	2
O	6	6
H	4	4
S	1	1

Now each side has the same number of atoms and is balanced.

Practice

1. Choose the correct missing compound in the following equation: $CH_4 + 2O_2 \rightarrow CO_2 +$ _____

    (1) H_2O

    (2) $2H_2O$

    (3) H_2O_2

    (4) $2H_2O_2$

Answer

1. **(2)** This equation is balanced because there are two Cs on the left side and two Cs on the right. There also are four Hs on both sides and four Os on both sides.

Properties of Matter

Let's now discuss the properties of matter.

Density

Density is the mass per unit volume of a material. You can calculate the density of a material by dividing the material's mass by its volume. For example, if a marble has a mass of 5 grams (g) and a volume of 1 cubic centimeter (cm^3), the density is $5g/cm^3$.

Consider if you placed both a wood block and a chunk of marble in a glass of water. The wood would float, and the marble would sink because the marble is denser than the water and the wood is less dense than the water.

Solvents and Solutes

If a spoonful of sugar is dissolved in water, a solute and a solvent are being used. The sugar is the *solute*, and the water is the *solvent*.

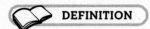 **DEFINITION**

A **solute** is the substance being dissolved. A **solvent** is the substance doing the dissolving.

Temperature can affect the rate at which a substance dissolves. If you want to dissolve more sugar, faster, you can heat the water. Other things you can do to affect the rate of dissolution are stirring the mixture and changing the size of the solute. If you ground the sugar into a fine powder, it would dissolve faster than, say, a sugar cube would.

Gases

Gases do not have a definite volume or shape. They fill the size of their container and will continue to spread out until they're equally distributed. Gases have specific characteristics with which you need to be familiar:

- **As temperature increases, pressure increases:** This occurs because as the temperature rises, the molecules of gas begin to move faster in the same amount of space. This causes the pressure to increase.

- **If the volume of a gas is decreased, pressure increases:** This occurs because if you take the same amount of gas and squeeze it into a smaller area, the molecules move faster, which again causes the pressure to increase.

- **As temperature increases, gases expand:** This occurs because as you heat a gas, the distance between the particles expands.

Practice

Question 1 refers to the following figure:

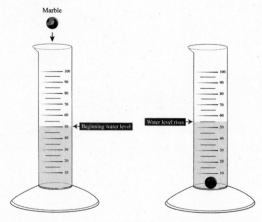

1. An experiment was conducted to determine the density of a marble. First, the student massed the marble with a triple beam balance to determine it had a mass of 10 grams. Second, the student filled the graduated cylinder with water as shown in the diagram and then dropped in the marble. Using the diagram, calculate the density of the marble.

   (1) 2 g/ml

   (2) 6.5 g/ml

   (3) .15 g/ml

   (4) .5 g/ml

Answer

1. **(1)** 10 g/5 ml = 2 g/ml. The formula for density is mass divided by volume. The mass of the marble is 10 grams, and the volume of the displaced water is 5 milliliters.

Physics

Physics is the study of matter, motion, and the interactions of objects and energy. In this chapter, we analyze motion, look at how forces affect matter, study waves and energy, and discover how machines make work easier.

The Science Test covers Newton's three laws of motion and the different types of simple machines as well as forces at work on different objects. Practice working different motion problems so you're familiar with these types of questions before test time.

In This Chapter

- Overviews of key areas of physics, including force, energy, simple machines, waves, and electricity
- Sample GED®-style questions to practice the skills on which you'll be tested
- Answers and explanations for all questions

Physics Problems

Let's discuss different motion problems.

Force and Motion

A course in physics will cover *force* (a push or pull acting on an object) and *motion* (a change in the position of an object with respect to time). Other terms you need to be familiar with include the following:

Momentum   The property a moving object has because of its mass and velocity.

Velocity   Speed in a given direction.

Work   The force times the distance.

You also need to be able to solve problems given in word problems. Here are the formulas you should know:

- Velocity (m ÷ s) = distance (m) ÷ time (s)

- Momentum (kg × m/s) = mass (kg) × velocity (m/s)

- Force (N) = mass (kg) × acceleration (m/s/s)

- Work (N × m) = force (N) × distance (m)

A typical force problem looks something like this:

> A 10 kg block is dropped from a building and is accelerating at 10 m/s/s. What force is acting on the block?

To solve this problem, you multiply the mass (10 kg) by the acceleration (10 m/s/s). So 10 kg × 10 m/s/s = 100 kg × m/s/s. (kg × m/s/s is known as a Newton.)

A typical velocity problem looks something like this:

> A car traveled 300 meters in 20 seconds. What is the velocity of the car?

To solve this problem, you need to use the velocity formula: velocity = distance ÷ time. So 300 m ÷ 20 s = 15 m/s.

Newton's Laws

Isaac Newton is known as the father of physics. Newton's three laws, which are the foundation of modern physics, changed our understanding of the universe because they show the relationship between the forces acting on an object and the motion due to these forces.

Newton's first law states that an object in motion stays in motion, and an object at rest stays at rest unless acted upon by an unbalanced force. For example, if you kicked a ball in space, the ball would continue moving forever. However, on Earth, the force of gravity acts on the ball to slow it down.

Newton's second law states that force equals mass times acceleration. For example, because a bus has a much bigger mass than a car, even if the two vehicles are moving at the same speed, the bus will require more force to move than the car.

Newton's third law states that for every action force, there exists an equal and opposite reaction force. For example, when an ax strikes a tree, the ax exerts a force to cut the tree and the tree exerts the same force to stop the ax.

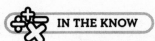 **IN THE KNOW**

Isaac Newton built the first light telescope, using mirrors rather than lenses. Known as the Newtonian reflector telescope, it is still in use today.

Power

Power is the rate at which work is done. The formula for power is work divided by time. (Remember, the formula for work is force times distance.) A typical power problem looks something like this:

> A 10 N force is applied to an object for 10 seconds. This moves the object 5 meters during the 10 seconds. Calculate the power used to move the object.

You can solve this problem in two steps. First you need to solve for work so take the 10 N force and multiply it by the 5 meter distance to get a work of 50 N × m. Then, solve for power by taking the work of 50 N × m and dividing it by the time of 10 seconds. So the power is 5 watts.

Practice

1. A 20 kg object is dropped from the top of a building and is accelerating at 5 m/s/s. What is the force acting on the object?

    (1) 20 kg × m/s/s

    (2) 15 kg × m/s/s

    (3) 25 kg × m/s/s

    (4) 100 kg × m/s/s

2. Which of the following is the best example of Newton's first law of motion?

    (1) A car accelerates as it goes down a hill.

    (2) A book in a car moves forward and slides off the seat as the car quickly stops.

    (3) Salt on a road helps the car gain friction and move forward.

    (4) You push a car forward on the road after it runs out of gas.

Answers

1. **(4)** Using the formula force = mass × acceleration, you can plug in the information to solve this problem. So 20 kg × 5 m/s/s = 100 kg × m/s/s.

2. **(2)** Newton's first law of motion states that an object in motion stays in motion. The example says there's a book on the seat of a car, and as the car quickly stops, the book flies forward and slides off the seat. The book was in motion because the car was in motion, so when the car stops, the book continues to move in the direction it was moving. Answer (1) is an example of a velocity question, and (3) and (4) are both examples of Newton's third law.

Energy and Work

Energy is the capacity to do work. We first look at kinetic and potential energy and then see how this energy can be used to move an object using simple machines.

Kinetic and Potential Energy

Kinetic energy is energy in motion. *Potential energy* is stored energy. A boulder sitting at the top of a hill has a great deal of potential energy due to its location at the top of the hill. Think about the amount of damage this boulder could do if it began falling. Once the boulder begins rolling down the hill, it has energy in motion, or kinetic energy.

Simple Machines

Machines help you lessen the amount of force you have to apply. There are six different simple machines: lever, pulley, wedge, inclined plane, screw, and wheel and axle.

Picture a seesaw, an example of a *lever.* A seesaw has a long board suspended on a fulcrum, or pivot point. Levers help lower the workload and make it easier to lift objects. The position of the fulcrum determines the amount of force needed to lift the object.

The following illustration shows two masses, one 100 kg and the other 5 kg. The fulcrum is not in the middle of the lever, but rather closer to the 100 kg mass because it is so much greater than the 5 kg mass. If instead both masses were equal, the fulcrum would be in the middle. The position of the fulcrum matters because the closer the fulcrum is to the mass, the easier it is to lift the object.

A lever.

A *pulley* is a system of ropes and a wheel that hoists an object upward, changing the direction of the movement. For example, if you needed to lift a refrigerator up a flight of stairs, you would have a hard time pushing the heavy appliance by hand. However, if you put a pulley at the top of the stairs and connect the rope to the refrigerator, you could pull on the rope and lift the refrigerator up the stairs. Using multiple pulleys together lessens the force needed but increases the distance because the amount of rope you need to lift the refrigerator is greater than the distance the refrigerator needs to be lifted.

In the following illustration, a simple pulley has a 100 N mass on the end. As you can see, it takes a 100 N force to pick up this mass with a pulley. This pulley doesn't lessen the force you need to pick up the mass, but rather changes the direction of the force.

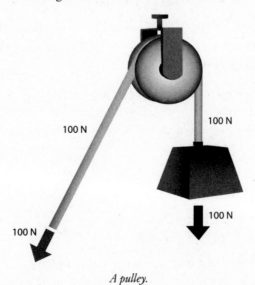

A pulley.

A *wedge* is a triangular-shape object that can be used to drive two things apart. An example would be an ax. You can split wood with an ax because of its shape. In the following illustration, you see a wedge splitting a piece of wood in half. The wedge is the triangular-shape object in the middle.

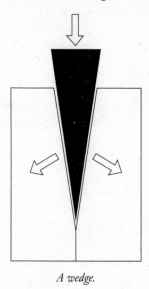

A wedge.

An *inclined plane* is like a ramp. It helps by reducing the amount of force needed to lift an object. By doing the work on the object over a greater distance, less force is used. For example, if you need to get your refrigerator into the back of a moving van, you could use an inclined plane, in the form of a ramp, to push the refrigerator into the van.

In the next illustration, you see a triangular-shape inclined plane with a mass resting on it. By using the inclined plane, you reduce the force needed but must move the object a greater distance.

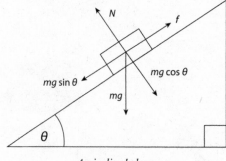

An inclined plane.

A *screw* is an inclined plane wrapped around a shaft, as shown in the next illustration. Again, the force is decreased, but the distance is increased. An obvious example is a simple hardware screw you would use at home to hold things together. To move the screw a few inches, you have to turn the handle around many times; you lessen the force but increase the distance.

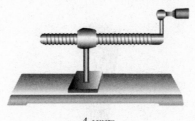

A screw.

A *wheel and axle* is a wheel attached to a rod that spins. A doorknob is a good example of a wheel and axle. Again, this lessens the force by increasing the distance. The next illustration shows a wheel and axle being used to raise a bucket. To raise the bucket a few feet, you have to turn the wheel many times, so again you lessen the force but increase the distance.

A wheel and axle.

Practice

1. A moving company is trying to get a 150 kg refrigerator to the top of a two-story building. To lessen the amount of work required, they connect the refrigerator to a double pulley system like the one shown here:

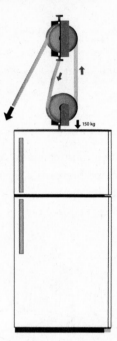

Which of the following statements is true about the minimum effort force required to lift the bucket if friction is ignored?

(1) It would take 0 kg of effort to lift the refrigerator.

(2) It would take 75 kg of effort to lift the refrigerator.

(3) It would take 150 kg of effort to lift the refrigerator.

(4) It would take 300 kg of effort to lift the refrigerator.

Answer

1. **(2)** It would take approximately 75 kg of effort because a pulley system is a type of simple machine that reduces the amount of effort needed. In this case, it would reduce the force by half, but the moving company would have to pull the rope twice as far as the height of the building.

Waves, Electricity, and Mass

In this section, we review the different types of waves, learn to understand electricity, and find out how and why matter cannot be created or destroyed.

Waves

A *wave* is an oscillation that travels from one place to another. Waves can move in the form of water, light, sound, and microwaves, to name a few. Waves are a traveling form of energy and an important concept in physics.

Any wave that travels through matter is a mechanical wave. There are two types of mechanical waves: transverse and compressional.

A *transverse* wave moves back and forth at right angles to the direction the wave is moving, like a wave in the ocean. Imagine if you took a jump rope and, holding one end, shook it up and down. You would be making a transverse wave.

A *compressional* wave moves forward and backward in the same direction the wave is moving. If you were to pull back on a spring and let it go, you would be making a compressional wave. An example of a compressional wave is a sound wave.

A typical wave.

In this illustration, one cycle of a wave is shown with the *crest,* the highest point, and the *trough,* the lowest point. The *wavelength* is the distance between the crest (or trough) of one wave and the crest (or trough) of another. *Frequency* is the number of wavelengths that pass a point in a second, measured in hertz (Hz).

Calculating wave speed is something you might be asked to do on the Science Test. The formula for frequency is wave speed divided by wavelength. An example problem might look like this:

If the speed of a wave is 10 m/s and it has a frequency of 5 Hz, what is the wavelength?

First, you must move the equation around. Instead of speed = wavelength × frequency, you have to isolate the wavelength to solve the problem. Because you need to solve for wavelength, you must move frequency to the other side of the equal sign. Now, wavelength = speed ÷ frequency. 10 m/s ÷ 5 waves per second = 2 m per wave.

Electricity

Electricity is the invisible flow of electric current through a wire or motor. Electric current comes from the flow of electrons and can do work like turn a motor or turn on a light. An *electric circuit* is the path the electricity travels. For example, if you turn on a light switch, the electric circuit is the path the electricity travels from the switch to the lightbulb.

Current (I) carries power and is measured in *amperes* (amps). *Resistance* (R) is the ability to resist current and is measured in *ohms*. *Voltage* (V), the difference in energy that's carried by charges in a circuit, is measured in *volts*. To solve for voltage, you use the formula $V = I \times R$.

Matter has electric charge because atoms are made of electrons, protons, and neutrons. Electrons have a negative charge, and protons have a positive charge. Like charges (+ +) repel one another, and unlike charges (− +) attract one another. The force around the charged particle is the *electric field*. As the distance between particles increases, the strength of the electric field decreases, and vice versa.

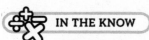 **IN THE KNOW**

> If you've ever touched a doorknob or light switch and received a small shock, you have experienced static electricity. This occurs when there's a buildup of electrons on one of the two objects, either you or the doorknob. The shock you feel was the electric current as it moves the excess electrons from you to the doorknob.

Conservation of Mass

Mass cannot be created or destroyed; however, it can change forms. Think of a boiling pot of water. If you leave the pot on the stove for hours, when you come back, all the water will be gone. This is an example of conservation of mass. Actually, the water isn't *gone;* it was vaporized and is now in the form of steam.

Another example is burning a log in a fireplace. When the log burns, it seems as if it is disappearing. However, the log turned into ash, smoke, and gas that escaped as the log burned. The mass is not destroyed; it just has been changed to a different form.

Remember, mass cannot be created or destroyed, although it may be rearranged.

Practice

1. A closed circuit with a 12-volt battery and a 200-ohm resistor produces a current of how many amperes?

   (1) 0.06 amps

   (2) 16.6 amps

   (3) 3,200 amps

   (4) 188 amps

Answer

1. **(1)** The formula is $V = I \times R$. First you have to rearrange the equation to solve for current (I). The rearranged equation is $I = V \div R$. $12 \div 200 = 0.06$ amps.

Earth and Space Science

In this chapter, we review both the land and the oceans. We discuss the theories of how the earth was made and what it's made of. Earth science, or geoscience, includes four major areas: geology, meteorology, oceanography, and astronomy. Geology is the study of the earth, meteorology is the study of the atmosphere, oceanography is the study of the oceans, and astronomy is the study of space or the universe.

The Science Test quizzes you on the layers of the earth, how the plates move, and what Earth looked like millions of years ago. The test also covers the atmosphere, including weather and climate as well as the layers the atmosphere is made of.

Plate Tectonics

Our planet is constantly changing. During this very slow process, mountains are being formed, ocean crust is melting, volcanoes are adding new rock, and earthquakes are shifting the earth. These processes as a whole are called *plate tectonics*. A plate is a single piece of the earth's crust (*lithosphere*), either land or ocean. For example, Australia would be a single piece of the earth's crust. Earth has many different plates, known as tectonic plates. The largest is the Pacific plate, but there's also the African plate, the Antarctic plate, and others.

In This Chapter

- Overviews of key areas of earth science; including plate tectonics; geologic time; and the earth's layers, atmosphere, and oceans

- Sample GED®-style questions to practice the skills on which you'll be tested

- Answers and explanations for all questions

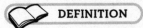 **DEFINITION**

Lithosphere is another name for the crust, the solid portion of Earth.

Plates interact in three ways: divergent plate boundaries, convergent plate boundaries, and transform plate boundaries.

A *divergent plate boundary* occurs when two plates move apart. A divergent plate exists in the middle of the Atlantic Ocean and is moving apart like a conveyer belt. As the plates spread apart, magma (molten rock) rises and fills in the gap. So the newest crust is right on the boundary, and older crust is found as you move outward from the boundary. This is known as *seafloor spreading.*

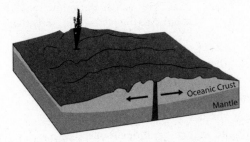

In a divergent plate boundary, the plates move away from one another.

A *convergent plate boundary* occurs when two plates move together. An example is an ocean plate sliding under a land plate. Convergent plate boundaries offset the activity of divergent plate boundaries, keeping the earth the same size. The earth doesn't get larger; instead, somewhere else plates are coming together, or converging. Volcanoes are oftentimes associated with this type of boundary.

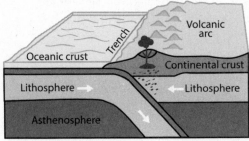

In a convergent plate boundary, the ocean crust slides underneath the continental, or land, crust.

In a *transform plate boundary*, the plates slide next to each other. Transform boundaries can occur on land or ocean crust. Because the plate boundaries aren't smooth, they don't slide evenly. Instead, they get stuck. Eventually, the stress builds to a point where the plates slip past each other, releasing a lot of energy in the process. This slow buildup and sudden release of energy is what causes earthquakes.

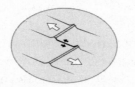 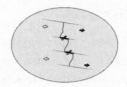

In a transform plate boundary, the plates slide next to each another.

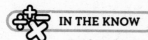

IN THE KNOW

Earthquakes are measured with a device known as a seismograph, which detects the earth's movement and records them as zigzag lines on paper. The stronger the movement, the larger the marks on the paper. The strength of an earthquake is measured on the Richter scale.

Practice

1. Scientists have observed that the ocean is growing larger by 3 centimeters every year. This growth could best be explained by which of the following processes?

   (1) A divergent plate boundary, which causes ocean floor spreading

   (2) A convergent plate boundary where two plates collide

   (3) A transform plate boundary along a fault zone

   (4) The process of subduction, where denser oceanic crust is sliding below less-dense continental crust

Answer

1. **(1)** Ocean spreading is found at divergent plate boundaries where the plates spread apart and magma fills in the gap.

Geologic Time

The earth we see today is different from what it looked like millions of years ago. Today we have seven continents: North America, South America, Asia, Europe, Antarctica, Australia, and Africa. However, millions of years ago, the planet had one large land mass known as Pangea.

Pangea.

Slowly, due to plate tectonic movements, this large land mass began to spread apart until the continents made their way to where they are today. In a few million more years, the continents will be in still different places.

We've already reviewed plate boundaries, but what's the driving force behind the movement of the plates? The answer is convection currents. Convection currents found in the mantle (a layer of the earth, discussed in the next section) cause the ocean plates to spread outward. Just as warm air rises, so does molten magma. As the magma rises, it carries the plates along with it.

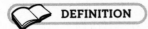 **DEFINITION**

Convection currents are currents that cause the plates to move. The extreme heat of molten rock causes it to rise up in the earth's mantle and spread out, moving the plates. As the magma rises, it cools and sinks again. This is a continuous motion that slowly moves the earth's plates.

Practice

1. The movement of the earth's crust is best explained by which of the following?

    (1) A magnetic current

    (2) A convection current

    (3) A conventional current

    (4) An oceanic current

Answer

1. **(2)** Convection currents cause the plates to move.

Composition of the Earth and Atmosphere

In this section, we study what the earth and the atmosphere are made of. Knowing the layers of the earth and the first two layers of the atmosphere is important for your success on the Science Test.

The Layers of the Earth

The earth is composed of the core, mantle, and crust. The atmosphere contains the troposphere, stratosphere, mesosphere, thermosphere, and exosphere (space).

The *core* is the earth's center, mainly made of nickel and iron. The core has a center, solid layer and an outer, liquid layer.

The *mantle* is found between the core and the crust and is made of silicon, iron, magnesium, aluminum, and oxygen. The mantle is semiliquid.

The *crust*, the outermost layer, is made of silicon, oxygen, aluminum, iron, calcium, sodium, potassium, and magnesium. The crust is solid and where all life exists.

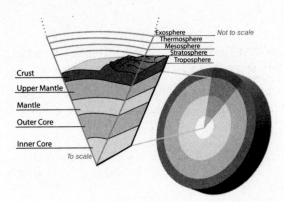

Earth's layers.

The atmosphere has five layers, but you most likely only need to know about the first two. You live in the *troposphere.* This layer is made of 78 percent nitrogen, 21 percent oxygen, and other trace gasses. Three quarters of the mass of all the layers is in this first layer, where all of Earth's weather occurs.

Moving outward is the *stratosphere.* The stratosphere is extremely important to life on Earth because it contains the ozone layer, which absorbs 99 percent of the ultraviolet light from the sun. Without the ozone layer, life on Earth would not be possible.

Weather and Climate

Weather is the state of the atmosphere at a specific place and time. If it's raining outside, that's weather. Climate is the average weather that occurs over many years. So just because it's raining outside right now doesn't mean the climate in the area is rainy.

Different types of air masses can occur. In a *cold front,* cold air wedges its way under warmer air. Because warmer air is less dense, it rises on top of the colder air. A cold front typically has a line of showers or a severe storm associated with it as the front moves through the area. A *warm front* occurs when warm air pushes its way beneath colder air. Typically, a warm front produces a long period of light rain. An *occluded front* is made of two cold air masses pushing warm air between them, with the warmer air rising on top. Typically, an occluded front produces a lot of rain as the two fronts collide.

Practice

1. A student is taking observations of the weather patterns in her area for 5 days. She collects the data and puts it into the following data table.

Day	Weather Observation
1	Zero precipitation; 100% cloud coverage
2	Zero precipitation; 100% cloud coverage
3	Severe storms followed by clear skies and cooler temperatures
4	Zero precipitation; no clouds
5	Zero precipitation; no clouds

What type of front does the student's data best indicate has occurred?

(1) Warm front

(2) Cold front

(3) Occluded front

(4) Stationary front

Answer

1. **(1)** A cold front has most likely moved through the student's area. During a cold front, cold air wedges its way under warmer air. Because warmer air is less dense, it will rises on top of the colder air. As the cold front moves through an area, typically a line of showers or a severe storm does, too.

Oceans

Seventy-one percent of Earth is covered with ocean. Oceans house tens of thousands of life-forms, contain many different ecosystems, and are important in regulating climate.

The uppermost layer of the ocean is known as the *euphotic zone*. Because the sun's rays can penetrate the water here, this is where most life exists, such as organisms like algae. Many different ecosystems are found in the euphotic zone.

The coral reefs are the most diverse of all the ocean ecosystems. Corals are tiny animals that build reefs, which provide shelter and food for many ocean creatures. Reefs also are important in protecting the shoreline from erosion. Reefs are found in warm, tropical waters that are shallow enough for sunlight to penetrate.

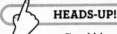 **HEADS-UP!**

Coral bleaching is a big problem today. Warmer water temperatures can cause coral to expel the algae zooxanthellae and turn white. The "bleaching" doesn't always mean death for the coral, but it does make it more vulnerable and the coral can die if the temperature doesn't cool down.

Another extremely biodiverse and important ocean ecosystem is the kelp forest. Whereas corals are found in warm, tropical waters, kelp is usually found in colder waters. Kelp forests provide food and shelter for many species.

Sea grass beds are another ocean ecosystem that provides food for many animals. Many different species of sea grasses grow, but all are salt tolerant.

The middle layer of the ocean is the *bathyal zone,* a dimly lit zone under lots of pressure from the layers above it that contains little oxygen and not a lot of life-forms.

The bottom layer of the ocean is the *abyssal zone.* It's completely dark, and few life-forms exist here due to the lack of oxygen and the extreme amounts of pressure.

The *benthic zone* is the ocean floor. This can be at the edge of the ocean right next to the beach where you walk or the very bottom of the deepest ocean. Many animals that bury themselves in the sand live in the benthic zone.

Practice

1. An ocean diver observes a coral reef with schools of fish, sponges, and ocean plants. The diver is swimming in which ocean zone?

   (1) Euphotic

   (2) Bathyal

   (3) Abyssal

   (4) Benthic

Answer

1. **(1)** The euphotic zone is the area of light, where lots of photosynthetic activity makes oxygen. The bathyal zone (2) is dimly lit without much oxygen. The abyssal zone (3) is completely dark with hardly any oxygen. The benthic zone (4) is the floor of the ocean. Answer (4) is not correct because we don't know if this is right at the shore, which would have a lot of oxygen, or at the deepest part of the ocean, with little to no oxygen.

Science Practice Test

The GED® Science Test presents questions in a variety of answer formats: multiple choice, fill in the blank, drag and drop, drop down, hot spot, and short answers. (We stick with multiple-choice items here.) You have 90 minutes to complete the Science Test; give yourself 40 minutes to complete this 25-question practice test.

If, after taking this practice test, you want to take another simulated test, several websites offer free GED practice tests. PBS Literacy Link (litlink.ket.org) is one such site.

Instructions

The Science Test is designed to measure your understanding of general science skills and concepts. You'll have sections in which you'll read a short paragraph and answer questions about what you read. You also will have to answer questions about graphs, data tables, and pictures. Use the information provided to answer the questions that follow. You can refer to the information as often as you want when answering the questions.

Remember, you have 40 minutes to complete the 25 questions on this practice test. Work carefully, but don't spend too much time on any one question. If you're having trouble with a question, make the best guess you can and move on. Don't skip any questions. Your score is based on the number of correct answers; there is no penalty for guessing.

When taking the practice test, try to simulate actual test conditions. Use a timing device of some sort and a couple No. 2 pencils with good erasers. Take the test in a place where you won't be interrupted, and follow test instructions. Start the timer after you've read the instructions and are ready to proceed to the first question.

Go on to the next page when you are ready to begin.

Questions 1 and 2 refer to the following paragraph and table:

A student performs a lab in which he measures plant growth each day for a week. He puts one plant in a dark closet, puts another plant in a room by a window, and puts the last plant outside. He wants to see if the amount of light affects the plants' growth. The following table outlines the information the student recorded.

	Plant in Dark	**Plant in Window**	**Plant Outside**
Day 1	10 cm	10 cm	10 cm
Day 2	10 cm	11 cm	12 cm
Day 3	10 cm	12 cm	15 cm
Day 4	10 cm	13 cm	18 cm
Day 5	10 cm	14 cm	21 cm

1. According to this information, what conclusion can the student draw?

   (1) The amount of light does not affect plant growth.

   (2) Plants grown in the dark die.

   (3) Plants grown in a window grow more than plants grown in the dark.

   (4) Plants grown outside require more water than plants grown in the dark.

2. Which of the following would be the best hypothesis for this experiment?

   (1) Plants grown in the dark do not increase in height.

   (2) Plants are called autotrophs.

   (3) Insects eat plants grown outside.

   (4) Plants need water to grow.

Questions 3 and 4 refer to the following graph:

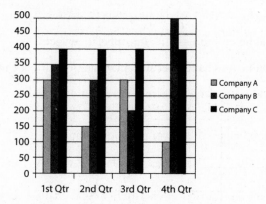

3. Which company had the most stable growth of the four quarters?

    (1) Company A

    (2) Company B

    (3) Company C

    (4) Companies A and B

4. Which company had the most growth in the fourth quarter?

    (1) Company A

    (2) Company B

    (3) Company C

    (4) Companies A and B

Questions 5 and 6 refer to the following paragraph:

Carbon cycles through the environment quickly. Every time you exhale, you have taken carbon that was in your body and expelled it into the atmosphere. Plants take the carbon out of the atmosphere and convert it to glucose. Carbon is also found in the ground in many rock formations.

5. Which conclusion can you make about carbon based on this paragraph?

    (1) Carbon is an important part of your body.

    (2) Oceans contain carbon.

    (3) Carbon combines with oxygen to form CO_2.

    (4) Plants require carbon to grow.

6. How would deforestation affect the carbon cycle?

    (1) There would be an increase in atmospheric carbon.

    (2) There would be an increase in atmospheric oxygen.

    (3) There would be no change because plants do not affect the carbon cycle.

    (4) Glucose production would decrease in remaining plants.

Refer to the following food chain to answer questions 7 and 8:

Grass → grasshopper → bird

7. Arrows represent the transfer of energy in a food chain. Every time an organism is eaten by another organism, the consumer uses 90 percent of the energy to survive and only passes on 10 percent of the energy to the next trophic level. Based on this information, what can you conclude?

    (1) Primary producers require more energy to survive.

    (2) Primary consumers must consume a greater number of organisms than secondary consumers to survive.

    (3) Secondary consumers must consume a greater number of organisms than primary consumers to survive.

    (4) Decomposers must consume the greatest number of organisms to survive.

8. If the grass has 1,000 calories, according to the 10 percent rule, how many calories will the bird have to offer from the 1,000 calories of grass?

    (1) 1

    (2) 10

    (3) 100

    (4) 1,000

9. Plants are able to convert the sun's energy into a usable form of food known as glucose. A plant can do this, but animals cannot due to a specialized organelle found only in plant cells. This process occurs in which organelle?

    (1) Chromosomes

    (2) Chlorophyll

    (3) Cell membrane

    (4) Lysosomes

10. Chemotherapy affects multiple systems in the body. A chemotherapy patient comes in complaining about a loss of eyesight and numbness in their hands and feet. Which body system is most likely being affected?

    (1) Nervous system

    (2) Optical system

    (3) Integumentary system

    (4) Endocrine system

11. Gregor Mendel experimented with pea plants and discovered how traits are passed from one generation to another. In Mendel's experiment, he crossed a tall pea plant (TT) with a short pea plant (tt). If four plants are produced from the two parent plants, which of the following phenotypical traits is most likely to be presented in the offspring?

    (1) Two tall plants, two short plants

    (2) One tall plant, three short plants

    (3) Four tall plants

    (4) Three tall plants, one short plant

12. Which of the following is the correct order of mitosis?

    (1) Prophase, metaphase, anaphase, telophase

    (2) Telophase, anaphase, metaphase, prophase

    (3) Telophase, metaphase, anaphase, prophase

    (4) Metaphase, anaphase, prophase, telophase

Use the periodic table to answer questions 13 and 14:

Group→	1	2	3	4	5	6	7	8	9	10	11	12	13	14	15	16	17	18
↓Period																		
1	1 H																	2 He
2	3 Li	4 Be											5 B	6 C	7 N	8 O	9 F	10 Ne
3	11 Na	12 Mg											13 Al	14 Si	15 P	16 S	17 Cl	18 Ar
4	19 K	20 Ca	21 Sc	22 Ti	23 V	24 Cr	25 Mn	26 Fe	27 Co	28 Ni	29 Cu	30 Zn	31 Ga	32 Ge	33 As	34 Se	35 Br	36 Kr
5	37 Rb	38 Cr	39 Y	40 Zr	41 Nb	42 Mo	43 Tc	44 Ru	45 Rh	46 Pd	47 Ag	48 Cd	49 In	50 Sn	51 Sb	52 Te	53 I	54 Xe
6	55 Cs	56 Ba		72 Hf	73 Ta	74 W	75 Re	76 Os	77 Ir	78 Pt	79 Au	80 Hg	81 Tl	82 Pb	83 Bi	84 Po	85 At	86 Rn
7	87 Fr	88 Ra		104 Rf	105 Db	106 Sg	107 Bh	108 Hs	109 Mt	110 Ds	111 Rg	112 Cn	113 Uut	114 Uuq	115 Uup	116 Uuh	117 Uus	118 Uuo

Lanthanides	57 La	58 Ce	59 Pr	60 Nd	61 Pm	62 Sm	63 Eu	64 Gd	65 Tb	66 Dy	67 Ho	68 Er	69 Tm	70 Yb	71 Lu
Actinides	89 Ac	90 Th	91 Pa	92 U	93 Np	94 Pu	95 Am	96 Cm	97 Bk	98 Cf	99 Es	100 Fm	101 Md	102 No	103 Lr

13. John is studying the differences in covalent and ionic bonds. He comes across a problem in his textbook about sodium and chlorine. Referencing his periodic table, John makes the conclusion that sodium and chlorine would most likely form what type of bond?

   (1) Neither a covalent nor an ionic

   (2) A covalent bond

   (3) An ionic bond

   (4) Both a covalent and an ionic bond

14. Which of the following elements are found in the same family or group?

   (1) Calcium and helium

   (2) Lithium and chromium

   (3) Beryllium and sulfur

   (4) Fluorine and chlorine

15. An athlete gets hurt on the football field, and the trainer brings the athlete a cold pack. Before he places the cold pack on the athlete's leg, he breaks the vial inside the pack. Instantly, the pack gets cold. This is an example of what type of reaction?

   (1) Endothermic

   (2) Exothermic

   (3) Physical change

   (4) pH change

16. Ammonia has a pH of approximately 11, whereas urine has a pH of approximately 6. How many more times acidic is urine than ammonia?

    (1) 5 times

    (2) 6 times

    (3) 1,000 times

    (4) 100,000 times

17. Which of the following equations is properly balanced?

    (1) $2NaOH + H_2SO_4 \rightarrow Na_2SO_4 + H_2O$

    (2) $2NaOH + 2H_2SO_4 \rightarrow Na_2SO_4 + 3H_2O$

    (3) $2NaOH + H_2SO_4 \rightarrow Na_2SO_4 + 2H_2O$

    (4) $NaOH + H_2SO_4 \rightarrow Na_2SO_4 + H_2O$

18. A 1,000 kg box is dropped from a bridge and is accelerating at 10 m/s/s. Using the formula force (N) = mass (kg) × acceleration (m/s/s), determine what force is acting on the box.

    (1) 10 N

    (2) 100 N

    (3) 1,000 N

    (4) 10,000 N

19. Lacey is riding on a roller coaster. It begins by lifting her to 20 meters, then drops 15 meters and goes into a loop with a height of 10 meters. After the loop, it turns sideways and goes into a spiral before it comes to a stop. At which point of the ride did Lacey have the most potential energy?

    (1) When the roller coaster was falling 15 meters

    (2) When the roller coaster reached 20 meters before the drop

    (3) At the top of the 10-meter loop

    (4) When the roller coaster came to a stop

20. A simple machine allows a person to do the same amount of work with less effort, but it takes more time. Which of the following is an example of a simple machine?

    (1) Bridge

    (2) Typewriter

    (3) Wheelchair ramp

    (4) Rope

21. Maricella is playing with a Slinky in physics class. Her friend Jorge holds one end of the Slinky while Maricella moves her end back and forth from left to right. What type of wave are Maricella and Jorge demonstrating?

    (1) Transverse wave

    (2) Compressional wave

    (3) Microwave

    (4) Wavelength

22. The ring of fire is a circle around the Pacific plate where many volcanoes are found. The volcanoes are found there because of what type of plate boundary?

    (1) Oceanic

    (2) Divergent

    (3) Convergent

    (4) Transform

23. A couple is going on a hot air balloon ride over the Grand Canyon. Which atmospheric layer will they reach?

    (1) Troposphere

    (2) Stratosphere

    (3) Mesosphere

    (4) Exosphere

24. You go on a fishing trip off the coast of Costa Rica. After a day of fishing, you decide to write an article in the local paper about the fishing trip. You describe the ocean layer where you were fishing as what?

    (1) Euphotic zone

    (2) Bathyal zone

    (3) Abyssal zone

    (4) Benthic zone

Question 25 refers to the following figure:

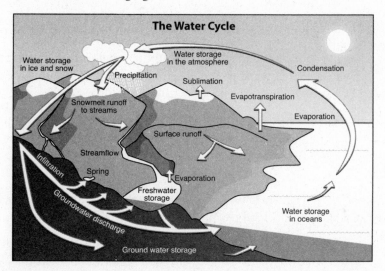

25. Water circulates through our planet in many ways. It falls to the ground in the form of precipitation, it evaporates from the ground or from plants in the form of evapotranspiration, and it infiltrates the soil. What is the name of the process that occurs when water vapor collects, condenses, and forms droplets that may fall back to the earth's surface?

    (1) Infiltration

    (2) Sublimation

    (3) Evapotranspiration

    (4) Condensation

Answers and Explanations

1. **(3)** The only answer that can be made directly from the data table is that plants located near a window grow more than plants grown in the dark. This is because the plant in the window went from 10 centimeters to 14 centimeters over the 5 days.

2. **(1)** This is the correct answer because a hypothesis is an educated guess about an experiment. The experiment is about plants and how much they grow in the dark, in a window, and outside. Therefore, the only hypothesis that can be right must have something to do with the experiment; in this case, plants grown in the dark do not increase in height.

3. **(3)** Company C is correct because its growth stayed at 400 during all four quarters, making it the company with the most stable (not changing) growth.

4. **(2)** Company B grew to 500, which was much greater than either company A or C.

5. **(4)** Carbon can be found in many places in the environment. The paragraph says plants take carbon out of the atmosphere and convert it to glucose. This is the only statement that can be concluded from the paragraph.

6. **(1)** The paragraph clearly states that plants take the carbon out of the atmosphere and convert it to glucose. Therefore, if deforestation is occurring, plants would not be removing carbon from the atmosphere, which would cause an increase in atmospheric carbon.

7. **(3)** Secondary consumers must consume a greater number of organisms because the higher you move up the food chain, the less energy is available to the next level.

8. **(2)** Every step up on the food chain has a decrease of 90 percent; only 10 percent moves on to the next level. If the grass has 1,000 calories, the grasshopper would have 100 calories, so the bird would have 10 calories left from the original 1,000 calories of grass.

9. **(2)** The organelles a plant has that an animal cell does not have are chloroplasts, chlorophyll, and a cell wall. Chlorophyll converts the sun's energy into glucose.

10. **(1)** The nervous system includes the brain, spinal cord, and nerves, all of which would function in eyesight and nerve feeling.

11. **(3)** Tt, Tt, Tt, Tt. When a tall (TT) plant is crossed with a short (tt) plant, the resulting offspring will all be tall (their phenotype) but be carriers of the short gene. This is because the tall plant only has a T to donate, and the short plant only has a t to donate. Each offspring gets one from each parent, so because the tall one gives the T and the short one gives the t, the offspring will all be Tt.

12. **(1)** The orders of mitosis are best memorized by PMAT: prophase, metaphase, anaphase, telophase.

13. **(3)** An ionic bond is a bond between a metal and a nonmetal. A covalent bond is a bond between two nonmetals.

14. **(4)** A family, or group, on the periodic table contains elements all found in the same column. For example, fluorine is right above chlorine in the same column and, therefore, in the same family or group.

15. **(1)** During an endothermic reaction, the temperature of the substance drops, or gets colder. When the trainer broke the vial in the ice pack, he caused an endothermic reaction.

16. **(4)** Each time you move up the pH scale, you multiply the value by 10. So in this case, going from 6 to 11 is five steps up the scale—from 6 to 7, from 7 to 8, and so on. Therefore, you need 5 zeros, or 100,000.

17. **(3)** $2NaOH + H_2SO_4 \rightarrow Na_2SO_4 + 2H_2O$. Look at how many atoms of each element are on the right side and how many are on the left. In this answer, two Na atoms are on each side, six Os, four Hs, and one S—it's balanced.

18. **(4)** To solve this, multiply the 1,000 kg box by the acceleration of 10 m/s/s to get 10,000 N (or kg × m/s/s).

19. **(2)** Potential energy is energy of position. Lacey has the most potential energy when she is at the highest point on the roller coaster, at 20 meters.

20. **(3)** An inclined plane is a ramp (in this case a wheelchair ramp) that lessens the force by doing the work on the object over a greater distance, using less force.

21. **(1)** A transverse wave moves back and forth at right angles to the way the wave is moving. An ocean wave moves up and down at a right angle to the direction the wave is moving (toward the beach).

22. **(3)** Convergent plates are when two plates move together, often forming volcanoes. This is because the one plate slides underneath the other plate, melts, and rises to the surface.

23. **(1)** The troposphere is the level of the atmosphere we live in. It contains 21 percent oxygen and is where the hot air balloon would stay.

24. **(1)** The euphotic zone is the uppermost layer of the ocean where the sun's rays can penetrate. This is where most life-forms are found.

25. **(3)** Condensation occurs when water vapor collects, condenses, and forms droplets.

Mathematical Reasoning Test

Part 4 consists of four review chapters—numbers, arithmetic, and number sense (Chapter 24); measurement and geometry (Chapter 25); data analysis, statistics, and probability (Chapter 26); and algebra, functions, and patterns (Chapter 27)—and a description of the Mathematical Reasoning Test (Chapter 28). Each chapter concludes with practice questions, most in traditional, four-option multiple-choice format. However, because the GED® is offered exclusively on computer, your actual Mathematical Reasoning Test also may include other types of question and answer formats, as discussed in Chapter 28.

Specific math terminology is needed to describe mathematical ideas and methods, and without such words, explaining how to "do" math would be difficult if not impossible. Throughout the following chapters, be sure to read the Definition sidebars to learn essential math terms you might not know.

Most of the problems on the Mathematical Reasoning Test ask you to apply math to everyday situations, such as finding percentages, determining measurements, reading charts or graphs, or recognizing patterns. Only rarely are you asked to do a "straight math" problem, such as adding two fractions or multiplying two decimals. You nonetheless may have to know how to do these things to solve the problem, so brush up if you need to.

Numbers, Arithmetic, and Number Sense

This chapter reviews the categories of numbers you should be familiar with for the Mathematical Reasoning Test, including counting numbers, whole numbers, integers, decimals, and fractions. You also learn to recognize the various categories of numbers and do arithmetic (add, subtract, multiply, and divide) with them. In addition, the chapter explores percents, ratios, and proportions. Percents and ratios are special ways of looking at fractions, and proportions are used to scale quantities up or down while preserving their relative size.

The chapter also reviews the meaning of the < (less than) and > (greater than) symbols that indicate the relative size of two numbers.

All of the numbers discussed are brought together in a "picture" called the number line. Distances between two numbers on the number line can be measured using the concept of absolute value.

The chapter concludes with a discussion of squares, cubes, roots, and radicals.

In This Chapter

- Overviews of numbers, arithmetic, and number concepts
- Sample GED®-style questions to practice the skills on which you'll be tested
- Answers and explanations for all questions

Counting Numbers, Whole Numbers, and Integers

The numbers you learned as a small child are the *counting numbers,* or natural numbers. You use counting numbers to count things: 5 apples, 10 fingers, and so forth. You learned your number facts for addition, subtraction, multiplication, and division for counting numbers in elementary school. This book assumes that you've mastered these facts for the first 10 counting numbers.

The counting numbers together with zero make up the *whole numbers.*

Numbers that are less than zero are *negative numbers.* Negative numbers have a short, horizontal line attached to the left of the number. If it's 10 degrees colder than 0, you say it's 10 below zero, or −10 degrees (read as "negative 10 degrees").

The integers consist of …, −3, −2, −1, 0, 1, 2, 3, …. The positive integers and counting numbers are different names for the same set of numbers. Pairs of integers that differ only in sign, such as 1 and −1, are *opposites.* When you add them, you always get 0. Zero is its own opposite.

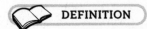 **DEFINITION**

> **Counting numbers** consist of 1, 2, 3, …. The "…" means "and so on, forever." **Whole numbers** consist of 0, 1, 2, 3, …. **Integers** are positive and negative whole numbers, including zero. **Opposites** are pairs of integers, such as 2 and −2, that add to make 0.

Unlike counting numbers, every nonzero integer has two parts: a sign and a magnitude. The *sign* is either positive or negative, and the *magnitude* is the numerical part without the sign. For instance, −10 has sign − (negative) and magnitude 10. The sign for a positive number is usually omitted, but is understood to be + (positive).

You now have seen three categories of numbers: counting numbers, whole numbers, and integers. Each category was built from its predecessor by attaching more numbers. First, the whole numbers were built from the counting numbers by attaching zero, and the integers were built by attaching opposites of counting numbers to the whole numbers. Before the end of the chapter, you'll see how fractions are built from integers and how decimal numbers are a convenient way of writing all these numbers.

When you add, subtract, multiply, or divide numbers, you do arithmetic. Here are some terms you need to know:

Sum   The result of adding numbers.

Difference   The result when you subtract one number from another.

Product   The result when two numbers are multiplied.

Factors   The numbers being multiplied.

Quotient   The result when one number is divided by another.

Dividend   The number being divided.

Divisor   The number doing the dividing.

If two integers have the same sign, add their magnitudes and put the common sign on the sum. For example, $8 + 7 = 15$, and $-7 + (-8) = -15$. The -8 is in parentheses because mathematicians don't like to see two signs right next to each other.

If two integers have opposite signs, subtract the smaller magnitude from the larger magnitude. Then attach the sign of the number with the larger magnitude to this difference. For example, $-8 + 10 = 2$ because $10 - 8 = 2$, and 10 (the number with the larger magnitude) is positive, so the answer 2 is positive. But $-8 + 6 = -2$ because $8 - 6 = 2$, and -8 (the number with the larger magnitude) is negative, so the answer -2 is negative.

To subtract integers, just add the opposite. Let's look at some examples:

$$6 - 9 = 6 + (-9) = -3$$

$$-2 - 7 = -2 + (-7) = -9$$

$$5 - (-4) = 5 + 4 = 9$$

$$-7 - (-9) = -7 + 9 = 2$$

Subtraction is an example of a technique used often in math. Instead of creating a new method to do a new problem, change the new problem to a problem that already has a method. Instead of having a new set of rules for subtraction, change the subtraction problem to an addition problem and use the addition rules you already have.

Multiplying integers is less complicated than adding them. If two integers have the same sign, their product is positive. If they have different signs, the product is negative. If either integer is 0, the product is 0. Thus, $4 \times 5 = 20$ and $(-4) \times (-5) = 20$, but $4 \times (-5) = -20$ and $(-4) \times 5 = -20$.

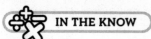 **IN THE KNOW**

When parentheses are used to enclose numbers, a multiplication sign isn't necessary. For example, $(-4) \times (-5) = 20$ has the same meaning as $(-4)(-5) = 20$.

The rule is the same for division. If two integers have the same sign and you divide, the quotient is positive. If they have different signs, the quotient is negative. So $20 \div 2 = 10$ and $(-20) \div (-2) = 10$, but $20 \div (-2) = -10$ and $-20 \div 2 = -10$. Furthermore, if the dividend is 0 and the divisor is nonzero, the quotient is zero, such as $0 \div (-5) = 0$. If the dividend is any number and the divisor is zero, the quotient is undefined, such as $8 \div (0)$ is undefined. Division by zero has no meaning.

You probably used the division symbol ($\div$) when you learned to divide in elementary school. However, the division bar, rather than the division symbol, is used most often in high school math. For example, $20 \div 10$ is written as $\dfrac{20}{10}$.

Decimals, Scientific Notation, and Rounding

Our number system uses 10 digits: 0, 1, 2, 3, 4, 5, 6, 7, 8, and 9. The prefix *deci-* means "10" in Latin (think of the word *decade*). A *decimal number* is a decimal point (.) with digits around it, like 29.365. Each of the digits occupies a place value. The names of the place values to the left and right of the decimal point are shown in the following figure.

Whole Numbers												Decimals				
Billions			Millions			Thousands			Units							
10^{11}	10^{10}	10^{9}	10^{8}	10^{7}	10^{6}	10^{5}	10^{4}	10^{3}	10^{2}	10^{1}	10^{0}	10^{-1}	10^{-2}	10^{-3}	10^{-4}	10^{-5}
Hundred Billions	Ten Billions	Billions	Hundred Millions	Ten Millions	Millions	Hundred Thousands	Ten Thousands	Thousands	Hundreds	Tens	Units	Tenths	Hundredths	Thousandths	Ten Thousandths	Hundred Thousandths

Place values.

Whichever column you start with in this figure, the place value of each digit is 10 times the place value of the digit to its right. For example, the value of a digit in the thousands column is 10 times what the value of that digit would be in the hundreds column.

Because decimals are based on the number 10, it's easy to multiply or divide a decimal number by 10. To multiply by 10, move the decimal point one space to the right. To divide by 10, move the decimal point one space to the left. To multiply by 100, move the decimal point two spaces to the right. To divide by 100, move the decimal point two spaces to the left, and so forth.

For example, look at the decimal number 29.365. Start with the rightmost digit, 5. It is in the thousandths place. This number would read "twenty-nine and three hundred sixty-five thousandths." To multiply this number by 100, move the decimal point two places to the right, yielding 2,936.5, or "two thousand nine hundred thirty-six and five tenths." To divide 29.365 by 10, move the decimal point one place to the left, yielding 2.9365, or "two and nine thousand three hundred sixty-five ten thousandths."

Any integer can be written as a decimal. Just place a decimal point after the integer. The integer −14 and the decimal −14.00 have the same value. So do the integer 7 and the decimal 7.00. Therefore, even if you see an integer written without a decimal point, you can think of it as a decimal number.

You can insert zeros at the front and back of a decimal number without changing its value. The number 0029.365000 is the same as 29.365. This is true because each zero multiplies its place value, and zero times any number is zero. As you'll see, this makes it easier to add and subtract decimals. Zeros inserted at the front of a decimal number are *leading zeros*, while those inserted at the back are *trailing zeros*.

The term *scientific notation* comes from science's use of very large numbers and numbers very close to zero. The distance (in miles) to the nearest star, other than the sun, is about 25.2 trillion miles. Scientific notation is used to compare astronomical distances because they are so large. At the other extreme, some physical constants in science are numbers very close to zero. Planck's constant—the energy of a photon divided by its frequency—would be written in decimal form as 33 zeros to the right of the decimal point, followed by 626. Scientific notation is the only reasonable way to write a number this small!

The numbers 1, 10, 100, 1,000, and so forth are "powers of 10." The number 10 is convenient because the powers of 10 can be determined by counting the number of zeros following the 1. For example, 10^3 (10 to the power 3) is $10 \times 10 \times 10$, which is 1,000, a 1 followed by three zeros.

The numbers $\frac{1}{10}$, $\frac{1}{100}$, $\frac{1}{1000}$, and so forth are also powers of 10. Because these numbers are less than 1, however, you use negative integers as powers of 10: $\frac{1}{10} = 10^{-1}$, $\frac{1}{100} = 10^{-2}$, $\frac{1}{1000} = 10^{-3}$, and so forth.

A number is written in scientific notation if it is a number between 1 and 10 (including 1 but not including 10) times a power of 10. The method for changing a number in decimal form to its scientific notation is best illustrated by examples.

Suppose you start with the decimal number 145.23. Move the decimal point two places to the left to create the number 1.4523, which is between 1 and 10. The number you started with is greater than 10, so you have to raise 10 to the power 2 (because you moved the decimal point 2 places to the left). Therefore, the scientific notation for 145.23 is 1.4523×10^2.

Now suppose that you start with the decimal number 0.0014523. This time you must move the decimal point three places to the right to get 1.4523, a number between 1 and 10. The number you started with is less than 1, so you have to raise 10 to the power −3 (because you moved the decimal point 3 places to the right). Therefore, the scientific notation for 0.0014523 is 1.4523×10^{-3}.

What about numbers greater than 1 and less than 10? What, for example, is the scientific notation for the number 4.61? Because this number is already between 1 and 10, there's no need to move the decimal point. In other words, you move the decimal point 0 places. Therefore, the scientific notation for 4.61 is 4.61×10^0.

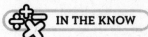   **IN THE KNOW**

> A decimal number is greater than or equal to 10, between 1 and 10, or less than 1. In these three cases, the powers of 10 are positive, zero, and negative, respectively, when the number is written in scientific notation.

The method for changing a number written in scientific notation to a decimal number reverses the procedure just described.

Suppose you start with the number 5.6038×10^4. Because the exponent is positive, the decimal number will be bigger than 10, so move the decimal point four places to the right, resulting in the decimal number 56,038.

Now suppose you start with the number 9.582×10^{-2}. Because the exponent is negative, the decimal number will be less than 1, so move the decimal two places to the left. You have to insert a leading zero to the original scientific form, making it 09.582×10^{-2}. Then, when you move the decimal point two places to the left, you get the decimal number 0.09582.

The difference in the *order of magnitude* of two numbers is the difference in the powers of 10 when the numbers are written in scientific notation.

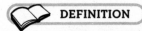   **DEFINITION**

> The **order of magnitude** of a number is the power of 10 when the number is written in scientific notation. Basically, the order of magnitude tells you whether a number is in the thousands, hundreds, tenths, hundredths, and such.

To find a difference in the order of magnitude of two numbers, just write the numbers in scientific notation and subtract the powers of 10. For example, to compare the orders of magnitude of 105 and 100,750, write 105 as 1.05×10^2 and 100,750 as 1.00750×10^5. The number 100,750 is 3 ($= 5 - 2$) orders of magnitude larger than the number 105. Or you could say the number 105 is 3 orders of magnitude smaller than the number 100,750.

The power of an earthquake is measured on the Richter scale. Richter scale numbers represent orders of magnitude. An earthquake of Richter number 8 is 100 times more powerful than one of Richter number 6 because they are 2 ($= 8 - 6$) orders of magnitude apart.

Add or subtract decimals the same way you would add or subtract whole numbers, but be sure to add or subtract digits of the same place value. A careful way to add decimals by hand is to arrange them vertically and line up the decimal points. To add the decimal numbers 6.2, 8.03, and 35.49, arrange them vertically, insert trailing zeros, and add:

$$
\begin{array}{r}
6.20 \\
8.03 \\
+35.49 \\
\hline
49.72
\end{array}
$$

When you subtract decimal numbers, you also need to line up the decimal points and insert trailing zeros. Then subtract just as you would if they were integers, but keep the decimal point where it is. For example, to find the difference 48.5 − 29.72, first insert a trailing zero to get 48.50 − 29.72. Then subtract as though you were subtracting 4,850 − 2,972, but retain the decimal point to get 18.78 as the difference.

To multiply decimals, multiply as though the numbers were integers, count the total number of places to the right of the decimal points in both factors, and place the decimal point that total number of places in from the right of the product.

To multiply 5.1 × 2.36, multiply 51 times 236 to get 12,036. The factors have a total of three digits to the right of the decimal points, so place the decimal point three places in from the right. The product is 12.036.

To divide decimals, move the decimal point of both the divisor and dividend the same number of places to the right until both are integers. Insert trailing zeros as necessary, and divide as you would integers.

To find the quotient $\dfrac{9.45}{2.1}$, insert a trailing zero on 2.1 to make it 2.10. Now move both decimal points two places to the right. Then, using long division, divide 945 by 210 to get 4.5 as the quotient.

There's a rule for rounding a decimal number to a particular place value. Call the digit in the place value you are rounding to the *rounding digit*. Look at the digit just to the right of the rounding digit. If this digit is less than 5, leave the rounding digit as it is and change each digit to its right to zero. If this digit is 5 or more, increase the rounding digit by 1 and change each digit to its right to zero. If the rounding digit is 9 and the digit to its right is 5 or larger, change the rounding digit to 0 and add 1 to the digit to its left.

The following examples illustrate this rule:

- **Round 4,746 to the nearest hundred:** The rounding digit is 7 (hundreds place). The digit to its right is 4, which is less than 5. Therefore, 4,746 rounds to 4,700.

- **Round 0.2653 to the nearest hundredth:** The rounding digit is 6 (hundredths place), and the digit to its right is 5, so round the 6 up to 7. Therefore, 0.2653 rounded to the nearest hundredth is 0.27.

- **Round 5.98 to the nearest tenth:** The rounding digit is 9 (tenths place), and the digit to its right is 8, so round 9 to 0 and 5 to 6. Therefore, 5.98 rounded to the nearest tenth is 6.0. You need the 0 even though 6.0 and 6 have the same value because 6 is 5.98 rounded to the nearest unit.

Fractions

Fractions are numbers such as $\frac{1}{2}, \frac{3}{7}, \frac{5}{5}$, and $\frac{10}{3}$. The top number is the *numerator*, and the bottom number is the *denominator*. A fraction cannot have a 0 in the denominator. The first two fractions are examples of proper fractions because the numerator is less than the denominator. The last two fractions are examples of improper fractions because the numerator is equal to or greater than the denominator.

Fractions often are used to represent parts of a whole. The denominator tells you the number of equal parts in the whole, and the numerator tells you the number of those equal parts you have. If you eat three pieces of eight equal-size pieces of a pizza, you have eaten (three-eighths) of the whole pizza.

A fraction also can be thought of as the result of a division. The fraction $\frac{1}{2}$ is the result of dividing 1 by 2. The fraction $\frac{3}{7}$ is the result of dividing 3 by 7. The fraction $\frac{5}{5}$ is the result of dividing 5 by 5, which equals 1. The fraction $\frac{10}{3}$ is the result of dividing 10 by 3, which equals $3\frac{1}{3}$.

If you divide a number by 1, the result is the same as the number. This means that an integer can be regarded as a special type of fraction—namely, one whose denominator is 1. For example, 17 is the same number as $\frac{17}{1}$. Fortunately, the rules of arithmetic work the same whether a number is regarded as an integer or a fraction.

Fractions have opposites (negatives), and they can be added and subtracted just like integers. Remember that when you add opposite number pairs, the answer is zero. For instance,

$$6+\left(-6\right)=0 \ \text{ and } \ \frac{2}{3}+\left(-\frac{2}{3}\right)=0.$$

A fraction is also paired with another number called its *reciprocal*. The reciprocal of a fraction is obtained by switching the numerator and denominator. The reciprocal of $\frac{5}{8}$ is $\frac{8}{5}$. The reciprocal of an integer such as –17 is $\frac{1}{-17}$ because –17 is the same as $\frac{-17}{1}$. A number times its reciprocal is 1. The number 0 doesn't have a reciprocal because no number times 0 equals 1. This is the reason division by zero is impossible.

A fraction is in reduced form if no number, other than 1, divides evenly into both its numerator and denominator. For example, $\frac{2}{3}$ is in reduced form while $\frac{4}{6}$ isn't because 2 divides evenly into both 4 and 6. To reduce a fraction that is not in reduced form, find a number that divides evenly into both the numerator and denominator of the fraction. The fraction $\frac{12}{28}$ reduces to $\frac{6}{14}$ because 2 divides evenly into both 12 and 28. But you can reduce $\frac{6}{14}$ further to $\frac{3}{7}$ if you divide by 2 again. This is as far as you can go because 1 is the only number that divides evenly into both 3 and 7. If your number facts are good, you might have realized to start with that you could divide both by 4 to get to the reduced form faster. The number 4 is the *greatest common factor* of 12 and 28.

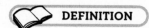 **DEFINITION**

Reciprocals are pairs of numbers that have a product of 1. The **greatest common factor** of two numbers is the greatest factor that will divide evenly into both numbers.

To multiply two fractions, multiply the numerators to get the numerator of the answer, and multiply the denominators to get the denominator of the answer. Then, if needed, reduce the product. For example, $\frac{3}{8} \cdot \frac{1}{5} = \frac{3 \cdot 1}{8 \cdot 5} = \frac{3}{40}$, which is in reduced form.

Now look at this multiplication problem: $\frac{2}{3} \cdot \frac{9}{14} = \frac{18}{42}$. You can reduce $\frac{18}{42}$ further by dividing the numerator and denominator by 6: $\frac{18 \div 6}{42 \div 6} = \frac{3}{7}$. Notice that in the original problem, there's a 3 in the denominator of the first fraction and a 9 in the numerator of the second fraction. Because 3 divides evenly into both of these numbers, you could divide both by 3 before multiplying. Similarly, 2 divides evenly into both 2 (the numerator of the first fraction) and 14 (the denominator of the second fraction). This procedure can be set up as follows:

$$\frac{2}{3} \cdot \frac{9}{14} = \frac{\cancel{2}^{1}}{\cancel{3}^{1}} \cdot \frac{\cancel{9}^{3}}{\cancel{14}^{7}} = \frac{1 \cdot 3}{1 \cdot 7} = \frac{3}{7}$$

When it's possible, dividing ahead of time like this makes it unnecessary to reduce as a second step.

The word *of* between two numerical quantities usually means *multiply* in math. Suppose, for example, that you and your friends order 3 pizzas and you eat $\frac{3}{8}$ of the total. There are 24 equal slices in 3 pizzas, so you eat $\frac{3}{8}$ of 24 slices. Multiply $\frac{3}{8}$ times 24, to get $\frac{72}{8}$, or 9 slices you eat altogether.

To divide one fraction by another, just multiply the first fraction by the reciprocal of the second. For instance, $\frac{2}{3} \div \frac{7}{8}$ is the same as $\frac{2}{3} \cdot \frac{8}{7}$, and both are equal to $\frac{16}{21}$. This is another example of doing a new problem by changing the form of the problem and using a method you already know.

Adding and subtracting fractions can be a little tricky, depending on whether the denominators of the two numbers are the same. If the denominators are the same, add or subtract the numerators and place the result over the common denominator. For example, $\frac{2}{7} + \frac{3}{7} = \frac{5}{7}$ and $\frac{8}{9} - \frac{3}{9} = \frac{5}{9}$. If necessary, answers can be reduced. For example, $\frac{7}{8} - \frac{3}{8} = \frac{4}{8} = \frac{4 \div 4}{8 \div 4} = \frac{1}{2}$.

When you add or subtract fractions that have different denominators, first find the *least common denominator.*

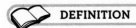 **DEFINITION**

> The **least common denominator** of two fractions is the least common multiple of the two denominators. This is the smallest number that is a multiple of both denominators.

Here are some examples of adding and subtracting two fractions with different denominators:

- $\frac{1}{4} + \frac{2}{3}$. The denominators are 4 and 3, and 12 is the smallest multiple of both. Because 12 is 3 times 4, multiply both numerator and denominator of $\frac{1}{4}$ by 3 to get $\frac{3}{12}$. Because 12 is 4 times 3, multiply both numerator and denominator of $\frac{2}{3}$ by 4 to get $\frac{8}{12}$. Add $\frac{3}{12}$ and $\frac{8}{12}$ to get the sum, $\frac{11}{12}$.

- $\frac{2}{5} + \frac{2}{15}$. The denominators are 5 and 15, and 15 is a multiple of both. Because 15 is 3 times 5, multiply both numerator and denominator of $\frac{2}{5}$ by 3 to get $\frac{6}{15}$. The denominators are now the same, so add $\frac{6}{15}$ and $\frac{2}{15}$ to get $\frac{8}{15}$.

- $\dfrac{3}{4} - \dfrac{7}{10}$. The two denominators are 4 and 10. Generate multiples of the larger denominator until you reach a multiple of the smaller one. The larger denominator is 10. The smallest multiple of 10 is 1 times 10, which is 10, but 10 isn't a multiple of 4. The next multiple of 10 is 2 times 10, which is 20. Because 4 goes into 20 (5 times), 20 is the least common denominator. Finish the problem as in the two previous examples to get the difference: $\dfrac{3}{4} - \dfrac{7}{10} = \dfrac{3 \cdot 5}{4 \cdot 5} - \dfrac{7 \cdot 2}{10 \cdot 2} = \dfrac{15}{20} - \dfrac{14}{20} = \dfrac{1}{20}$.

Ratios

Ratios provide a method of comparing two numbers. For example, if I am 50 years old and you are 25 years old, the ratio of our ages is 50 to 25. You could write this as the ratio $\dfrac{50}{25}$, which reduces to $\dfrac{2}{1}$. Therefore, you could say that I've lived 2 years for each 1 year you've lived.

Unit pricing at the supermarket is another example of using ratios to make comparisons. The brand-name cereal may cost $4.25 for 15 ounces while the store brand costs $2.50 for 11.5 ounces. By comparing the ratios $\dfrac{4.25}{15} = 0.28$ and $\dfrac{2.5}{11.5} = 0.22$, you can determine that you save about 6 cents an ounce by buying the store brand.

Suppose 42 people are at a dance—24 boys and 18 girls. You could say that $\dfrac{18}{42}$ of those at the dance are girls and $\dfrac{24}{42}$ are boys. If you're interested in comparing the number of girls to the number of boys, you could look at the ratio $\dfrac{18}{24}$. By reducing $\dfrac{18}{24}$ to $\dfrac{3}{4}$, you could say that there are three girls to every four boys at the dance.

Percents are fractions or ratios that have denominators of 100. Using 100 as a standard denominator makes comparing numbers easier because you have to look at only the numerators to determine which number is greater. You encounter percents on a regular basis in your daily life. Sales tax is 6% of the price of an item; the electronics store is offering 30% off the price of high-definition TVs; a professional quarterback completes 60% of his passes, and so forth. The word *percent* means "for every 100." So 6% sales tax means the tax is 6 cents for every 100 cents (1 dollar), 30% off the price means 30 cents off for every 1 dollar, and a 60% completion rate means 60 completed passes for every 100 passes thrown.

To change a fraction to a percent, do the division implied in the fraction. This gives you a decimal number, which you then multiply by 100. For example, to change $\dfrac{3}{5}$ to a percent, first divide 3 by 5 and get 0.6. Then multiply 0.6 by 100% by inserting a trailing zero to 0.6, moving the decimal point 2 places to the right, and then attaching a % sign. The answer is 60%.

When you use a percent in a computation, you can change the percent to a decimal. To change a percent to a decimal, move the decimal two places to the left and drop the percent sign.

Percents are often used to describe discounts or mark-ups on prices. If an item you want to buy is 15% off, you pay only 85% (100% − 15%) of the original price. Therefore, you would pay only 0.85 times the original price of the item.

 **GOOD IDEA**

If a discount is described as a percent off, subtract that percent off from 100% and multiply the result by the original value to obtain the sale price of the item.

Adding chain percents taken off a single item gives incorrect results. If a store offers 25% off and when you get there you get another 10% off, your final discount isn't 35% off. Suppose, for example, you buy a $100 item. With a 25% discount, your item now costs $75. The extra 10% off is taken off $75, not $100. Therefore, you get only $7.50 more off instead of $10. Your item's final cost would be $67.50, and not $65.

A *proportion* is a statement that two ratios are equal. In the earlier dance example, the ratio of 18 girls to 24 boys equals the ratio of 3 girls to 4 boys: $\frac{18}{24} = \frac{3}{4}$. This statement is a proportion. You also could say that 18 girls to 24 boys is proportional to 3 girls to 4 boys.

Proportions are important in geometry because they preserve shape. When you enlarge a photograph of a person's face, the whole face is larger, but the parts of the face are proportional to the face in the original photo. The mirrors in the funhouse of an amusement park compress the face to look fat or stretch it to look long. Neither of these reflections is proportional to the actual face.

A proportion consists of four numbers: the two numerators and the two denominators of the two ratios. In the dance example, $\frac{18}{24} = \frac{3}{4}$. You also can write a proportion using colons. In this case, 18:24 = 3:4. The outside numbers (18 and 4) are the *extremes* of the proportion. The two inside numbers (24 and 3) are the *means* of the proportion. In a proportion, the product of the means equals the product of the extremes. In this case, 18 × 4 = 3 × 24. Both products are 72. Applying this fact is called *cross-multiplying*.

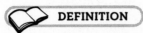 **DEFINITION**

If you write a proportion as $a:b = c:d$, a and d are the **extremes,** and b and c are the **means.**

If you know any three of the numbers in a proportion, you can determine the fourth. Suppose, for example, that a basketball player typically makes 8 of 10 free throws. How many free throws would you expect this player to make if she takes 20 free throws? If you let x stand for the number of free throws the player makes out of 20, you have the proportion: $\dfrac{x}{20} = \dfrac{8}{10}$. Cross-multiply to get $x \cdot 10 = 20 \cdot 8$, or $x \cdot 10 = 160$. To find the value of x, divide 160 by 10, to get 16. A player who typically makes 8 of 10 free throws can expect to make 16 of 20.

This method always can be applied to solve a proportion if you know three of the numbers. Call the missing number x, cross-multiply, and divide by the number that multiplies x.

The Number Line and Absolute Value

Given two numbers, call them a and b, there are three possibilities:

- The two numbers are equal ($a = b$).

- The first number is smaller than the second ($a < b$).

- The first number is larger than the second ($a > b$).

The symbols < and > are used to compare the sizes of numbers. For example, 3 < 6 and 12 > 4.

A *number line* provides a way of picturing the location of the numbers according to their size. Start with the number 0 on the number line. Positive numbers are to the right of zero, and negative numbers are to the left of zero. The numbers get larger as you move from left to right on the number line. The following number line illustrates these ideas and points out a few number locations. (A number line is only a visual aid, and no attempt has been made to show the exact locations of numbers in this figure.)

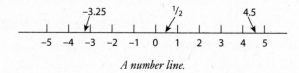

A number line.

Notice that on the number line, 5 and −5 are the same distance from 0 (namely, 5 units). The concept of distance is expressed as a non-negative number. The distance between a number and zero is the *absolute value* of the number. The absolute value of a positive number is just the number itself, while the absolute value of a negative number is its opposite (the positive number). The absolute value of zero is 0. The absolute value of a number is always greater than or equal to zero.

The symbol for absolute value is | |. Using this notation, you would write the absolute value of 5 as $|5|$ and the absolute value of -5 as $|-5|$. In math notation, $|5| = 5$ reads "the absolute value of 5 equals 5," and $|-5| = 5$ reads "the absolute value of -5 is 5."

The absolute value symbol is a grouping symbol, like parentheses. For example, $|8 - 12|$ is equal to $|-4|$, which is 4. Don't make the mistake of taking the absolute value of 8, which is 8, and then subtracting the absolute value of 12, which is 12, to get -4.

More generally, the distance between any two numbers on the number line is the absolute value of the difference between the two numbers. The distance between 7 and 12 is 5 because the absolute value of $7 - 12$ is 5 $\left(|7 - 12| = |-5| = 5 \right)$.

Squares, Cubes, Roots, and Radicals

The *square* of a number is the number multiplied by itself. Thus, 16 is the square of 4 because $4 \cdot 4 = 16$, and it's the square of -4 because $-4 \cdot -4 = 16$. *Perfect squares* are numbers such as 1, 4, 9, 16, 25, 36, and so forth.

The *square root* of a number is a number that, when multiplied by itself, equals the given number. Every positive number has two square roots that are equal in absolute value but opposite in sign. For example, the two square roots of 16 are 4 and -4. The square root of 0 is 0.

The number 4 is the *principal square root* of 16. You use the square root radical sign $\left(\sqrt{} \right)$ to indicate you want the principal square root. If the number under the radical sign is a perfect square, you find its principal square root. Thus, $\sqrt{16} = 4$ (not 4 and -4). Also, when the number under the radical sign has a factor that's a perfect square, you can *simplify* the radical expression by writing it as the product of two radical expressions, one of which contains the perfect square.

For example, $\sqrt{12} = \sqrt{4 \cdot 3} = \sqrt{4} \cdot \sqrt{3} = 2 \cdot \sqrt{3} = 2\sqrt{3}$. In this case, $\sqrt{3}$ is left as is because 3 is not a perfect square nor does 3 contain a factor that is a perfect square.

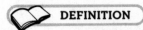 **DEFINITION**

The **principal square root** of a positive number is the positive number that, when multiplied by itself, equals the given number.

The *cube* of a number is the product when the number is used as factor three times. Thus, 27 is the cube of 3 because $3 \cdot 3 \cdot 3 = 27$, and -27 is the cube of -3 because $-3 \cdot -3 \cdot -3 = -27$. *Perfect cubes* are numbers such as 1, 8, 27, 64, 125, and so forth.

Practice

You may use a calculator for some of the practice questions that are in this chapter; Chapters 25, 26, and 27; and on the practice test in Chapter 29. The GED Testing Service uses an on-screen TI-30XS Multiview Scientific Calculator for the Mathematical Reasoning Test. Features of this calculator are described in Chapter 28.

 1. Jackson leased a new car for 3 years. He agreed to pay $1,900 down and a $269 payment each month. He also agreed to pay $0.125 per mile he drove over 30,000 miles. During the 3-year lease period, Jackson drove the car 32,458 miles. Excluding taxes, what was the cost of leasing this car for 3 years?

(1) $5,435.25

(2) $9,991.25

(3) $11,891.25

(4) $13,741.25

 2. Susan drove to her mother's house at an average speed of 36 miles per hour. The trip there took a half hour. If it took her 20 minutes to return, what was her average speed, in miles per hour, coming home?

(1) 40

(2) 46

(3) 50

(4) 54

 3. A $1,200 computer is on sale at 20% off. How much would you save by purchasing the computer on sale?

(1) $20

(2) $96

(3) $240

(4) $960

 4. A pancake recipe calls for $\frac{3}{4}$ cup of flour for each batch. You have 3 cups of flour and enough of the other ingredients to make six batches of pancakes. How many batches of pancakes can you make? Write your answer in the answer box: ☐

5. Jack and Jill were picking weeds in the garden. Jack picked $\frac{1}{3}$ of the weeds, and Jill picked $\frac{1}{5}$ of them. What fraction of the weeds did they pick together?

(1) $\frac{1}{4}$

(2) $\frac{1}{8}$

(3) $\frac{8}{15}$

(4) $\frac{4}{5}$

 6. Simplify the following expression completely:

$\sqrt{200}$

(1) $10\sqrt{2}$

(2) $2\sqrt{50}$

(3) $5\sqrt{40}$

(4) 100

Answers

1. **(3)** Add the three costs: down payment ($1,900), total monthly payments (36 × $269 = $9,684), and mileage over 30,000 (2,458 × $.125 = $307.25) to get $11,891.25.

2. **(4)** If it took Susan a half hour to get to her mother's house with an average speed of 36 miles per hour, her mother must live 18 (distance = speed × time) miles away. It took 20 minutes, or $\frac{1}{3}$ of an hour, to return, so time $= \dfrac{\text{distance}}{\text{speed}} = \dfrac{18 \text{ miles}}{\frac{1}{3} \text{ hour}} = 54$ miles per hour.

3. **(3)** Twenty percent of $1,200 is 0.20 × $1,200 = $240.

4. **(4)** To determine the number of batches of pancakes you can make with 3 cups of flour, divide 3 by $\frac{3}{4}$ to get four batches. Although you have enough of the other ingredients to make six batches, the amount of flour limits your total yield to four batches.

5. **(3)** This problem requires you to add two fractions without a calculator. The least common denominator is 15. The fraction $\frac{1}{5} = \frac{3}{15}$, and $\frac{1}{3} = \frac{5}{15}$. Then, $\frac{3}{15} + \frac{5}{15} = \frac{8}{15}$.

6. **(1)** Simplify the radical: $\sqrt{200} = \sqrt{100} \cdot \sqrt{2} = 10\sqrt{2}$.

Measurement and Geometry

This chapter opens with tables that summarize units of length, liquid volume, weight, and temperature, in both the customary (English) system and the metric system. It's assumed you're familiar with these measurements and their relationships.

That information is followed by definitions of geometric concepts and objects, organized around lines, angles, polygons, triangles, quadrilaterals, circles, and solid figures. You likely are familiar with many of these definitions, which, not surprisingly, you are expected to know for the Mathematical Reasoning Test.

Important facts about triangles, including the well-known Pythagorean theorem, are reviewed next. You may have to use these facts to answer certain questions on the Mathematical Reasoning Test.

Next, are explanations of how to use formulas for determining the area, perimeter, and volume of geometric objects. These formulas are described in Chapter 28 and are available for easy reference during the actual Mathematical Reasoning Test.

The chapter ends with a general discussion of lines in a coordinate plane. A fuller discussion of lines can be found in Chapter 27.

In This Chapter

- Overviews of measurement and geometry
- Sample GED®-style questions to practice the skills on which you'll be tested
- Answers and explanations for all questions

Common Measurements

You should know certain measurement facts involving length, weight, volume, and temperature when you take the Mathematical Reasoning Test. This information is summarized in the following tables of customary and metric measurements. Sample problems for each group of units are given as well.

Units of Length

Customary	Metric
Foot is the basic unit	Meter is the basic unit
12 inches make 1 foot	100 centimeters make 1 meter
3 feet make 1 yard	1000 millimeters make 1 meter
5,280 feet make 1 mile	1000 meters make 1 kilometer

When converting to smaller units, you should multiply. When converting to larger units, you should divide.

Let's look at some sample problems:

Doreen wants to fence in her flower garden, which has a perimeter of 60 feet. Fencing comes in 2-yard sections. How many sections of fencing will Doreen need?

There are 3 feet to a yard, so 60 feet is $60 \div 3 = 20$ yards. Because each section is 2 yards, Doreen will need 10 sections of fence.

Tyrese is reading a map that has a scale of 1 centimeter equals 5 kilometers. The map distance to his destination is 8 centimeters. How far away is his destination?

Because each centimeter on the map represents 5 kilometers, a map distance of 8 centimeters represents $8 \times 5 = 40$ kilometers.

Units of Liquid Volume

Customary	Metric
Gallon is the basic unit	Liter is the basic unit
4 quarts make 1 gallon	100 centiliters make 1 liter
2 pints make 1 quart	1000 milliliters make 1 liter

Sample problems:

Bob and Jack's ice cream costs $3 a pint, and Chicken Farm ice cream costs $5.75 a half gallon. Which ice cream is less expensive?

Change a half gallon to pints so you can compare pints to pints. A gallon is 4 quarts, so a half-gallon is 2 quarts. A quart is 2 pints, so 2 quarts is 4 pints. Four pints of Bob and Jack's ice cream costs $12, compared to $5.75 for Chicken Farm, so Chicken Farm is less expensive.

Zoe needs to take 3 milliliters of medication every other day. How many centiliters of her medication will she take in 30 days?

Because she takes her medication every other day, Zoe will take $15 \times 3 = 45$ milliliters of medication in 30 days. Given there are 10 milliliters to a centiliter, this amounts to 4.5 centiliters over 30 days.

Units of Weight

Customary	Metric
Pound is the basic unit	Gram is the basic unit
16 ounces make 1 pound	1000 milligrams make 1 gram
2,000 pounds make 1 ton	1000 grams make 1 kilogram

Sample problems:

A 1-liter bottle of product X weighs about 0.7 kilogram. How many grams do three such bottles weigh?

Given there are 1000 grams (g) per kilogram (kg), multiply as follows:

$$3 \text{ bottles} \times \frac{0.7 \text{ kg}}{\text{bottle}} \times \frac{1000 \text{ g}}{\text{kg}} = 3 \text{ bottles} \times \frac{0.7 \text{ kg}}{\text{bottle}} \times \frac{1000 \text{ g}}{\text{kg}} = 2100 \text{ g} .$$

Notice that you can cancel like units the same way you do factors when multiplying fractions.

The Chins want to buy stone to landscape their front yard. They need to buy 3 tons total. Their pickup truck will carry 750 pounds per trip. How many trips will they have to make in their truck to carry all the stone home?

Given there are 2,000 pounds per ton, 3 tons is 6,000 pounds. Divide 6,000 by 750 to get 8 trips.

Units of Temperature

Customary	Metric
Degrees Fahrenheit is the unit	Degrees Celsius is the unit
Water freezes at 32°F	Water freezes at 0°C
Water boils at 212°F	Water boils at 100°C

Sample problem:

The formula for changing Celsius temperature to Fahrenheit is $F = \frac{9}{5}C + 32$. If it is 20° Celsius in Paris, what is the Fahrenheit temperature?

Substitute 20 for C in the formula: $F = \frac{9}{5}(20) + 32 = \frac{9}{\cancel{5}^{1}}\left(\cancel{20}^{4}\right) + 32 = 36 + 32 = 68$. The temperature is 68° Fahrenheit.

Geometry Terminology

The geometry of flat shapes, such as triangles, rectangles, and circles, is called *plane geometry*. *Solid geometry* is the study of three-dimensional figures, such as prisms, spheres, cylinders, cones, and pyramids.

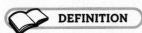 **DEFINITION**

Plane geometry is the study of two-dimensional figures. **Solid geometry** is the study of three-dimensional figures.

You see geometry all around you. A yield sign is shaped like a triangle. A stop sign has an octagon shape. The U.S. Department of Defense in Washington, D.C., is headquartered in a building the shape of a pentagon. Cereal boxes, water glasses, and ice-cream cones are models of geometric solids. The Great Pyramids of Egypt are probably the best-known examples of that shape.

Congruence (≅) is a central concept in geometry. Two line segments are congruent if they have the same length. Two angles are congruent if they have the same degree measure.

A *polygon* is a closed figure whose boundary consists of line segments connected end to end. Two polygons are congruent if they have the same size and shape. Two polygons can have the same shape but different sizes. In this case, they are *similar* (~).

In the following table, each entry consists of a name, a math symbol or description, and a figure for the named object.

Geometric Concepts and Objects

Item	Symbol/Description	Figure
Lines		
Line	$\overleftrightarrow{AB}$	
Segment	$\overline{AB}$	
Ray	$\overrightarrow{AB}$	
Parallel lines	$\overleftrightarrow{AB} \parallel \overleftrightarrow{CD}$	
Perpendicular lines	$\overleftrightarrow{AB} \perp \overleftrightarrow{CD}$	
Transversal	t	
Angles		
Angle	$\angle A$	
Degree measure	45°	

continues

Geometric Concepts and Objects (continued)

Item	Symbol/Description	Figure
Right angle	90°	90°
Acute angle	less than 90°	
Vertical angles	formed by intersecting lines	$b°$ $a°$ $c°$ $d°$ $a = c$ and $b = d$
Correspondings ≅ ∠s	formed by t and $\parallel$ lines	t $a°$ $b°$ $d°$ $c°$ m $w°$ $x°$ $y°$ $z°$ n $a = w, b = x, d = y,$ and $c = z$
Alternate interiors ≅ ∠s	formed by t and $\parallel$ lines	t $a°$ $b°$ $d°$ $c°$ m $w°$ $x°$ $y°$ $z°$ n $d = x$ and $c = w$
Obtuse angle	greater than 90° (but less than 180°)	
Supplements	sum is 180°	1 2

Item	Symbol/Description	Figure
Complements	sum is 90°	 1 2
Polygons		
Triangle	3 sides	
Quadrilateral	4 sides	
Pentagon	5 sides	
Hexagon	6 sides	
Octagon	8 sides	
Triangles		
Isosceles	2 $\cong$ sides	
Equilateral	3 $\cong$ sides	
Scalene	no $\cong$ sides	

continues

Geometric Concepts and Objects (continued)

Item	Symbol/Description	Figure
Acute	3 acute angles	
Obtuse	1 obtuse angle	
Right	1 right angle	
Quadrilaterals		
Parallelogram	2 pairs || sides	
Rectangle	4 right angles	
Square	rectangle with 4 ≅ sides	
Rhombus	4 ≅ sides	
Trapezoid	only 1 pair of || sides	

Item	Symbol/Description	Figure
Circles		
Center	O	
Circumference	distance around circle	
Radius	length r	
Chord	$\overline{AB}$	
Diameter	$\overline{CD}$	
Solids		
Rectangular prism	shaped like a box	
Pyramid	sides come to a point	
Cylinder	shaped like a can	
Cone	shaped like a funnel	
Sphere	shaped like a ball	

Important Triangle Facts

You need to know several important facts about triangles for the GED test.

The measures of the interior angles of any triangle sum to 180°. Suppose you know that two interior angles of a triangle have measures 28° and 63°. These two measures sum to 91°, so the measure of the third interior angle is $(180 - 91)° = 89°$.

The sum of the lengths of any two sides of a triangle must be greater than the length of the third side. This constraint is the *triangle inequality*. Basically, to make a triangle, the length of the longest side must be less than the sum of the lengths of the other two sides and greater than their difference. Suppose two sides of a triangle have lengths 5 and 12. If the third side has length x, then $7 < x < 17$.

If the measures of two angles of a triangle are unequal, the two sides opposite the angles are unequal and the greater side is opposite the greater angle.

The base angles of an isosceles triangle are congruent. Suppose that one of the base angles is 38°. Then the other base angle is also 38°, so the vertex angle must be 104° because $180° - 2 \times 38° = 180° - 76° = 104°$.

If you know that the vertex angle of an isosceles triangle has measure 50°, you can find the measure of a base angle by subtracting 50° from 180° to obtain 130° and then divide by 2 to get 65°.

An equilateral triangle is also *equiangular*. Because the sum of the measures of the three interior angles is 180°, each interior angle measures 60° $(180° \div 3)$.

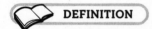 **DEFINITION**

A triangle is **equiangular** if all three of its interior angles have equal measure.

Recall that the square (second power) of a number is the number times itself. This fact underlies the *Pythagorean theorem*. Applicable to only right triangles, it states that the square of the length of the hypotenuse of a right triangle is equal to the sum of the squares of the lengths of the legs. Angle C is the right angle in the right triangle $\triangle ABC$ in the following figure. If a, b, and c are the side lengths, the Pythagorean theorem says $a^2 + b^2 = c^2$.

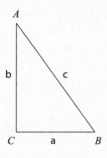

$$c^2 = a^2 + b^2$$

If the legs of a right triangle have lengths 3 and 4, the hypotenuse has length 5, because $3^2 = 9$, $4^2 = 16$, $9 + 16 = 25$, and $5^2 = 25$. If the legs of a right triangle have lengths 5 and 12, the hypotenuse has length 13. (Work it out!)

Suppose both legs of a right triangle are 1 unit long. The Pythagorean theorem says that the square of the length of the hypotenuse is 2 $\left(1^2 + 1^2\right)$. This means the length of the hypotenuse is a number that equals 2 when you multiply it by itself. No whole number times itself equals 2. Nor is any decimal number times itself, although $1.414^2 = (1.414)(1.414) = 1.999396$ is very close to 2. You use $\sqrt{2}$ to represent the positive number whose square is 2: $\sqrt{2} \cdot \sqrt{2} = \left(\sqrt{2}\right)^2 = 2$.

Unless a number is a perfect square, such as 25 or 16, use a calculator to get an approximate decimal value for its positive square root. The following problem can be solved using the Pythagorean theorem. Recall that every positive number has two square roots that are equal in absolute value but opposite in sign. However, for Pythagorean theorem problems, you need to consider only the positive square root because distance and length are non-negative quantities.

A sliding board is 8 feet long, and the ladder from the ground to the top of the slide is 6 feet. If the ladder is perpendicular to the ground, approximately how far, in feet, is the bottom of the slide from the bottom of the ladder?

The slide is the hypotenuse of the right triangle formed by the ladder, the slide, and the ground. Let x stand for the desired distance, in feet. Then $8^2 = 6^2 + x^2$, or $64 = 36 + x^2$.

So $x^2 = 64 - 36 = 28$ and $x = \sqrt{28} \approx 5.3$.

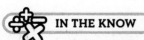
IN THE KNOW

The $\approx$ symbol means "is approximately equal to." So the desired distance in the preceding problem is about 5.3 feet.

It's also true that if the square of the length of the longest side of a triangle is equal to the sum of the squares of the lengths of the other two sides, the triangle is a right triangle. You might be asked, for example, whether a triangle with side lengths 4, 5, and 6 is a right triangle. Square the two smaller numbers and add them: $4^2 + 5^2 = 16 + 25 = 41$. Then square the largest number, $6^2 = 36$. Because $41 \neq 36$, this triangle is not a right triangle.

Perimeter, Area, and Volume

Perimeter, area, and *volume* are measures of the size of geometric objects. You measure perimeter when you determine how much fencing you need around your yard. The amount of wall you have to paint is an area. The amount of mulch you need to cover the garden to a 3-inch depth is a volume.

Perimeter is a one-dimensional measure, measured in feet, miles, centimeters, or other unit of length. Area is a two-dimensional measure, measured in square feet (ft^2), square centimeters (cm^2), and so forth. Volume is a three-dimensional measure, measured in cubic feet (ft^3), cubic centimeters (cm^3 or cc), and so forth.

The number π (pi) is the ratio of the circumference to the diameter of a circle. On the GED test, use the approximate decimal value of π, 3.14, to calculate the circumference (perimeter), area, or volume of a circle. The area of a circle of radius 5 inches is approximately $(3.14)(5^2) = (3.14)(25) = 78.5$ in^2.

The Mathematical Reasoning Test provides an online mathematics formula sheet for your reference during the test. Among other things, the formulas for perimeter, area, volume, and surface area of most of the shapes in the table shown earlier in this chapter are on this formula sheet. Here are the formulas:

Area of *a:*

Square	$A = side^2$
Rectangle	$A = length \times width$
Parallelogram	$A = base \times height$
Triangle	$A = \frac{1}{2} \times base \times height$
Trapezoid	$A = \frac{1}{2} \times (base_1 + base_2) \times height$
Circle	$A = \pi \times radius^2$ (π is approx. 3.14)

Perimeter of *a:*

Square	$P = 4 \times \text{side}$
Rectangle	$P = 2 \times \text{length} + 2 \times \text{width}$
Triangle	$P = \text{side}_1 + \text{side}_2 + \text{side}_3$
Circle	$C = \text{circumference} = \pi \times \text{diameter or } 2\pi \times \text{radius}$

Volume of *a:*

Cube	$V = \text{edge}^3$
Rectangular prism	$V = \text{length} \times \text{width} \times \text{height}$
Right prism	$V = \text{area of base} \times \text{height}$
Pyramid	$V = \left(\frac{1}{3}\right) \times \text{area of base} \times \text{height}$
Square pyramid	$V = \left(\frac{1}{3}\right) \times \text{base edge}^2 \times \text{height}$
Cylinder	$V = \pi \times \text{radius}^2 \times \text{height}$
Cone	$V = \left(\frac{1}{3}\right) \times \pi \times \text{radius}^2 \times \text{height}$
Sphere	$V = \left(\frac{4}{3}\right) \times \pi \times \text{radius}^3$

Surface area of *a:*

Cube	$SA = 6 \times \text{edge}^2$
Rectangular prism	$SA = 2 \times \text{length} \times \text{width} + 2 \times \text{length} \times \text{height} + 2 \times \text{width} \times \text{height}$
Right prism	$SA = \text{perimeter of base} \times \text{height} + 2 \times \text{area of base}$
Pyramid	$SA = \text{area of 3 lateral sides} + \text{area of base}$
Cylinder	$SA = 2 \times \pi \times \text{radius} \times \text{height} + 2 \times \pi \times \text{radius}^2$
Cone	$SA = \pi \times \text{radius} \times \text{slant height} + \pi \times \text{radius}^2$
Sphere	$SA = 4 \times \pi \times \text{radius}^2$

The entire formula sheet is shown in Chapter 28. Examples of how to apply these formulas are in the practice questions at the end of this chapter and in the practice test in Chapter 29.

Coordinate Geometry

A *coordinate plane* is formed by two perpendicular number lines that cross at their zero points, called the *origin*. The horizontal number line is the *x axis*, and numbers on this axis get larger as you move from left to right. The vertical number line is the *y axis*, and numbers on this axis get larger as you move from lower to higher.

A point is located in a coordinate plane using an *ordered pair* of numbers. The first number, or *x coordinate*, is measured along the *x* axis. The second number, or *y coordinate*, is measured along the *y* axis. The following figure shows a coordinate plane with the following points:

point A (1,4)

point B (−2,3)

point C (4,−1)

point D (−4,−2)

point E (3,0)

point F (0,−3)

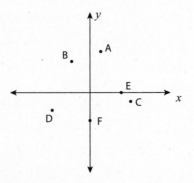

 **IN THE KNOW**

Any point with a *y* coordinate of 0 is on the *x* axis, while any point with an *x* coordinate of 0 is on the *y* axis.

An aspect about a line in a coordinate plane you need to be able to find is its *slope* (the amount of "tilt" from the horizontal). The formula for finding the slope of a line is on the formula sheet in Chapter 28. For horizontal and vertical lines, it's easier not to use the formula. Look at the line through the two points (−3,2) and (5,2) in the coordinate plane in the following figure. The line is perfectly horizontal. Because a horizontal line has no tilt, its slope is 0. Next, look at the line through the points (1,−7) and (1,5), also shown in the figure. The line is perfectly vertical. A vertical line is completely tilted, so its slope is undefined.

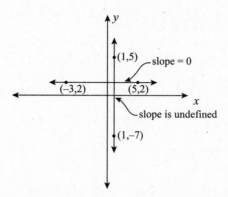

Now use the formula for slope from the formula sheet with the point (−5,2) and the point (7,−3), where $x_1 = -5$, $y_1 = 2$, $x_2 = 7$, and $y_2 = -3$:

$$\text{slope} = \frac{y_2 - y_1}{x_2 - x_1} = \frac{-3 - 2}{7 - (-5)} = \frac{-5}{12}$$

The following figure shows that the line through the points (−5,2) and (7,−3) slants downward from left to right. This occurs because its slope is negative.

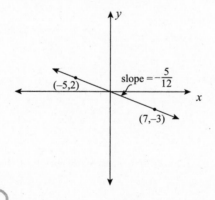

IN THE KNOW

A line with a positive slope slants upward as you move left to right. A line with a negative slope slants downward as you move left to right.

The slope of a line tells you important information about the line. The slope is the *rate of change* of the line, meaning it tells you how fast the *y* values are changing relative to the *x* values. In other words, the slope tells how far you go up (or down) for each unit you move right. For a slope of $\frac{-5}{12}$, you go down 5 (because the numerator is −5) for every 12 steps right. If the slope had been positive, you would have gone up 5 for every 12 steps right.

For any two points on a line, you can express the slope of the line as follows:

$$\text{slope} = \frac{\text{vertical change between the two points}}{\text{horizontal change between the two points}}$$

No matter which two points on the line you choose, the slope of the line is the same value.

There's more on the coordinate plane and line graphs in Chapter 27.

Practice

 1. A base angle of an isosceles triangle measures 34°. What is the degree measure of the vertex angle? Write your answer in the answer box: ☐

 2. The profile of a sliding board has the shape of a right triangle. The bottom of the ladder and the bottom of the slide are 4 feet apart and the slide is 7 feet long, as shown in the following figure:

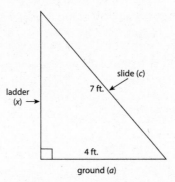

The height, in feet, of the ladder is closest to which of the following lengths?

(1) 5.0

(2) 5.4

(3) 5.7

(4) 6.0

 3. If the area of a circle is 196π, what is its diameter?

(1) 7

(2) 14

(3) 28

(4) 34

4. The roof of a house has the shape of an isosceles triangle, as shown in the following figure:

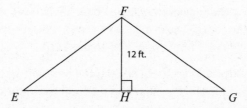

The 12-foot perpendicular line from the peak divides the base of this triangle in half. The sides of the roof have slopes of $\frac{3}{4}$ and $-\frac{3}{4}$. Find the length, in feet, of $\overline{EG}$.

(1) 16

(2) 24

(3) 30

(4) 32

   5. The Kraangs' dining room has 12-foot ceilings, and the floor has the shape of a rectangle with dimensions 20 feet by 25 feet, as shown in the following figure. Ignoring space taken up by doors and openings, find the total amount, in ft², of wall area in the dining room.

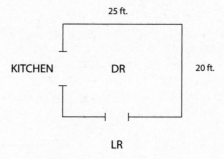

(1) 500

(2) 540

(3) 1,080

(4) 1,200

Answers

1. The correct answer is 112°. An isosceles triangle has two base angles that have the same measure and a vertex angle. Because one base angle has a measure of 34°, so does the other one, and the sum of these measures is 68°. The sum of the measures of all three angles is 180°, so subtract 68° from 180° to get 112°.

2. **(3)** The slide, ladder, and ground between the bottoms of the slide and the ladder form a right triangle, so use the Pythagorean theorem to find x, the length of the missing leg (the ladder).

$$a^2 + x^2 = c^2$$
$$4^2 + x^2 = 7^2$$
$$16 + x^2 = 49$$
$$16 + x^2 - 16 = 49 - 16$$
$$x^2 = 49 - 16$$
$$x^2 = 33$$
$$x = \sqrt{33}$$
$$x \approx 5.7$$

3. **(3)** The formula for the area of a circle is πr^2. First, find the radius of the circle by substituting into the area formula and solving for r.

$$A = \pi r^2$$
$$196\pi = \pi r^2$$
$$\frac{196\pi}{\pi} = \frac{\pi r^2}{\pi}$$
$$196 = r^2$$
$$r^2 = 196$$
$$r = \sqrt{196}$$
$$r = 14$$

Next, find the diameter by multiplying the radius by 2: $14 \times 2 = 28$.

4. **(4)** The slope of a line is the vertical change *(FH)* divided by the horizontal change *(EH)*. The vertical change is 12 feet, and the horizontal change is *EH*. Therefore, $\frac{12}{EH} = \frac{3}{4}$. Solve this proportion by cross-multiplying: $3 \times EH = 48$, so $EH = 16$. *EG* is twice as long as *EH*, so $EG = 32$.

5. **(3)** Each of the four walls has an area of 12 × the length of the wall. Two walls have areas of $12 \times 25 = 300$, for 600 ft². The other two walls have areas of $12 \times 20 = 240$, for 480 ft². The four walls have a total area of 600 ft² + 480 ft² = 1,080 ft².

Data Analysis, Statistics, and Probability

Data analysis, statistics, and probability play a large role in today's digital world. The advent of computers makes it possible to tabulate data into statistical summaries that one could only dream about doing 50 years ago. As the twenty-first century moves forward, being able to extract evidence and make decisions from information is an essential skill.

Data Analysis

For the Mathematical Reasoning Test, data analysis involves answering questions by studying graphic representations of data. Following are examples that illustrate these types of visual presentations.

Bar graphs are useful for showing frequency counts in various categories. A bar graph consists of rectangles situated on a horizontal axis. The heights of the rectangles are proportional to the counts in the categories. The vertical scale also could show the percentage of the total in each category. The following figure shows the number of first-, second-, and third-class passengers and crew on the maiden voyage of the *Titanic*.

In This Chapter

- Overviews of charts, tables, graphs, statistics, and probability
- Sample GED®-style questions to practice the skills on which you'll be tested
- Answers and explanations for all questions

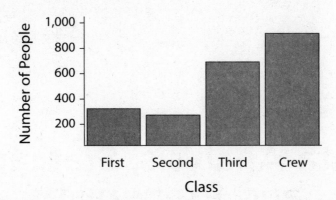

To read the graph, check the scale to determine the units and the amount corresponding to each category. A glance at this graph tells you that the largest group was the crew, followed by third class, then first-class passengers. Second-class passengers were the smallest group.

Circle graphs are most useful in showing how a total is divided into parts. The graph is a circle that's divided into pie-shape pieces proportional to the number or percentage in each category. The following circle graph shows the percentage breakdown of the *Titanic* passengers and crew.

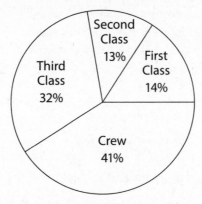

Note how easy it is to see that first- and second-class passengers together make up about a quarter of the total count.

Line graphs show plotted points connected by line segments. They are a good way of showing change over time. The following line graph shows the monthly natural gas usage for a year in a home where natural gas provides heat and hot water.

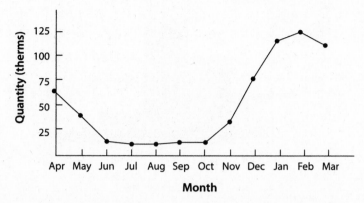

The graph shows that the greatest natural gas usage occurred in February.

Dot plots (or *line plots*) show dots (or other appropriate symbols) placed above values on a number line. The number of dots above a value shows the number of times that particular value occurs in the data set. The following dot plot shows the number of a variety of fish in an aquarium.

Key: Each dot represents one fish

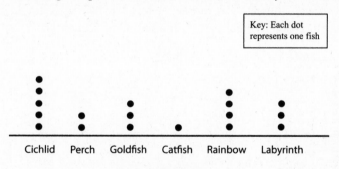

Fish in the Aquarium

As you can see from the dot plot, cichlid is the most plentiful fish in the aquarium.

Histograms summarize data by showing frequencies or percentages of the occurrence of data within intervals. The intervals have equal width and cover from the least to the greatest data values. The endpoints of the intervals are selected to ensure each data value clearly falls within one and only one interval. The height of a rectangular bar over an interval corresponds to the frequency or percentage of the data values within that interval. A histogram's bars are (usually) side by side with no space in between. The following histogram displays the number of pizzas pizza store employees can make in an hour.

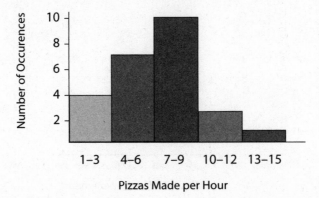

The graph shows that pizza store employees can make, on average, 7 to 9 pizzas per hour.

A *scatter plot* is a graph of ordered pairs of data from two numerical variables plotted on a coordinate grid. The scale for one of the variables is along the horizontal axis, and the scale for the other variable is along the vertical axis. Each ordered pair is a *data point* in the scatter plot. The data points are not connected by line segments. The following graph is a scatter plot of the number of visitors to an amusement park over a period of 12 months.

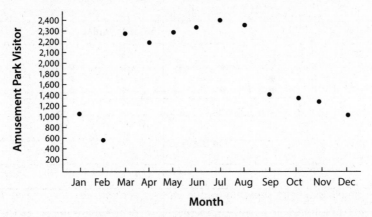

The scatter plot shows more people visit the amusement park between March and August.

A coordinate plane can be used to graph a function (see Chapter 27 for a discussion of functions). Such a graph provides a visual image of how one variable depends on another. For example, the following graph shows the distance a person is from home as a function of the length of time the person has been walking in one direction.

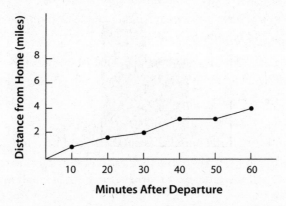

You can tell whether the person is walking faster (steep slope) or more slowly (gradual slope) or not moving at all (zero slope) by just looking at the slopes of the segments.

Tables provide a simple way to summarize data. The following table shows a household budget broken into various spending categories.

Household Budget

Category	Monthly Budget
Rent	$1,200
Food	$600
Clothing	$150
Utilities	$300
Insurance	$250
Auto	$400
Entertainment	$300
Miscellaneous	$250

The table shows that after rent, food is the costliest budget item.

Statistics

Statistics involves collecting, summarizing, and analyzing data. For the Mathematical Reasoning Test, the statistics you need to know is limited to ways of numerically describing a data set, such as a group of test scores.

Any set of numbers has a greatest (maximum) value and least (minimum) value. The difference between the maximum and minimum is the *range*.

The *mean* is a measure of *central tendency,* a number that represents the "center" of a data set. The mean is the arithmetic average of the numbers. Add all the numbers and divide by the number of numbers to reach the mean.

The *median* is another measure of central tendency. Put the numbers in order from least to greatest (or greatest to least). If the number of numbers is odd, there is a middle one, the median. If the number of numbers is even, there is a pair of middle numbers, and the median is their average. In either case, half the numbers are smaller than or as small as the median and half are as large or larger.

The *mode* is also a measure of central tendency. This is the number (or numbers) that occurs with the greatest frequency that's more often than that of any of the other numbers.

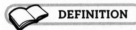

DEFINITION

The **range** of a data set is the maximum value minus the minimum value. The **mean** of a data set is the sum of the numbers divided by the number of numbers. The **median** of a data set is the middle number or the average of the middle pair of numbers when the numbers are in order from least to greatest. The **mode** of a data set is the number(s) that occurs with the highest frequency.

Consider the following 15 test scores:

52, 55, 61, 62, 74, 74, 79, 82, 82, 82, 86, 89, 93, 93, 95

The range is 43 (= 95 − 52). Adding the 15 test scores gives a total of 1,159. Dividing by 15 gives a mean of 77.3, rounded to the nearest tenth. The median is 82, the eighth number in the ordered list of numbers. And the mode is 82 because 82 occurs three times in the list. This frequency is higher than that of any other number.

Now suppose the highest score, 95, was not in the list. Then the two middle numbers would be 79 (the seventh) and 82 (the eighth). The median in this case would be 80.5, the average of 79 and 82.

A *box plot* is a visual depiction of data using summary information. The box plot shows a rectangular box above the horizontal axis. The median is indicated with a vertical line in the interior of the box. The minimum value is at the end of the horizontal line extending from the left end of the box, and the maximum value is at the end of the horizontal line extending from the right end of the box. Five vertical lines determine four groups from left to right, starting at the minimum value position in the box plot. Each group contains approximately 25 percent of the data values.

The following figure shows the box plot for the 15 test scores. (Box plots can be oriented vertically also.)

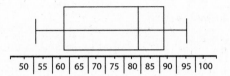

Probability

Probability is a way of measuring uncertainty. It is associated with chance processes. For purposes of this discussion, a chance process results in a single *outcome* that cannot be determined beforehand. So, you can't say with certainty exactly what the outcome will be. However, you can have notions about the possible outcomes. For example, flipping a fair U.S. coin and observing the up face is a chance process. You don't know for sure whether the coin will land face up ("heads") or face down ("tails"), but you do know there are two possible *equally likely* outcomes: heads on the up face or tails on the up face.

 **IN THE KNOW**

In a chance process, equally likely outcomes have exactly the same chance of occurring.

If you toss a fair six-sided die and observe the up face, you have six possible equally likely outcomes: 1 dot showing on the up face, 2 dots showing on the up face, and so on up to 6 dots showing on the up face (hereafter, abbreviated as 1, 2, 3, 4, 5, or 6).

An *event* is one or more outcomes. If all the possible outcomes are equally likely, the probability of an event is the number of ways that event can occur divided by the total possible number of outcomes. Here are examples:

The probability of heads on one flip of a fair coin is $\frac{1}{2}$ because there are two possible outcomes (heads or tails), and one is heads.

The probability of observing an up face with less than three dots in the toss of a fair six-sided die is $\frac{2}{6}$ or $\frac{1}{3}$, because there are six possible outcomes and two of them (1 and 2) show less than three dots on the up face.

If you draw one card from a well-shuffled standard deck of 52 playing cards, the probability of drawing a picture card (king, queen, or jack) is $\frac{12}{52}$ or $\frac{3}{13}$ because there are 52 cards altogether and 12 of them are picture cards.

If a spinner has eight equal-size sectors numbered 1 through 8, the probability of the needle pointing to 2, 4, or 6 when it stops spinning is $\frac{3}{8}$ because there are 8 possible outcomes and 3 of them are favorable to the desired outcome.

Here are some facts about probability you should know and examples illustrating them:

The probability of an event is a number between 0 and 1, including both 0 and 1.

The probability of an *impossible event* is 0. What is the probability of observing 7 dots on the up face in one toss of a fair six-sided die? A six-sided die doesn't have 7 dots on any of its faces, so the probability is 0.

The probability of a *certain event* is 1. What is the probability of observing less than 7 dots on the up face in one toss of a fair six-sided die? The probability is 1 because all of the possible outcomes show less than 7 dots.

The probability of an event *not* occurring is 1 minus the probability that the event does occur. What is the probability that on one toss of a fair six-sided die, the up face is *not* a 1 or a 2? This means the up face is 3, 4, 5, or 6. Therefore, the probability is $\frac{4}{6}$ or $\frac{2}{3}$. From a previous example, the probability of observing 1 or 2 on the up face is $\frac{1}{3}$. So the probability of observing 3, 4, 5, or 6 on the up face is $1-\frac{1}{3}=\frac{2}{3}$, which is the same as already determined.

If you're asked to find the probability of one event *or* another occurring as a result of the same chance process, the number of favorable outcomes is the sum of the number of outcomes favorable to each event, as long as *no outcome is counted twice*. For example, in one toss of a fair six-sided die, the probability of observing an up face where the number of dots is even or prime is $\frac{5}{6}$. This is true because of the six possible outcomes, 2, 4, and 6 are even and 2, 3, and 5 are prime. You count 2 only once, so the number of favorable outcomes is 5, not 6.

If you have a sequence of two events, you can find the probability of the first event *and* the second event occurring by multiplying the probabilities of the individual events, as long as you have determined the probability of the second event *by taking into account that the first event has already occurred*. For example, if you draw two cards, one after another *without replacement* (meaning you don't put the first card back in before you draw the second card), from a from a well-shuffled standard deck of 52 playing cards, the probability that both are picture cards is $\frac{12}{52}\cdot\frac{11}{51}$, which reduces to $\frac{11}{221}$.

This is true because the probability the first card is a picture card is $\frac{12}{52}$. Because the card drawn is not replaced, 51 cards are left and 11 picture cards, so the probability that the second card is a picture card is $\frac{11}{51}$. Now suppose, the first card is replaced before the second card is drawn. The probability that both cards are picture cards is $\frac{12}{52} \cdot \frac{12}{52}$, which reduces to $\frac{9}{169}$.

Independent events do not affect each other's probabilities, so multiply their probabilities to find the occurrence of the events. For example, the probability of getting three heads when you flip three coins is $\frac{1}{2} \cdot \frac{1}{2} \cdot \frac{1}{2}$ or $\frac{1}{8}$.

To determine the number of outcomes for a sequence of chance processes, multiply the number of ways each can occur. For example, the number of possible outcomes when you flip three coins is $2 \cdot 2 \cdot 2$ or 8 because there are 2 ways for the first coin to come up, 2 ways for the second coin to come up, and 2 ways for the third coin to come up. Using H for "heads" and T for "tails," the 8 outcomes are HHH, HHT, HTH, HTT, THH, THT, TTH, and TTT.

Practice

Questions 1 through 4 refer to the following table:

Value	Frequency
10	5
23	1
36	6
44	2
52	6

1. What is the range of the data set? Write your answer in the answer box:

2. What is the mean of the data set? Write your answer in the answer box:

3. What is the median of the data set? Write your answer in the answer box:

4. What is the mode of the data set? (If more than one mode, separate the values with commas.) Write your answer in the answer box:

5. If a family has two children who are not twins, what is the probability that both are boys? (Assume single boy or girl births are equally likely.)

(1) $\frac{1}{8}$

(2) $\frac{1}{4}$

(3) $\frac{1}{2}$

(4) $\frac{3}{4}$

 6. According to the following table, what percent of the Johnson family budget is used for housing, food, or clothing? Write your answer in the answer box: [____]

Johnson Family Budget (Percent of Income)

Category	Monthly Budget
Housing	31%
Food	18%
Transportation	12%
Clothing	9%
Utilities	8%
Entertainment	6%
Insurance	4%
Miscellaneous	12%

7. The following table shows the number of people who survived and the number who died, by class, when the *Titanic* sank. Approximately what percent of those who died were first-class passengers?

	Class			Crew	Total
	First	**Second**	**Third**	**Crew**	**Total**
Survived	202	118	178	212	710
Died	123	167	528	673	1,491
Total	325	285	706	885	2,201

(1) 5.59%

(2) 8.25%

(3) 14.8%

(4) 38.7%

 8. Which of the following answer choices can *not* be determined from the graph shown?

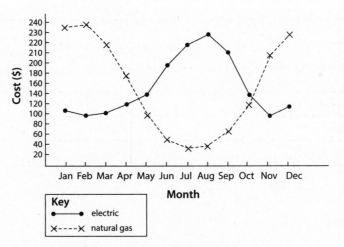

(1) Electric costs are highest in the summer months.

(2) Natural gas costs are lowest in the winter months.

(3) The total monthly costs (both natural gas and electric).

(4) The amount of natural gas used in August.

 9. The mean of 5, 8, 17, 24, and *x* is 18.6. Determine the value of *x*. Write your answer in the answer box:

Answers

1. **(42)** The range is maximum − minimum = 52 − 10 = 42.

2. **(34.45)** The mean is the sum of the numbers divided by the number of numbers. Multiply each number by its frequency to get the sum and add the frequencies to get the number of numbers:

$$\frac{5 \cdot 10 + 1 \cdot 23 + 6 \cdot 36 + 2 \cdot 44 + 6 \cdot 52}{(5 + 1 + 6 + 2 + 6)} = \frac{689}{20} = 34.45$$

3. **(36)** The numbers are ordered from least to greatest, so the median is the middle value or the average of the pair of middle values. There are 20 numbers, so the median is the average of the tenth (36) and eleventh (36) numbers. Thus, the median is 36.

4. **(36, 52)** Two numbers occur with a frequency of 6, which is higher than that of any other number. Thus, the modes are 36 and 52. (Data that have two modes are *bimodal*.)

5. **(2)** Multiply the probability that the first child is a boy and the probability that the second child is a boy to obtain $\frac{1}{2} \cdot \frac{1}{2} = \frac{1}{4}$.

6. **(58)** Add the three percentages, 31%, 18%, and 9%, to get 58%.

7. **(2)** Of the 1,491 who died, 123 were first-class passengers, or about 8.25%.

8. **(4)** The amount of natural gas used cannot be calculated because the problem does not tell the cost per unit volume.

9. **(39)** The mean of the 5 numbers is 18.6, so their sum is 18.6 × 5 = 93. Thus, $x = 93 − (5 + 8 + 17 + 24) = 93 − 54 = 39$.

Algebra, Functions, and Patterns

You'll be pleased to know that not everything that would be covered in two years of high school algebra courses is tested on the Mathematical Reasoning Test. This chapter highlights some of the main concepts and skills in algebra you'll see on the test. These ideas have been selected because having a strong understanding of them increases your likelihood of having a successful result on the Mathematical Reasoning Test.

Variables, Notation, and Order of Operations

Algebra gives you a general way of analyzing numbers and their relationships. Suppose, for example, you wanted to multiply a number by 2 and add 3 to the result. You could express this idea for a single number, say 5. If you multiply 5 by 2, and add 3 to the result, you get 13. All this does is give you an answer to a computation. It does not express the idea of multiplying by 2 and then adding 3.

One way of expressing this idea for any number is to start by calling the number x. A letter that you use to stand for a number is a *variable*. Its value is unknown. To show that you

In This Chapter

- Overviews of variables, order of operations, exponents, polynomials, rational expressions, equations, functions, systems of equations, and word problems

- Sample GED®-style questions to practice the skills on which you'll be tested

- Answers and explanations for all questions

multiply x by 2, write $2x$. When multiplying a number and a variable, no dot or times sign is necessary. The number 2 is the *numerical coefficient*.

To show that you add 3 to the result, write $2x + 3$. This is an *algebraic expression*. Other examples of algebraic expressions are $y^2 + 5$, $2x - 1$, $6x^2 - x + 2$, and $\dfrac{x^3 + 6x^2}{x^2 + 4}$.

 **DEFINITION**

> A **variable** is a letter that stands for a number. When a number and a variable are multiplied, the number is the **numerical coefficient**. An **algebraic expression** is a number; a variable; or the result of adding, subtracting, multiplying, dividing, or applying exponents to numbers and variables.

How do you know $2x + 3$ means multiply a number by 2 and then add 3 instead of add 3 to the number and then multiply the result by 2? Mathematicians agreed long ago to the *order of operations*. This convention specifies a set order in which addition, subtraction, multiplication, division, and applying exponents are done.

The convention for ordering math operations has the acronym PEMDAS. First look at the MDAS part. These four letters stand for *multiplication*, *division*, *addition*, and *subtraction*. Of these four, M and D have the same status and are done first, from left to right. The A and S also have the same status and are done next, left to right. The following examples help clarify these ideas:

$$5 \times 4 \div 10 = 20 \div 10 = 2$$

(Multiply 5 times 4 to get 20 and then divide 20 by 10 to get 2.)

$$12 \div 2 \times 6 = 6 \times 6 = 36$$

$$5 + 4 - 6 = 9 - 6 = 3$$

$$2 - 6 + 4 - 12 = -4 + 4 - 12 = 0 - 12 = -12$$

The MD combination precedes the AS combination in PEMDAS because all multiplication and division must take place before any addition or subtraction. The following examples illustrate this rule:

$$3 \times 5 + 2 = 15 + 2 = 17$$

(Multiply 3 times 5 to get 15 and then add 2 to get 17. *Do not* add 5 and 2 first to get 7 and then multiply by 3 to get 21.)

$$8 + 3 \times 5 - 10 \div 2 = 8 + 15 - 5 = 23 - 5 = 18$$

$$3 - 2 \times 8 \div 4 + 6 = 3 - 16 \div 4 + 6 = 3 - 4 + 6 = -1 + 6 = 5$$

The E in PEMDAS stands for exponents. An *exponent* is a raised number attached to a *base*, which is a number, variable, or grouped quantity just to the exponent's left. A positive integer exponent means the exponent's base is used as a factor that many times. For example, $2^4 = 2 \cdot 2 \cdot 2 \cdot 2$, which equals 16. You say 2^4 is an *exponential expression* and read it as "2 to the fourth power." Also, 2^3 is read "2 to the third power" or, more commonly, "2 cubed," and 2^2 is read "2 to the second power" or, more commonly, "2 squared."

E precedes MDAS because raising numbers to powers must be performed before multiplication, division, addition, or subtraction. Here are examples:

$$2 \cdot 3^2 = 2 \cdot 9 = 18$$

(First, square 3 to get 9 and then multiply 9 by 2 to get 18. *Do not* multiply 2 times 3 to get 6 and then square 6.)

$$5 - 6 \cdot 2^3 = 5 - 6 \cdot 8 = 5 - 48 = -43$$

(First, cube 2 to get 8. Next, multiply 6 and 8 to obtain 48. Then subtract 48 from 5 to get −43.)

$$(-3)^2 + 4 \cdot 5 = 9 + 4 \cdot 5 = 9 + 20 = 29$$

(First, square −3 to get 9. Next, multiply 4 and 5. Then add 9 and 20 to obtain 29.)

Exponents precede negation, as shown here:

$$-3^2 + 4 \cdot 5 = 9 + 4 \cdot 5 = 9 + 20 = 11$$

(First, square 3 to get 9. Next, apply the negative sign to get −9. Then multiply 4 and 5. Finally, add −9 and 20 to obtain 11. *Do not* start by squaring −3 to get 9. There are no parentheses around −3, so the exponent 2 applies only to 3, not to −3.)

Finally, P in PEMDAS stands for parentheses. First, perform all operations within parentheses (or any other grouping symbol such as brackets, braces, division or fraction bars, absolute value bars, and radicals). In most cases, no times sign is needed when a quantity in a grouping symbol is multiplied by a number. The examples that follow illustrate this convention:

$$3(1 + 4)^2 = 3 \cdot 5^2 = 3 \cdot 25 = 75$$

(First, add 1 and 4 in parentheses to get 5. Next, square 5 to get 25. Then, multiply 25 by 3 to get 75.)

$$6 + 5(3 \cdot 4)^2 = 6 + 5 \cdot 12^2 = 6 + 5 \cdot 144 = 6 + 720 = 726$$

(First, multiply 3 and 4 in parentheses to get 12. Next, square 12 to get 144. Then, multiply 144 by 5 to get 720. Finally, add 6 and 720 to obtain 726.)

$$\sqrt{9+16} = \sqrt{25} = 5$$

(First, add 9 and 16 under the radical to get 25. Then find the positive square root of 25 to obtain 5.)

Here are other examples.

$$\frac{5}{8} - \frac{7-6}{7+1} = \frac{5}{8} - \frac{1}{8} = \frac{4}{8} = \frac{1}{2}$$

$$5|9-12| = 5|-3| = 5 \cdot 3 = 15$$

Look at the meaning of a few more expressions with PEMDAS in mind, this time with variables:

$$(x + 3)^2$$

Add 3 to the number that x stands for, then square the result. This is *not* the same as squaring x, squaring 3, and adding the results. See why not by trying it for $x = 1$. This is one of the most common mistakes made by beginning algebra students—all because the PEMDAS convention is not followed.

$$5 - 2x$$

This is not equal to $3x$ because you have to multiply the number x by 2 before subtracting the result from 5.

$$2(x + 3)$$

This is not equal to $2x + 3$ because you have to multiply *each* term inside the parentheses by 2, not just the first term. This rule is the *distributive property* of real numbers, so $2(x + 3) = 2 \cdot x + 2 \cdot 3 = 2x + 6$.

$$7x^2$$

Because exponents come before multiplication, the exponent 2 means square the number x first, then multiply the result by 7. If x were the number 2, then $7x^2 = 7 \cdot 2^2 = 7 \cdot 4 = 28$; and not $(7 \cdot 2)^2 = 14^2 = 196$.

HEADS-UP!

When a variable is raised to the first power, don't write the power 1 (for example, $x^1 = x$).

Evaluating and Simplifying Algebraic Expressions

An algebraic expression is any arrangement of numbers and variables. It's important to realize that an algebraic expression is not an equation because there is no equal sign. Equations are covered later in this chapter.

When you *evaluate an algebraic expression*, you are given a number to substitute for the variable. Then you do the calculations, being sure to follow the order of operations. Here are examples:

Evaluate $6x - 5$ when $x = 2$. $6x - 5 = 6(2) - 5 = 12 - 5 = 7$.

Evaluate $x^2 - 3x + 4$ when $x = -1$. $x^2 - 3x + 4 = (-1)^2 - 3(-1) + 4 = 1 + 3 + 4 = 8$.

Evaluate $\dfrac{x^3 + 6x^2}{x^2 + 4}$ when $x = 4$. $\dfrac{x^3 + 6x^2}{x^2 + 4} = \dfrac{(4)^3 + 6(4)^2}{(4)^2 + 4} = \dfrac{64 + 96}{16 + 4} = \dfrac{160}{20} = 8$.

In an algebraic expression, *terms* are connected to each other by indicated addition (+) or subtraction (−). If no addition or subtraction is indicated, the expression itself is a term. For example, $2x$ has one term, and $6x - 5$ has two terms. *Like terms* must look exactly alike with the exception that their numerical coefficients can be different. Numbers that have no variable factors are *constants*. All constants are like terms. Like terms containing variable factors have exactly the same variables with matching exponents. Some examples of like terms are 10 and −8, $2x$ and $3x$, $6y$ and y, and $4x^2y^3$ and $3x^2y^3$. *Unlike terms* are terms that do not meet the requirements for like terms. For instance, $6x$, and −5 are unlike terms.

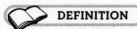 **DEFINITION**

An algebraic **expression** is a number, a variable, or the result of adding, subtracting, multiplying, dividing, or applying exponents to numbers and variables. In an algebraic expression, **like terms** are constant terms or terms that have exactly the same variable factors with the same corresponding exponents.

You can *simplify* an expression by performing operations with terms. To add or subtract like terms that contain variable factors, add or subtract the numerical coefficients and use the result as the numerical coefficient of the variable factors. To add or subtract unlike terms, simply indicate the addition or subtraction. Here are examples:

Simplify $2x + 3x$. The expression $2x + 3x$ consists of like terms $2x$ and $3x$. They are like terms because they contain the same variable x (raised to the same power 1). Thus, $2x + 3x = 5x$.

Simplify $6y - y$. Be careful here because you can't just subtract $y - y$. To follow the order of operations you have to multiply the first y by 6 first. Think of y as $1 \cdot y$, so $6y - 1y = 5y$.

Simplify $3x^2 + 5x$. This can't be simplified further because the exponents on x are not the same.

When an algebraic expression contains a mixture of like terms, systematically combine matching like terms as illustrated in the following examples:

Simplify $3x^2 + 10 - 2x + 3x^2 + 5x - 8$. To facilitate the simplifying process, mentally rewrite minus signs as $+ -$ and give the $-$ (negative sign) to the number that follows it. In this case, you would think of $3x^2 + 10 - 2x + 3x^2 + 5x - 8$ as $3x^2 + 10 + -2x + 3x^2 + 5x + -8$. This algebraic expression has three sets of like terms: $3x^2$ and $3x^2$, $-2x$ and $5x$, and 10 and -8. Combining like terms results in $6x^2 + 3x + 2$. It's customary to write the result in descending powers of x.

Simplify $10x^2 - 50x + 20x^2 + 25 - 10x + 2x^2 - 40$. $10x^2 - 50x + 20x^2 + 25 - 10x + 2x^2 - 40 = 32x^2 - 60x - 15$.

When you multiply or divide terms that have variable factors, you must follow rules for exponents. If you multiply 3^3 by 3^2, you are using 3 as a factor five times because $3^3 \cdot 3^2 = (3 \cdot 3 \cdot 3)$ $(3 \cdot 3) = 3 \cdot 3 \cdot 3 \cdot 3 \cdot 3 = 3^5$. In general, to multiply two exponential expressions that have the same base, add the exponents and attach the sum as an exponent on the common base. Symbolically, this rule is $x^m \cdot x^n = x^{m+n}$. Applying this rule to the problem just discussed yields $3^3 \cdot 3^2 = 3^{3+2} = 3^5$, the same result.

To divide two exponential expressions that have the same base, subtract the exponent in the denominator from the exponent in the numerator and attach the difference as an exponent on the common base. Symbolically, this rule is $\dfrac{x^m}{x^n} = x^{m-n}$. For example, $\dfrac{x^6}{x^2} = x^{6-2} = x^4$. In this case, you subtract the exponents to get x^4, which results because two of the six factors of x in the numerator cancel with the two factors of x in the denominator, leaving four factors of x in the numerator.

Finally, when you have a "power to a power," such as $\left(x^3\right)^2$, which means x^3 used as a factor twice, multiply the exponents to obtain, in this case, $\left(x^3\right)^2 = x^{3 \cdot 2} = x^6$. Stated in general, this rule is $\left(x^m\right)^P = x^{mp}$. When the exponential expression has a numerical coefficient included in the parentheses, raise the coefficient to the indicated power. For example, $\left(5x^3\right)^2 = 5^2 x^{3 \cdot 2} = 25x^6$.

When multiplying or dividing terms that have variable factors, multiply or divide the numerical coefficients, and use the result as the numerical coefficient of the product or quotient of the variable factors. Here are examples:

What is the product of $\left(5xy^2\right)^2\left(2x^2y^3\right)^3$?

$$\left(5xy^2\right)^2\left(2x^2y^3\right)^3$$

$$=\left(5x^1y^2\right)^2\left(2x^2y^3\right)^3 \qquad \text{Think to yourself: The exponent on } x \text{ is 1.}$$

$$=\left(5^2x^{1\cdot2}y^{2\cdot2}\right)\left(2^3x^{2\cdot3}y^{3\cdot3}\right) \text{ Practice doing this step mentally.}$$

$$=\left(25x^2y^4\right)\left(8x^6y^9\right)$$

$$=200x^{2+6}y^{4+9} \qquad\qquad \text{Practice doing this step mentally.}$$

$$=200x^8y^{13}$$

Simplify $\dfrac{\left(-4x^2\right)^3}{\left(2x^3\right)\left(8x^2\right)}\cdot\dfrac{\left(-4x^2\right)^3}{\left(2x^3\right)\left(8x^2\right)}=\dfrac{\left(-4\right)^3x^6}{16x^5}=\dfrac{-64x^6}{16x^5}=-4x^{6-5}=-4x^1=-4x$.

Working with Polynomials

A *polynomial* is an algebraic expression that consists of one or more terms that contain no variable expressions as divisors and whose variable factors have only whole number exponents. For example, $6x-5$, and x^2-5x+4 are polynomials, but $\dfrac{x^3+2x^2}{x^2-4}$ is not.

Polynomials consisting of only one term are *monomials,* those consisting of exactly two terms are *binomials,* and those consisting of exactly three terms are *trinomials.* Beyond three terms, no special names are used. So, for example, $3x^2$ is a monomial, $6x-5$ is a binomial, and x^2-5x+4 is a trinomial.

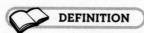 **DEFINITION**

> A **polynomial** is an algebraic expression that consists of one or more terms that contain no variable expressions as divisors and whose variable factors have only whole number exponents. **Monomials** are one-term polynomials, **binomials** are two-term polynomials, and **trinomials** are three-term polynomials.

You add, subtract, multiply, and divide polynomials using your skills in performing these operations with terms. Here are examples:

- **Add:** $(6x - 5) + (4x + 9)$. If no symbol or a + sign immediately precedes a polynomial enclosed in parentheses, remove the parentheses and rewrite the polynomial without changing any signs. Then collect like terms. Thus, $(6x - 5) + (4x + 9) = 6x - 5 + 4x + 9 = 10x + 4$.

- **Subtract:** $(10x + 4) - (6x - 5)$. If a − sign immediately precedes a polynomial enclosed in parentheses, remove the parentheses and the − sign and rewrite the polynomial, but with all the signs changed. Then collect like terms. Thus, $(10x + 4) - (6x - 5) = 10x + 4 - 6x + 5 = 4x + 9$.

- **Multiply:** $3x \cdot 4x^2$. Multiply the numerical coefficients, and follow the rules for exponents for the variable factors. Thus, $3x \cdot 4x^2 = 12x^3$.

- **Multiply:** $2x(5x - 1)$. Using the distributive property, multiply *each* term inside the parentheses by $2x$. Thus, $2x(5x - 1) = 2x \cdot 5x - 2x \cdot 1 = 10x^2 - 2x$.

- **Divide:** $\dfrac{-18x^5}{6x^2}$. Divide the numerical coefficients and follow the rules for exponents for the variable factors. Thus, $\dfrac{-18x^5}{6x^2} = -3x^3$.

- **Divide:** $\dfrac{-18x^5 + 30x^2}{6x^2}$. Divide *each* term in the numerator by $6x^2$. Thus, $\dfrac{-18x^5 + 30x^2}{6x^2}$

$$= \frac{-18x^5}{6x^2} + \frac{30x^2}{6x^2} = -3x^3 + 5.$$

- **Multiply:** $(2x + 1)(x + 3)$. Multiply each term of the second binomial by each term of the first binomial to obtain four *partial products* and then simplify the result. Thus, $(2x + 1)(x + 3) = 2x \cdot x + 2x \cdot 3 + 1 \cdot x + 1 \cdot 3 = 2x^2 + 6x + x + 3 = 2x^2 + 7x + 3$.

The FOIL method is an efficient way to remember how to multiply two binomials. **F** stands for "multiply the *first* terms in each binomial," **O** stands for "multiply the two *outer* terms," **I** stands for "multiply the two *inner* terms," and **L** stands for "multiply the *last* terms in each binomial." The following figure illustrates FOIL using the preceding example:

Applying FOIL yields $2x \cdot x + 2x \cdot 3 + 1 \cdot x + 1 \cdot 3$, from which you obtain $2x^2 + 6x + x + 3 = 2x^2 + 7x + 3$.

Here are three special products of binomials to know:

$$\left(x+y\right)^2 = x^2 + 2xy + y^2 \text{; for example, } \left(x+3\right)^2 = \left(x+3\right)\left(x+3\right) = x^2 + 6x + 9.$$

$$\left(x-y\right)^2 = x^2 - 2xy + y^2 \text{; for example, } \left(x-1\right)^2 = \left(x-1\right)\left(x-1\right) = x^2 - 2x + 1.$$

$$\left(x+y\right)\left(x-y\right) = x^2 - y^2 \text{; for example, } \left(x+2\right)\left(x-2\right) = x^2 - 4.$$

Just as in arithmetic, you use factoring to undo multiplication. Here are examples of factoring out the greatest common monomial factor:

Factor $3x - 6$. Factor out the common factor 3 from $3x - 6$ to obtain $3x - 6 = 3 \cdot x - 3 \cdot 2 = 3(x - 2)$.

Factor $x^3 + 2x^2$. Factor out the common factor x^2 from $x^3 + 2x^2$ to obtain $x^3 + 2x^2 = x^2 \cdot x + x^2 \cdot 2 = x^2 (x + 2)$.

Here are examples of using trial and error and your knowledge of FOIL to factor trinomials of the form $ax^2 + bx + c$ as the product of two binomials:

 HEADS-UP!

If the first and last terms of a trinomial are positive, the second terms in the trinomial's two binomial factors have the same sign as the trinomial's middle term. If the trinomial's first term is positive and its last term is negative, the second terms in the trinomial's two binomial factors have opposite signs.

Factor $x^2 - 5x + 4$. The first terms in the two binomial factors are both x. The last terms have the same sign as -5 with a product of 4 and a sum of -5. Thus, $x^2 - 5x + 4 = \left(x- \ \right)\left(x- \ \right) = \left(x-1\right)\left(x-4\right).$

Factor $x^2 + 6x + 9$. The first terms in the two binomial factors are both x. The last terms have the same sign as $+6$ with a product of 9 and a sum of 6. Thus, $x^2 + 6x + 9 = \left(x+ \ \right)\left(x+ \ \right) = \left(x+3\right)\left(x+3\right).$

Factor $x^2 - 2x - 3$. The first terms in the two binomial factors are both x. The last terms have opposite signs with a product of -3 and a sum of -2. Thus, $x^2 - 2x - 3 = \left(x- \ \right)\left(x+ \ \right) = \left(x-3\right)\left(x+1\right).$

Factor $x^2 + 6x - 40$. The first terms in the two binomial factors are both x. The last terms have opposite signs with a product of -40 and a sum of $+6$. Thus, $x^2 + 6x - 40 = \left(x+ \ \right)\left(x- \ \right) = \left(x+10\right)\left(x-4\right).$

Factor $2x^2 + 7x + 3$. The first terms in the two binomial factors are x and $2x$. The last terms have the same sign as +7 with a product of 3. Thus,
$$2x^2 + 7x + 3 = (2x + \quad)(x + \quad) = (2x + 1)(x + 3).$$

Here are examples of factoring polynomials of the form $x^2 - y^2$ (the difference of two squares):

Factor $x^2 - 1$. The first terms in the two binomial factors are both x. The last terms have opposite signs with a product of −1 and a sum of 0. Thus,
$$x^2 - 1 = (x + \quad)(x - \quad) = (x + 1)(x - 1).$$

Factor $x^2 - 4$. The first terms in the two binomial factors are both x. The last terms have opposite signs with a product of −4 and a sum of 0. Thus,
$$x^2 - 4 = (x + \quad)(x - \quad) = (x + 2)(x - 2).$$

Working with Rational Expressions

A *rational expression* is an algebraic fraction in which both the numerator and denominator are polynomials. For example, $\dfrac{x^3 + 2x^2}{x^2 - 4}$ is a rational expression. Because division by zero is undefined, values of a variable that cause the denominator of a rational expression to evaluate to zero are excluded as possible values for the variable. For $\dfrac{x^3 + 2x^2}{x^2 - 4}$, x cannot assume the value 2 or −2 because the denominator, $x^2 - 4$, equals zero when x equals 2 or −2.

 **HEADS-UP!**

You can't divide any number by 0. But zero divided by any number except 0 is 0.

Some algebraic fractions can be reduced. Here is an example:

Reduce $\dfrac{x^3 + 2x^2}{x^2 - 4}$. Factor the numerator and denominator and then cancel common numerator and denominator factors. Thus,
$$\frac{x^3 + 2x^2}{x^2 - 4} = \frac{x^2(x + 2)}{(x + 2)(x - 2)} = \frac{x^2\cancel{(x+2)}}{\cancel{(x+2)}(x - 2)} = \frac{x^2}{(x - 2)}.$$

Addition, subtraction, multiplication, and division of rational expressions mimic the corresponding operations with arithmetic fractions. Here are examples:

- **Add:** $\dfrac{2x+1}{x+1}+\dfrac{x-2}{x+1}$. The denominators are the same: add the numerators and place the sum over the common denominator. Thus,

$$\frac{2x+1}{x+1}+\frac{x-2}{x+1}=\frac{(2x+1)+(x-2)}{x+1}=\frac{2x+1+x-2}{x+1}=\frac{3x-1}{x+1}.$$

- **Subtract:** $\dfrac{3x-1}{x+1}-\dfrac{x-2}{x+1}$. The denominators are the same: subtract the second numerator from the first numerator and place the difference over the common denominator. Avoid sign errors by placing numerators in parentheses. Thus,

$$\frac{3x-1}{x+1}-\frac{x-2}{x+1}=\frac{(3x-1)-(x-2)}{x+1}=\frac{3x-1-x+2}{x+1}=\frac{2x+1}{x+1}.$$

- **Multiply:** $\dfrac{5x}{x+1}\cdot\dfrac{x+3}{x-1}$. Multiply the numerator factors to get the numerator of the product, and multiply the denominator factors to get the denominator of the product. Thus, $\dfrac{5x}{x+1}\cdot\dfrac{x+3}{x-1}=\dfrac{5x(x+3)}{(x+1)(x-1)}=\dfrac{5x^2+3x}{x^2-1}.$

- **Divide:** $\dfrac{2x}{x-3}\div\dfrac{x+3}{x}$. Multiply the first algebraic fraction by the *reciprocal* of the second algebraic fraction. Thus, $\dfrac{2x}{x-3}\div\dfrac{x+3}{x}=\dfrac{2x}{x-3}\cdot\dfrac{x}{x+3}=\dfrac{2x^2}{x^2-9}.$

Solving Linear Equations and Inequalities

An *equation* is a statement that one quantity equals another. Equations can be true or false. The equation $2 + 2 = 4$ is a true equation, but $2 + 3 = 4$ is a false equation. An equation with a variable in it is neither true nor false: $2x - 7 = 11$ is neither true nor false. If $x = 9$, the equation is true because $2(9) - 7 = 18 - 7 = 11$, but if x is any other number, the equation is false.

A *solution* is a number that makes an equation true when you substitute it for the variable (it *satisfies* the equation). An equation is *linear* if the variable appears in the equation as raised to the first power only (has no explicit exponent). Figuring out what number makes a linear equation true is *solving* the equation.

Some equations can be easily solved by inspection. For example, when you look at the equation $6x = 30$, think: "What number multiplied by 6 yields 30?" The answer is 5, so $x = 5$. When you have to solve an equation in a multiple-choice question, you can substitute each answer choice until you find the one that makes the equation a true statement (called *backsolving*). Backsolving doesn't help, however, if the solution to the equation doesn't answer the question asked, or if the question is not in multiple-choice format.

Fortunately, there's a more structured method for solving a linear equation. Work through the following example that illustrates the method. Your goal is to undo what has been done to the variable. Isolate the variable on one side of the equation, and make 1 its coefficient. Solve the equation $5x + 2 = 17$. Think of the two sides of the equation as scales and the = sign as the balance point. Take 2 away from both sides, and you still have balance, so the resulting equation reads $5x = 15$. The equations $5x + 2 = 17$ and $5x = 15$ are *equivalent equations* because they have the same solution. Divide both sides of the second equation by 5. This maintains the balance, and the new equivalent equation is $x = 3$, the solution. This process *transforms* the original equation to one whose solution is evident. Note that although it's not necessary, it is best to isolate the variable on the left side when you solve an equation.

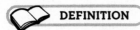 **DEFINITION**

An equation is **transformed** if you add a number to both sides, subtract a number from both sides, multiply both sides by a nonzero number, or divide both sides by a nonzero number. When you transform an equation, you get an equivalent equation. **Equivalent equations** have the same solution.

Look at these examples:

Solve $2x - 3 = 7$. Add 3 to both sides to get $2x = 10$. Divide both sides by 2 to get $x = 5$.

Solve $8 - 3x = -1$. Subtract 8 from both sides to get $-3x = -9$. Divide both sides by -3 to get $x = 3$.

Here are detailed examples that require more steps:

Solve $5x + 8 = 2x - 37$.

$5x + 8 = 2x - 37$	The variable appears on both sides of the equation.
$5x + 8 - 2x = 2x - 37 - 2x$	Subtract $2x$ from the right side to remove it from that side. To keep the balance, subtract $2x$ from the left side, too.
$3x + 8 = -37$	Simplify.
$3x + 8 - 8 = -37 - 8$	8 is added to the variable term. Subtract 8 from both sides.
$3x = -45$	Simplify.
$\dfrac{\cancel{3}x}{\cancel{3}} = \dfrac{-45}{3}$	You want the coefficient of x to be 1, so divide both sides by 3. On the left, side the 3s cancel out.
$x = -15$	On the right side, you have $-45 \div 3$, which is -15.

Solve $5(x + 7) = 65$.

$$5(x+7)=65$$

$5x+35=65$ Use the distributive property to remove parentheses.

$5x+35-35=65-35$ 35 is added to the variable term. Subtract 35 from both sides.

$5x=30$ Simplify.

$\dfrac{\cancel{5}x}{\cancel{5}}=\dfrac{30}{5}$ You want the coefficient of x to be 1, so divide both sides by 5.
On the left side, the 5s cancel out.

$x=6$ On the right side, you have $30 \div 5$, which is 6.

Solve $2x - 7y = -37$ for y.

$2x-7y=-37$ Treat x terms as constants because y is the variable of interest.

$2x-7y-2x=-37-2x$ Subtract $2x$ from the left side to remove it from that side.
To keep the balance, subtract $2x$ from the right side, too.

$-7y=-2x-37$ Simplify.

$\dfrac{-7y}{-7}=\dfrac{-2x-37}{-7}$ Divide both sides by -7.

$y=\dfrac{2}{7}x+\dfrac{37}{7}$ Simplify.

You already learned about proportions as a special type of equation in Chapter 24. A *proportion* is an equation that says two ratios are equal, such as $\dfrac{3}{8}=\dfrac{15}{40}$. When you solve a proportion, one of the four numbers is unknown and represented by a variable, say x. For example, to solve $\dfrac{2}{7}=\dfrac{x}{21}$, cross-multiply to get $7x = 42$, and divide both sides by 7 to get $x = 6$.

An *inequality* is a statement that expresses a comparison between two unequal quantities. An example of a simple inequality is $x < 3$ (a number is less than 3). Just as with equations, an inequality may be true or false. A solution to an inequality is a number that, when substituted for the variable, makes the inequality true. The inequality $x < 3$ has an infinite number of solutions: 2, 1, 0, −15, and 2.9, to name a few. This situation is different from equations because all the equations you've seen so far have only one solution.

Three other inequality symbols besides $<$ (is less than) are $\leq$ (is less than or equal to), $>$ (is greater than), and $\geq$ (is greater than or equal to). The difference between $x < 3$ and $x \leq 3$ is that 3 is not a solution to the first inequality, but it is a solution to the second one: 3 is less than or equal to 3 because it equals 3.

The inequality $x < 3$ is already solved because the solutions are evident (all numbers less than 3). Suppose instead that you have the task of solving the inequality $4x - 5 < 7$. You solve this inequality just as you'd solve the corresponding equation $4x - 5 = 7$. First, add 5 to both sides, resulting in the inequality $4x < 12$. Then, divide both sides by 4 to get the inequality $x < 3$.

Solving inequalities is just like solving equations, but there is one very important difference: when you multiply or divide both sides of an inequality by a negative number, you must *reverse* the direction of the inequality. The reversal is necessary because, for instance, $3 < 4$, but when you multiply or divide both sides by -1, $-3 > -4$. For example, suppose you want to solve the inequality $-5x < 20$. To get a coefficient of 1 for x on the left side, divide both sides by -5. The result is the inequality $x > -4$.

 **GOOD IDEA**

As with equations, it's best to isolate the variable on the left side of the inequality. For example, change $7 < 3x + 2$ to $3x + 2 > 7$.

The examples that follow illustrate solving inequalities:

Solve $6x + 1 > 13$. Subtract 1 from both sides to get $6x > 12$. Then divide both sides by 6 to get $x > 2$.

Solve $8 - 5x \geq -2$. Subtract 8 from both sides to get $-5x \geq -10$. Then divide both sides by -5 to get $x \leq 2$.

Solve $x - 5 < 3x - 19$. Subtract $3x$ from both sides to get $-2x - 5 < -19$. Add 5 to both sides to get $-2x < -14$. Divide both sides by -2 to get $x > 7$.

You can graph the solutions to an inequality on a number line. Again, consider $x < 3$. Recall that the values increase as you move from left to right on a number line. Because the solutions are all numbers less than 3, you want to show all numbers to the left of 3 on the graph. The open circle on the following graph shows that 3 is *not* on the graph. The arrowhead pointing to the left shows that the graph continues indefinitely in that direction.

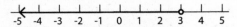

Solving Quadratic Equations

A *quadratic equation* has the standard form $ax^2 + bx + c = 0$, where x is a variable and the coefficients a, b, and c are constants with $a \neq 0$. For example, $x^2 + 6x - 40 = 0$ is a quadratic equation in which $a = 1$, $b = 6$, and $c = -40$ (keep a $-$ sign with the number that follows it); $2x^2 + 7x + 3 = 0$ is a quadratic equation in which $a = 2$, $b = 7$, and $c = 3$; and $4x^2 - 36 = 0$ is a quadratic equation in which $a = 4$, $b = 0$, and $c = -36$. A value that makes a quadratic equation true is a *root* of the equation. In terms of real numbers, a quadratic equation either has two real roots, one real root, or no real roots.

Here are examples of solving quadratic equations:

Solve $x^2 + 6x = 40$. You can solve this equation by the technique of factoring. First, put $x^2 + 6x = 40$ in standard form by subtracting 40 from both sides to obtain $x^2 + 6x - 40 = 0$. Factor the left side of this equation to get $(x+10)(x-4) = 0$. Set each factor equal to zero, and solve each of the resulting linear equations for x: $x + 10 = 0$ gives $x = -10$ and $x - 4 = 0$ gives $x = 4$. Therefore, the two roots of $x^2 + 6x - 40 = 0$ are -10 and 4.

Solve $2x^2 = -7x - 3$. You can solve this equation by using the quadratic formula $x = \dfrac{-b \pm \sqrt{b^2 - 4ac}}{2a}$. (This formula is available to you on the mathematics formula sheet during the actual GED test.) First, put $2x^2 = -7x - 3$ in standard form by adding $7x$ and 3 to both sides to get $2x^2 + 7x + 3 = 0$. Identify the coefficients a, b, and c: $a = 2$, $b = 7$, and $c = 3$. Substitute the coefficients into the quadratic formula, and evaluate.

$$x = \frac{-b \pm \sqrt{b^2 - 4ac}}{2a} = \frac{-7 \pm \sqrt{7^2 - 4(2)(3)}}{2(2)} = \frac{-7 \pm \sqrt{49 - 24}}{4} = \frac{-7 \pm \sqrt{25}}{4} = \frac{-7 \pm 5}{4},$$

which yields $\dfrac{-7+5}{4} = \dfrac{-2}{4} = -\dfrac{1}{2}$ or $\dfrac{-7-5}{4} = \dfrac{-12}{4} = -3$. Therefore, the two roots of $2x^2 = -7x - 3$ are $-\dfrac{1}{2}$ and -3.

Solve $4x^2 = 36$. Because $b = 0$ in this quadratic equation, there is a simple way to solve it. First, solve for x^2 by dividing both sides by 4 to obtain $x^2 = 9$. Then, find the two square roots of 9 to determine that the two roots of $4x^2 = 36$ are 3 and -3.

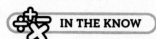 **IN THE KNOW**

For the quadratic equation $ax^2 + bx + c = 0$, if $b^2 - 4ac > 0$, there are two real roots; if $b^2 - 4ac = 0$, there is one real root; and if $b^2 - 4ac < 0$, there are no real roots.

Functions

A *function* is a set of ordered pairs for which each first component (*input* or x value) is paired with exactly one second component (*output* or y value). Thus, in a function, no two distinct ordered pairs have the same first component but different second components. So for example, (9,−3) and (9,3) cannot both be ordered pairs of the same function. (See the "Coordinate Geometry" section in Chapter 25 for a discussion of ordered pairs.) A function's *domain* is the set of all possible input values, and its *range* is the set of all possible output values.

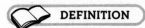 **DEFINITION**

A **function** is a set of ordered pairs for which each first component is paired with exactly one second component. The set of first components is the **domain** of the function, and the set of second components is the **range** of the function.

Commonly, an equation is used to tell you how to get the output value y when you know the input value x. Such equations begin with "$y =$." It's conventional to refer to this equation as the *function*. So for example, you can say, "the function $y = 2x − 6$" or "the function $y = x^2$." Another notation for functions is to use $f(x)$, which is read as "f of x," in place of y. You can speak of "the function $f(x) = 2x − 6$" or "the function $f(x) = x^2$." Because $y = f(x)$, this notation under-scores that the value of y depends on the value of x. It's customary to refer to x as the *independent variable* and to y as the *dependent variable*. Note the notation $f(x)$ does not mean f times x.

You can generate a table of ordered pairs for the function $y = 2x − 6$ by substituting convenient values for x into $y = 2x − 6$ and computing the corresponding y values. For instance, when $x = 1$, substitute 1 for x to get $y = −4$; similarly, when $x = 2$, $y = −2$; and so on. Here is a table of selected x values paired with their corresponding y values for the function $y = 2x − 6$.

x	y = 2x − 6
−2	−10
−1	−8
0	−6
1	−4
2	−2
3	0
4	2

Notice that the table of ordered pairs exhibits a definite pattern: as x goes up by 1, y goes up by 2. We revisit this idea shortly.

You can graph these ordered pairs as points in the coordinate plane: (−2,−10), (−1,−8), and so on. Note that these 7 points seem to line up. If you were to plot points in between these (by using fractional values for x), they, too, would fall right in line. This is because $y = 2x - 6$ is an example of a *linear function*—its graph is a line.

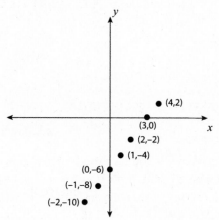

Other examples of linear functions are $y = 5x - 4$, $y = -2x + 3$, $y = \dfrac{3}{4}x - 1$, and $y = 3x$.

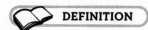 **DEFINITION**

In a function if x is raised to the power 1 and not to any higher power, the function is **linear.**

In general, a linear function has the form $y = mx + b$, where m is the *slope* of the graph of the function and b is its *y-intercept*, which is the value of y at the point where the graph crosses the y-axis. For $y = 5x - 4$, and $b = -4$, and for $y = -2x + 3$, $m = -2$ and $b = 3$.

The slope of the function $y = 2x - 6$ is 2. This slope tells you how y changes relative to changes in x. It's the *rate of change* of the function. For $y = 2x - 6$, y goes up by 2 when x goes up by 1. (This is the pattern you observed earlier in the table of values for the function $y = 2x - 6$.) For $y = -2x + 3$, y goes down by 2 when x increases by 1. For $y = \dfrac{3}{4}x - 1$, y increases by 3 when x increases by 4. Recall from Chapter 25 that a line with a positive slope slants upward as you move left to right while a line with a negative slope slants downward as you move left to right. (See "Coordinate Geometry" in Chapter 25 for an additional discussion of slope and rate of change.)

Because $y = b$ when $x = 0$ in $y = mx + b$, $(0,b)$ is on both the line and the y-axis. Therefore, the point $(0,b)$ is where the graph of $y = mx + b$ crosses the y-axis. For example, the function $y = 2x - 6$ has y-intercept -6, so its graph crosses the y-axis at $(0,-6)$.

An x-intercept is a point where the graph of a function crosses the x-axis. It is a value of x that corresponds to $y = 0$. For the function $y = 2x - 6$, solve the equation $0 = 2x - 6$ to determine that the x-intercept is 3. So its graph crosses the x-axis at $(3,0)$.

The intercepts for the graph of the function $y = 2x - 6$ are shown in the following figure.

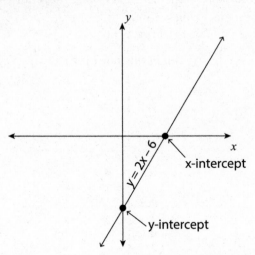

Now consider the function $y = -2x + 3$. The slope is -2, and the y-intercept is 3. Graph this function by first plotting the point (0,3). Because the slope is -2, you can get a second point by starting at (0,3) and moving 2 units down and 1 unit right to the point (1,1). Because you know the graph is a line, you need to plot only two points to draw the line. Here is the graph of $y = -2x + 3$.

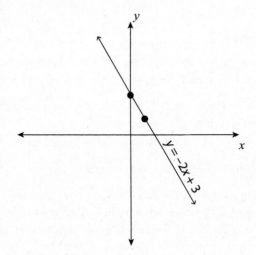

The function $y = \dfrac{3}{4}x - 1$ has slope $\dfrac{3}{4}$ and y-intercept -1. Graph this function by first plotting the point $(0,-1)$. From that point, move 3 spaces up and 4 spaces to the right to get a second point $(4,2)$. The graph of $y = \dfrac{3}{4}x - 1$ is shown in the following figure.

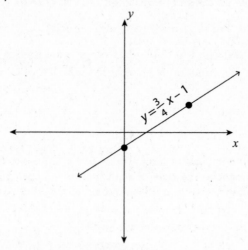

The function $y = 3x$ has slope 3 and y-intercept 0. This function is a *proportional function*, and 3 is its *constant of proportionality*. A distinguishing feature of proportional functions is that their graphs always pass through the origin. Here is the graph of $y = 3x$.

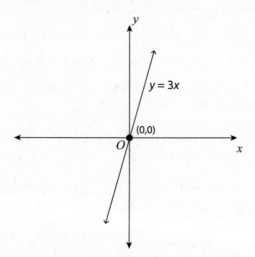

A quadratic function has the form $y = ax^2 + bx + c$, where x is a variable and the coefficients a, b, and c are constants with $a \neq 0$. The roots of the corresponding quadratic equation $ax^2 + bx + c = 0$ are the *zeros* of $y = ax^2 + bx + c$. If the zeros are real numbers, their values are the x-intercepts of the graph of $y = ax^2 + bx + c$. The graph is a *parabola* (a bowl-shape curve).

The parabola is symmetric about the vertical line $x = -\dfrac{b}{2a}$. When $a > 0$, the parabola opens upward, and the value of y when x equals $-\dfrac{b}{2a}$ is the *minimum value* of the function. The point on the graph where the minimum value occurs is the *vertex* of the parabola. The function is decreasing to the left of its vertex and increasing to the right of its vertex. When $a < 0$, the parabola opens downward, and the value of y when x equals $-\dfrac{b}{2a}$ is the *maximum value* of the function. The point on the graph where the maximum value occurs is (again) the *vertex* of the parabola. In this case, the function is increasing to the left of its vertex and decreasing to the right of its vertex.

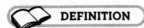 **DEFINITION**

> A **quadratic function** has the form $y = ax^2 + bx + c$ with $a \neq 0$. The graph of a quadratic function is a **parabola**. The **zeros** of a quadratic function are the *roots* of the corresponding quadratic equation $ax^2 + bx + c = 0$..

Here are examples:

Graph $y = x^2 - 2x - 3$. The graph of the function $y = x^2 - 2x - 3$ is a parabola that opens upward. The parabola is symmetric about the vertical line $x = 1 \left(= -\dfrac{b}{2a} = -\dfrac{(-2)}{2(1)} \right)$ and opens upward. When $x = 1$, the minimum value of the function is $y = x^2 - 2x - 3 = (1)^2 - 2(1) - 3 = 1 - 2 - 3 = -4$. Thus, the vertex of the parabola is $(1, -4)$. Because $x^2 - 2x - 3 = 0$ implies $(x-3)(x+1) = 0$, which yields 3 and -1 as roots, the x-intercepts of the graph of $y = x^2 - 2x - 3$ are 3 and -1. The graph is shown in the following figure.

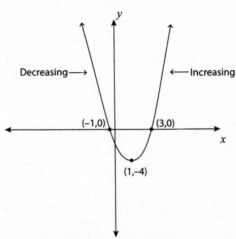

Graph $y = -x^2 + 4$. The graph of the function $y = -x^2 + 4$ is a parabola that opens downward. The parabola is symmetric about the vertical line $x = 0$ $\left(= -\dfrac{b}{2a} = -\dfrac{(0)}{2(1)} \right)$. Note the vertical line $x = 0$ is the y-axis. When $x = 0$, the maximum value of the function is $y = -x^2 + 4 = -(0)^2 + 4 = 0 + 4 = 4$. Thus, the vertex of the parabola is (0,4) Because $-x^2 + 4 = 0$ implies $x^2 - 4 = (x - 2)(x + 2) = 0$, which yields 2 and -2 as roots, the x-intercepts of the graph of $y = -x^2 + 4$ are 2 and -2. The graph is shown in the following figure.

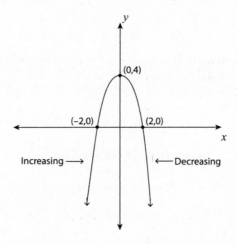

IN THE KNOW

If the quadratic equation $ax^2 + bx + c = 0$ does not have real number roots, the graph of the quadratic function $y = ax^2 + bx + c$ will not intersect the x-axis.

You can use functions to represent real-life behavior. For example, if you sell pencils for 10 cents each, the amount of money you make is a function of the number of pencils you sell. The formula in this case is $y = 0.10x$, where x is the number of pencils you sell and y is the amount of money (in \$) you make. The distance an object falls to the ground is a quadratic function of the amount of time it falls. This is not a linear function because gravity causes falling objects to increase their speed as they fall. You'll see more real-life functions in the practice test (see Chapter 29).

Solving a System of Two Simultaneous Linear Equations

For purposes of this section, a linear equation with two variables has the form $ax + by = c$, where x and y are variables and the coefficients a, b, and c are constants. A pair of two such linear equations is a *system* when the two equations are considered simultaneously, as when you are seeking their common solution. That is, when you are trying to find an ordered pair (x, y) that satisfies both equations at the same time. Here is an example of a system of two simultaneous linear equations:

$$x - y = 7$$
$$3x + 2y = -4$$

To solve the system by the method of *substitution*, solve the first equation, $x - y = 7$, for x in terms of y to obtain $x = y + 7$. Next, eliminate x by substituting $(y + 7)$ for x in the second equation, $3x + 2y = -4$. Then, solve for y.

$$3(y+7)+2y = -4$$
$$3y+21+2y = -4$$
$$5y+21 = -4$$
$$5y+21-21 = -4-21$$
$$5y = -25$$
$$\frac{\cancel{5}y}{\cancel{5}} = \frac{-25}{5}$$
$$y = -5$$

Finally, solve for x by substituting -5 for y in the equation, $x = y + 7$, to obtain $x = -5 + 7 = 2$. Thus, the ordered pair $(2, -5)$ is the solution to the system.

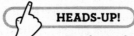 **HEADS-UP!**

For the method of substitution, it makes no difference which equation you solve first or for which variable.

To solve the system by the method of *elimination*, transform the first equation, $x - y = 7$, by multiplying both sides of the equation by 2 to obtain $2x - 2y = 14$. (The goal is to produce opposite coefficients on the variable y so it can be eliminated by adding the two equations.) Next, eliminate y by adding the second equation, $3x + 2y = -4$, to the transformed equation and then solve the resulting equation for x.

$$2x - 2y = 14$$
$$3x + 2y = -4$$
$$5x + 0 = 10$$
$$5x = 10$$
$$\frac{\cancel{5}x}{\cancel{5}} = \frac{10}{5}$$
$$x = 2$$

Finally, solve for y by substituting 2 for x in the equation, $x = y + 7$, to obtain $2 = y + 7$, which yields $y = -5$. Thus (as previously obtained), the ordered pair $(2,-5)$ is the solution to the system.

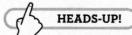 **HEADS-UP!**

> For the method of elimination, it makes no difference which variable you eliminate first. Also, you might find it necessary to use multiplication to transform *both* equations in order to produce opposite coefficients for one of the variables.

Graphically, as shown in the following figure, $(2,-5)$ is the point of intersection of the graphs of the two lines whose linear equations are $x - y = 7$ and $3x + 2y = -4$.

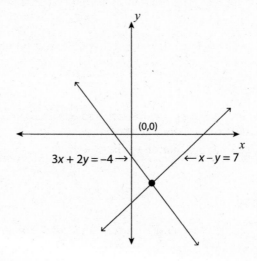

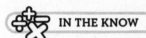 **IN THE KNOW**

The graphs of the two equations in a system of two simultaneous linear equations are two lines. If the two lines have different slopes, they will intersect in one common point. In this first case, the ordered pair that corresponds to the point of intersection is the unique solution to the system. If the two lines have the same slope and the same y-intercept, they coincide, meaning they have all points in common. So in this second case, the system has an infinite number of solutions. If the two graphs have the same slope but different y-intercepts, the two lines are parallel, meaning they have no points in common. Thus, in this third case, the system has no solution.

Solving Word Problems

Here are the steps to solving a word problem using algebra:

1. Be absolutely clear about what the problem wants you to find.

2. Think about what kinds of things you need to know to answer the question in the problem. Sometimes this requires looking up or knowing a formula.

3. Match what you need to know with the information the problem gives you. Let variable expressions stand for what the problem is asking you to find (usually in terms of x or some other convenient letter).

4. Write an equation that relates the quantity you are to find with other quantities in the problem.

5. Solve the equation.

6. Reread what the problem asks you to find, and be sure you've answered the question.

The following sections offer examples of word problems you might encounter on the GED test.

Consecutive Integers

Consecutive integers are, loosely speaking, integers "in a row." You have a starting number, and you count up one number at a time until it's time to stop. For example, 3, 4, 5, and 6 are four consecutive integers starting with the number 3 and −4, −3, and −2 are three consecutive integers starting with −4.

Suppose you are asked to find three consecutive integers with a sum of 45. You could guess and check: $10 + 11 + 12 = 33$, which is too small. This method might take many tries to get the correct three numbers. Eventually, you might determine that $14 + 15 + 16 = 45$.

A more reliable method for solving this problem is to let the variable n stand for the starting number. The next number is one more than n, or $n + 1$, and the third number is one more than that, or $n + 2$. The three numbers n, $n + 1$, and $n + 2$ add up to 45, so $n+(n+1)+(n+2)=45$. The solution n to this equation and the next two numbers provide an answer to the original question.

To solve this equation, you should first simplify the left side. The new equation would be $3n + 3 = 45$. You can then subtract 3 from both sides, getting $3n = 42$, and then divide both sides by 3 to get $n = 14$. Therefore, the three consecutive integers that add to 45 are 14, 15, and 16.

Geometry Problems

Geometry word problems often require you to use a formula for length, area, or volume, but in reverse. For example, instead of being given a length and a width and being asked to find the area, you're told what the area is and asked to find the length and width. The following examples illustrate this idea.

Problem 1:

The area of a circle is 400 in². To the nearest tenth of an inch, what is the diameter of this circle?

Use the mathematics formula sheet (see Chapter 28) to find that the formula for the area of a circle is πr^2, where r is the length of the radius.

Omitting the units (in²), substitute 400 for area and 3.14 for π. The resulting equation is $400 = 3.14r^2$. Then $r^2 = \dfrac{400}{3.14}$ and $r = \sqrt{\dfrac{400}{3.14}}$, which is 11.3, rounded to the nearest tenth. But wait a minute! This is the radius, not the diameter, which is double the radius of 11.3. The diameter is two times that or 22.6 inches.

 **HEADS-UP!**

Don't assume the solution to an equation is always the answer to the problem.

Problem 2:

A rectangle is 4 feet longer than it is wide. The perimeter of the rectangle is 36 feet. What are the dimensions of the rectangle?

Let w stand for the rectangle's width, in feet. Then $w + 4$ is the rectangle's length, in feet. Use the mathematics formula sheet to find the formula for the perimeter of a rectangle as twice the rectangle's width plus twice the rectangle's length. Omitting units (feet), this gives you the equation $2x + 2(x+4) = 36$ or, equivalently, $2x + 2x + 8 = 36$. Combine $2x + 2x$ to get $4x$, and subtract 8 from both sides to get $4x = 28$. Then divide both sides by 4 to get $x = 7$ for the width and $x + 4 = 7 + 4 = 11$ for the length. The dimensions of the rectangle are 7 feet by 11 feet.

Motion Problems

A motion problem is one that relates distance, speed, and time. The primary formula is $d = rt$, where d = distance, r = speed, and t = time. The two related formulas are $t = \dfrac{d}{r}$ and $r = \dfrac{d}{t}$. These formulas express familiar ideas if you drive an automobile. If you travel for 3 hours at an average speed of 50 miles per hour, you will drive 150 miles ($150 = 50 \times 3$). If you drive 120 miles in 2 hours, your average speed is 60 miles per hour $\left(60 = \dfrac{120}{2}\right)$. And finally, if you travel 110 miles at an average speed of 55 miles per hour, it will take you 2 hours $\left(2 = \dfrac{110}{55}\right)$.

Problem 1:

> A truck leaves a warehouse at 10 A.M. traveling at an average speed of 50 miles per hour. Two hours later, another truck leaves the same warehouse on the same highway traveling in the same direction at an average speed of 70 miles per hour. If both trucks continue at their respective speeds without making any stops, at what time will the second truck catch up with the first?

> Let t = the time, in hours, the first truck travels until the second truck catches up with it. When the second truck catches up with the first, the two trucks will have gone the same distance, but the second truck's time travel is 2 hours less. The distance traveled by the first truck is $50t$, and the distance traveled by the second truck is $70(t-2)$. Because these distances are equal, you have the equation $50t = 70(t-2)$. This is equivalent to $50t = 70t - 140$. Subtract $70t$ from both sides to get $-20t = -140$ and then divide both sides by -20 to get $t = 7$. The second truck will catch up with the first one 7 hours after the first one leaves the warehouse, or at 5 P.M.

Problem 2:

> Two people walk away from each other in opposite directions. The first person walks at an average speed of 4 miles per hour, while the second person walks at an average speed of 3 miles per hour. How far apart will they be in 30 minutes?

> Thirty minutes is one half of an hour, so $t = 0.5$. The distance the first person walks is $4 \times 0.5 = 2$ miles, and the distance the second person walks is $3 \times 0.5 = 1.5$ miles. Because they're walking in opposite directions, they will be 3.5 ($= 2 + 1.5$) miles apart in 30 minutes.

Practice

1. Simplify the following expression.

$$10 - 4(3-5)^3 + 2^3 - (-22)$$

   (1) 40

   (2) 52

   (3) 60

   (4) 72

2. What is the product of $\left(2xy^2\right)^3\left(-3x^2y^3\right)^2$?

   (1) $-6x^7 y^{12}$

   (2) $-72x^7 y^{12}$

   (3) $72x^7 y^{12}$

   (4) $72x^{12} y^{36}$

3. Which inequality is graphed on the number line shown?

   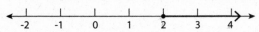

   (1) $x < 2$

   (2) $x \le 2$

   (3) $x > 2$

   (4) $x \ge 2$

4. Ten less than three times a number equals one more than two times the same number. What is the number? Write your answer in the answer box: ☐

5. Solve for x: $3x - 1 = 4(5-x)$.

   (1) 1

   (2) $\dfrac{10}{7}$

   (3) 3

   (4) 5.25

6. What is the slope of the line that has equation $6x + 3y = -15$?

    (1) -2

    (2) $-\dfrac{1}{2}$

    (3) $\dfrac{1}{2}$

    (4) 2

 7. If $x^2 + 5x - 14 = 0$, what are the values of $x - 1$?

    (1) $-8, -3$

    (2) $-8, 1$

    (3) $-7, 2$

    (4) $-6, -2$

 8. What is the x value of the solution to the system $\begin{array}{l} 2x - y = -5 \\ x + 4y = 11 \end{array}$?

    (1) -3

    (2) -1

    (3) 1

    (4) 3

Answers

1. **(4)** Follow the order of operations.

$$10 - 4(3-5)^3 + 2^3 - (-22) = 10 - 4(-2)^3 + 2^3 - (-22)$$
$$= 10 - 4(-8) + 8 - (-22)$$
$$= 10 + 32 + 8 + 22$$
$$= 72$$

2. **(3)** Perform the indicated operations, being sure to follow the rules for exponents.

$$\left(2xy^2\right)^3 \left(-3x^2y^3\right)^2 = 8x^3y^6 \cdot 9x^4y^6 = 72x^7y^{12}$$

3. **(4)** The circle at 2 is filled in ($x = 2$) and the arrow is pointing to the right ($x > 2$), so $x \geq 2$ is the correct choice.

4. **(11)** Let x equal the number. Ten less than three times x is $3x - 10$. One more than two times x is $2x + 1$. Solve the equation $3x - 10 = 2x + 1$. First, subtract $2x$ from both sides to get $x - 10 = 1$. Next, add 10 to both sides to get $x = 11$.

5. **(3)** First distribute the 4 on the right side of the equation to obtain $3x - 1 = 20 - 4x$. Then add $4x$ to both sides to get $7x - 1 = 20$. Add 1 to both sides to get $7x = 21$. Finally, divide both sides by 7 to get $x = 3$.

6. **(1)** To identify the slope, put the equation in $y = mx + b$ form by solving for y.

$$6x + 3y = -15$$
$$6x + 3y - 6x = -15 - 6x$$
$$3y = -6x - 15$$
$$\frac{3y}{3} = \frac{-6x - 15}{3}$$
$$y = -2x - 5$$

The slope is -2, the coefficient of x.

7. **(2)** First, solve $x^2 + 5x - 14 = 0$ by factoring.

$$x^2 + 5x - 14 = 0$$
$$(x + 7)(x - 2) = 0$$
$$x + 7 = 0 \text{ or } x - 2 = 0$$
$$x = -7 \text{ or } x = 2$$

Next, substitute both values, one at a time, into the expression $x - 1$ to obtain $-7 - 1 = -8$ and $2 - 1 = 1$. Therefore, the correct choice is $-8, 1$.

8. **(2)** To solve the system by eliminating y, multiply the first equation, $2x - y = -5$, by 4 to obtain $8x - 4y = -20$. Next, add the second equation, $x + 4y = 11$, to the transformed equation and then solve the resulting equation for x.

$$8x - 4y = -20$$
$$\underline{x + 4y = 11}$$
$$9x + 0 = -9$$
$$9x = -9$$
$$\frac{9x}{9} = \frac{-9}{9}$$
$$x = -1$$

Taking the Mathematical Reasoning Test

The computer-delivered Mathematical Reasoning Test has 46 questions to be completed in 115 minutes. According to the "Assessment Guide for Educators: Mathematical Reasoning" (available from gedtestingservice.com), about 45 percent of the test questions address quantitative problem-solving and about 55 percent focus on algebraic problem-solving.

Overview

The Mathematical Reasoning Test consists of two parts, Part I and Part II, with a 3-minute break between the two parts. Part I consists of 5 questions that do not allow the use of a calculator. Part II consists of 41 questions for which calculator use is allowed. The testing service provides an embedded, on-screen TI-30XS Multiview Scientific Calculator for your use during Part II. Currently (2017), if you prefer, you may bring a handheld TI-30XS Multiview Scientific Calculator to use for test questions that allow the use of a calculator. Only the TI-30XS Multiview Scientific Calculator is permitted for use on the GED® test. (See the "TI-30XS Multiview Scientific Calculator" section later in this chapter for a discussion about this calculator.)

In This Chapter

- Overview of the Mathematical Reasoning Test
- Tips on navigating the types of questions
- Pointers on using the formula reference sheet, Æ Symbol Tool, TI-30XS Multiview Scientific Calculator, and more

You can move back and forth among the questions within each individual part of the test. However, you must submit your answers to Part I before you can move on to Part II, and you are not allowed to revisit questions in Part I after you have begun Part II. Even though the two parts are distinct, they are not timed separately. You must manage your time so you complete both the noncalculator and the calculator parts in the allotted 115 minutes. For that purpose, the testing software has a time clock you can use to keep track of your time. The clock appears in the upper-right corner of the test screen.

Question Types

Here are the question types you'll encounter on the Mathematical Reasoning Test:

- **Multiple-choice questions:** You use the mouse to click on one of four possible answer choices. You can change your answer by clicking on a different choice.

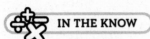 **IN THE KNOW**

> For purposes of clarity, most of the Mathematical Reasoning questions in this book require you to select from a list of answer choices and show the answer choices labeled with numbers. These numbers do not appear on the computer screen when you take the actual test.

- **Fill-in-the-blank questions:** You click in the answer box provided and type your answer to the question. You may need to type in a numerical answer, or you may need to enter an expression or equation using the keyboard or the on-screen symbol tool (see the later "Æ Symbol Tool" section for a description of this tool). You can change your answer by using the Backspace key and then typing a new answer.

- **Drop-down questions:** You click on a box labeled "Select …" that's embedded in a sentence or mathematical expression. This action opens a drop-down menu of answer choices. Scroll down and click on your answer choice to complete the sentence or mathematical expression. Repeat this process for each "Select …" box in the question. You can change your answer by clicking the "Select …" box again and choosing a difference answer.

- **Hot-spot questions:** You click on a graphic image (for example, a number line, coordinate grid, graph, or chart) to answer the question. You can change your answer by clicking on a different location on the image.

- **Drag-and-drop questions:** You click on an answer, drag it to the location of your choice, and drop it. Repeat this process for each answer you need to move. You can change an answer by dragging it to a different location or back to its starting point.

There is no set number for each question type, nor do the question types appear in a specific order. However, according to GED FAQs (at gedtestingservice.com), more than 50 percent of the GED test questions are multiple choice.

GOOD IDEA

Before you take your GED test, go to the online GED test tutorial (at gedtestingservice.com/2014cbttutorialview) to practice the various question types.

Erasable Note Boards

Erasable note boards, measuring $8\frac{1}{2}$ by 14 inches, and erasable markers are provided at the testing center for your use during the GED test. You can have only three note boards at a time, but you can ask for additional note boards as needed during the test. Marking on your note boards before the test begins is not allowed.

Formula Reference Sheet

An on-screen formula reference sheet is available for your use during the Mathematical Reasoning Test. The formula sheet provides geometric formulas for area, perimeter, surface area, and volume of geometric shapes; formulas used in algebra; and definitions for the mean and median of a data set. You click on the Formula Sheet button at the top of the screen to view the sheet. Here's what information it provides:

Mathematics Formula Sheet

Area of *a:*

Square	$A = s^2$
Rectangle	$A = lw$
Parallelogram	$A = bh$
Triangle	$A = \frac{1}{2}bh$
Trapezoid	$A = \frac{1}{2}(b_1 + b_2)h$
Circle	$A = \pi r^2$

Perimeter of *a:*

Square	$P = 4s$
Rectangle	$P = 2l + 2w$
Triangle	$P = s_1 + s_2 + s_3$
Circle	$C = \text{circumference} = \pi d \text{ or } 2\pi r$

Volume of *a:*

Rectangular prism	$V = lwh$
Right prism	$V = Bh$
Pyramid	$V = \dfrac{1}{3} Bh$
Cylinder	$V = \pi r^2 h$
Cone	$V = \dfrac{1}{3} \pi r^2 h$
Sphere	$V = \dfrac{4}{3} \pi r^3$

Surface area of *a:*

Rectangular prism	$SA = 2lw + 2lh + 2wh$
Right prism	$SA = Ph + 2B$
Pyramid	$SA = \dfrac{1}{2} Ps + B$
Cylinder	$SA = 2\pi rh + 2\pi r^2$
Cone	$SA = \pi rs + \pi r^2$
Sphere	$SA = 4\pi r^2$

(*P* is perimeter of base with area *B*, *s* is slant height, $\pi \approx 3.14$)

Algebra:

Slope of a line	$m = \dfrac{y_2 - y_1}{x_2 - x_1}$
Slope-intercept form of the equation of a line	$y = mx + b$
Point-slope form of the equation of a line	$y - y_1 = m(x - x_1)$
Standard form of a quadratic equation	$ax^2 + bx + c = 0$

Quadratic formula	$x = \dfrac{-b \pm \sqrt{b^2 - 4ac}}{2a}$
Pythagorean theorem	$a^2 + b^2 = c^2$
Simple interest	$I = Prt$
	(I = interest, P = principal, r = rate, t = time)
Distance formula	$d = rt$
Total cost	total cost = (number of units) × (price per unit)

Data:

Mean	The mean equals the sum of the data values divided by the number of data values.
Median	The median is the middle value in an odd number of data values, or the arithmetic average of the pair of middle values in an even number of data values.

Æ Symbol Tool

The Æ Symbol Tool button is available at the top of the screen (next to the Calculator button) during the Mathematical Reasoning Test. You use this tool to enter mathematical symbols in fill-in-the-blank questions. The available symbols are shown in the following figure, where the = symbol is shown as selected.

Π	f	≥	≤	≠	2	3	|	×	÷	±	∞
√	+	-	(	)	>	<	=				

TI-30XS Multiview Scientific Calculator

Even if you have experience using calculators, you'll benefit by familiarizing yourself with the TI-30XS Multiview Scientific Calculator.

During the test, an on-screen calculator reference document is available for your use anytime the calculator is available. This document provides detailed descriptions and examples of how to operate the TI-30XS Multiview Scientific Calculator. It shows you how to perform basic arithmetic, calculate with percentages, compute using scientific notation, enter numbers as common fractions and mixed numbers and perform calculations with these fractional representations, and compute using powers and roots.

The Calculator button is in the blue toolbar above the question. After you click on the button, you can click at the top of the calculator window to drag the calculator to a convenient location on the screen.

 **GOOD IDEA**

Before you take your GED test, log on to the online tutorial at gedtestingservice .com/2014cbttutorialview. There, you can practice opening, closing, moving, and sizing the on-screen Formula Sheet; inserting symbols into an answer box using the Æ Symbol Tool; and using the TI-30XS Multiview Scientific Calculator and Calculator Reference document.

Mathematical Reasoning Practice Test

The Mathematical Reasoning Test is designed to assess your math skills in the following categories: number sense and computation, geometric measurement, data analysis and statistics, and algebraic expressions and functions. This chapter provides a 23-question, half-length Mathematical Reasoning practice test. Calculators may be used on 20 of the questions only, as indicated by a calculator icon. This practice test is not separated into Part I (calculator allowed) and Part II (calculator not allowed) like the actual Mathematical Reasoning Test.

For this practice test, you should allow yourself $57\frac{1}{2}$ minutes (half of the actual test's allotted 115 minutes), and you should not use a calculator unless the question is marked with a calculator icon. Read the explanations of all the questions—even those you get right. If you are still uncertain about how to get the correct answer for a question, go back to the chapter covering that topic and reread the appropriate material.

 **GOOD IDEA**

Many online resources can help you enhance your preparation for the GED® test. Just enter "math ged" in your search engine. Two resources you definitely should use are the free GED Mathematical Reasoning practice test at gedtestingservice.com/freepractice/download/GED_Math/GEDMathPracticeTest.html and the free Mathematical Reasoning item sampler at gedtestingservice.com/itemsamplermath. Another helpful site is PBS Literacy Link at litlink.ket.org, which offers two free 25-question practice math tests.

Instructions

You will have $57\frac{1}{2}$ minutes to complete the 23 questions on this practice test. Work carefully, but don't spend too much time on any one question. If you are having trouble with a question, make your best guess and move on. Your score is based on the number of correct answers; there is no penalty for guessing.

When taking the practice test, try to simulate actual test conditions. Get a timing device of some sort and a couple No. 2 pencils with good erasers. Go to a place where you won't be interrupted, and follow the test instructions. Start the timer after you've read the instructions and are ready to proceed to the first question. While taking the test, you can refer to the formula reference sheet in Chapter 28 as needed.

Go on to the next page when you are ready to begin.

1. The heights of the five starters on the basketball team are 67 inches, 71 inches, 79 inches, 70 inches, and 79 inches. What is their median height, in inches?

    (1) 67

    (2) 70

    (3) 71

    (4) 79

2. A square is to be drawn on a coordinate plane. The corners are at $(-2,3)$, $(4,3)$, and $(4,-3)$. Mark the fourth corner on the coordinate plane grid.

3. Simplify $2x^3x^3$.

    (1) $2x^3$

    (2) $2x^6$

    (3) $8x^6$

    (4) $2x^9$

4. A map has a scale of 2 inches equals 10 miles. If the map distance between Center City and Sun City is 5 inches, approximately how many miles apart are the two cities? Write your answer in the answer box:

5. The shadow of a woman standing next to a tree is 3 feet long, and the shadow of the tree is 12 feet long. If the woman is 5 feet, 6 inches tall, how tall, in feet, is the tree?

(1) 15

(2) 22

(3) 25

(4) 28

 6. A pile of sand at a concrete plant is a cone shape. It is 15 meters high, and the circular base has a diameter of 40 meters. What is the volume of this sand, in meters^3?

(1) 630

(2) 6,280

(3) 12,560

(4) 25,120

7. Kaia is in the market for a new car. The sticker price for the car she is interested in is $45,000. One dealer offers her 15% off the sticker price. Another dealer offers her 20% off. How much money will Kaia save if she buys the car from the second dealer?

(1) $450

(2) $900

(3) $1,125

(4) $2,250

8. Find the value of the missing x coordinate if $(x, -4)$ and $(2, -1)$ lie on a line that has slope $\frac{3}{7}$. Write your answer in the answer box: ☐

Questions 9 and 10 are based on the following table, which summarizes responses of 90 boys and girls who were surveyed about their favorite color.

Color	Boys	Girls	Total
Black	5	3	8
Blue	18	22	40
Green	8	8	16
Red	12	6	18
White	2	6	8
Total	45	45	90

9. What percent of the boys chose blue as their favorite color?

   (1) 18%

   (2) 20%

   (3) 40%

   (4) 60%

 10. What percent of those choosing red were girls?

   (1) 6%

   (2) 12%

   (3) $33\frac{1}{3}\%$

   (4) $66\frac{2}{3}\%$

 11. Show the location of the y-intercept of the graph of $3x + y = 7$. Mark your answer on the coordinate plane grid.

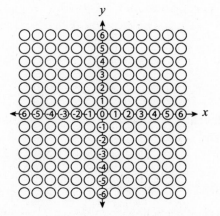

 12. Two roommates went by car to a movie theater, which is 20 miles from their apartment. Due to heavy traffic, it took them 40 minutes to get there. What was their average speed in miles per hour?

   (1) 24

   (2) 30

   (3) 32

   (4) 40

13. Grandparents left a large piece of property with a creek running through it to their two grandchildren. The property is rectangular in shape, and the creek runs diagonally from one corner of the property to one of the long sides, dividing the property into two portions, as shown in the following figure. The elder grandchild inherits the larger portion of land, while the younger one inherits the smaller portion. Using the dimensions shown in the figure, determine how much more land, in feet², the older grandchild inherits than the younger one.

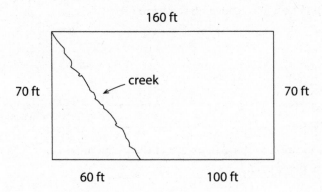

(1) 2,450

(2) 4,500

(3) 6,000

(4) 7,000

 14. Otis bought a table that was discounted 33%. If t represents the original price of the table, what was Otis's cost?

(1) 0.67t

(2) $t + 0.33$

(3) $t - 0.33$

(4) 0.33t

 15. Currently, the ratio of Jaeden's age to Kiernan's age is 5:3, and the sum of their ages is 32. In 10 years, the ratio of their ages will be:

(1) 5:3

(2) 15:11

(3) 15:13

(4) 25:21

16. To drive from Silver City to Urbana, you have to go 15 miles due north to Wakefield. Then you turn left and go due west 10 miles to Urbana. If there were a road directly from Silver City to Urbana, how far a drive, in miles, would this be (to the nearest mile)?

(1) 15

(2) 16

(3) 17

(4) 18

 17. The following table shows the percentage of students enrolled in each course who would recommend the course to a friend. Which conclusion *cannot* be drawn from the information?

Class	Percent Recommending
Biology	88%
British Literature	46%
Calculus	38%
Chemistry	72%
Economics	61%
Psychology	71%

(1) Psychology is the third-highest recommended course.

(2) Chemistry and Psychology are recommended at about equal percentages.

(3) Less than half of the students in Calculus would recommend it to a friend.

(4) More students would recommend Biology than Economics.

 18. The surface area of a sphere is 400π in². What is the sphere's diameter, in inches?

(1) 10

(2) 20

(3) 30

(4) 40

19. Twenty less than a number is five more than one-half of the same number. What is the number? Write your answer in the answer box: ⬚

20. Eight cards are dealt face down on a table: two spades, three hearts, one diamond, and two clubs. Two cards are drawn randomly, one after the other, from the cards on the table. If the first card drawn is a spade and it is not put back on the table before the second card is drawn, what is the probability that the second card drawn is a heart?

    (1) $\dfrac{1}{7}$

    (2) $\dfrac{1}{4}$

    (3) $\dfrac{3}{8}$

    (4) $\dfrac{3}{7}$

21. The half-life of radioactive material is the length of time it takes the substance to be halved due to the emission of radiation. If the half-life of a radioactive substance is 50 years, what fraction of the original amount will remain after 150 years?

    (1) $\dfrac{1}{16}$

    (2) $\dfrac{1}{8}$

    (3) $\dfrac{1}{4}$

    (4) $\dfrac{1}{2}$

22. If $5x + 3 = 2(x - 3)$, what is the value of x? Write your answer in the answer box:

    ⬚

23. A rectangle's length is 3 feet longer than twice its width. The area of the rectangle is 44 feet². The rectangle's length is how many feet?

    (1) 4

    (2) 5.5

    (3) 7

    (4) 11

Answers and Explanations

1. **(3)** The median of a list of 5 numbers is the middle number if the numbers are in order. Ordered from least to greatest, the numbers are 69, 70, 71, 79, 79. Thus, 71 inches is the median height.

2. The correct answer is (–2,–3). The point (4,3) is 6 units to the right of (–2,3), and (4,–3) is 6 units below (4,3). Therefore, the fourth corner should be 6 units below (–2,3), or at (–2, –3). The point (–2,–3) should be marked.

3. **(2)** $2x^3x^3 = 2x^{3+3} = 2x^6$.

4. The correct answer is 25. A map distance of 5 inches is 2.5 times greater than 2 inches. Therefore, the actual distance is 2.5 times 10 miles, or 25 miles.

5. **(2)** Because the lengths of objects and their shadows are proportional, the easiest way to do this problem is to observe that the shadow of the tree is four times longer than the shadow of the woman, so the tree is four times taller than the woman. Four times 5 feet, 6 inches is 22 feet.

6. **(2)** Use the formula for the volume of a cone from the formula sheet. The height is 15 meters. Given the diameter is 40 meters, the radius is 20 meters. Using 3.14 for π gives

$$V = \frac{1}{3}\pi r^2 h \approx \frac{1}{3}(3.14)(20 \text{ m})^2(15 \text{ m}) = \frac{1}{3}(3.14)(400 \text{ m}^2)(15 \text{ m}) = 6{,}280 \text{ m}^3.$$

7. **(4)** The second dealer offers Kaia the car for an extra 5% off the sticker price. Five percent of $45,000 is $(0.05)(45{,}500) = \$2{,}250$.

8. The correct answer is –5. Letting $(x,-4) = (x_2,y_2)$ and $(2,-1) = (x_1,y_1)$, substitute into the slope formula $m = \dfrac{y_2 - y_1}{x_2 - x_1}$, and solve for x:

$$\frac{3}{7} = \frac{-4 - (-1)}{x - 2}$$

$$\frac{3}{7} = \frac{-4 + 1}{x - 2}$$

$$\frac{3}{7} = \frac{-3}{x - 2}$$

$$3(x - 2) = 7(-3)$$

$$3x - 6 = -21$$

$$3x - 6 + 6 = -21 + 6$$

$$3x = -15$$

$$\frac{3x}{3} = \frac{-15}{3}$$

$$x = -5$$

9. **(3)** There were 45 boys surveyed. Of those 45, 18 chose blue as their favorite color, and 18 of 45 is 40 percent.

10. **(3)** Red was the favorite color of 18 of those surveyed. Of those 18, 6 were girls; and 6 of 18 is $33\frac{1}{3}\%$.

11. The correct answer is (0,7). The y-intercept is the value of y when x equals zero. If $x = 0$, the equation would read: 3 (0) + y = 7, or y = 7. The point (0,7) should be marked.

12. **(2)** Forty minutes is $\frac{40}{60}$ or $\frac{2}{3}$ of an hour. Because average speed is distance divided by time, divide 20 miles by $\frac{2}{3}$ hour to obtain 30 mph. It's worthwhile to note that 60 mph is a mile a minute. In this case, it took 40 minutes to go 20 miles, and this is half a mile a minute, so their average speed was 30 mph.

13. **(4)** The creek divides the property into a triangle and a trapezoid. According to the formula sheet, the area of a triangle is $\frac{1}{2}bh = \frac{1}{2} \times$ (base) $\times$ (height), and the area of a trapezoid is $\frac{1}{2}(b_1 + b_2)h = \frac{1}{2} \times$ (base₁ + base₂) $\times$ (height). The figure shows that the base of the triangle is 60 feet and its height is 70 feet, so the area of the triangle is $\frac{1}{2} \times$ (60 ft) $\times$ (70 ft) = 2,100 ft². The height of the trapezoid is also 70 feet, and its two bases have lengths of 160 feet and 100 feet, so its area is $\frac{1}{2} \times$ (160 ft + 100 ft) $\times$ (70 ft) = 9,100 ft². Subtract to get 9,100 ft² – 2,100 ft² = 7,000 ft².

14. **(1)** Given the table was discounted 33 percent, Otis paid 100% – 33% = 67% of the original price. This is 0.67t.

15. **(2)** Let 5x = Jaeden's current age, and 3x = Kiernan's current age. Then 5x + 3x = 32, so 8x = 32 and x = 4. Thus, Jaeden's current age is 5x = 5(4) = 20, and Kiernan's current age is 3x = 3(4) = 12. In 10 years, Jaeden and Kiernan will be 30 and 22, respectively, and the ratio of their ages will be $\frac{30}{22} = \frac{15}{11}$, which is 15:11.

16. **(4)** Because due north and due west form a right angle, the three cities form a right triangle. The distance from Silver City to Urbana is the hypotenuse of this right triangle. The legs of this right triangle are 15 and 10 miles. According to the Pythagorean theorem, hypotenuse² = 15² + 10² = 225 + 100 = 325. Therefore, the length of the direct route is $\sqrt{325}$, which is 18, to the nearest mile.

17. **(4)** This conclusion cannot be drawn because the table doesn't provide any information about *numbers* of people.

18. **(2)** Using the formula for the surface area of a sphere from the formula sheet (and omitting the units), solve $4\pi r^2 = 400\pi$ for r:

$$4\pi r^2 = 400\pi$$

$$\frac{\cancel{4\pi}\, r^2}{\cancel{4\pi}} = \frac{\cancel{400\pi}^{\,100}}{\cancel{4\pi}}$$

$$r^2 = 100$$

$$r = \sqrt{100}$$

$$r = 10$$

The diameter is twice the length of r, so the sphere's diameter is 20 inches. (-10 is also a solution, but it is rejected because r cannot be negative.)

19. The correct answer is 50. Let $x =$ the number. Solve the following equation for x:

$$x - 20 = \frac{1}{2}x + 5$$

$$x - 20 - \frac{1}{2}x = 5$$

$$\frac{1}{2}x - 20 = 5$$

$$\frac{1}{2}x - 20 + 20 = 5 + 20$$

$$\frac{1}{2}x = 25$$

$$x = 50$$

20. **(4)** After the first card is drawn, seven cards are left: one spade, three hearts, one diamond, and two clubs. Three of these seven are hearts, so the probability the second card drawn is a heart is $\frac{3}{7}$.

21. **(2)** Given the half-life is 50 years, the original amount will be cut in half three times over a period of 150 years to $\frac{1}{2}$ in 50 years, to $\frac{1}{2} \cdot \frac{1}{2} = \frac{1}{4}$ in 100 years, and to $\frac{1}{2} \cdot \frac{1}{2} \cdot \frac{1}{2} = \frac{1}{8}$ in 150 years.

22. The correct answer is −3. Solve the given equation:

$$5x + 3 = 2(x - 3)$$
$$5x + 3 = 2x - 6$$
$$5x + 3 - 2x = 2x - 6 - 2x$$
$$3x + 3 = -6$$
$$3x + 3 - 3 = -6 - 3$$
$$3x = -9$$
$$\frac{\cancel{3}x}{\cancel{3}} = \frac{-9}{3}$$
$$x = -3$$

23. **(4)** Let W = the rectangle's width. Then $2W + 3$ = the rectangle's length. Using the formula for the area of a rectangle (and omitting the units), solve the following equation for W and then determine $2W + 3$, the rectangle's length:

$$LW = A$$
$$(2W + 3)W = 44$$
$$2W^2 + 3W - 44 = 0$$
$$(2W + 11)(W - 4) = 0$$
$$W = -5.5 \text{ (reject) } W = 4$$
$$2W + 3 = 2(4) + 3 = 8 + 3 = 11$$

Index

Symbols

A

D

F

G

I

J–K

L

multiple adjectives, commas and, 45
muscular system, 272

N

Native Americans, 168
natural numbers, 330
natural selection, 277
negative numbers, 330
nervous system, 272
neutral substances, 286
neutrons, 281-282
Newton, Isaac, 244-245, 293
   three laws of motion, 294-295
nitrification, 255
nitrogen cycle, 255-256
nitrogen fixation, 255
nonfiction/informational passages, 63-78
   articles, 64-65
      main ideas, 65-66
      practice questions, 66
      supporting details, 65-66
      topic sentences, 65
   autobiographies, 73
   biographies, 73-74
      practice questions, 74
   consumer documents, 71
      contracts, 71-72
      practice questions, 72
   details, 64
   historical documents, 76-77
      practice questions, 77
   main ideas, 64-66
   memoirs, 73
   miscellaneous nonfiction, 67
   op-eds, 75
      practice questions, 76
   passage structures, 67
   questions, 67
   viewpoints, 64
   workplace documents, 68-69
      practice questions, 69
nuclei, 268

numbers, 329-345
   absolute value, 341
   categories of, 329-330
   counting, 330
   cubes of, 342
   decimals, 332
      leading zeros, 333
      multiplication, 332
      rounding digits, 335
      scientific notation, 333
   fractions, 336
      denominators, 336
      greatest common factors, 337
      least common denominators, 338
      multiplication, 338
      numerators, 336
      reciprocals, 337
   magnitude, 330-331
   negative, 330
   number lines, 341
   opposites, 330
   order of magnitude, 334
   practice questions, 343-344
   principal square roots, 342
   ratios, 339-341
      cross-multiplying, 340
      making comparisons using, 339
      percents, 339
      proportions, 340
   scientific notation, 333
   square roots of, 342
   squares of, 342
   whole, 330
numerical coefficients, 378

O

observation, scientific method, 242
occluded fronts, 310
oceanography, 305, 311-312
   euphotic zones, 311
   kelp forests, 312
ohms, 302